CHURCHILL'S DECEPTION

THE DARK SECRET THAT DESTROYED NAZI GERMANY

LOUIS C. KILZER

SIMON & SCHUSTER
New York   London   Toronto   Sydney   Tokyo   Singapore

SIMON & SCHUSTER
Rockefeller Center
1230 Avenue of the Americas
New York, New York 10020

Designed by Karolina Harris
Manufactured in the United States of America

10 9 8 7 6 5 4 3 2 1

Library of Congress Cataloging in Publication Data
Kilzer, Louis C.
Churchill's deception: the dark secret that destroyed Nazi Germany/Louis
C. Kilzer
    p.   cm.
Includes bibliographical references and index.

   1. World War, 1939–1945—Diplomatic history. 2. Churchill, Winston, Sir,
1874–1965. 3. World War, 1939–1945—Secret service—Great Britain. 4. Hess,
Rudolf, 1894–1987. 5. History—Errors, inventions, etc. I. Title.
D750.K55 1994
940.54'8641—dc20   94-3178
                                    CIP
ISBN: 0-671-76722-4

Photo Credits
Photo 1 courtesy of the Collections of the Library of Congress; photos 2, 3, 7, 8
courtesy of the Minneapolis *Star-Tribune*; photos 4, 5, 9, 11, 12, 14, 15 by Wide
World Photos; photo 6 courtesy of U. S. Army Photographs; photos 10, 13 by
Globe Photos.

"My Father" is reprinted from *Moabit Sonnets* by Albrecht Haushofer, translated
by M. D. Herter Norton, by permission of W. W. Norton & Company, Inc.
Copyright © 1978 by W. W. Norton & Company, Inc.

To Elizabeth, Alexander and Xanthe

MY FRIEND Mark Smith first pointed out the improbability of the Hess medical records. Without that, this book would not have been possible. Much is also owed to my agent, Jane Dystel, and editors Paul Aron and Dominick Anfuso. At the National Archives in Washington, I received welcomed help from archivists John Taylor, Robert Wolfe and Katherine Nicastro. In the former Soviet Union I was aided by Oleg A. Rzheshevsky, of the Institute of History, Academy of Sciences; Oleg I. Tzarev, of the KGB; Alexander S. Orlov, of the Institute of Military History, Defense Ministry; Sergei A. Tsyplyaev, MP, All-Union Parliament; and Nikolai N. Yakovlev, of the Institute of Sociology, Soviet Academy of Sciences. Sergei V. Tsyganov and Vitaly Konzuhkov, editors in the Novosti Press Agency, helped me as interpreters. Historian Harold Deutsch lent his perspective to the book. Hugh Thomas was generous with his time. In Minneapolis, Brian Richard Boylan, Robert T. Smith and Robert Evans helped me with critical readings of early manuscripts.

Contents

Preface		11
1	Typhoon	19
2	Quixotic	27
3	Revelations	64
4	Breath of Evil	79
5	Toward War	106
6	War	130
7	En Finir	155
8	Often Only Losers	165
9	Genius	184
10	Wrought by Criminals	204
11	Conspiracies	226
12	The Hess Mission	251
13	Deal	278
Notes		291
Bibliography		315
Index		321

Preface

It should have been discovered by a great historian or a lucky journalist, someone, at least, who was supposed to find such things. The Second World War and the Cold War that followed had, after all, been two of the most studied events of the century.

But an unknown Welsh doctor, baffled by telltale X rays and his own observations, found the dark secret of the two great wars, and evidence of the crime behind them. The doctor himself would not hit upon the proper explanation of his findings, though his search for answers changed his life.[1]

Hugh Thomas had nothing grandiose on his mind when he landed the job as the consultant in general surgery at the British garrison in Berlin in 1972. The garrison was small, mostly young and decidedly symbolic. As any Berliner knew, the Western presence in their city was merely a show-the-flag operation. Should the East-West contest ever erupt in real shooting, Berlin would go first. Wargamers in the States didn't even consider holding the city, a relic buried deep inside East Germany.

Predictably, a society not sure of living for tomorrow lived for today. There was a gaiety at ground zero—a merriment that bedeviled Thomas on his discovery path. Berlin, the former seat of the Third Reich, was on the longest continuous festival in modern times.

As such, the city was ripe for a young surgeon whose official duties—treating a broken nose might make for an exciting day—should have left him with plenty of time to explore. But Thomas was intrigued by one aspect of his job description that seemed not at all routine. He hadn't known it before he arrived, but he quickly learned that his job extended beyond the personnel of the garrison. For part of each year the British had control of Spandau Prison, where the major Nazi war criminals who weren't hanged had been sentenced. Being the garrison's doctor, Thomas would minister to any prisoner's medical needs during the months the British controlled Spandau.

This should not have been too taxing. By the time Thomas got to Spandau, all the war felons had been released. Save one.

And he was an odd one, intriguing to Thomas. From almost all reports, the seventy-nine-year-old prisoner was immeasurably insane. He had refused to defend himself at Nuremberg, citing amnesia. Then, just when an amnesia defense might have worked in his favor, he said he had been faking and wanted the judgment of the court. He then sat down to absently read a book. Some noted that he seldom turned a page.

Spandau had not resolved his mental malady. The prisoner was fond of taking long walks around a small prison courtyard, where he would mumble to himself, head bowed, hands clasped behind his back. It was said he had logged enough miles to get him to China had walls not constrained him.

This was not to say he couldn't carry on a coherent conversation. He was particularly adept at discussing matters concerning Adolf Hitler.

Thomas was not disappointed with his lonely ward, for he already knew part of the prisoner's remarkable story. The man pounding the turf inside Spandau was Rudolf Hess, the former Deputy Führer of the Third Reich, the head of the Nazi Party and Hitler's closest friend.

The legend of Hess was both rich and peculiar. Thomas knew the general outline. In May of 1941, this man—one of the most powerful in the world—had jumped into the cockpit of a plane, piloted it across the English Channel and then bailed out somewhere over western Scotland.

The surprised British wanted to know what he was doing jumping into the Isles at a time Great Britain and Germany were locked in a bitter war. He had come to hammer out a peace, he said. He was quickly placed under the scrutiny of psychiatrists, while the British had a good laugh at Hitler's expense. Hitler, according to the legend, had known none of his deputy's plans. He was furious. But the titillating news of Hess's exploits slowly faded until it was permanently dispatched from the front pages six weeks later when Hitler invaded the Soviet Union.

And that was precisely what concerned Josef Stalin's suspicious mind. Stalin, never one for coincidences, found the Hess venture particularly annoying. Somehow the Soviet Premier got the notion that the Hess mission had something to do with Hitler's onslaught against the Red Army.

Stalin would mostly only fume over Hess, until in late 1942 when something then unknown convinced him firmly that there was a black hand involved in the mission. His cold heart froze solid toward the West, and the Cold War was born, a result of a man who would walk in circles.

After the war, many thought Hess should be treated leniently, his having sought peace, after all. Stalin saw things differently. To him, Hess was *the* war criminal. He wanted Hess dead. In compromise, the Deputy Führer received a life sentence.

Thomas knew some of the circumstances that brought Hess to his fate as the lone prisoner in Spandau. But he told himself they were professionally irrelevant. Thomas was a medical man, and he wanted to know the medical history of his most important potential patient. Unfortunately, in Berlin of 1972, Hess's medical paper trail was thin. Apparently, Hess had not had a complete physical since he entered Spandau twenty-seven years before.

In search of clues, Thomas found a book on Hess in the garrison's library. He learned that Hess had led a medically interesting life, having a penchant for serious injury. The book noted that Hess had been wounded at least twice during the First World War, once almost mortally.

That injury was caused by a high-powered rifle shot to his left lung. Thomas had seen such wounds before—in Belfast during IRA clashes—and he knew they were ugly. Not only would there be a gash as the bullet entered, but an even bigger scar as it exploded out the back. Ribs would most likely splinter, and even in the chance event that a bullet managed to both enter and leave the chest between ribs, the force of the blast would cause the two adjacent ones to stretch and deform.

But external scarring and even rib displacement were not Thomas's main concerns. Lung damage was. A lung shot creates massive interior injury to the soft tissues, leaving behind a hard, fibrous path through the chest. This internal scar never goes away. Directly observable in 1973 by X ray or autopsy, its effects could be indirectly seen by any doctor. There at least would be a shortness of breath during exercise. Walking to China, for instance, would be difficult.

Thomas filed this and some other matters away, and waited for the day that he could give his notorious patient a thorough examination.

He soon found that no such examination could be made in the confines of Spandau. Thomas saw Hess once or twice there at monthly get-togethers with the medical staffs of the four occupying powers. Yet these meetings were more excuses to imbibe than to practice medicine.

Whatever power was in charge of the prison on a particular month would prepare a lavish lunch that attempted to outdo in some respect that of its immediate predecessor. The Russians would improve their borscht, the British their steak-and-kidney pudding. True, when the medical staffs arrived they did look at Hess, but the protocol did not extend to the rigor of actually having the prisoner disrobe.

Instead, the staffers headed as quickly as possible for the luncheon offerings, where doctors toasted to their patient's good health. May it continue. This was Berlin, after all. People got drunk.

But Thomas wanted more than free drinks and food. He wanted something more systematic for patient Hess, such as X rays and the like. His commander finally asked for Hess to be taken to a hospital and given a more-or-less complete physical examination. The Russians, predictably, drew the line at drinking to Hess's health in the Spandau anteroom. Having Hess served by a real hospital—in the absence of some sort of emergency—could be seen as coddling the prisoner. The Russians knew many ways to treat prisoners, and coddling wasn't one of them. Particularly this prisoner.

Finally, though, the Soviets relented, afraid apparently of a propaganda loss if something preventable did happen to Hess after they had refused to give him a real medical checkup.

When the big day arrived to take Hess out of Spandau, the media—which had somehow learned of the not unimportant fact that the former Deputy Führer could again be seen—had the place surrounded, dangling from trees, peering from the bushes, cruising in cars. Soldiers lined the way with automatic weapons. Hitler's heir was out and about in Germany. There was general pandemonium.

At the hospital, an anxious medical staff awaited. Of course, officials from all four occupying powers had to be present.

Finally, the ambulance arrived.

The Russian delegation was led by a boorish man named Voitov who generally amused everyone by shouting "Stop! No comfort!" to any gesture that was offered, such as guiding Hess with a hand on his elbow. Thomas wrote that Voitov "looked like a hack cartoonist's idea of a typical K.G.B. agent: the single button which held the jacket of his bright blue suit together threatened constantly to do horrible damage to his sagging pot-belly."

Of course, someone had prepared a fine buffet for the affair. Salmon sandwiches were popular. Liquor flowed.

Thomas abstained. Amid all the commotion and theater, there was medicine to be practiced. Hess first had an eye examination. His glasses, it showed, were worse than useless. He emerged, spirits apparently rising from all this attention, and prepared for radiology, the crux of the examination. For that, he had to drink a lamentable mixture called a barium meal. Barium would help outline internal organs.

Thomas and the examiner donned lead body shields for the X-ray room. Voitov was there, without shield. Fearful of possible nuclear harm to his private parts, Voitov's vigilance waned, and he fled to the safety of whiskey sours.

Some thirty or so minutes later, the X-ray negatives were processed and some of the assembled medical personnel broke away from the adjacent party to actually look at them. Nothing extraordinary showed up.

The staff waited for the barium to work itself down further in the digestive tract to the large intestines. But Hess's digestion was not up to the challenge, and the doctors huddled to come up with a solution. They decided to feed the prisoner some of their salmon, which he wolfed down with such crassness that Thomas was confused. The Hess he had read about in books was somewhat urbane, not one to dispense with utensils and shovel food to his mouth from a bowl. Then again, he had been a prisoner for thirty-two years. People change.

The salmon gambit worked. Soon new X rays of the lower intestines were snapped onto lighted boards. Again, nothing irregular was seen.

After the examination was finished and most of the doctors and Voitov were milling far from the patient, Thomas casually approached the prisoner in a changing area. Hess removed his hospital shift and for a time was naked in front of Thomas.

Instinctively, the doctor glanced at his torso, curious about the chest injury.

"For an instant," Thomas reported, "I froze in disbelief."

There were no scars.

Not the best plastic surgeon of his day could have hidden vicious scars made by a high-velocity military bullet, or so Thomas thought. Thomas went to examine the X rays taken that day, and those taken at an earlier time during a medical emergency.

There was no fibrous tissue track through the lung and no rib damage of any sort.

Thomas knew that left two possibilities. The first was that Rudolf Hess had not, in fact, suffered any First World War injuries. Thomas checked the German archives for Hess's original medical record and went as far as engaging Ilse Hess, Hess's wife, in a roundabout conversation about her husband's health. The records said Hess had suffered the injuries. And so did Ilse. Not only did he have extensive scars, but—just as Thomas expected—he had some difficulty breathing at altitude.

That left the other possibility as the best solution. The man in Spandau Prison was not Rudolf Hess.

Much of Dr. Hugh Thomas's life has since been spent trying to reconcile this possibility with history. Challenges to his medical evidence have been weak, and support has been strong. After reviewing the evidence, seventy-six thoracic surgeons from the Royal College of Surgeons of Edinburgh voted seventy-six to zero that the Spandau prisoner—he died in 1987—could not have been the Hess of history. Among other inconsistencies, the subject's left lung was absolutely intact. (Other scars were also missing, including one left by a well-known wound Hess suffered when his forehead intercepted a beer mug during a Munich beer hall brawl.)

A few years after his original discovery, Thomas branched from the purely medical and scientific into historical issues. And here he was not on as firm a ground. In 1977, Thomas rightly wrote that Spandau Prisoner No. 7 was not Rudolf Hess. Then he made a less-than-scientific leap. If Prisoner No. 7 was not Rudolf Hess, then Nazi Germany had sent over a double, Thomas reasoned.

However, just as there were two possibilities to explain the lack of scarring, there are two possibilities to explain how an impostor had settled into Spandau Prison.

This book is about that other, much darker, option.

1 :⁣ *Typhoon*

It had been the most important year in a hundred years and he was where he always wanted to be, at the center. But May Day, 1941, held little joy for Winston Spencer Churchill.

Twenty months had passed since German panzers swept into Poland, igniting the Second World War. It had been nearly a year since Hitler invaded the West, just as Churchill became Prime Minister. There had been gloom and resignation at first, then great optimism, now uncertainty.

The old bulldog had taken over at the very worst of times. The government—and that included Churchill—at first thought the only way out for England would be a deal with Adolf Hitler. These were, after all, pragmatic men. They knew when they were beaten.

It had taken the Nazi Führer less time to rout the British from the Continent than it had taken him to defeat the Poles. The fleeing Tommys had even left almost all of their weapons behind as they scrambled aboard ships and boats and anything that would float at Dunkirk. Back in Great Britain, they were an army in name only. If Hitler had chosen to come, he could have. The cliffs of Dover would have offered as much resistance as the British army.

But Hitler did not come, for reasons Churchill grew to understand, though most of the rest of the world didn't. And in not coming, Hitler provided the Prime Minister with a hope, thin but real, that if he could just stall the Nazi Führer long enough England could win this war. She could even advance her position.

The period of Churchill's stall was war at its most obscure. Hitler, its instigator, desperately tried to stop it, despite possessing overwhelming superiority in arms, while Churchill, with almost no forces at all, wanted it to continue.

On the surface, it was indeed absurd. Joseph Kennedy, who had returned to America after serving as ambassador to Great Britain, summed up the prospects in testimony before the House Foreign Affairs Committee: "I don't see how 1,500,000 men can drive 6,000,000 men, armed to the teeth, from anyplace unless there is a revolution."[1]

There was no need for Kennedy to explain something everyone knew—most Germans were in love with their Führer. Revolution was not likely.

This is how logical men, in America and inside the Kremlin, were reading events. But what must be true on paper might not be true in the shadow war. Churchill had a veiled weapon, the Secret Intelligence Service (SIS), and he was betting that shadow warriors could counter two hundred German divisions. Seldom before had a great nation wagered its very existence on deception.

And seldom before had a grand plan been so simple and elegant: America and Russia would fight the war that England couldn't. And then they would step aside.

Only days after becoming Prime Minister, Churchill's worried son had asked if there was any way the British could win this war. Of course, said his father, "I shall drag the United States in."[2] And he set about trying to accomplish this by every trick in that impressive black bag of the SIS.

He sent scores of agents to North America to try to convince an American President, which was easy, and then the American people, which was more difficult, that this was a war they must fight.

Deceptions are best if they are simple, and this one was as simple as they come: the Americans were to be frightened into war. Adolf Hitler was to be portrayed as a demon—which he was—who was seeking to conquer the world—which he wasn't. After the war, when American secret agents got hold of the Reich files that should have contained details of Hitler's plot to take over Latin America just before the final thrust to Roosevelt's Hyde Park, they were embarrassed to discover how strictly Eastern European Hitler's real estate ambitions were.

Churchill's bravado with his son was a good stiff-upper-lip performance by the newly installed Prime Minister, but an America, dragged or otherwise provoked to war, would not be sufficient to save Great Britain. Even before becoming Prime Minister, the old warrior spelled out his vision in unmistakable terms.

"What is wrong with this simple proposal?" he had asked. "I beg His Majesty's Government to get some brutal truths into their heads. Without an effective Eastern front, there can be no satisfactory defense of our interests in the West, and without Russia there can be no effective Eastern front."[3]

The British government had every reason to believe that, given the proper incentive, Hitler would solve the brutal truths by attacking the Bolsheviks. That was, after all, the plan Churchill had known about since 1936, when Hitler and his entourage treated visiting British agents and nobles to the inner workings of an Eastern blitzkrieg, right down to Stuka bombers and darting tanks. And it was the plan that Churchill had heard about eight months earlier when, even before all the guns quieted in France, Hitler instructed his generals to open their maps of the Ukraine. In fact Hitler had signed Directive No. 18 the past December for the biggest, most daring battle in world history, Barbarossa, the invasion of the Soviet Union.

But as Churchill sat at 10 Downing Street contemplating his plans for the Empire, Hitler's Luftwaffe was raining steel hell on England, obliterating in these night raids of early 1941 whole sections of the industrial heart of the Isles. This certainly was a curious way to prepare an attack on the Soviet Union.

In the North Atlantic, Hitler was sinking millions of tons of shipping that Great Britain had no realistic chance of replacing. And in North Africa and Baghdad there was danger of an even greater sort.

Churchill was taking a savage beating by inferior German forces led by a superior German general named Erwin Rommel. And since the security of the great oil fields of the Middle East was—as the American chiefs of staff were already sensing—the true heart of

British foreign policy, Churchill was beside himself.

After a series of humiliating African Theater defeats and retreats, an exasperated Prime Minister could not restrain his sarcasm. In an April 21, 1941, note to his generals the bulldog explained: "Twenty-five thousand men with 100 [field] guns and ample supplies are expected to be able to hold a highly fortified zone against 4,500 men at the end of 700 miles of communications, even though those men be Germans. . . ."[4]

His army was not fighting, at least not well, his generals were hard of hearing and the German dictator was not behaving. If things didn't change, and soon, Hitler might win the day.

That was certainly how Josef Stalin saw it. In his Spartan apartment inside the Kremlin, the Russian dictator felt he knew that the increasing talk of a German invasion of the USSR was phony. Stalin, one Russian historian summarizes, believed that "Germany could not wage a war on two fronts. And to open up a second front against Russia, when it seemed that Great Britain was pretty close to [defeat] was illogical. . . . He thought that it would delay the war until 1942. . . .

"By the end of May [1941] the Germans captured Crete and their planes landed in Iraq and Syria. And so it seemed in Moscow that the next step for the Germans must be to jump over the sea to Iraq and Syria and then to Egypt. The idea was to seize the oil channels from Syria. And Britain without any oil and gas couldn't continue the war."[5]

It was the winning strategy. And simple. In chess terms, Britain had left its queen exposed. Why should not Hitler simply take it? Instead of pushing 140 German divisions into Russia, Hitler could simply move a fourth that many south and win certain success in the Persian Gulf, to the cheers of the local population, no less. Stalin was so convinced of Hitler's sanity that he was ignoring the 3,300 German tanks massed at his border. Germany, he thought, would not advance east until Britain was out of the war.

In the Reichschancellory in Berlin, Adolf Hitler saw the same chess board, and came to the same conclusion. He did not want to attack until Great Britain was neutralized. But he hoped it would not have to be in the manner envisioned by Stalin. As Winston Churchill already knew well, the Nazi Führer did not really want to snatch the British Queen, or King or, really, the British anything. But Hitler was not a fool.

Hitler's plans to destroy Soviet Bolshevism rested upon an assumption; an assumption that was shaking the Führer to his uncrowded soul. It was called England. She must be out of the war or "neutralized" before the invasion of Russia. Beyond his racism, beyond his fanatical anticommunism, Hitler—as Stalin sensed—had a bedrock position against ever taking Germany into a two-front war. It was an obsession without peer for Hitler.

Several months earlier Hitler had spelled out his frustrations to one of his top generals. Franz Halder, the chief of staff of the German army, summed up Hitler's predicament: "The Führer," Halder wrote in his diary, "is greatly puzzled by Britain's persisting unwillingness to make peace. He sees the answer (as we do) in Britain's hope on Russia and therefore counts on having to compel her by main force to agree to peace. Actually that is much against his grain. The reason is that a military defeat of Britain will bring about the disintegration of the British Empire. This would not be of any benefit to Germany. German blood would be shed to accomplish something that would benefit only Japan, the United States, and others."[6]

This was a theme he repeated constantly. England was stalling.

On July 13, 1940, Halder, after speaking to Hitler, wrote that "England has some hopes about Russia. . . ."[7] On July 31, Halder wrote, based on conversations with Hitler: "Britain's hope lies in Russia and the United States. . . ."[8] On October 4, Hitler told Mussolini that "Great Britain placed her hopes in America and in Russia."[9] On January 9, 1941, Hitler said: "What kept England going were the hopes it vested in the United States of America and in Soviet Russia."[10]

Adolf Hitler was quite willing to oblige the British by wrestling Russia into the war, but only after his bedrock position was met. Before launching this adventure, Hitler wanted a satisfactory guarantee that the British would not invade Germany's unprotected rear while Hitler's forces were occupied in the Soviet Union. In case anyone in Great Britain misunderstood this, Hitler decided to make the point quite clear.

At the first of the year he ordered Reichsmarschall Hermann

Göring to carry out mass air raids "more systematically than hith-erto."[11] German TNT was presently driving home his message. Hitler also intensified the North African campaign, demolished Great Britain in Greece and Crete, and threatened Iraq.

It was a message Winston Churchill was getting. And he was get-ting it at a time that his other hope—a quick American interven-tion—was evaporating.

Antiwar leader and aviation hero Charles Lindbergh had warned a few weeks earlier that America was "being led toward war with ever-increasing rapidity and with every conceivable subterfuge,"[12] a view seconded by Boston Archbishop William O'Connell, who de-clared that "secret maneuvers behind the scenes of government are drawing us nearer to war."[13]

Polls showed that the students were not alone. Dr. George Gallup reported on February 16, 1941, that 61 percent of Americans would not favor war even if Germany sank an American merchant ship.

The bottom line was that Churchill had Roosevelt but not Amer-ica. And now even Roosevelt was proving vexing. In fact, Roo-sevelt's attitude was troubling Churchill perhaps most of all. The American President did not seem amenable to a plan merely to pre-serve the Empire's status quo, much less recoup its lost glory.

In a recent cable, Roosevelt told Churchill that he understood why the British were fighting in North Africa, Greece, Crete and elsewhere. Yet he said the British should not fear retreating from those same places. "In the last analysis," Roosevelt wrote, "the Naval control of the Indian Ocean and the Atlantic Ocean will in time win the war."[14] The implication—that the Middle East and North Africa were not important in this war—was deadly ominous to Churchill. To preserve or even expand its influence on the re-gion was a key British objective of the Second World War. The Pres-ident was not seeing the same chess board as Stalin, Hitler and Churchill.

Churchill was nearly devastated. He wrote to his foreign secre-tary, Anthony Eden: "It seems to me as if there has been a consid-erable recession across the Atlantic, and that quite unconsciously we are being left very much to our fate."[15] Alexander Cadogan, the British Foreign Office under secretary who had recently confided to his diary that "the real battle of the war is coming in N. Africa"[16] noted "days of awful gloom" following the President's message, of which Churchill, "tired and depressed, had taken a jaundiced view."[17]

Churchill was preparing a dire response to the President. "We are far from wishing to add to our territory," Churchill, who had clearly understood the undertone of the president's message, would shortly write, "but only to preserve our life and perhaps yours. . . . I cannot take the view that the loss of Egypt and the Middle East would be a mere preliminary to the successful maintenance of a prolonged oceanic war. . . . I adjure you, Mr. President, not to underrate the gravity of the consequences which may follow from a Middle Eastern collapse."[18]

In case the President wasn't getting it, Churchill told him that if the United States "cannot take more advanced positions now, or very soon, the vast balances may be tilted heavily to our disadvantage." To avoid that, the United States should "immediately . . . range herself with us as a belligerent Power."[19]

Meanwhile, Iraqi troops were attacking British troops at Basra, while occupying the Mosul oil fields. The British oil lines were bending. If the Iraqis advanced further, there could be catastrophe.

So on May Day, 1941, there was a gloomy Prime Minister, under a typhoon of German steel at home, retreating armies everywhere, a solid victory nowhere, an American President wanting his country in the war, but not knowing just how or when, and who, once in the war, might have objectives entirely different from England's. And then there was a German dictator, playing a solid opening.

It was time for a drastic gambit.

For nearly a year, Hitler and his minions had made repeated contacts with powerful peace forces operating inside Great Britain, forces that believed in the absurdity of this war. The Nazis had contacted the British Peace Party in Rome, Madrid, Switzerland—anywhere possible—to persuade it to finally act. The party must tame or even overthrow Winston Churchill.

Hitler thought he knew the Peace Party's strength. The landed nobility of the British Empire had no reason to wish Germany harm—the British King was by kinship German, after all—and had every reason to want the Bolsheviks crushed. The Reds were the real threat to the established order in Britain, not the Germans.

But every time Hitler thought the Peace Party would act, it pulled back, ceding power to that damned warmonger at 10 Downing Street.

As the invasion of the Soviet Union grew closer, Hitler's patience shortened. If he had to, he would crush the island. He would snatch the queen left exposed on the chess board.

Hitler's analysis of the situation in Great Britain was perceptive. There was a powerful Peace Party in England whose members were precisely those that Hitler thought. And they were indeed in a position to subdue Winston Churchill, though it would have to be done subtly. They were also, as Hitler guessed, growing weary of the German Blitz and apprehensive that Hitler's assault on the Soviet Union might be delayed, or canceled.

The Führer had read the tea leaves correctly in all cases, save one. What he didn't know was that the man who ran the Peace Party was his old nemesis, Winston Churchill.

It was Churchill's grandest deception, and he had built it, nurtured it, coaxed it along, so that if he ever needed it—as he did now—it might prove decisive.

The risks were great, but if he could somehow make it work, then finally the German threat would abate. Engaged with the Soviet Union, Hitler would have little time for England. Or Iraq.

The plan had another advantage. It was not merely a deception. In many ways, the agreement made between Hitler and the fictitious party would be treated as binding. England would not, in fact, attack the German rear, just as Hitler hoped. Churchill saw advantage in this. Since his goals were not really European anyway, he did not know why he should waste resources there.

However, there was a beautiful caveat. Churchill at any time could reverse the situation. He, after all, was not a signatory. Far from it. He was the uncompromising bulldog.

There would be many surprises along the way and the final stage of the deception would begin with a great mistake. But that was for the future. What was important was to get on with it.

Britain would deal with the devil.

2 ⁘ *Quixotic*

AT THIS TIME MY SOLE AND SURE HOPE OF VICTORY DE-
PENDED UPON OUR ABILITY TO WAGE A LONG AND INDEF-
INITE WAR UNTIL OVERWHELMING AIR SUPERIORITY WAS
GAINED, AND PROBABLY OTHER GREAT POWERS WERE
DRAWN IN ON OUR SIDE.

—*Winston S. Churchill writing of the spring of 1941*[1]

On May 10, 1941, Churchill received FDR's response to his plea
that the United States should enter the war. Roosevelt should have
saved himself the effort. His message to Churchill didn't even mention, much less agree with, Churchill's analysis of strategic peril.[2]

As the day drew on, the news got worse. The Admiralty called a
press conference to tally its losses. Since the war began, Great
Britain and her negligible allies had lost 6.1 million tons of shipping,
some 1,508 ships. And the toll was increasing. More ships and tonnage had been recently sunk than at any time since Dunkirk; thirty
thousand more tons of shipping were sent to the bottom on May 10
alone. The toll was as impossible for England to comprehend as it
was for its shipyards to replace. The sea war, as everything else, was
going Hitler's way.

The night brought special horrors. Reichsmarschall Göring decided that May 10 was an appropriate date to send another bloody
Führergram to Winston Churchill and the Peace Party.

Just after dusk on this Saturday night—Hitler was fond of weekends for dramatic moves—wave after wave of Luftwaffe bombers greeted Londoners with more tons of phosphorus, iron and TNT than any city had ever suffered in one bloody raid. Seven hundred acres of London's center were incinerated; Commons was destroyed, the House of Lords set ablaze. Westminster Hall, Westminster Abbey, Grey's Court Hospital and Queen's Hall were severely damaged. Two thousand fires raged unchecked because bombers wiped out water lines. A third of central London's streets were rendered impassable. In all, 1,436 British civilians perished, more than on any other day of the war.[3]

The Führer's telegram was simple to read: he had both the power and—if forced—the resolve to crush the island.

A Small Event

While Londoners were receiving the full force of Hitler's message in the late evening of May 10, a strange and seemingly small event was unfolding further north. A single raider flying a Messerschmidt ME-110, a short-range German fighter, had coursed through Germany and Holland and was making an improbable dash across the North Sea. He appeared headed on a course that would bring him to a spot near Glasgow in western Scotland.[4] It seemed impossible. No ME-110 could make it that far and ever hope to return.

Royal Air Force radar men noted the invader about 10 P.M. and alerted a young RAF wing commander. The commander, the Duke of Hamilton, did not seem overly concerned about the crazy pilot and his plane and decided against sending interceptors.[5]

As the intruder neared landfall its pilot was disturbed that a cloud cover that had been predicted was nowhere in sight. Even though it was twilight, if the British sent up interceptors it could be murderous. Also troubling the pilot was his failure to pick up a radio signal that was to guide him to his destination. The lone pilot decided to take precautions. He throttled up his 1,000 horsepower twin engines, pointed the stick down, and commenced to hedgehop over dark British terrain, often only sixteen feet above ground, "skimming over trees, men, beasts and houses."[6] With a compass strapped to his thigh and a head full of maps and photos he had studied for weeks, the pilot gambled that he could still make his destination unmolested. Many heard the plane roar overhead; no one could do anything about it.

Since the plane was neither a reconnaissance craft or a bomber, people watching the flight wondered what the man flying it could possibly want. Why wasn't he down with the rest of the Luftwaffe, terrorizing London?

Four hours after he took off from an air base in Augsburg, Germany, the pilot said fate and luck finally brought him to his destination. He had hoped, he said, to arrive near Dungavel House, south of Glasgow. Dungavel House, oddly, was the estate of the Duke of Hamilton, the same Duke who had decided not to send up interceptors. Finding his destination did not solve the pilot's problems. In fact, he was in serious trouble, not with interceptors, but with his vision. "I circled over the spot," near Dungavel House, he later recalled, "for a long time, but I could not see a suitable landing place."[7]

Apparently, someone had told him that there would be a landing site near the Duke's estate. This pilot, after all, had committed the entire route to Dungavel House to memory just in case the radio beacon failed, as it had. And he somehow had managed to have extra fuel tanks on his plane. Such a careful man was not likely to overlook the critical issue of landing. Something, though, had gone wrong. He found no landing strip.

The pilot was forced to ponder an unsettling option: parachuting. Though clearly the most practical choice in the absence of a place to land, it had one significant drawback—the pilot, brave and skilled as he was, had never parachuted nor even been instructed on the rudiments of parachuting. This was something quite unexpected.

The pilot thought to himself that parachuting must be simple enough; one merely opens the canopy, stands and jumps. He soon found this simple scenario gravely violated the laws of physics. Traveling at 280 miles an hour, the pilot was hurled back into his seat by tornado-strength winds. He tried again, but Newton prevailed. He hit upon an idea: "I . . . climbed several thousand feet, threw the plane over on its back and switched off the engine." Newton, it seems, might just allow a man to fall from a cockpit. And, indeed, it was so.

"Just as I was falling out, I righted the machine again, switched on the engine and sent the plane hurtling to earth while I fell clear."[8] His German parachute worked just in time to prevent serious injury. The strange visitor from Germany arrived with only an injured ankle.

David McLean, a Scottish plowman, was the first to see him. "I was in the house and every one was in bed, late at night, when I heard a plane roaring overhead," McLean recounted a day later. "As I ran to the back of the farm I heard a crash and saw the plane bust into flames in a field about 300 yards away.

"I was amazed and a bit frightened when I saw a parachute dropping slowly downward through the gathering darkness. Peering up at it I could see a man swinging from the harness. I immediately concluded that this was a German airman bailing out and I raced back to the house for help."[9]

Armed with a pitchfork, McLean rushed the enemy. Lying on the ground and clutching his ankle, the German nonetheless cut a proper sort of image. McLean was obviously impressed. "He smiled and as I assisted him to his feet he thanked me," McLean said. He helped the pilot "into the house. By this time my old mother and my sister had got out of bed and had made tea." The pilot, dressed in the uniform of a Luftwaffe captain, declined the offer of tea—"I never drink tea as late as this"—and asked, instead, for water. While they all awaited the arrival of authorities who could make sense of this, McLean took the measure of his guest. "I could see," he said, "from the way he spoke that he was a man of culture. His English, although it had a foreign accent, was very clear. . . .

"He was a striking man, standing over six feet in height and wearing a magnificent flying suit. His watch and identity bracelet were of gold." But it was the visitor's self-confidence that most astounded McLean. "He seemed to treat what seemed to us a most hazardous flight as a pleasure trip. He seemed quite confident that he would be well-treated and repeatedly expressed how lucky he had been to land without a mishap."

Apparently, the German didn't consider the injured ankle much of problem. "He showed us pictures of his little boy of whom he spoke most proudly," McLean said.

Most on this night agreed that the mysterious visitor was no ordinary pilot newly delivered into the potentially angry arms of an enemy. He was neither frightened, anxious nor confused. He seemed, in fact, in control. "He was most gentlemanly in his attitude to my old mother and my sister and stiffly bowed when he came in and before he left. He thanked us profusely for what we had done for him," said McLean. "He was anxious about only one thing and that was his parachute. He said to me: 'I should like to keep that parachute, for I think I owe my life to it.' "

Soon a constable, inebriated and a bit hostile, arrived brandishing a pistol. Two men from the Signal Corps also joined in, and the stranger was finally delivered to the Home Guards—be he prisoner, visitor or guest.

Unlike the plowman, these more seasoned fighters might be less impressed with the enemy flier. But it was not so. The German had his way with them. Guardsman Jack Paterson found the German absolutely calm. He only asked for a cup of milk and gave the mug to his captors as a souvenir, saying: "I left Germany in a Messerschmidt 110 destroyer. Although I'm a skilled pilot, I am really a German Army Officer." As with everybody save the drunk constable, Paterson was impressed. The prisoner, he said, "was immaculately dressed. His uniform was made of the finest material and he wore very fine leather top-boots."

Before they ceded their ward to other hands, the two were convinced that anyone carrying himself as this one did must be "somebody high in the Nazi ranks." The pilot said his name was Captain Alfred Horn.

Horn told his captives that he came in a German uniform, unarmed. Even the plane was without ordnance: "I have no bombs in my plane so you need not worry," he told Guardsman Robert Gibson. In fact, when the plane was later examined, its main gun was still packed in grease. There were no shells.

The point was clear: the German had not come as a spy, but as something else. From all impressions, whatever this mission, it seemed official. Sometime during these first hours—accounts have varied—Captain Horn made a request. He said he had a message— a very important message—for the Duke of Hamilton. The German said he wanted to be taken to the Duke's nearby estate as quickly as that sort of thing could be arranged.

Word of this unusual request was relayed to the Duke—he was still on duty, guarding the Scottish skies—but the Duke declined the invitation, at least for the moment. Nor was the German taken to see the Duke. Bureaucratic instinct had taken hold, and there were procedures to be followed. In a room in Guard headquarters, Captain Horn was asked to place his personal effects on a table. There emerged a letter addressed to the Duke of Hamilton (it remains lost or not available), a visiting card from a professor named Albrecht Haushofer and another from Albrecht Haushofer's father, a Professor Karl Haushofer.

It wasn't until the next day, when the Duke of Hamilton finally presented himself to the German, that Captain Horn revealed his true identity. After asking others to leave the room, the German turned toward the Duke, and, according to one version, said: "I saw you at the Olympic Games in Berlin. You lunched with us. I don't know if you recognize me—but I am Rudolf Hess."[10] That was far too much to accept on faith alone. Officials quickly tried to verify the strange visitor's identity by searching his forehead for a scar left from the wound Hess received during a Munich beer hall brawl—the injury had been well reported in English papers. The scar, which would miraculously disappear by the time Prisoner No. 7 arrived at Spandau, was in place.[11]

It was the beginning of the legend. Rudolf Hess—Deputy Führer of the Third Reich, the head of the Nazi Party, and Adolf Hitler's friend and confidant—had arrived in Great Britain in the middle of the Second World War. From all appearances, all his actions, his demeanor, his confidence, he was a man who thought he was expected, or at least felt sure that he could ingratiate himself to the enemy. And no version of events disputes this: Hess clearly thought he would soon be flying back to Germany.

"My friend Albrecht Haushofer told me you were an Englishman who would probably understand our point of view," he told the

Duke. He had come with proposals for peace between the two great Nordic nations. He wanted to begin negotiations with the Duke's "party." Hamilton's reply must have sent a shudder through the Deputy Führer: "There is now only one party in this country."[12] The Peace Party, Hess was learning, was a chimera.

Obviously, the arrival of the Deputy Führer of the Third Reich on the rolling hills of Scotland was no small event. Once word leaked, if it did, it would be a sensation. The world knew little of the Nazi leaders, except that they were maniacal and wanted to conquer the world. For most, that was quite enough. The world would not understand what the leader of the Nazi Party was doing sipping warm milk with Home Guardsmen in Scotland. This was, after all, the same empire Hitler was literally burning to the ground.

Hess had expected a meeting and a quick trip back. But beginning with the missing landing strip, things had gone awry. Worse, word was beginning to leak. Something major had happened in the British Isles on May 10, 1941, and the flattening of central London was only part of the story.

Hitler Reacts

Hess did not return to Germany, not on May 10, not on May 11, not even on May 12. Berlin received no message as to his whereabouts. The Deputy Führer might just as well have evaporated into the ether.

Hitler faced a problem. The Deputy Führer of the Third Reich had sallied forth into the western sky. Then nothing. Hitler didn't know what was happening.

Versions of what occurred within the Hitler entourage in the forty-eight hours after the Hess sortie are varied. Accounts do, though, agree on a few things. Before he flew away, Hess wrote a letter addressed to Hitler and pressed it into an adjutant's hand with the order to deliver it to Hitler at Obersalzberg, where the Führer had his mountain chalet, should Hess not return to Augsburg. When the Deputy Führer did in fact fail to return, the adjutant rushed the document to Obersalzberg and, after some confusion, was ushered in to see the Führer, who promptly ripped open the letter and began to read. Hitler was either immediately outraged, as some said, gasping in amazement, fulminating against his friend and confidant; or, as others maintained, he remained strangely subdued.[13] The letter did not survive the war, though Hess's secretary recalled that it began with the words: "My Führer, when you receive this letter, I shall be in England."[14]

If he was aware of the planned flight—as many of Hess's close associates maintained to the end—Hitler at least put on a good show that he was not. Months earlier, the Führer secretly authorized Hess to put out peace feelers to Great Britain's Peace Party; with both Hess and Hitler agreeing that they should tap the young director of the Berlin Geopolitical Institute, Albrecht Haushofer, for some of the most sensitive arrangements because Haushofer had such extraordinary contacts among the British. He commenced the task somewhat reluctantly, but eventually hit upon the idea of establishing correspondence with the Duke of Hamilton and proposing a high-level meeting in a neutral country.

Haushofer, and his father, Professor Karl Haushofer, did far more than write a few letters to advance connections with the British Peace Party, but it was the Duke of Hamilton that appeared to be foremost on Hitler's mind as he sat in his chalet called the Berghof.

Hitler summoned the young professor to Obersalzberg and sequestered him in a room, demanding that he write out everything he knew of Hess's intent to fly to Scotland. Haushofer said he knew nothing of that matter, and wrote about old Peace Party contacts that Hitler himself had authorized. However, those at the Berghof that day, people who knew little or nothing of the back-channel peace contacts, were left with the impression that the Führer was in the dark about peace contacts, the whole enterprise being a surprise to him.

The impression he left to his guests was one thing, the impression the Hess mission might have on the world was quite another. Hitler knew that Hess was carrying to the British proposals that Hitler believed in, and ones he thought responsible leaders on the Isles would accept. Hitler and Hess had discussed and formulated the Nazi master plan during their twenty-one-year alliance. No one in Germany was better equipped to represent the Führer than Rudolf Hess. Yet despite that close bond, Hitler could wait only so long to see if his deputy's effort would meet with success. The problem was simple—each hour that Hess was unaccounted for sharply increased the chances that his deputy would fall into the dreaded hands of Winston Churchill. Once that happened, Hitler's entire game could be lost.

If Churchill found out about the myriad behind-the-scenes peace contacts Haushofer and Hess had made with British citizens of high standing, Churchill would act, the conspirators would be exposed, and months of delicate back-channel efforts would be wiped out. Though the landed classes of England might want an understanding with the Germans, the working and middle classes certainly did not. They would follow their blood, sweat, toil and tears Prime Minister. There could be an uprising that would mean the end of Hitler's ultimate dream of an Anglo-German alliance.

There would be another unhappy consequence if Hess fell into Churchill's grasp, perhaps nearly as bad as the first. Hess would be at Churchill's mercy, and mercy was not Churchill's long suit. The British could extract from Hess information about the coming invasion of the Soviet Union, perhaps dealing Germany a mortal blow. Short of that, but not far short, the British could claim that Hess had fled the Third Reich to confess Nazi crimes: atrocities, a deranged hierarchy and even Hitler's thirst for world domination. There would be no end of trouble.

The more he heard nothing but silence from Great Britain, the more worried Hitler became. Finally, he could wait no longer. With the chance that his deputy was in Churchill's hands, Hitler had to discredit Hess before Hess was made to discredit him. Two days after Hess disappeared, Hitler authorized a radio announcement that Rudolf Hess, suffering from a "progressive disease" and being therefore "stringently forbidden" from flying, had nevertheless taken off from an airport in Augsburg at 6 P.M., May 10, 1941, and was presumed to have "crashed somewhere or suffered an accident." Further, the communiqué said that Hess left behind a letter for Hitler that indicated "mental disintegration" and "hallucinations." Hitler, according to the official report, had ordered the arrest of the adjutants who had knowledge of the flight and who had failed to prevent it or report it.[15]

The initial explanation to the German people was perplexing. Officials at the American embassy cabled Washington that the announcement "created an immediate sensation and led to widespread speculation" among Germans about the meaning of the affair. Hess, the officials reported, "was probably more widely respected in Germany than any other leading Nazi and was regarded as a sincere, comparatively moderate and trusted collaborator of Hitler."[16]

Meanwhile, the British were staying mum, issuing no statements. Officials gave every indication of wanting the mission to be kept as quiet as possible. It was as if the Nazis were right and Hess had crashed unseen into the North Sea.

Scoop

Eric Schofield, the general manager of the *Glasgow Daily Record*, was walking his dog near a plane crash site on May 11, 1941, when he noticed an unusual number of people milling about and conversing on what should have been a sleepy spring Sunday.[17] A year before, a downed German plane would have been interesting. But now it was hardly news. So Schofield grew curious about these Scots' excitement over the German plane's wreckage. He asked: "What's everyone talking about?"

He was told the usual. A German airman had parachuted from a doomed plane the night before. The wreckage was just ahead. Schofield asked what was so unusual about *that*.

"Ah, I'm coming to that," the man replied. "This fellow flies here all the way across Scotland in some new type of Messerschmidt plane no one has seen before. A plane that's got no ammunition for its guns! That's the first thing. Next, he couldn't hope to get away again because the boys up at the R.A.F. camp say a plane of this sort can't carry enough juice to take it back to Germany.

"And the pilot's not the usual sort of Jerry airman, either. He's old, nearly fifty. And then he's not wearing the usual sort of uniform. It's made of special cloth. McLean was telling us that he'd never seen the like of it. Also, he's got a gold watch, and a gold bracelet, and boots that McLean says are as soft as a leather glove. He's a pot all right, a proper pot."

After a pause came the kicker: "And another thing. He was asking for the Duke of Hamilton."

Such a tale told to a newspaperman was something impossible to ignore. Schofield rushed to a phone to call the news desk. Sitting there, enjoying a lazy weekend morning, was Max McAuslane, a part-time editor. Schofield relayed the curious story. McAuslane knew immediately that this was news. He dispatched a reporter to the scene, then called the paper's top editor, who decided on a hunch to cut short his weekend and return to the office.

The reporter uncovered a provocative story, though it didn't answer the key questions: who was the German and why did he want to see the Duke? McAuslane sensed that this was not only an unusual story, but perhaps an important one. So he put on the other hat he wore around the *Record*—that of a reporter—and played an old reporter's ruse. He decided to take the story that had been turned in and show it to the military censor, a routine and even unnecessary step. He would ask innocently if there was any reason on earth this could not be printed in the next morning's paper. McAuslane knew that if something was askew, a low-level bureaucratic functionary could almost be counted upon to unwittingly show his hand.

It happened much as McAuslane guessed. The censor, after discussing matters with his superiors, said the story could not be published. Period. McAuslane asked for an explanation. The censor said dissuasively that the story was "rubbish." Might be, prodded McAuslane, but the *Record* was full of rubbish about which the government took little interest. The censor did not respond with any humor. The story was not to be printed. Period. After that, McAuslane and the paper's freshly returned editor, Clem Livingstone, knew for sure that the story of the parachuting German was not only interesting. It was surely important.

Their instincts had not failed them so far, nor would they for the rest of this remarkable day. Livingston, on still another hunch, decided to call a radio monitoring service that kept track of broadcasts from the Continent. He asked the service to note any odd news emanating from the Third Reich.

On Monday evening, the hunch paid off. The service called Livingstone. There was an odd radio broadcast from Berlin. It said that Deputy Führer Rudolf Hess, suffering some sort of hallucinations, had taken off in an airplane and had perhaps crashed into the sea.

Livingstone, somehow, knew immediately the meaning of the broadcast. The dapper pilot asking to see the Duke of Hamilton was the third most powerful man in the German Reich. Rudolf Hess was in Scotland.

What Livingston lacked, of course, was proof. Again the *Record* improvised. Livingstone rummaged through the newspaper morgue looking for photos of Hess look-alikes; imposing men with dark hair and prominent eyebrows—Cary Grant, Tyrone Power and the like. Of course, he found one of Hess himself. He gave them to a reporter and sent him out to McLean's house. The reporter was to ask if any of these men was the mysterious visitor.

If one member of the McLean household identified Hess as the pilot, the reporter was to telephone with the cipher "Thumbs up, once." If two identified Hess, the message would be "Thumbs up, twice." And if all three identified Hess, he would say: "Thumbs up, three times."

The reporter went to the McLeans' farm and spread out the pictures. Later, from a nearby phone, he called Livingstone. "Thumbs up, three times," he said.

With that, the *Record* decided to print the story, damn the censor. Even a very lucky newsman could only expect one such scoop in a lifetime.

Rudolf Hess in England

In London, officials knew time was also their enemy. They had apparently sought to keep the whole matter quiet, but events conspired against them.

Rumors were rampant in Glasgow, the Germans were already issuing bizarre radio announcements and the *Record* was set to publish. There was nothing left to do. London had to say something. The British government issued a dispatch. It began with the words "Hess One." Then the Teletype machine spewed out "a few wrong letters and figures jumbled up" before writing the important words: "Rudolf Hess in England."[18]

London's sparse announcement contained no specifics, suggested no motive, discussed nothing concerning the Duke of Hamilton. That revelation would be one of many *Daily Record* scoops. Yet the British statement ignited a firestorm around the world. Hitler's deputy was in Scotland, the same man referred to by the press as the "conscience of the party."

The *Daily Record*'s phone rang off the hook. Presses stopped and new Linotype was set; front pages would contain little but coverage of Rudolf Hess and his mysterious mission. Radio news played nearly nonstop.

American diplomats, as baffled as everyone else, began collecting anything they could on what was already being called "the Rudolf Hess Affair." From France came word that "the Hess 'escape' has stirred the hopeful imagination of many of the simple people of France who see in it the first ray of hope of possible internal dissensions within Nazi Germany with all that this implies for the future of France."[19] The American delegation in Copenhagen reported that the "flight has made an overwhelming impression in all German circles the more so as he [Hess] had enjoyed great popularity, confidence and respect of the German people."[20]

John Gilbert Winant, the American ambassador to the Court of St. James, noted that "Hess was more completely devoted to Hitler and the Nazi cause than any other man in Germany. Sincere anti-Nazis who talked with me had less complaint to make against him than any of the control group." Winant, obviously seeking a traditional motivation, was finding none. Hess, he said, "was happily married and devoted to his wife and child. His father . . . was a successful merchant in Egypt and he [Hess] was well educated. . . . Both the women in Germany and the Nazi youth hold him in great respect."[21]

From all over the globe—from Egypt, Turkey, the Soviet Union, even Japan—American diplomats were telling the State Department that the Hess mission not only captured the imagination of the locals, but suggested that something extraordinary, perhaps even an almost unthinkable peace, was at hand.

The picture of Hess the American side—not yet in the war—was getting was of a serious and responsible leader, someone certainly capable of charming a British farmer and a few constables and Home Guardsmen, but someone also very unlikely to encounter any of them.

The German leadership didn't know what to make of London's tepid announcement, but could not afford to take chances. Knowing finally that Hess was indeed being held by the British, there was no doubt at Obersalzberg, the Reichschancellory or Nazi Party headquarters that difficult things could shortly follow. Hess was in government hands, and that meant Churchill's hands. The British Prime Minister could pick up the palette and begin painting a brutal picture. The Nazis redoubled efforts to discredit Hess.

Suddenly, Hess—the sycophantic follower of the Führer—was said to be "a sick idealist who fell victim to the 'delusion' that he could bring about peace by this dramatic action." His mad mission, Germans were assured, would have no effect on the prosecution of the war.[22] In short, Hess was smitten by mystics and astrologers and was, essentially, out of his mind.

Silence

The Germans were about to be confounded.

For some reason, Churchill, the old bulldog, was not fighting. One popular anecdote holds that the Prime Minister, upon hearing that the Deputy Führer of the Third Reich had dropped in for a visit, said: "Hess or no Hess, I'm going to see the Marx Brothers." Which, legend has it, he did.

And it wasn't just Churchill who was apparently missing a prime chance to wound Britain's enemy. There was silence throughout the Empire. Hess was not, as the Germans expected, portrayed as a hero who fled the Nazi regime with a head full of secrets. He did not reveal atrocities or plans for world conquest. And he certainly didn't talk of an invasion of the Soviet Union.

The whole world waited for word. No word came.

The British sent Foreign Secretary Anthony Eden to try to explain things to Ambassador Winant. Winant then cabled Washington that he had learned "in strictest confidence" the British bottom line on the Hess mission. First of all, Winant wrote, Hess was acting on his own and not as "an agent for his Government. . . .

"Apparently," Winant said, "Hess had in mind, for some time coming to England. Eden told me that from what information [Ivone] Kirkpatrick had been able to give he had become obsessed with this idea." That idea being that he could single-handedly convince the British people to come to terms with Hitler. Hess had already written a memorandum in which he said "he was certain Germany would be victorious because of their enormous military strength, but that there had already been great slaughter and he believed that continuing the fighting would take an enormous toll of life."[23]

Why Eden had told this story to Winant in confidence is a puzzle, because the British were soon doling it out to every journalist in town. It was as if the British wanted to attach a new nuance to the dictionary definition of "quixotic." It should, they seemed to be advocating, be synonymous with the term "Hess mission."

The New York Times absorbed the point quickly. Its May 15 story repeated everything about the quixotic Hess mission, commenting: "Out of the many theories and explanations advanced concerning the Rudolf Hess exploit there emerged yesterday one point upon which both Britain and German informed sources agreed—that Adolf Hitler's deputy and confidant had flown to Scotland on a self-inspired peace mission." The *Times* had a very interesting observation. It described the two countries' propaganda lines as "dovetailing" into one another.[24]

They were, indeed. If the British wanted to portray Hitler's deputy as a misguided, though sincere, self-motivated emissary, the Germans were not about to deny it. That was the precise message they were trying to get out. German propaganda went through another quick contortion.

The *Times*, again, caught the line. A story in the same edition was headlined: "BERLIN CALLS HESS A PEACE 'MESSIAH.' " The report said that Hess had sent letters to various German leaders that "indicated that [he] believed that through his personal initiative peace could be brought about if the 'truth' were taken to Britain. His motive, it was authoritatively declared, appears to have been humanitarian—the wish to prevent the two great Nordic peoples of Europe from 'tearing each other to pieces.' " German sources reported to the *Times* that Hess was "100 percent German and National Socialist, as well as a brave soldier. . . . [Hess would not] do anything to harm the Fatherland, nor was he in any sense a traitor. . . ."[25]

Guardian Angel

London's actions mystified the world.

When he first heard of the Hess mission, German propaganda master Joseph Goebbels confided to his diary that it was "a hard, almost unbearable blow . . . dreadful and unthinkable."[26] The propaganda minister was particularly fearful of "atrocity stories" being revealed somehow from Hess's mouth.

On the night of May 12, with nothing yet coming from London, Goebbels predicted ominously: "the storm will, of course, break during the next few hours. . . ." A day later, Goebbels marveled that "Churchill has little to say about the *real motives*. . . . If I were the English Propaganda Minister, I would know exactly what to do [emphasis added]."

Twenty-four hours after that, Goebbels admitted that he was confused. On one hand, he wrote, "London is cunningly letting us wait for an official statement, and thus allowing free rein to the lies." On the other hand, he noted that "there is no indication of an underlying grand strategy at this stage. I would be making more of it if I were the English Propaganda Minister. Churchill is being very reticent."[27]

As it became obvious that the British were content to follow the Berlin line, Goebbels basked in his good fortune. London seemed willing to let the defection of the Deputy Führer of Germany simply die quietly. "It seems we have a guardian angel watching over us," Goebbels wrote. "We are dealing with dumb amateurs over there."[28] What the British were saying of Hess was "precisely what we wanted to hear." Reflected Goebbels: "Duff Cooper [his British counterpart] is worth his weight in gold from our point of view. He is really uniquely stupid. What I would have made of this case!"[29]

While Goebbels basked in what he saw as the perfect stupidity of the British, other leaders were also trying to make sense of the affair. They were less sanguine.

In Rome, Italian Foreign Minister Count Galeazzo Ciano, Mussolini's son-in-law, was dubious about the Hess tale from its inception, and grew more so as the days passed. After the first German announcement of Hess's probable crash, Ciano knew something strange was underfoot. He wrote in his diary: "A strange German communique announces the death of Hess in a plane accident. I cannot conceal my skepticism about the truth of this version. I even doubt whether he is dead at all. There is something mysterious about it. . . ."[30]

The next day, German Foreign Minister Joachim von Ribbentrop arrived to try to prepare Mussolini, Germany's central ally, for the expected propaganda barrage from London. Don't worry, was Ribbentrop's core message. Despite Hess's failings—Ribbentrop said there were many—he was a patriot and would not disclose any secrets. Therefore, he assured the Duce, anything "printed in his name is false."[31] But, in fact, nothing was printed in Hess's name.

In Italy, as around the world, leaders soon noted the absence of the expected broadside from London. By May 15, Ciano sensed that London's handling of the affair was more than merely mysterious. "Contrary to expectations," he wrote, "the speculation of Anglo-American propaganda on the Hess case is quite moderate. The only documents that are really harmful are the German dispatches, confused and reticent."[32] By the sixteenth, Ciano marveled that the British press was playing up Hess as a man on a peace mission.

Two weeks later, Mussolini met Hitler for general discussions. When, in private, Hitler brought up the name of his deputy, the Nazi dictator broke into tears.[33] Hitler cried when his mother died.

He cried when, on a hospital bed in 1918, he learned that Germany had lost the First World War. Now, in discussing his lost deputy and friend, Hitler cried again.

Across the Atlantic, there was a rapid American response to the Rudolf Hess Affair.

Sitting in the White House was a President firmly convinced that Adolf Hitler had a master plan that included the defeat of England, the appropriation of her fleet, and the use of those ships against the United States. If he got the ships, Adolf Hitler would gain material resources Germany could not otherwise have equaled for a decade, if, in fact, it ever could. Sooner or later—with sooner being his reputation—Hitler would use the fleet to transport troops and supplies to South America, from where he could launch attacks northward. If he wanted to control the world, as Roosevelt believed, Hitler would eventually have to subdue America.

This was a theme Roosevelt had been preaching to a mostly unconvinced nation for months. It was far better, he argued, to help Churchill stop the madman in Europe than for Americans to have to do it later in the Western Hemisphere. With Hess in Churchill's hands, Roosevelt's spirits rose. Very soon, evidence of the master plan would emerge, and America would wake up.

If past history was controlling, Roosevelt should have been right. From the beginning of their correspondence to the first reports about Hess being in Great Britain, Churchill had never missed a chance to stoke the President's fears of Nazi intentions in North and South America. He had even braced Roosevelt with the consequences of a British armistice with Hitler. The image of the capital ships *Hood* and *Prince of Wales* and the rest falling into Hitler's hands was terrifying to Roosevelt. Churchill told Roosevelt of the result of a peace diktat managed by Adolf Hitler:

"You must not be blind to the fact that [in that circumstance] the whole remaining bargaining counter with Germany would be the fleet, and if this country was left by the United States to its fate no one would have the right to blame those then responsible if they made the best terms they could for the surviving inhabitants. Excuse me, Mr. President, putting this nightmare bluntly. Evidently I could not answer for my successors who in utter despair and help-lessness might well have to accommodate themselves to the German will."[34]

It was not an isolated case. Churchill returned to the theme every time he thought it could prod America closer to full involvement.

Roosevelt waited—as did cabinet secretaries, senators and representatives who had been pushing the President's line—for confirming words from Rudolf Hess. On the other side, Lindbergh, Montana Senator Burton Wheeler and other America Firsters also waited expectantly for word from London.

When nothing emerged but silence interspersed with a few stilted and uninformative communiqués, an unease developed in Washington. As early as May 14 newspapers noted that American officials "could find no satisfactory explanation of the Hess episode and felt that the whole story had not been told yet."[35] A day later, an impatient President decided to act. In a telegram sent to Churchill marked "no distribution," the President made clear his desires:

"If Hess is talking, or does so in the future, it would be very valuable to public opinion over here if he can be persuaded to tell your people what Hitler had said about the United States, or what Germany's plans really are in relation to the United States or to other parts of the Western Hemisphere, including commerce, infiltration, military domination, encirclement of the United States, etc.

"From this distance I can assure you that the Hess flight has captured the American imagination and the story should be kept alive for just as many days or even weeks as possible.

"If he says anything about the Americas in the course of telling his story, it should be kept separate from other parts and featured by itself."[36]

Though he didn't say it, the President must have known what Goebbels and all shadow warriors knew: the British could put anything they wanted into the Deputy Führer's mouth. Roosevelt's reference to persuasion would not be easy to miss or to misunderstand.

After receiving such a direct suggestion from the President of the United States, and knowing that revelations from Hess might greatly speed the process of bringing America into the war, Churchill would surely act. The silence from London would end. Hess would issue authoritative reports on Nazi plans in the Americas.

But it was not to be. Three days after he received Roosevelt's urgent request, Churchill cabled Roosevelt with a bland and unhelpful report. Churchill said that officials had had three interviews with the Deputy Führer.

"At the first interview . . . Hess was extremely voluble, and made long statement with the aid of notes. First part recapitulated Anglo-German relations during past thirty years or so. . . . Second part emphasized certainty of German victory. . . . Third part outlined proposals for settlement.

"Hess said that the Führer had never entertained any designs against the British Empire, which would be left intact save for the return of former German colonies, in exchange for a free hand for him in Europe. But condition was attached that Hitler would not negotiate with present Government in England. This is the old invitation to us to desert all our friends in order to save temporarily the greater part of our skin. . . .

"He added however that Germany had certain demands to make of Russia which would have to be satisfied, but denied rumors that attack on Russia was being planned."

Also, in keeping with the developing legend, Churchill told Roosevelt that Hess "declared that this escapade is his own idea and that Hitler was unaware of it beforehand. If he is to be believed, he expected to contact members of a 'peace movement' in England, which he would help to oust the present Government."[37]

There was *nothing* in this message about Nazi designs on the United States, South America or anyplace else. On the same date, Roosevelt confidant Sumner Welles, under secretary of state, asked Lord Halifax, British ambassador to the United States, for information about Hess. Halifax, Welles reported, "said he had not as yet received any report from his Government, although he had urgently cabled for one."[38]

The American President was being stonewalled. And he knew it and refused to believe Churchill was telling the truth.[39]

The reference to the "peace movement" wanting to topple Churchill should have prodded the President into wondering how the Deputy Führer of Germany got such a notion. But there is no evidence that it did.

Other news reaching Washington added to the mystery of the British lassitude. On May 19, two days after Churchill's response to Roosevelt, America's German ambassador told Washington that anti-Hitler elements in Germany were as perplexed as everyone else about British behavior. The British were crazily missing a grand opportunity.

The ambassador said members of the anti-Nazi underground "have approached, complaining of the way the affair is being handled by the British radio to which listening in is increasing. They complain that the British radio is minimizing the incident indicating that Hess has disclosed nothing of importance. . . . They remark that if it were merely stated that Hess was continuing to write, thereby establishing the presumption that disclosures of Hess' misdeeds, projects and prospects might be forthcoming, it would cause eventual difficulties for the regime here."[40]

Yet the British were paying little heed to either German opposition to Hitler or to the President of the United States. As such, a bottom line was becoming clear: the only reason Winston Churchill would pass up the opportunity to bring America closer to the war was if something much more important was at stake. There was only one thing more important than American involvement in the war.

Eastern Suspicions

Stalin began to take a new look at the chess board. Was there something he had missed?

Three days after Rudolf Hess parachuted into plowman McLean's field, Stalin began taking actions. The Russian General Staff ordered seven Soviet armies to move secretly west into what, in military terms, would form Russia's operational echelon for the possible fight ahead. Military historian Bryan Fugate has reflected:

"The hefty size of the operational echelon belies the assumption that the general staff was caught napping by the German attack [six weeks after the move order]. Quite the contrary, the careful positioning of the operational echelon on what would become the flanks of [Germany's] Army Group Center would cause the Wehrmacht no end of difficulty in the summer of 1941."[41]

Stalin made many mistakes in 1941, but a few things he did right. Taking the Hess flight seriously enough to temper his strategic views was one of them.

Americans in Moscow were learning of Soviet suspicions. On May 20, the American military attaché in Moscow sent to his superiors this intelligence report: "Yugoslavia Military Attache stated the Chief of the Red Army said to him the Soviets will fight Germany later and are waiting for the United States to enter war, and that the Soviet Government distrusts England and suspects Hess flight as effort to turn war against U.S.S.R."[42]

The Japanese ambassador, shortly after meeting with Soviet Foreign Minister V. M. Molotov, was asked whether Russia would continue sending supplies to Germany as envisioned by the non-aggression pact of 1939. His cryptic response reflects the thinking of the Soviet leadership: "Germany now has 140 fully trained and equipped divisions on the Soviet frontier, the Soviets have 110, of which only 34 are fully trained and equipped. I think the cooperation will steadily increase."[43] Stalin was stalling.

While Stalin saw dark designs behind the Hess mission, most Americans were simply confused. One, however, did show a very special interest in the affair. FBI Director J. Edgar Hoover, as early as May 15, sent the State Department a memorandum of a conversation with an unnamed source "close to the German embassy."[44]

"It appeared," the memo read, "according to the German individual, that there had been two definite groups in Britain, that is to say, the Churchill conservative group and the former remnants of the Cliveden Set, among which the Duke of Hamilton appears to have been a convert. He stated it appears Hess was trying to contact this particular peace sect and bring them the 'idea' of terminating this present conflict.

"The German individual stated that he knows Hess very well, and that Hess has always been a great believer in the Anglo-Saxon race. He advised that Hess has expressed himself on numerous occasions—'What a pity it is that England and Germany don't get together in an alliance, as they are naturally of the same stock, race and background, and hence should unify their action in the world.' "

Hoover had hit upon two keys to understanding the Hess riddle:

how the Nazi hierarchy actually viewed the British, whom they were so fond of bombing, and how the top Nazis felt about a powerful "peace sect" that not only operated in Britain, but could actually represent England in negotiations. There is no evidence, however, that the information stirred even a paper clip at Foggy Bottom.

The director, however, was not deterred. On May 22, he sent a memorandum to the State Department with important information. In fact, if this information had been correctly analyzed, the most prominent Soviet spy penetration of Western intelligence of the twentieth century might have been exposed.

The information Hoover possessed—though he didn't know it— had just been routed to Moscow by a ring of Soviet moles operating in Great Britain.

Hoover described his remarkably well-informed source as merely an "individual prominent in Soviet circles."[45] Hoover wrote:

"A Russian source has advised with respect to the arrival of Rudolph [sic] Hess in Scotland that in his opinion this occurrence was predicated upon instructions of Adolf Hitler for the purpose of arranging a contact with Liberal Communists or the remnants of the Cliveden set so that they, in turn, could contact Prime Minister Churchill and thereby influence the British government to negotiate a peace with Germany and thereafter combine forces with Germany to attack Russia.

"It was stated that the Russian position was very plain, as a constant rearmament program had been in effect in that country for some time, although Russia is not disposed to picking a quarrel with Germany at the present time."

The Final Silence

One man who in late May knew exactly what was going on was huddled in the Reichschancellory in Berlin with his generals, plotting final details of the greatest land battle in history. While those generals were likely contemplating the concussion of war, Adolf Hitler may well have been reflecting on silence. There had been plenty of that since his deputy arrived in Scotland.

The world knew much of the British silence. Most were paying little note to another, equally portentous, silence. The British had not been the first to quiet. That honor fell to Hitler.

While on May 10, 1941, Göring's bombers pulverized central London, the night of May 11 was quiet. In fact, May 10, 1941—the day Hitler's deputy arrived in Great Britain—was both the height and the sudden end of the German Blitz. The massive raids were never to return. London had been spared. Hitler had sent a message, something akin to an exclamation point followed by a question mark.

Trained American observers immediately took note. "German air operations over Britain were on a minor scale. . . . Daylight May 12: German air operations were reduced to a minimum with a few scattered planes observed over land but no raids were reported."[46] Over the next six weeks, the Americans continually reported the same: the Luftwaffe was missing in action. There was no explanation for why Hitler had suddenly cut off the attack immediately after his fiercest barrage.

While American observers in England wondered where the Luftwaffe had gone off to, observers in Germany were wondering about the absence of the Royal Air Force. Following the Hess flight, the indefatigable Goebbels began noting the quiet skies. It was almost as though, above Europe, there was a cease-fire.

May 17: "Middling air raids on Hannover. Air-raid warning in Berlin, but no bombs."[47] May 18: "Middling raid on Dusseldorf." May 19: "Mass raid on Cologne." May 20: "No air raids on either side." May 22: "No air activity on either side." May 23: "No air activity on either side." May 24: "No air activity on either side." May 25: "Minor enemy air raids on West Germany. Very little activity on our side." May 26: "Very little air activity on either side. The weather is too bad. The public seems to believe that the lack of air activity has something to do with their readiness for peace. This is, of course, pure nonsense." May 28: "No air activity on either side."

The procession of no or little air activity reports continued for Goebbels. Finally, even the propaganda minister began to believe that the silence meant that general peace was about to break out.

On June 8, he wrote that "talk of peace is everywhere. There must be something behind it." By June 9, he noted, "Peace rumors are still circulating."

He soon, however, learned of the final attack plans for the Soviet invasion. And he was confused. By mid-June, with the bulk of the Reich's forces in the East, Goebbels expected the British to have their way with the lightly fortified West. Though there were some raids, they seemed remarkably slender to Goebbels. "It is odd," Goebbels wrote, "that the English are not attacking us more at the moment, while we are labouring under a handicap."[48] On the eve of the invasion, Goebbels noted again the actions of the beneficent British. "For a long time now the RAF has not been attacking in the kind of force that we had feared," Goebbels wrote. "One skirmish after another. No one can explain it."[49]

Actually, someone could. Adolf Hitler had for some time begun to change his view of the success or failure of the Hess mission. The more the British handled the affair with silence, the greater grew Hitler's conviction that the Peace Party was responsible. The Rudolf Hess Affair might have finally, improbably, unpredictably accomplished Hitler's goal. Winston Churchill was appearing to be a Prime Minister, reined in.

The British had done nothing to discourage this view and everything to promote it. On May 22, 1941, Sir Archibald Sinclair announced in the House of Commons that the Duke of Hamilton was cleared of all wrongdoing in the Hess matter. There had been, Sinclair declared, no communications between Hess and Hamilton.[50]

That certainly must have been choice to Adolf Hitler. The Führer had personally authorized these communications and had been kept informed. The Peace Party approaches conducted by Albrecht Haushofer had been inspired by Hitler and Hess. Now the British were saying that one of the leading British conspirators was totally absolved. If the British were looking for a way to tell Hitler that the back channel was safe, despite the inconvenience of Hess's house arrest, they could hardly have found a better way than loosing Sinclair in the House of Commons.

Two days after Sinclair's announcement, the British released fourteen million leaflets saying that if Germany soon invaded *En-*

gland "it may easily be some weeks before the invader has been totally destroyed."[51] Invade England? Not only were the British apparently trying to keep quiet about the Nazis' true intentions, they
actually appeared to be helping in the deception. Bloody lucky.

In fact, there was so much the British did—and didn't do—during this period, that Joseph Goebbels was right to marvel. Those
dumb amateurs across the Channel were, as he said, clearly worth
their weight in gold.

Americans began hearing about this strange and growing German
faith in the mysterious British Peace Party. From sources other than
J. Edgar Hoover. The American embassy in Rome cabled Washington in early June that German intelligence was convinced that
"there is reason to expect Churchill Government may soon fall and
hope is placed in opposition of Astor and Beaverbrook. In fact,
someone is in Rome now doing a little London business for Ribbentrop."[52] Lord Beaverbrook, minister of British aircraft production,
was one of Hitler's favorite Peace Party members.

The same day—June 7, 1941—even Goebbels began to take notice of word from London: "Growing criticism of Churchill in London. But some of it contrived."[53]

He was right, of course. The criticism was contrived. But these
were fluid times and the propaganda minister did not follow
through on the thought.

A little over a week later, General Halder, deep in preparation for
the onslaught of the Soviet Union, was briefed on what dangers
might lurk at the Wehrmacht's rear. Those dangers were the general's worst fear—the specter of Great Britain springing a trap in the
West while he was least able to cope with it. Fresh from meetings
with the Führer, Baron Ernst von Weizsäcker, German state secretary, reassured Halder and the rest of the German High Command
about what to expect in the West:

"Britain will at first feel relieved by the news of our attack on
Russia and will rejoice at the 'dispersal of our forces.' But a rapid
advance of German troops will soon bring disillusionment, for the
defeat of Russia cannot but lead to a marked strengthening of our
position in Europe," was how Halder recorded Weizsäcker's re-
marks.

"As to Britain's readiness for an accord with us, [Weizsäcker] has this to say: The propertied classes will strive for a settlement, leaving us a free hand in the east, but it would involve renunciation of our claims to Holland and Belgium. If these tendencies are to prevail, Churchill has to be overthrown, as he relies on the support of the Labor Party, which is not interested in a peace concluded by the propertied classes."[54]

It was a strange idea—that Churchill was in June 1941 relying on the Labour Party—but it couldn't have been more timely for the British. The Nazi Führer's faith in the Peace Party—that is, the propertied classes—was apparently restored.

As for the sometimes befuddled Goebbels, trying hard to figure out all the signals from England—the silence on Hess, the inexplicable failure of England to attack when Germany was most vulnerable, and the rumors of an Anglo-German Peace—it was left to the Führer to make the explanation. On June 22, 1941, as the big guns of Barbarossa were taking aim against the Soviet Union, Hitler showed Goebbels his hand. "*The Führer,*" wrote Goebbels in his diary entry of that date, "*has high hopes of the peace party in England. Otherwise, the Hess Affair would not have been so systematically killed by silence* [emphasis added]."[55]

Barbarossa

Just before dawn on June 22, 1941, began the mightiest battle in history. Germany stormed into the great Russian expanse with 3.3 million soldiers, 3,300 tanks, 600,000 other motorized vehicles and half a million horses. Army Group North sped through the Baltic states, recently subjugated by Stalin. It was to cut off Leningrad, securing the Baltic Sea for shipment of iron ore to Germany from Scandinavia. Army Group Center aimed toward Moscow.

To Hitler, that was a feint, hiding his main objective. The key rested on the flanks. Hitler was a great student of the American Civil War general William T. Sherman, and appreciated that general's strategy of huge flanking movements to cut off an enemy's resources while capturing them for himself. He called Sherman the first great modern general. Hitler welded Sherman's doctrines to his own overall political objectives and ordered his forces to capture the agricultural heartland in the Ukraine, then take the Crimea, the Caucasus and the Soviet oil fields.

This measure, Hitler told his generals, "can be said to be absolutely essential for Germany. Under present circumstances no one can guarantee that our only important oil producing region [that is, Romania] is safe from air attack. Such attacks could have incalculable results for the future conduct of the war."[56]

Once this objective was met, the war would be over. England would have to acknowledge a fait accompli.

One day before the killing started, when the whole world suspected that a German-Russian clash was only moments away, an American writer approached the truth behind it. Anne McCormick, observing the rising German-Soviet tensions, wrote: "In some way Hess is a symptom and symbol of this clash. In some way his flight is associated with the present crisis. Even if it is completely unreal, another war of nerves, he is somehow involved in the plot to create the impression that Germany must fight Russia or against her."[57]

London worked feverishly to blunt such suspicions. The Hess mission not only had nothing to do with the German invasion of Russia, they claimed. Instead the invasion itself was only a precursor to much graver times. With apparently a straight face, Winston Churchill told Franklin Roosevelt that the "invasion of Russia is no more than a prelude to an attempted invasion of the British Isles . . . and the subjugation of the Western Hemisphere to his [Hitler's] will and to his system."[58]

Churchill knew this was nonsense. Germans had personally briefed the English about their plans for over seven years, Hess being the latest and most astounding example. The British Empire and the United States were not German objects for conquest. Besides, the British had broken the German code and from that knew that no aggression against the Isles was planned. Churchill was merely doing what he had been doing for over a year, lying to Roosevelt about the fundamental facts of the war.

Eight days after Barbarossa began, the Führer visited the headquarters of the German High Command, expanding on the Peace Party theme. Halder recorded the Führer's comments in a shorthand that sometimes left out words, but seldom meanings. "Britain's domestic political scene: possibility of Churchill's overthrow by Conservatives with a view to forestalling a Socialist-Communist revolution in the country. Lloyd George, Hoare."[59]

Hoare's full name was Samuel Hoare, Churchill's ambassador to Spain. As much as any other person Samuel Hoare had been the leading "Peace Party" contact for Rudolf Hess. On the morning that Hess flew to Scotland, Albrecht Haushofer had even called Hoare to make sure peace-loving interests in Great Britain were ready for discussions somewhere.

Now, deep inside Soviet territory, the Führer was apparently mentioning Hoare and David Lloyd George, the British Prime Minister during the First World War and a supposed Peace Party advocate, as possible replacements for Churchill. As the Germans rolled east, the Führer's assessment of the Hess mission had totally changed from the dark hours of May 11 and 12. Even though his deputy had fallen into the hands of his bitterest enemy, it was clear that enemy could do nothing about it. Hess had succeeded. Strangely, it was a success for Hitler, who didn't know with whom he was dealing, and for Churchill, who did.

Bernhard

At the time, only a handful of people at best knew anything of this. The full scope of the deception would be impossible to know then, or for fifty years since. To the world, Rudolf Hess had ceased to exist. The only thing of import was the question: could Hitler be stopped?

One person, though, came mysteriously close to untangling the affair. Using logic and a knowledge of the ways of realpolitik, Georg Bernhard had an insight. On the day after Hitler explained the Peace Party to his High Command, Bernhard wrote in *The New York Times* about the meaning of the Hess mission:

> It is now apparent to everybody that Rudolf Hess flew to England with the full consent of Adolf Hitler. It was his job to bring peace between Germany and England. The war between Ger-

many and Russia has solved the mystery of Rudolf Hess, if it ever was a mystery.

The whole affair sounds like a detective story. As a matter of fact it is one, the kind of detective story that could only have been written in Berlin. In Berlin this sort of thing is called by another name, "grosse Politick." During the [First] World War the German High Command was made up of every imaginative clique. They forged all kinds of plans against the British Empire with Afghanistan, Persia and Arabia as theaters of war. And in this connection we should not forget that it was General Ludendorff who arranged to send Lenin and his comrades in a sealed train to Russia where they carried out the successful Bolshevik revolution.

What happened this time? The original idea behind the whole trick is of historic importance: the Nazi leaders in Berlin had become convinced that with the decision of the United States to go to the limit in helping Britain it would be impossible to defeat that country. In particular the German leaders no longer believed that Britain could be successfully invaded. Consequently they decided to make peace.

The question then was, how? Even in Berlin it was apparent that a simple peace offer would not be successful, that the world would look upon it as a confession of German weakness. . . . On the other hand, a peace offer which admitted that the Germans needed peace with England in order to shift fronts and to begin the "holy war" against bolshevism—that seemed to the Berlin leaders to have large possibilities.

. . . the German leaders believed they would bring about a deep split in English, and eventually in American, public opinion by playing upon the fear of bolshevism and the deep, though admittedly justified, lack of confidence in Communists and their revolutionary alma. The German leaders did not expect a change of heart on the part of Prime Minister Churchill, but after all, they argued, Churchill was a member of a democratic government. He could be overthrown. . . .

Only very few people know what really happened in England after Hess arrived. But the outcome of the whole affair is a masterful achievement for Winston Churchill. For the important thing from England's standpoint was that Germany should march against Russia. That could have been accomplished only by making Berlin believe that the immediate result of a German attack on Russia would be the reshuffling of the British Cabinet without Churchill.

Whatever form it took, Bernhard concluded that Churchill was "able to bring about a decisive turning point in the war."[60]

But the world was moving too fast, and the war was changing too much, for Georg Bernhard to be heard above the din of war. Or even British silence.

Publicly, the British insisted that the story was just as they had said: the Hess mission was one of a quixotic idealist trying naively to make the world at peace with Adolf Hitler.

Obliterate

The great German Barbarossa offensive rolled eastward, seemingly invincible, ever expanding. Stalin and Marshal Georgi Zhukov huddled in the Kremlin, wondering—as Churchill had done little more than a year earlier—what terms they might offer to achieve an honorable surrender.[61] Hitler's plan to cut off Moscow from the Ukraine and the Caucasus had cast a gloom over the Kremlin. Stalin had expected Hitler to come to Moscow, and that is where he had his strongest forces.

From the beginning, the war seemed to go wrong. Over two thousand Soviet planes were destroyed on the ground during the battle's first two days. The White Russian capital of Minsk fell six days after Barbarossa began. Everywhere the Red Army was forced back.

"It is probably no overstatement," Halder optimistically wrote in his diary, "to say that the Russian campaign has been won in the space of two weeks."[62]

The Wehrmacht was not the only German organization crashing into Russia. Six weeks before the campaign even began—on the day after Hess arrived in Scotland and the day the skies of Great Britain were emptied of the Luftwaffe—Adolf Hitler issued a fateful order. When the German Wehrmacht entered the Soviet Union, the army was to be closely followed by special troops under the command of

Reichsführer SS, Heinrich Himmler. These troops were called the Einsatzgruppen.

The Einsatzgruppen, Hitler said, were to perform "special tasks" against Russian Jews and others.[63] As the army moved east, these mobile killing units proved as efficient as the Wehrmacht. Hundreds of thousands of Jews—often with father, mother and children lying down upon other bodies in mass graves—were administered "special treatment."

The Holocaust had begun.

The Einsatzgruppen and the Wehrmacht were very successful in the Soviet Union, though not as successful as General Halder had anticipated. Russia did not collapse in two weeks. The Russians lost hundreds of thousands of troops, but had millions to spare. And they managed, unlike the British at Dunkirk, to escape with most of their heavy guns.

This was not as frustrating to Hitler as it was to his generals. Hitler continued to want to go south, toward the vital oil resources, while his generals wanted to finish off the Red Army, not, apparently, realizing that the Red Army without petroleum would hardly be an army at all.

The generals were insistent. Heinz Guderian, an Army Group Center Commander, argued that "the troops would go to Moscow. The season was very hot and dry and, therefore, good for the further conduct of operations in the same direction. The streets and the railways had all the direction to Moscow. . . . Moscow is the center of Russia, the center for communications, the center for telegraph and telephone wires, the center for radio, for the government, for many economical branches."[64] The rest of the OKH, the Army High Command, joined in. Capture of a city and the destruction of the forces that would protect it, they argued, should be the objective of the war.

In September 1941, Hitler, the former corporal, succumbed to his generals' advice. It was the worst military mistake of his life. Hitler ordered Army Group North and Army Group South to dispatch a decisive mass of their forces toward Moscow. Two giant pincers would descend on the Russian capital while Army Group Center rammed straight ahead.

Stalin and Zhukov grew relieved. At last, the Germans were behaving as expected. There would be no early surrender.

The move toward Moscow seemed to invigorate the Führer, and soon he was believing that his generals had been right after all. The war, he thought, would soon be over. Hitler issued an order that took away the breath of those same generals. He ordered the discontinuance of all munitions production in Germany and decided to disband and demobilize forty divisions stationed on the Eastern Front.[65]

The German generals did their best to ignore the demobilization order, but munitions factories were, in fact, converted to civilian production. Halder said "it took Germany a year" to recover from that mistake, and Albert Speer, head of Nazi war production, confirmed that account. Said Speer: "Ammunition production had been heavily cut"[66] because "in fall of 1941 . . . an early end of the Eastern campaign was being confidently expected."[67] Some generals tried to tell Hitler that, even after the Russian collapse, there was still Great Britain to worry about. A general pointed out that Rommel was still engaged with the British in North Africa. Hitler responded: "The African Theater of Operations was unimportant."[68]

Hitler's reasoning was transparent. A collapse of Russia would mean peace with England as well. In fact, he was possibly correct in that. It was one of the many hedges Churchill worked into the Peace Party bargain.

Soon, though, in the snows in front of Moscow, Hitler suffered his first significant reverse. The German advance was stopped as Stalin's hidden reserves breached the front. Stalin did not have the initiative, but, for the first time, neither did Adolf Hitler. Hitler would never again issue orders to disband divisions.

It seemed an unlikely time for the Rudolf Hess matter to surface. As far as the British were concerned, he was long forgotten and should remain that way. Georg Bernhard's perceptive points had flashed, then faded. The Deputy Führer was irrelevant to the great events taking place. He was history.

Yet on November 5, 1941, thirty-two days before the Japanese attack at Pearl Harbor sparked America to war, the code of silence was broken. Washington was told a sliver of truth about the Hess affair.

It certainly wasn't the whole truth, there were distortions, but on two major points the revelations showed that Rudolf Hess was not history, not irrelevant and not going to easily disappear.

The American military attaché at the London embassy cabled U.S. Brigadier General Sherman Miles, head of U.S. military intelligence, with some stark new information about Hess. Its source, he said, was "someone whose intimate acquaintance with the affair is unquestionable."

"I have," attaché Raymond Lee wrote, "every reason to consider this is the correct story. Will you please not duplicate this memorandum and show it only to such individuals as are really entitled to read it, as it would be a pity if it were traced back, through me, to my informant." He described his information as "an interesting bit of history."[69]

The British informant told the American that much of the Hess story was, really, quite true.

"Hess landed and was captured just as the papers described. He was taken to a hospital and there told the doctor that 'I am Rudolf Hess.' The doctor laughed and said, 'Yes, we have a fellow in the hospital here who thinks he's Solomon,' but Hess persisted that he was Hess and demanded to see the Duke of Hamilton.

"The Duke appeared, talked with Hess and reported to authorities: 'Yes, I think it's Hess, but don't take my word for it. I met him up on a platform during the Olympic Games and maybe shook his hand—I can't really remember if I did or not—but I didn't know him at all—never carried on a conversation with him. I've seen his pictures often enough and this man certainly looks like Hess. . . .

"After Hamilton, Ivone Kirkpatrick, who has been secretary in the British Embassy in Berlin for a long time, and who knew Hess, went up to see the man. Kirkpatrick confirmed that it was indeed Hess."

Then came the unexpected.

"Hess said he flew to the Duke to tell him that Germany was about to fight Russia." Hess said that he "knew the Duke would see immediately that it would be absurd and awful for England to continue to fight Germany any longer. For, if England continued fighting from the west, we should have to destroy England after we destroyed Russia."

Left out of this was any mention of the long Nazi preparation for this flight, the contacts in foreign countries, the letters from Haushofer, the calls to Madrid. Hamilton was not picked randomly for an unannounced visit. Yet there was quite enough here for most anyone to be impressed. Rudolf Hess, the highly placed informant was telling the Americans, had brought with him plans for the Russian invasion—plans the British had kept all to themselves.

Stalin would not have been pleased to know this, what with German troops trying presently to relieve him of both country and life. Nor would FDR be overjoyed. Though the President had expected something of this nature, Churchill had personally assured him that there was nothing to the Hess mission. Specifically, he had told the President that Hess brought no mention of possible war with Russia.

In his secret communiqué Captain Lee expanded further. Hess, he said, had expected the Duke to go right to the head of the British Peace Party: none other than King George himself.

Once the King knew "about our plans to fight the Bolsheviks . . . the King could have made a peace with us."

Kirkpatrick asked Hess about the probable reaction of Churchill. The Deputy Führer was not impressed. "Oh, nonsense," said Hess. "Who does the Churchill Government represent? Nobody but those fools who want to destroy Germany and therefore drag down the whole civilized world before the Bolshevik menace. The King could have made a peace with us, of course."

However abbreviated and crudely paraphrased, the entire Nazi belief in an upper-class Peace Party cabal was being outlined to the Americans. Why anyone in Great Britain at this time, or any time, would do this is unanswerable.

Lee trusted the informant, and his trust was well placed. Lee's communiqué to Washington contained many less important details of the Hess arrival in Great Britain that were not released until after the war, sometimes many years after the war. The informant was obviously in a key position to get good information. He even said he had personally spoken with Hess on several occasions, relaying that the Deputy Führer talked openly, seemingly unguarded, just as if he was talking with an ally.

"I can tell you anything you want to know," said Hess, who no doubt—if the British were smart and not, in fact, dumb amateurs—was made to feel that he was talking to an ally. No better way to get information than that.

Finally, Lee got to a second major revelation, no less shattering than the first. During Hess's early stay he was observed by a psychiatrist. The doctor asked him about his fears. Hess didn't have any, except that he didn't want to be poisoned. But, asked the psychiatrist, did he not fear the Jews in Germany?

"*No,*" Hess responded. "*We are obliterating the Jews* [emphasis added]."

It is unclear what happened after General Miles received the Lee communiqué. There are no notations that would suggest it was sent or summarized to anyone higher in the U.S. government. There are no declassified indexes showing anything pertaining to Hess left the U.S. Army intelligence staff in the months following November 5, 1941.

Perhaps the message was filed and lost. Perhaps its import was not immediately of concern to military intelligence. Japanese-American relations were at the time crumbling and a Pacific strike was expected. Perhaps there is no quick explanation.

A year after Lee's communiqué—in October of 1942—Stalin would raise the Hess issue to the highest level. Rudolf Hess suddenly, somehow, threatened the whole Grand Alliance. Stalin alleged that the Hess mission had something to do with the attack on the Soviet Union. It was not a mere "interesting bit of history."

Certainly with that, Roosevelt would be given everything important on the Deputy Führer's mission. His communications with the bulldog, however, show that he was still quite in the dark.

Lee's message, Hoover's sources, the great enigma of the British silence, the deceiving of a President and a Führer, and all the other ingredients of the Rudolf Hess Affair would not become a focus of the Americans during this war.

But once the war ended, perhaps there would be an occasion to revisit the case, to find out why Stalin had been so upset by Hess that he sent his country toward the Cold War, to examine what Hess had really brought to Britain, to delve into the master plan of Adolf Hitler without the prism of British propaganda.

In defeated Germany of 1945, American agents again acquired the trail toward the truth that Hoover and Lee and Bernhard and others had sensed in 1941. But now they would deal with known sources and key documents, and they would come close to the truth.

3 : *Revelations*

WHEN ONCE THE TERMS WE OFFERED TO GREAT BRITAIN
ARE MADE PUBLIC THERE WILL BE AN UPROAR THROUGH-
OUT THE KINGDOM.

Adolf Hitler, September 2, 1942[1]

As the autumn leaves turned in Germany in 1945, Rudolf Hess
reentered the arena of spotlights and controversy. The issue was the
trial of the major surviving Nazi war criminals at Nuremberg. Of
course, everybody was interested in how Rudolf Hess had survived
his stay in British hands. When the British finally brought him to
Nuremberg—Hess was the last defendant to arrive—almost to the
person, his former friends and colleagues said he was, somehow,
changed. Not physically. He was gaunt, but recognizable. Yet to his
fellow Germans, he seemed void, mad, as if part of his mind had disappeared. To some prosecutors, however, the man who showed up
at Nuremberg claiming that he remembered nothing of his past was
an evil man. Nothing else.

His British hosts for the previous four and a half years had somewhat reluctantly agreed to bring him to the trials. A few compas-
sionate men lobbied for leniency. A man who sought peace before
the big killings started certainly deserved consideration. Russian
prosecutors, however, were getting orders to view the case far differently. The master at the Kremlin wanted Hess dead.

It was a contest that would leave America somewhat in the middle. So as American agents fanned out over Germany to gather ev-

idence on the Nazi leadership, they were in a very good position to obtain information that could arbitrate the issue of Hess's guilt. Soon, they began finding disturbing facts that would never—could never—be presented to the Military Tribunal. Piece by piece, they were uncovering the great British forgery.

Haushofer

Deep in the Bavarian woods south of Munich, American agents were trying to find an old mansion on a hill. Its patriarch was little known to the world, though famous to those who studied Nazi foreign policy—a man, in fact, without whom the Second World War may never have happened. The agents' intelligence report does not say exactly how many were searching that day, though it appears at least three were in the group. It was late September 1945, and there were still major holes in the Allies' understanding of exactly what went on inside the Nazi hierarchy. The man they sought had many of the answers.

Finally, the agents came upon a dirt road leading to the estate. They noted that someone, probably prudently, had removed a road sign identifying the place. The agents pressed on. They walked up the hill and knocked on the door. A person—the Americans didn't identify him or her—let them in and asked them to wait. Soon Karl Haushofer, an old man who bore the twin titles of general and professor, appeared. He probably did not cut the image of an architect of German foreign policy. He greeted the Americans in a dressing gown, wool socks and flannel slippers.

The Americans were obviously not fans of the former general of the First World War. Their eventual report would be replete with sarcastic digs such as those that occasionally made their way into OSS reports. It was unfortunate that the agents didn't take more time with ancient Haushofer—whose second title stemmed from his professorship in geopolitics at the University of Munich. He was a truly remarkable man who knew many secrets. The Americans would leave with at least some of them. In fact, before the day was over, they would learn a key answer to the riddle of Rudolf Hess.

The agents didn't know that when their interview began. They were more interested in events that happened long before the war, when the seeds of Nazi foreign policy sprouted.

There was little that Haushofer could say this day to persuade the Americans that he was anything but an immensely evil man, one of the "most influential personalities of Nazi Germany," the creator of Nazi foreign policy and an implicit co-conspirator in the Holocaust. Their comments made clear they were sizing his neck for the noose.

Haushofer's problem was simple: as a professor in Munich after the Great European War, he had acquired two problematic students. One had studied under him, while the other received special tutoring. The first was Rudolf Hess, the second Adolf Hitler.

There surely must have been some pleasantries exchanged before the grilling started, but the agents apparently deemed them too unimportant to report. According to the record of their interview, the interrogation of General Karl Haushofer began with a question both singular and open-ended. It was this: "Hitler?"

"Oh, no," said the seventy-five-year-old Haushofer. An agent noted skeptically: "His face assumed a pained expression."[2]

The Americans didn't know how absolutely genuine Haushofer's pain was. His dalliance with the Führer and the Nazi Party had already led to the murder of his son, Albrecht, four months earlier, by a commando squad under orders of the master of death himself, Heinrich Himmler. Millions had been killed by Himmler's SS, yet Albrecht Haushofer's death was unique. It was the very last murder Himmler personally ordered, and, to Himmler, was probably the most deserving, for without Albrecht Haushofer, the Third Reich may have won.

The old general knew this and it was not a knowing without burden. Five years earlier, the whole world was different, lighter, more open, and Haushofer and his son were leading lives some would call charmed. They were two key advisors to Hess and, to a lesser extent, to Hitler when Hess and Hitler seemed on top of the game, re-creating a big German presence in Central Europe, without much opposition.

Hess had met Haushofer shortly after the First World War and was smitten by the professor's political ideas. A short time later, Hess attended a beer hall rally where a fiery mustachioed man named Adolf Hitler was speaking. Hess was overwhelmed by Hitler's fierce oratory, passion and conviction. While Haushofer soon became almost a father to Hess, Hitler became his leader, or, as the Germans say, his Führer. In 1920, Hess introduced the great men of his life to each other, and they immediately found common ground. Haushofer's ideas formed whole chapters of Nazi foreign policy.

Haushofer's ideas were varied, but one idea both he and Albrecht shared was the wisdom in and, in fact, the historical necessity of a close German-Anglo alliance. Hitler adopted that position.

The Second World War should have been a grand time for Karl Haushofer, what with Hitler testing his ideas on a world scale. Few academics had ever been so honored. But Haushofer's great theories became dust as the Third Reich imploded, and the war became all too mortal. When excuses needed to be made during the last months, Karl Haushofer and his son were easy targets. The SS sent Karl Haushofer to Dachau. It was not a grueling stay, he was treated well,[3] but, from whatever perch in such a hell, Haushofer could not have missed what many of his countrymen had willed away. Theory had become a crime that was almost unimaginable.

Dachau was a steep fall for a man who had enjoyed access to the Nazi inner circles. Hitler had even once kissed the hand of Haushofer's Jewish wife.[4]

The professor had been fooled by the Nazis but he was not a habitual fool. Time had moved on and the world had changed. Nineteen forty-five was no year to be linked to Adolf Hitler. Haushofer, in his warm slippers with an oak fire likely warming the great room, tried his best to distance himself from the Führer.

He had, he explained, far more contact with Hess and, in fact, had used the Deputy Führer to try to implant only good ideas inside the Führer's raging mind. Alas, to no avail. Hitler, he said, was "an angry man with excited eyes whom only Hess could calm."

Yes, Haushofer told them, he taught Hitler "geo-politics," but the Nazi Führer "never understood." And how could he? The Führer, Haushofer said, "knew no feelings of friendship. His resentment of anyone else's superiority was colossal." Explained Haushofer, again: "I was only able to influence him through Hess."

This tactic was sound. Although Hitler was irredeemable, the jury was quite literally out on Hess. If the British insisted that the Deputy Führer was a dreamy peace-seeker in the midst of scoundrels, the professor should have equal rights.

Hess and Haushofer had exchanged a mountain of correspondence as they thought out German foreign policy. Most of it dealt with the need for an Anglo-German understanding. Perhaps this connection to the Deputy Führer could actually help Haushofer.

The American agents were, of course, not impressed with the general's pleas of innocence. The foreign policy Haushofer had advocated had not been tranquil. He had advised that Germany renounce the Versailles treaty that ended the First World War. Hitler did so. He had suggested the reunification of the German-speaking peoples in Austria and the Sudetenland. Hitler had not varied from that. Haushofer had also thought that the Reich should obtain formerly German territories in Poland. When Hitler did that, with the German invasion of Poland, he sparked the world war.

Haushofer protested that Hitler embellished these ideas, pursuing them in far too military a fashion. Haushofer had favored diplomacy. The American interrogators did not seem to appreciate gray lines. They knew that Haushofer was behind the major Nazi ideal of German unity. That was crime enough.

Haushofer did not dispute most of what the Americans offered. The professor had wanted a united Germany. And so what? Explaining the dismemberment of Czechoslovakia, Haushofer said: "This annexation goes hand in hand with my theories. The Germans of the Sudeten area had the right to join the Reich; because they had been persecuted."

The old gentleman probably did not help his standing with his interrogators with his next set of answers. Was it not true, the Americans wondered, that his theories had a profound effect upon Nazi Foreign Minister Joachim von Ribbentrop? Yes, Haushofer said, "I taught him to read the cards."

"What do you mean by reading the cards?" one of the questioners asked.

"I taught him his basic political principles," Haushofer responded. Since Ribbentrop would be first on the gallows precisely because of his basic political principles, it was a questionable admission.

Earlier in the interview, when the Americans lightly broached the subject of Rudolf Hess and his "mission," Haushofer easily deflected the inquiry by taking the high dry ground occupied by the British. The Hess affair, he explained, was "the escape of a heroic and idealistic man from an unbearable situation."

But by the end, the old man was wearing down. When the Americans asked about his son Albrecht's connection with Hess, there emerged a somewhat different Haushofer, less defensive, more resigned. Albrecht's death had been a blow like none other. It symbolized the utter failure of the old professor's vision and his life.

The agents asked Haushofer what exactly was Albrecht's role in Nazi Germany? This was the exchange:

"(Haushofer): He was the founder of the Geopolitical Institute in Berlin.

"Question: And . . . officially?

"(Haushofer): Nothing at all. Lord, he had a desk at the Foreign Office where he was consulted about certain matters. He was sent abroad from time to time but only because he had such good connections, only because he had such good connections.

"Question: Where were these connections?

"(Haushofer): Well, everywhere—in France, England, Switzerland . . . he was always very welcome. . . ."

And didn't those connections pertain to the Hess mission?

The answer was rather interesting.

"In 1941," Haushofer said, "Germany put out peace feelers to Great Britain through Switzerland. Albrecht was sent to Switzerland. There he met a British confidential agent—a Lord Templewood, I believe. In this peace proposal we offered to relinquish Norway, Denmark and France. A larger meeting was to be held in Madrid. When my son returned, he was immediately called to Augsburg by Hess. A few days later Hess flew to England."

The agents remarked: "Compare with the above '. . . the escape of an idealist from an unbearable situation!' "

It was something to exclaim about. It would mean that there was an official German government contact with the British government about a "peace conference," a German proposition to return its Western conquests, a call to Augsburg, and then a decision by Hess within days to leave. From this scenario, Hess begins to resemble a plenipotentiary, not a lone idealist.

From their abbreviated report, it appears the agents didn't ask Haushofer exactly who this Lord Templewood was. Perhaps they already knew. Lord Templewood—a title he gained later in the war, and for good reason—was Samuel Hoare. Hoare was Churchill's man, the individual the British Prime Minister specifically and in great haste sent into that hotbed of intrigue called Madrid in the same week that Churchill became Prime Minister. Hoare was His Majesty's ambassador to Spain.

Hoare was also Hitler's man. He was the same Samuel Hoare that Hitler would mention to his generals as a possible replacement for Churchill. He was a perfect member of Churchill's "Peace Party."

The scenario outlined by Haushofer could hardly have seemed real to the Americans. How could Hitler at his most ascendant moment offer at the beginning of negotiations, or anytime, the surrender of his hard-won victories? Was Adolf Hitler actually proposing a peace with Great Britain that would roll back the Wehrmacht without shots being fired?

Further, was Churchill—or renegades in his government—listening?

Haushofer began offering answers. "We had been sending our [British] friends private letters through Portugal," Haushofer said, "and I assume that some of these were intercepted by the [British] Secret Services which must have written the answers which induced Hess to fly to England for the expected peace conference. . . ."

It was a cold and clear insight, and, in the end, the only logical one.

The Americans left General Haushofer's estate without discovering who were the British "friends" the Nazis were contacting about a peace conference—friends so powerful that the Germans assumed they could secure a peace conference on British soil.

Nor did the Americans, apparently, gain any insight into what the British Secret Intelligence Service might have wanted to gain with Hess in Great Britain, if not his services as a plenipotentiary.

They did, however, leave knowing that Albrecht would not be available for questioning.

"The Gestapo killed him with a shot in the back of the neck," his father explained. "My younger son buried him with his own hands."

The Americans bid the professor farewell and left to write their report.

Obersalzberg

Elsewhere in Germany Americans were finding evidence about Albrecht Haushofer and the Hess affair. The best evidence would shortly vanish.

As they overran Germany in the spring of 1945, the Allies discovered diaries kept by both Albrecht and Karl Haushofer. The diaries were officially logged and their import was noted. Both these men helped shape Nazi foreign policy. One of them, Albrecht, was the prime mover of the Rudolf Hess Affair. With these diaries in hand, there could today be no question about the reasons for the Hess flight to Scotland. Those would be spelled out.

Unfortunately, both sets of diaries disappeared, without copies. The contents are unknown.[5]

But other writings were being found and, for a while at least, preserved. On November 27, 1945, the American political advisor for Germany announced in a cable to the State Department that he was sending Washington microfilm of "letters and material from the personal files of Albrecht Haushofer, founder of the Geopolitik Institute, concerning discussions and correspondence between Haushofer and Rudolf Hess in September, 1940, regarding peace feelers to England.

"Document No. 8, a personal memoranda, datelined Obersalzberg, 5 May 1941, is from Haushofer to Hitler, and concerns Haushofer's English connections and the possibility of their being used as contacts for peace discussions."[6]

The political advisor knew the import of Document No. 8, for he *specifically* noted that it was written only five days *before* Hess flew to Scotland. That's precisely when Hitler was *not* supposed to know a thing about what Haushofer was doing with his "English connections."

It was therefore, perhaps, a charade when Hitler appeared stunned upon hearing that his deputy had jumped a plane to England. If nothing else, it was superfluous of him to order Albrecht Haushofer to Obersalzberg to write out details of the British peace contacts about which the Führer had already been fully briefed.

It would be best, of course, to read exactly what Haushofer wrote in his peace contact memorandum to the Führer. But, alas, the microfilm cannot be found in the files of the U.S. National Archives. A stamp shows the records were received by the State Department on December 11, 1945. But a handwritten note partially covering the stamp says "enclosure removed 12-14-45."

It is history's loss.

On the day Albrecht wrote the peace contact memo to the Führer, Hitler was huddled with his generals designing the great move east. However, he broke away from his military conference to spend four and a half hours in private discussions with Rudolf Hess. No official record of those discussions has been found.[7]

However, there was a witness. He was at a distance and not directly involved, though he heard snippets as the two men walked and pondered. Those snippets are somewhat interesting. Alfred Leitgen, Hess's adjutant, said he heard the words—he didn't know from which speaker—"Albrecht Haushofer" and "Hamilton." Then he snatched a fragment of a sentence: "No problems at all with the airplane." Next, he heard Hitler distinctly declare: "My God, won't it be incredibly dangerous." Finally, he heard this fragment from Hess: "simply declared insane!"[8]

Halder on Hess

Sometime before Albrecht Haushofer's writings to Hitler were discovered, other Americans—this time conducting a review of Allied strategic bombing—were beginning to learn how far Hitler was willing to go to make peace with England. And, of course, Hess's name was quick to surface.

The informant this time was General Franz Halder, chief of staff of the German army from 1938 to September 1942. As such, he was integral to the planning of three of the greatest events of the war: the September 1, 1939, invasion of Poland, which started it; the May

10, 1940, German invasion of the West, which crushed France and sent English armies fleeing from Dunkirk; and the June 22, 1941, German invasion of the Soviet Union, which sparked the Holocaust.

This period also encompassed the flight of Rudolf Hess to Scotland.

Interviewing him at a detention center of the Twelfth Army group at Wiesbaden, Americans in 1945 would for the first time learn of Hitler's inner strategy as he directed the High Command. In the end, they would learn an element of the Hess affair that professor Haushofer either didn't know, which is unlikely, or was wise enough to forget.

Halder told his American interrogators of the beginning of the war when Hitler tried out his blitzkrieg tactics on a brave but outmatched Poland shortly after she had received defense guarantees from France and England.

Hitler, Halder said, believed the assurances given to Poland by the great Western powers were chimeras. Being himself unprepared for a major war, Hitler told his generals, "I would be a complete idiot if I would take the country into a world war because of the lousy Polish conflict."[9]

Hitler, the Americans noted in their report, told the army chief of staff "a number of times that it was beyond doubt that England and France were merely bluffing." And, indeed, to the world it appeared Hitler might have a point. Though France and Germany encouraged Poland in her dispute with Hitler over a strip of land called the Polish Corridor, the Western countries lifted not a finger to help the Poles when Hitler made his move. German Stuka bombers and Panzers had their way with Poland. France and England busied themselves polishing up the Maginot Line.

The Allies did, however, declare war on Germany. In the end, that would be no small event. But at first, it made for a very pathetic war. The Second World War was initially so lacking in battles that journalists were bent on calling it the "phony war."

Hitler agreed. After the Polish surrender, Halder told the Americans, "it was the general understanding in Berlin that the war would soon come to an end. Peace negotiations were conducted through a number of different channels.

"The most important one was the contact with the British Foreign Secretary established by the late Ambassador of Germany to the Holy See, von Hassell. Halder himself was associated with this move and was informed about all the details of the negotiations. Other conversations were initiated by Göring through Sweden and by a lawyer from Munich [Herr Muller] through Switzerland."

The revelation that there had been peace negotiations with British Foreign Secretary Halifax should have put the Americans on notice that, as with the agents who questioned Karl Haushofer, this was not to be an ordinary interview.

The initial peace negotiations ended, Halder said, because the British were demanding the removal of Hitler and Hitler didn't feel like being removed, what without a shot being so far fired in the West. Hitler, instead, conceived a plan to attack the West, and when it was finally sprung, its rapid success astonished everyone: Führer, field marshal and private alike.

After catching his breath, Hitler (Halder said) began thinking of ways to pull off his greatest goal: the destruction of Soviet Bolshevism.

The problem was, England was still in the war, fighting however ineffectually. How to deal with her?

The Americans interviewing Halder would learn something special. One of the key commanders of the Second World War would reveal the crux of Hitler's strategy.

"Hitler's grand strategy throughout was to avoid a war against England. He made repeated attempts to gain England's cooperation in a war against Russia. He felt that he needed all European economic resources for such an undertaking.

"All the measures taken since the end of the Polish campaign were aimed at convincing Britain of the futility of its war against Germany. The invasion of Norway, the conquest of France and the Low Lands, the massing of troops at the Channel, and the air offensive against Britain were all intended to break England's will to continue the war."

The heads of the American agents may have been spinning at this point, because here a respected German general who had no love lost for the Führer—he had been unceremoniously sacked by Hitler after the Russian campaign faltered—was describing the major events of the war not in terms of Hitler's maniacal obsession for world conquest, but in terms of an obsession to gain British approval for a more limited goal: the crushing of the Soviet Union.

That the invasion of Norway, Blitz of the West, Battle of Britain and even the threatened invasion of the British Isles were not military objectives in themselves, but only means to accomplish a quite different objective, would have been an idea not easy to assimilate.

If those who had interviewed General Haushofer had heard this, they possibly would have understood how Hitler could offer to give up the West. He simply hadn't intended to take it in the first place.

Halder was not, however, through with his revelations. He explained to the Americans just how far the German Führer was prepared to go to accomplish the goal of a Nazi-Anglo understanding:

"Still believing, however, in some fundamental 'anti-bolshevist' solidarity between Germany and England, Hitler dispatched Rudolf Hess to inform the British of his determination to wage war against Russia and to submit to them his 'last offer' to participate in the venture.

"The British 'double-crossed' Hitler, and informed Moscow of the nature of Hess' mission. At that point Hitler's hand was forced. He felt that Russia was alerted, and that further delays would be only to Russia's advantage."

There it was, clearly stated to the Americans. Hitler not only had sent Hess, but had armed him with details of the Russian invasion and with his "last offer." Presumably, the "last offer" was the one mentioned by Haushofer—Hitler's willingness to return his Western conquests.

The Americans, though they didn't note it in their report, should have been troubled by the word "double-crossed." For that word implies a still further, even more dangerous, element.

It is possible to be double-crossed only after there has been an initial understanding. If Halder was right, then the British were expecting the Nazi Party chief at a peace parley, just as Haushofer had said.

It was beginning to appear that when the brave RAF wing commander, the Duke of Hamilton, picked up the radar blip of a lone raider approaching the coast of Scotland on May 10, 1941, he was actually tracking an invited guest.

Mr. Webster will not soon be correcting his dictionary. Rudolf Hess's mission was not quixotic, after all. At least not according to the chief of staff of the German army.

General Halder had been wrong about one thing. Great Britain had not notified the Soviet Union of the plans Hess brought. That was the last thing Winston Churchill would have done.

Churchill wrote after the war that his government had learned about the planned assault from various sources, though certainly not from Rudolf Hess. Churchill said he struggled to find the perfect words to get across to Stalin the gravity of the situation. Finally, after much thought and revision, Winston Churchill settled on this paragraph to tell Joseph Stalin that Germany was prepared to attack along a thousand-mile front:

"I have sure information from a trusted agent that when the Germans thought they had got Yugoslavia in the net—that is to say, after March 20—they began to move three out of the five Panzer divisions from Romania to Southern Poland. The moment they heard of the Serbian revolution this movement was countermanded. Your Excellency will readily appreciate the significance of these facts."[10]

That was it, the sum total of Churchill's official warnings to Stalin about the coming German onslaught. Unfortunately, there was no mention of an invasion in the invasion warning. Nor was there a warning in the invasion warning.

Churchill sent this message on April 3 to Sir Stafford Cripps, the British ambassador in Moscow, with instructions that he should hand it to Stalin. Cripps was so unimpressed with the invasion warning that he didn't even acknowledge receiving it until April 12, and then only to complain that "so short and fragmentary a commentary" would only confuse the Russians. "I greatly fear that delivery of Prime Minister's message would be not merely ineffectual but a serious tactical mistake," Cripps warned London.[11] Churchill, though, insisted that Stalin be given the message, and a reluctant Cripps finally followed orders on the nineteenth. As Cripps had predicted, Stalin was not impressed.

• • •

If the Americans in Germany in 1945 had compared reports, dusted off Captain Lee's communiqué to General Miles and J. Edgar Hoover's messages to the State Department, then retraced the history of May and June 1941 through embassy cables, notes between the President and Churchill, and the simple chronology of the period, they just might have arrived at some interesting conclusions.

They would have seen at least this pattern: Hitler had sent Hess to Great Britain, and it was not done on the spur of the moment, but had been carefully planned. Further, someone on the other end was also involved. With this alone, the American agents could have spared the history books from some of the blatant distortions and lies that the British wove into the Hess affair.

But it is unlikely the Americans could have solved the riddle. Though they were being told that Hitler had sought peace with Great Britain and even offered to surrender conquered territory if that would help bring the British along, this idea would not have been easy to accept. Everything the Americans had heard about Hitler would argue against him doing anything of the sort. Moreover, though fingerprints of the British secret services were all over the Hess affair, the Americans had not a clue as to what the British were doing enticing the Deputy Führer to Scotland. They knew one thing, though: it clearly wasn't to embarrass the Germans. What then?

The Americans in Germany in 1945 can be forgiven for not solving the puzzle. It is not solved officially to this day. Many British historians throw up their arms in disgust at the very mention of the matter. Perhaps some of them have been rather too close to their subject. A few more hearty British writers have seen enough circumstantial evidence to believe that someone in Great Britain was indeed flirting with the Nazis. Not surprisingly, suspicion falls first on the Duke of Hamilton.

But he was young at the time and not nearly a big enough player to bring all of this about. No, these accounts—very well done, containing many signposts—have suspected that the prime mover was the Duke of Windsor. Windsor, whose German sympathies before the war are not hard to document, was the former King Edward VIII. He abdicated in 1936 to marry a divorced American, Mrs. Wallis Simpson.

These accounts are mostly united on one particular: if there was a Peace Party operating in Great Britain, then it was a renegade operation and traitorous. The traitors, of course, miraculously avoided prosecution even after their dirtiest deed was exposed by plowman McLean and the Glasgow newsmen. It is the picture of a Byzantine cabal operating from Buckingham Palace to embassies in Madrid and Washington.

The conspiracy theory gets very complicated and, at times, borders on the absurd. The grand conspiracy line was meant for Hitler to consume, not Britons who should know better. There is a different route to a final answer.

One man who reportedly suspected skulduggery, though he couldn't prove it, was a veteran of the shadow wars. Sir Maurice Oldfield, a postwar chief of MI6, the British foreign intelligence service, always thought his government had lied about the Hess Affair. But even from his position, he never thought he could get his hands on the whole truth. So he stole what he could from Foreign Office files in the 1950s to ensure that not all official records would be destroyed or altered.[12]

Much of the remaining Hess documents are locked up in Britain until 2017, and the idea that even then the whole story will be revealed is merely an act of faith. For if the Prime Minister did intrigue with Hitler, however artfully, in an escalation of a war that went on to kill tens of millions, when, perhaps, another result was possible, then it is a secret worth keeping for all time.

One reason many today have not picked up on the thread, much less the diligent American agents in 1945, is partly because of some great myths that seem to always attach themselves to great personalities.

Many have a distorted view of Hitler, whose abiding and omnipresent evil makes even slight revisions dangerous to careers. Churchill, the god, is another example.

But to really understand what happened, and how and why, it is necessary to learn what these men truly thought. And to do that means returning to the beginning.

4: *Breath of Evil*

A SAPIENT LEGEND FROM THE ORIENT TELLS US THAT
THE SPIRITS OF EVIL POWER LIE IMPRISONED IN THE
OCEAN'S NIGHT, SEALED IN BY THE HAND OF AN ANXIOUS
GOD, TILL ONCE IN A MILLENNIUM LUCK MIGHT GRANT
THE DECISION TO A SINGLE FISHERMAN WHO COULD SET
FREE THOSE BOUND IF HE DID NOT PROMPTLY FLING
BACK HIS FIND INTO THE SEA. THAT FATE HAD BEEN DE-
CREED FOR MY FATHER. IT ONCE LAY WITHIN THE
STRENGTH OF HIS WILL TO PLUNGE THE DEMON BACK
INTO ITS DURANCE. BUT MY FATHER BROKE AWAY THE
SEAL. HE DID NOT SEE THE RISING BREATH OF EVIL. HE
LET THE DEMON SOAR INTO THE WORLD.

—*Albrecht Haushofer, 1945*[1]

Lebensraum

The demon emerged in Munich, 1919.

The city was a menagerie of Reds of every stripe, anarchists, be-
wildered democrats, resentful nationalists, all preparing for pitched
battles for the heart of a country that had just lost a war and over
two million dead.

Only a year earlier it appeared that Germany might win the
World War. Generals Erich Ludendorff and Paul von Hindenburg
led the Kaiser's armies into the fiercest land battles history had
ever seen. And the West retreated. But the offensive stalled as did
the will of the people back home, for Germany was facing more

than France and England. A seemingly inexhaustible supply of
American men and machines poured into the battlefields from the
West, strengthening flagging Allied resolve, while an equally per-
vasive stream of ideology marched from the East, clothed in red,
and ready for a brutal new world. American might and Red dedica-
tion would change for decades the calculus of European death.

The Kaiser had abdicated, ceding power to moderate socialists,
but instantly opening a path for the Reds of Munich, Stuttgart,
Berlin and most points German. These crazy-quilt forces of the far
left did what they did best: they marched, murdered and demanded dictatorship. Thousands died. Bavaria for a time became a
Soviet republic. That was before equally murderous and idealistic
Free Corps from the right took back the government.

It was a rough start for the Weimar Republic.

The Free Corps had their roots in the Pan-German movement
that began before the First World War. Composed mostly of young
men who had just left the military, the Free Corps groups of 1919
were united by a belief in German glory and German destiny and
the righteousness of the German racial *Volk*—that pastoral body
which derived its essence from German land.

Naturally, the Free Corps opposed all things international that
could threaten the *völkisch* heart, primarily international capitalism
and international Bolshevism. The philosophical outlook was mys-
tical rather than rational, but, however ill-formed, the movement
was deep and made deeper by the wounds of the treaty the Allies
imposed June 28, 1919, on Germany at Versailles.

The territorial and colonial concessions the Allies won—and
even the ruinous reparations they later demanded—were not the
most bitter parts of the Versailles treaty for those of the new right.
That distinction was left for the section that ascribed all war guilt
to Germany. Whatever else they thought about the bungling
Kaiser, Germans of the *völkisch* movement knew he had not alone
taken the world into war.[2]

The new groups were generally united by something more than
fervent nationalism. They carried the pungent odor of anti-Semitism. There were many reasons why Germany had lost the war,
most having to do with Allied tanks and factories and soldiers, but
collapse of support at home and the labor strikes that followed must

be counted among them. And when the new nationalists looked at who was behind those events they thought they saw a Jewish face.

No nationality or race in Europe had a monopoly of the new left. Germans of every class were part of the movement. But would-be Free Corpsmen had no need to look far to find Jewish names attached to leftist designs.

In Munich the name that was most on their minds during this period was Kurt Eisner, who had led the Red takeover of the city. Eisner was a small, elderly Jew who wore "a black floppy hat which, large as it was, couldn't contain a shock of wild hair. Epically untidy, he was a living cartoon of the bomb-throwing Red."[3]

Eisner, who had spent nine months in prison for his role in engendering German strikes, would be a symbol of hatred for the budding anti-Semites, and following his assassination in February 1919, he would become a martyr of the German left as well.

Into this riot of hatred, hope and utopianism came Major General Karl Haushofer, formerly Germany's military representative to Japan, a veteran of the killing fields, and now a retired officer making a new life for himself as lecturer at the University of Munich in the field christened geopolitics. It was a bad time to be almost anything in Munich, but it was a good time for geopolitics, for that airy-sounding subject promised answers to the two leading questions of the time: why had Germany lost the war, and how could she regain her stature?

Haushofer's theories had at their base a pastoral and agrarian quality that was a perfect match for the *völkisch* paradigm of the Bavarian right—one that held that a people's will sprang from the land to become an almost superhuman force. Nations, he taught, had become great only after they had secured an agricultural bedrock. Without the ability to feed itself, a nation could never be free of dependence on foreign powers, and, therefore, could never fully develop an independent national spirit.

From this immutable principle sprang the need for conquest, for colonies, for Lebensraum, or "living space."

Lebensraum was by definition geographical and great nations had to pay special heed to the natural laws of geography, said Haushofer. Looking back, Haushofer saw that the German debacle in the Great European War stemmed from a wrong geopolitical view. Germany had been seeking its living space in foreign colonies, and one close look at the map would show that such a policy would engender an enemy Germany could ill afford.[4]

In order to defend its colonies, Germany would have to first get to them, and to do that she would need suitable sea power. And Great Britain—whose only true defense was the sea—would view almost any sea power as unsuitable, no matter how reasonably Germany pleaded its case. Simply, an empire based on an island would always view the world through the prism of the sea.

Geopolitically, Germany could do one of two things: she could try to beat Britain at her own game in her own arena by commanding the Channel and the North Sea, or she could find an alternative for her living space. The first choice was dubious, not to say expensive. The second held promise.

Germany, after all, was a Continental power cloistered mostly in Central Europe. From that vantage point, it was easy to see the vast territories in Eastern Europe. When the stern mathematics of land and population dictated a need for living space, why not look eastward at the sparsely populated and highly productive lands of the Ukraine?

To be sure, Great Britain would not look kindly at a Germany seeking its Lebensraum in Continental Europe. She preferred a Bismarckian power balance in Europe that kept all parties in check while she concentrated on maintaining, or recouping, her Empire. But Britain was no longer the undisputed queen of the waves. There were two powers that were naturally—geographically—of far more concern to England than Germany: the Empire of the Sun and the United States. Both were formidable and inexorably growing more so.

Hess

One of the first to fall under Haushofer's influence was a strapping twenty-four-year-old lieutenant who had fought tenaciously during the war.[5]

Born in the English-held city of Alexandria, Egypt, Rudolf Hess was the son of a reasonably successful importer. Before the war, he had sought an education in mathematics and natural sciences. His practical father had steered him to study business in Switzerland and, until the war, this remarkable man was destined to be a merchant of rugs and vases and metals.[6]

But the gunfire attracted Hess as much as he attracted gunfire, and he jumped into the war, at the chance of danger, and wasn't disappointed. His Bavarian infantry unit suffered extreme casualties fighting at Verdun and elsewhere. American officials later trying to chronicle events said he was wounded five times.[7] That could be too much, but it is clear that at least twice during the war he nearly died, once from a bullet wound that exploded through his lung and exited his back.[8]

While recovering from a gas attack, Hess volunteered for even more hazardous duty: the air corps. He was trained with all dispatch and in the fall of 1918 joined Fighter Squadron 35 on the Western Front. Flying, of course, would earn Hess his great fame. But this war ended before any German pilots could make it over Great Britain.

Hess arrived in postwar Munich the same month that Eisner died. Fierce battles sparked by that event were waging and the region slipped to within a breath of civil war.

Hess, as did many a veteran who had spilled blood for the fatherland, aligned himself with the Free Corps and joined a paramilitary group called the Thule Society[9] that sought a German nationalist socialism, the end of capitalism, suppression of international Communism and a virulent anti-Semitism—more or less a typical hodgepodge of the day. He had not lost his penchant for injury. An American intelligence report says that during one brawl in May of 1919 he sustained some sort of serious leg wound.[10]

But Hess was more than a mere street fighter. The ever-aspiring scholar had developed during the war an interest in history that the ideologues could not alone satisfy. Hess sought and gained entry into the University of Munich. Soon, a fellow member of the air corps told Hess of a remarkable man with remarkable theories, a general, in fact, who was starting a lecture series on geopolitics.

Hess asked the friend to make the introduction.[11]

Rudolf Hess and Karl Haushofer became almost instantly attached. Hess treated Haushofer as a second father and Haushofer more or less adopted the young lieutenant as his third son.

Haushofer's theories were infectious. He spoke with a decided nationalist accent. Through an understanding of geopolitics—Haushofer defined it as the study of "the relationship of the sacred qualities of the earth to man's political efforts"[12]—Germany could lift itself off the ground, surrender the burden of war guilt, and, with the proper allies, emerge again.

The message was not anti-Semitic, for Haushofer would not count himself a member of that horde, but geopolitics of the time talked in the language of race and racial destiny. So his theories were not antithetical to politics of the *Volk*, being, instead, perfectly positioned to attract a man like Hess, half mystic and half rationalist. Geopolitics was codified in the language of reason.

Hitler

As Rudolf Hess was absorbing the evolving theories of Karl Haushofer, another veteran of the World War was gaining an indoctrination by fire in Munich politics. He would eventually prove to be Hess's best friend and Haushofer's best and most dangerous student. But in 1919, Adolf Hitler knew neither man.

The son of an abusive Austrian customs bureaucrat named Alois and a gentle mother named Klara, Hitler had lived in shadows before the Great War. Perhaps the secret that propelled Hitler can be gleaned from listening to his father's 1903 obituary: "The sharp word that fell occasionally from his lips could not belie the warm heart that beat beneath the rough exterior. At all times an energetic champion of law and order and universally well informed, he was able to pronounce authoritative on any matter that came to his notice."[13]

Freed of the father who could authoritatively master any subject and who, like Hess's father, insisted on a practical education, Adolf Hitler attempted to do something very impractical. He sought to be an artist, an endeavor his father, who punctuated his authoritative will with the short end of a whip, had expressly forbidden.[14]

The small-town son of a minor bureaucrat went to Vienna. He found it a magical city. Not unlike Midwestern Americans who find themselves in New York pursuing chancy dreams, Adolf Hitler had the bravado that comes from growing up in a small pool where seemingly anyone can succeed. And like those counterparts in America, Adolf Hitler soon found himself over his head.

Some personal habits that would mark him for the rest of his life developed in his bohemian days in Vienna. As with Winston Churchill, Adolf Hitler detested morning, preferring to rise at noon and work well into the night. But unlike his future foe, Hitler never developed a taste for either tobacco or alcohol, and he found that life as a vegetarian suited him well.

"Adolf had brought starvation to a fine art," recalled his best and only friend from that time, August Kubizek. "To be sure, in Vienna he generally lacked the money for food. But even if he had it, he would prefer to starve and spend it on a theatre seat."[15] Hitler was an intense man with little humor, willful and driven, but to exactly what end Kubizek had no idea. He wrote poetry, sketched and scrounged for cheap opera tickets. Along the way, ideas formed in the teenager's head that could not be contained. Hitler talked to Kubizek as though before an audience of hundreds, on subjects great and small, but all with an intensity that mesmerized—there really is no better word—Kubizek. It was not the lulling, undulating voice—not then, at least—but the eyes. "Never in my life have I seen any other person whose appearance . . . was so completely dominated by the eyes," Kubizek recalled. "They were the light eyes of his mother, but her somewhat staring, penetrating gaze was even more marked in the son and had even more force and expressiveness, especially when Adolf was speaking. . . . In fact Adolf spoke with his eyes, and even when his lips were silent one knew what he wanted to say. When he first came to our house and I introduced him to my mother, she said to me in the evening, 'What eyes your friend has!' And I remember quite distinctly that there was more fear than admiration in her words."[16]

In Vienna, Hitler also demonstrated something else that probably cannot be overlooked. He was amazingly asexual. To Kubizek this was astounding, because, to his regret, women were drawn to

Hitler and not to his sidekick. Some women would actually turn and stare at Hitler after he passed them on the street, a behavior very much frowned upon at the time. "I was all the more surprised at this as Adolf did nothing to provoke this behavior; on the contrary, he hardly noticed the ladies' encouraging glances, or, at most, would make an annoyed comment about them to me. . . . Did he not understand these unequivocal invitations, or did he not want to understand them? I gathered it was the latter, as Adolf was too sharp and critical an observer not to see what was going on around him, especially if it concerned himself."[17]

For four years Kubizek was with Hitler, and he never saw Hitler physically involved with a woman. Once, after an opera, a woman had a suggestive note delivered to the man with the intense eyes. Hitler read it and was contemptuous, passed it over to Kubizek, and said that Kubizek should keep the proposed rendezvous. Kubizek was chagrined. Why couldn't he attract such attentions? Of course, he wouldn't keep the rendezvous. He said he knew at least that much about women.[18]

Years later, as they tried to decipher the mission of Rudolf Hess, the Soviet intelligence services would settle on the notion that there was a homosexual clique at the center of Nazi power, with Hess, the family man, part of it. Some others would tell the same to American secret agents. But at this time in Vienna, between 1904 and 1908, Kubizek saw nothing of the sort. In fact, he said he saw the opposite. Once the two friends were taken to dinner by a wealthy businessman. When they emerged from the restaurant the businessman bid them an apparent farewell. Hitler asked his friend if he had seen anything unusual about the man. Kubizek hadn't. Hitler showed Kubizek a business card the man had slipped into his hand with a hotel address and room number scribbled on the back. The man, Hitler explained, was a homosexual. Back in their apartment, the two young men burned the card. Hitler had always railed against homosexuals, Kubizek said. From everything Kubizek saw, Hitler was a true ascetic.

Two events that changed the direction of Hitler's life came close together during these early Vienna days.

First, Hitler's grand bid to study at the Academy of Fine Arts—

he had predicted getting accepted would be "child's play"[19]—was rejected by a committee that did not approve of his drawings. He was told that he should consider architecture instead of art. Hitler was bitterly disappointed, but still hopeful.

Shortly after this, though, Hitler returned home to visit ailing Klara. A doctor took Hitler aside and told him that his mother had cancer. "His long, sallow face contorted," Dr. Edward Bloch recounted. "Tears flowed from his eyes. Did his mother, he asked, have no chance? Only then did I recognize the magnitude of the attachment that existed between mother and son."[20] On December 21, 1907, Klara Hitler died while the future German dictator held her head in his lap.

When Dr. Bloch came to sign the death certificate he was stricken by the scene. "In all my career," he said, "I never saw anyone so prostrate with grief as Adolf Hitler."[21]

"It was a dreadful blow," Hitler would later write. "I had honored my father, but my mother I had loved."[22]

Hitler returned to Vienna, but it had lost its allure. Kubizek was soon accepted to a conservatory to study music. That must have been particularly cruel for Hitler, for he could get nowhere with his art, while his faithful lapdog was on his way to certain success. With Kubizek out of the city one summer, Hitler left the apartment they had kept together, and vanished into a world hard and cruel, learning more about the art of starvation than was healthy for him or the world. He worked as a common laborer, when he was lucky, and went hungry when he was not. Often he lived as a tramp, sleeping in doorways and taverns, developing hatred for Vienna, a city "which first avidly sucked men in and then so cruelly crushed them."[23]

He lived for a time in a homeless shelter. He made the rounds of soup kitchens. He was reduced to actual begging.[24]

Such destitution had two decisive effects on Hitler: first he developed a keen insight into poverty and the fear of poverty and the instincts of the working classes trying to avoid poverty. He developed a genuine kinship with the working man that, whatever else can be said about him, he carried with him to his death. That this kinship with the disadvantaged can legitimately be defined as compassion is only one of Hitler's enormous contradictions.

But what has never been obscured is the second outcome. Living at the bottom had made the seventeen-year-old resentful of those at the top. And Adolf Hitler began to think that those who had unjustifiably made it to the top and kept him on the bottom were the Jews.

"I owe it to that period that I grew hard and am still capable of being hard," Hitler wrote. "And even more, I exalt it for tearing me away from the hollowness of comfortable life; for drawing the mother's darling out of his soft downy bed and giving him 'Dame Care' for a new mother; for hurling me, despite all resistance, into a world of misery and poverty, thus making me acquainted with those for whom I was later to fight."[25]

Exactly how Hitler came to blame his condition on Jews is one of the remaining mysteries, because it was forever wrapped inside a mind that balanced so many contradictions. Historian John Toland, whose work on Hitler cannot be equaled, reports that two of Hitler's closest associates during this period were Jewish—as were the brokers of his art.

From where, then, did Hitler's hate arise? Toland says one can only guess. He offers this:

"Perhaps [it was] an art dealer or pawnshop operator; perhaps an official at the Academy of Art; perhaps some combination of these things; or even something which lay dormant in the recesses of his mind. There could have been a dawning hatred of Dr. Bloch. . . . It is not at all uncommon for a bereaved son to blame a doctor, consciously or unconsciously, for the death of a beloved parent."[26] Dr. Bloch was Jewish.

In one shelter, Hitler met a man who encouraged his art. And with his help Hitler finally began earning a living from his vocation. He made enough money to leave Vienna and travel to Munich, where he said he intended to study art and architecture.

If Vienna had been an artist's bohemia, Munich was a politician's. Hitler became entranced with the radical political theories that ran rampant in the city, while he continued a marginal freelance business in his art.

Hitler wrote that upon seeing Munich he was transfixed: "A *German* city!" he wrote in *Mein Kampf*. "What a difference from Vienna! I grew sick to my stomach when I even thought back on this Babylon of races."[27]

Munich, however, did not solve Hitler's central problem: he was both poor and without prospects. Munich could turn against a person in such a plight as surely as could Vienna.

Vision

On June 28, 1914, a Serbian assassin murdered Archduke Franz Ferdinand. Soon the dominos of war began to fall and the continent was engulfed in flames.

War was sudden freedom for Hitler. His undeniably intelligent and creative mind had before the war been so hammered down that no one would have predicted anything but a bad and insignificant end for the Austrian.

The fighting meant everything to someone with nothing left to lose. It was a chance at a radically new life. Hitler enthusiastically enlisted and was assigned to the Sixteenth Bavarian Reserve Infantry Regiment.

There was no doubting the young man's courage. As Hess had done, Hitler relished the front line, volunteering, in fact, for the most deadly assignment that line possessed: running messages from one command to another over an area so pierced with flying lead that it was at the very boundary of no-man's land.

For this and other acts, Hitler had won an Iron Cross, 1st Class— the near equivalent to the American Medal of Honor.

By the end, Hitler's uniform was weighted with honors. To go with the Iron Cross, 1st Class, was the Iron Cross, 2nd Class; the Military Cross, 3rd, with swords; the Regimentsdiplom for bravery; and a service medal, 3rd class. Added to these was a medal, much lower than the others, but one many veterans respected most—the one awarded to a soldier wounded in combat.[28]

Adolf Hitler had beaten death so often that for the rest of his life he would show no fear of it. It was a lack of "leadership ability"— his commanding officer said—not a lack of bravery that held Hitler to the rank of corporal.

At the end of the war, Adolf Hitler's company was hit by mustard gas, the first time it had experienced it. Soon Hitler's "eyes turned into glowing coals." He lost his sight and was transferred to a hospital in the rear.[29] He suddenly saw a German army unlike that on the front lines. In the rear there was dissension. Troops resisted moving forward. Calls of revolution were everywhere. Germany neared chaos.

News from Berlin was desperate. There were demands that the Kaiser abdicate—some factions advocating for a new German democratic republic, others for a Red German soviet.

Through it all, the twenty-nine-year-old corporal slowly began recovering his sight. Adolf Hitler wanted to get well so that he could get back to the front. The rear was all too confusing. But he would never make it back to the front during this war. On November 9, 1918, a pastor entered Hitler's hospital to announce the end. The House of Hohenzollern had fallen; Socialists had taken over the government. Germany's cause was lost. Four years of blood sacrifice—Hitler's first unit had suffered 80 percent casualties in the first weeks alone—were erased. The pain, the risks, the lost lives amounted to nothing. The man who twenty-one years later would start another war to avenge this one again went blind. A doctor said it was the response of a "hysterical psychotic."[30]

The issue of Jews coursed through the mind of the blinded Hitler. He drew deductions, irrational and deadly: the Jews were responsible for Germany's calamity. They carried German passports and had German citizenship, but they considered themselves merely part of the diaspora, opportunistic citizens whose true allegiance was to Palestine, or to the capitalists or to the Reds. Never to Germany. Wherever there was a strike that hurt the soldier, a Red Jewish agitator was present. Soldiers who encouraged others to turn back from the front were Jewish. The capitalists from America who financed Germany's humiliation were Jewish. The rot of Europe—from finance capital to Bolshevism—was Jewish and anti-German.

Jews had fought beside Hitler during the war, but he forgot them. Hitler, without sight, became a savage anti-Semite, more extreme and bitter than even when he left Vienna.

His was a vision clearly seen and firmly felt, but it was the vision of a blind man. Hitler on his hospital cot thought he would never again see, but he made a pact with himself. Should he again be able to view the world, it would be through the eyes of a politician, not an artist. Almost as soon as he made the pledge—he called it a miracle—he regained his lost sight. Germany had gained a future leader of a different kind.

"Kaiser William II," Hitler later wrote, "was the first German Emperor to hold out a conciliatory hand to the leaders of Marxism, without suspecting that scoundrels have no honor. While they still held the imperial hand in theirs, their other hand was reaching for the dagger. There is no making pacts with Jews; there can only be the hard: either—or. I, for my part, decided to go into politics."[31] Vision recovered, political will resolved, Adolf Hitler headed back into the chaos that was Munich.

On the surface, he was not unlike thousands of others, a beaten man with an uncertain future. But unlike most, Hitler stayed attached to the army, still a corporal, employed at the margins. There were no longer external enemies for the German army to oppose, so it busied itself tracking internal ones. They were not in short supply. Naturally this army, composed of those who had refused to walk away, was partial to the German right, the *völkisch* parties of the Free Corps that had also kept faith. Yet the army was still German, and the Germans were still orderly; something that could not be said of the Free Corps. They were as loud, disorderly and as violent as the others. So the army set upon cataloging them together with the Reds, though more sympathetically.

The army could have done nearly anything with Adolf Hitler; he could have been discharged, sent elsewhere, or asked to surveil the Communists or anarchists. With an Iron Cross, 1st Class, he would not be scrubbing floors. The army seemed to settle upon a proper course for this stout warrior lacking leadership skills. Hitler landed the unimportant task of spying on a few fringe *völkisch* groups. On September 12, 1919, Adolf Hitler took up his first assignment. He was to ingratiate himself to a tiny group called the German Workers' Party, attend a meeting or two, learn the membership and report back. Nothing much was expected.

Formed earlier in the year by mechanic Anton Drexler, the German Workers' Party—if an organization with six members can be called a party—was sponsored by the Thule Society, the group that had earlier attracted Rudolf Hess. The Thule Society, more obscure than mysterious, gave the splinter group at least the semblance of political mass. Thule leaders knew that the Free Corps movement lacked appeal to the working class. The *völkisch* movement had been primarily middle-class, a fact that allowed the Reds free rein in attracting common workers. The purpose of the German Workers' Party was to win back the workers.

Well schooled in the spreading dogma of the Reds, German workers were attracted to socialism and its promise: more money, less work and more equality. They were not, however, attracted to the idea that their society should be less German. The workers remained German, not internationalists. Most retained Christianity, in its plethora of variations. They were not ready, as the Communists seemed to insist, to tear down everything to build something wholly different. That was both too radical and too disorganized. Besides, Germans liked being German.

The German Workers' Party had a kernel of an idea that would later flourish throughout Western Europe. Germany should be a socialist state with a nationalist character.

None of this was at all fleshed out when Adolf Hitler showed up as a spy in a beer hall in Munich to begin his political career. Hitler stood well back of the thin crowd, listening to the chatter and wanting to go home. There was little substance here; every wild idea got equal play. Finally a professor took the podium and suggested that Bavaria secede from Germany. That was too much for Adolf Hitler. This was not a time for Germany to commit suicide.

Hitler propelled himself, almost accidentally, toward the front. He became the politician of his vision. Drexler described the moment: Hitler took command "in a way which it was a joy to watch. He gave a short but trenchant speech in favor of a greater Germany which thrilled me and all who could hear him. When the speaker had finished I rushed towards him, thanked him for what he had said and asked him to take the pamphlet I had away with him to read. It contained, I said, the rules and basic ideas of the new movement; if he was in agreement with them, he could come again in a week's time and work in a smaller circle, because we could do with people like him."[32]

It was Hitler's first public speech, and it showed immediately that this man who was considered unable to lead men was at least capable of hypnotizing them. A few days later, Adolf Hitler joined the German Workers' Party. He was member No. 7.[33]

The party's socialist beliefs were completely in keeping with Hitler's strong anticapitalist Vienna-bred leanings, those that come naturally to one who had waited in soup lines while the idle elite queued for the Wagnerian operas he so desperately wanted to attend. But as important as socialism to the German Workers' Party was anti-Semitism. In February 1920, the party spelled out its platform, oddly balancing racism and socialism. It held that no Jew could "be a member of the nation," and that no nonmembers could vote or hold any official position, or in any other way enjoy the protection of the state—a line in perfect keeping with the Third Reich's eventual Nuremberg laws. But the platform had the elements Hitler believed in that made it a "party of the right" only in the sense that it was nationalist and anti-Semitic, not that it was economically reactionary.

In fact, like many of the strange contradictions that Hitler balanced in his mind, the platform was revolutionary. It called for "the nationalization of all businesses which have been formed into corporations," and "profit sharing" with employees in all industrial enterprises, "insurance for old age" and "expropriation of land for communal purposes without compensation," educational reform that would allow poor children with talent a university education, and special restrictions "prohibiting child labor."[34] The Third Reich would eventually amend the most radical of these proposals, but the key social welfare programs that remained would shame any American New Dealer. Hitler's program would evolve into the paradigm of Europe's postwar social activism, though his name, understandably, would not be mentioned in that context.

Putsch

Hess and Haushofer were walking through Munich one night in 1920 when young Hess asked the professor to attend a beer hall meeting where a mercurial Austrian was to speak. Haushofer resisted but eventually relented. Hess had never heard this man with the short-cropped mustache speak before, but he was transfixed for over two hours. This man, this corporal, this Austrian, was the future of Germany. Of this, Hess had no doubt.

Hess joined the party and soon was splitting time between Haushofer and Hitler. Through these months Rudolf Hess was pulled toward the blue-eyed Austrian who spoke directly to his soul and the former major general who satisfied his intellect. Haushofer counseled against getting too close to Adolf Hitler, but already knew he was losing his dear student. "I had a moral influence on him, but there was a competition between the political influences and the scientific influences," he would later say.[35] Hess hedged his bets. He kept close to both Haushofer and Hitler, who found the younger man's appreciation of history and intellect stimulating. Hess, in turn, began to tutor Adolf Hilter in the fine points of Haushofer's geopolitical theories. They began taking hold, but the real learning would occur when Haushofer had the chance to teach the future German Chancellor directly.

Hess and Hitler were soon involved in one raucous beer hall fight after another, while their party, renamed National Socialist German Workers' Party—better known as the Nazi Party—began to build membership on the power of Hitler's vocal cords. In one of these brawls, Hess actually used his head—literally—to intercept a beer mug aimed at Adolf Hitler, receiving still another wound that required stitches.[36] Rudolf Hess was a resilient punching bag.

As Adolf Hitler was just beginning to assimilate the theories of geopolitics, he was very much honing a public speaking manner that arguably became the most effective in history.

He had the ability to connect with Germans, to understand them and to talk to them simply though passionately in the language of both resentment of the past and optimism for the future. In part, it was because of who he was. A seemingly simple man, a poor corporal of the war, bedecked in simple clothes but wearing the highest badge of military bravery. Hitler was one of them, only somehow of a purer essence, one that radiated compassion on one hand and unbound fury on the other. In just this vessel, Munichers found vent for emotions they had before only vaguely known they possessed.

The Hitler the world would eventually know from film clips—the gesticulating Führer ranting from the podium—was not the Hitler that greeted the people of Munich in 1921, or the Hitler that entranced Rudolf Hess. The Hitler of the 1920s worked crowds of hundreds, not tens of thousands, and he had a way of connecting with them almost individually, as though each was his personal friend, his Kubizek. This was Hitler's genius and his greatest power. He was never talking over people, only to them, and with a wit and presence that could silence a heckler with a slight movement of a forearm.

Invariably he began his beer hall speeches slowly in an almost self-deprecating voice, but clear and logical and easy to follow, the talk of a common man with scars. Then his tone of irony would build, slowly, and the crowd would find Hitler's ever-present humor somehow relaxing but portentous, for the instant he saw he had them in his grasp, he became the German ultrapatriot, overcome with galvanizing resentment: a wolf, wounded, enraged, determined. He told them why Germany was wounded: Germany's hyperinflation that was wrecking the pensions of the elderly, the vile reparations demanded by countries who wanted to turn Germans into slaves, in short, the omnipresent humiliation of an unfair peace, were laid by Hitler at the feet of the "November Criminals," those slackers back home who had betrayed the fatherland when it most needed them: the capitalists and the Reds—all, in the end, controlled by the true serpent of evil: International Jewry.

An early follower—Harvard-educated Ernst "Putzi" Hanfstaengl—described the end of one of Hitler's beer hall speeches. It had started, as so many, with a raucous crowd, unmannered, more intent on drink than erudition. But then the magician took the stage, and sparkled.

"I looked round at the audience," Hanfstaengl recalled. "Where was the nondescript crowd I had seen only an hour before? What was suddenly holding these people, who, on the hopeless incline of the falling mark, were engaged in a daily struggle to keep themselves within the line of decency? The hubbub and mug-clattering had stopped and they were drinking in every word. Only a few yards away was a young woman, her eyes fastened on the speaker.

Transfixed as though in some devotional ecstasy, she had ceased to be herself and was completely under the spell of Hitler's despotic faith in Germany's future greatness. . . .

"The audience responded with a final outburst of frenzied cheering, hand-clapping, and a cannonade of table-pounding. It sounded like the demoniacal rattle of thousands of hailstones rebounding on the surface of a gigantic drum."[37]

Hitler's lifestyle augmented his image. Though he could have had more, he chose to live simply in a tiny one-room apartment without any amenities: a champion of the workers. It was probably not a ploy. On one level, Hitler was a simple man, preferring plain surroundings.

His Vienna habits survived. Hitler rose late and—very un-Germanly—was incapable of keeping a schedule. A friend said he "had the Bohemian habits of a man who had grown up with not real roots. He was hopelessly unpunctual. . . ."[38] When he did eventually pull himself together and make it to the office or a coffee shop, he "never stopped talking all day, committed nothing to paper, issued no directives and was the despair of his staff."[39] He also kept up other habits he had learned in Vienna. Women did not sleep over at his room, nor did he sleep elsewhere. He was not so much a man as he was a Führer.

As Hitler's popularity with the people of Munich grew, so did the influence of the former "debating society." He was the main Nazi draw, the one sure way it had for raising funds. In that, politics of Germany in the 1920s was no different from politics anywhere else.

Hitler, of course, knew this fact as surely as he knew that he was not born to be a second to Anton Drexler in an obscure Bavarian political party. He wanted control, and it was hard to deny him. Drexler had not invited Hitler into the party only to have him seize it, but there was really nothing he could do. As the party gained membership, those new members had allegiance to the man who inspired them and not to an unexciting party hack. By 1921, with the party's existence absolutely dependent on his persona, Hitler wrestled control from Drexler—wrestled being an exaggeration, for it was done so easily—and won the title of party Führer, with "dictatorial powers" on many issues.[40]

An element that would distinguish Hitler's fledgling party from others was already shaping up in the early 1920s. The party's meetings were frequently disrupted by Red agitators and others, and Hitler decided to stomp that problem out. He organized bands of young followers to police Nazi rallies. The Brown Shirts, or SA, always had a decidedly violent bent, and were therefore politically useful when Hitler wanted to bluff or bully. Not only could they protect the Nazi rallies, they could disrupt those of his competitors.

Though the Brown Shirts grew in numbers, they did not always grow in discipline. Hitler found it wise to have a more dependable, orderly and slightly older—though much smaller—group assigned directly to his service and protection. In 1922 the Nazis formed the Schutzstaffel for such a purpose. It would later be known and feared by its abbreviation, the SS.

The event that almost hastened Hitler's rise, only later to threaten it entirely, began on January 11, 1923, when the French, in a dispute over reparation payments, occupied the Ruhr. The Ruhr was the heart of German industry and its subjugation was, however politely the French put it, a loss of German sovereignty. The occupation so inflamed German nationalism that Hitler's popularity and fanaticism grew exponentially. During the next nine months, Hitler attracted thirty-five thousand new party members and tens of thousands more were listening and agreeing with what they heard. It was a time of sharp division between the Bavarian government and the Reich government in Berlin, between the swelling nationalist movement and the left, between Hitler and other would-be leaders of the right.

Hitler grew bolder, sensing his power but not his limits. The French action was coalescing a huge well of resentment that Hitler sought to tap. He was thirty-four years old; impetuous, daring and naive. A meeting of the Bavarian leadership in a convenient beer hall provided just the opportunity Hitler needed to attempt a shortcut to power. It was an audacious plan to effectively kidnap the state's leadership, convince its members that the time had come for a National Socialist Bavaria, and then seize power in Bavaria and, perhaps, all of Germany. It was so crazy that it almost worked. After storm troopers surrounded the hall, Hitler strode in, "climbed on a chair . . . made a sign to the man on his right, who fired a shot at the ceiling."[41] Hitler then proclaimed a National Socialist revolution, and took the Bavarian leaders away to a side room.

There, he tried persuasion, beginning with the not-too-subtle remark "No one leaves the room alive without my permission."[42] Eventually, after another shot had been fired at the great hall's ceiling—by Hitler himself—and after his oratorical and terroristic skills had been used to the limit, Hitler was finally able to bring his "guests" to the podium, where they announced that, yes, they had thrown their lot in with Hitler.

Brown Shirts and old soldiers hugged and celebrated the arrival of Germany's savior, someone who could curb hyperinflation, get the French out of the Ruhr, unite Germany and restore the mighty Reich. Since Germany had absolutely no means to do any of this, it was probably lucky for Hitler that the plan failed from the weight of its own absurdity.

One problem was that Bavarian leader Gustav Ritter von Kahr slipped away and renounced his shotgun marriage with the National Socialists. After that, things went fast awry. Sensing defeat, Hitler decided utter audaciousness was in order. Against overwhelming odds, he marched side by side with the great General Ludendorff, who had become a Nazi sympathizer, into the armed teeth of police and troops. To even matters somewhat, perhaps two thousand National Socialists, some armed, followed behind.

The opposing forces were at first frozen.[43] Then shots rang out. Four police and fourteen Nazi followers were killed, Hitler sustained a dislocated shoulder, the future Luftwaffe commander Hermann Göring was shot in the leg, General Ludendorff was arrested and the Nazi revolution was ended.

During the attempted Putsch, Hess had seized several Bavarian political leaders, herded them to the south and held them as hostages. With the collapse of the coup, Hess fled to Austria, but eventually returned, was arrested and promptly charged—as was Hitler—with high treason.

The army was the deciding political force in Bavaria, and since it had encouraged Hitler's foray into politics, the incipient Führer probably knew he would not be meeting soon with the hangman.

But he feared he might meet with what to him was an even worse fate: obscurity.

Landsberg

When Hitler had first been incarcerated in Landsberg Prison, forty miles west of Munich, it was as though his world had ended. His room was amenable, brighter and more spacious than many rooms he had rented in the past. But that did not help. Hitler was disconsolate, horrified by his terrible failure. He refused to eat. He lost weight and almost the will to live. Anton Drexler visited and was stunned. "I found him sitting like a frozen thing at the barred window of his cell," he said.[44]

But his trial, which gave him a chance again to sharpen his oratory, revived Hitler. The trial was publicized throughout Germany and, though not on page one, was reported in most major Western newspapers. Hitler again had a platform.

He took over the trial, assuming all guilt for himself. The overmatched court was on the defensive, and Hitler was again a champion. Thousands who had not known of him before learned of Hitler then, a man unjustly prosecuted. He defiantly pleaded his cause before his judges:

"The army which we have formed grows from day to day; it grows more rapidly from hour to hour. Even now I have the proud hope that one day the hour will come when these untrained bands will grow to battalions, the battalions to regiments and the regiments to divisions, when the old cockade will be raised from the mire, when the old banner will once again wave before us: and the reconciliation will come in the eternal last Court of Judgment, the Court of God, before which we are ready to take our stand. Then from our bones, from our graves, will sound the voice of that tribunal which alone has the right to sit in judgment upon us. For, gentlemen, it is not you who pronounce judgment upon us, it is the external Court of History which will make its pronouncement upon the charge which is brought against us. The verdict that you will pass I know. But that Court will not ask of us, 'Did you commit high treason or did you not?' That Court will judge us . . . as Germans who wanted the best for their people and their fatherland, who wished to fight and to die. You may pronounce us guilty a thousand times, but the Goddess who presides over the Eternal Court of History will with a smile tear in pieces the charge of the Public Prosecutor and the verdict of this court. For she acquits us."[45]

The court, however, could not acquit the volatile Austrian. There were four dead policemen, after all. Instead, it sentenced Hitler to five years of minimum security time, which quickly dissolved into a mere thirteen months.

But this was not to be a footnote in history. The time Hitler spent in prison would be the most crucial period of his life, for it was during these days that the Nazi leader found the intellectual structure that would steer the world to war sixteen years later. It was during this time that Hitler and Hess wrote *Mein Kampf.*

Imprisonment drove Hess and Hitler into a close bond. It was actually a dream for Hess to be so close for so much time to the man with whom he was obsessed. Hess was becoming Hitler's new Kubizek, devoted, unquestioning, willing to put up with Hitler's tempestuous moods. He soon became Hitler's closest confidant as well as his secretary, which was exactly what Hitler needed, someone to pluck order out of the chaos of his mind.

This was not hard time. Hanfstaengl reported that Hitler had actually won over the guards, who greeted him with "Heil Hitlers" when he visited.[46] "He and Hess had not so much cells as a small suite of rooms forming an apartment." Besides the space, there was relative freedom. "People were sending presents from all over Germany and Hitler had grown visibly fatter on the proceeds," Hanfstaengl noted. Hanfstaengl suggested that Hitler exercise, a suggestion Hitler was profoundly opposed to. "It would be bad for discipline if I took part in physical training. A leader cannot afford to be beaten at games," Hitler said.[47] Hanfstaengl also noticed a dynamic developing between Hess and Hitler. "There was a very close bond between the two during this period, and for the first time I heard them speak to each other on 'thou' terms, although later in public they did not."[48]

From inside Landsberg, Hess and Hitler decided to undertake a systematic study of Germany's condition. Hess had just the man for such an audacious scheme. Old Professor-General Karl Haushofer knew everything there was to know about geopolitics, a subject Hitler not only needed to learn but wanted to as well. It wasn't often that Hitler opened his mind to the thoughts of others. But at Landsberg he would, becoming so enthralled with the process that he boasted that in prison he was finally earning his university degree, courtesy of the German government. Hess and Hitler determined to write a book—its final title was *Mein Kampf*—that would eventually contain the blueprint of Nazi madness.

Karl Haushofer, despite all the distancing he would later attempt at Nuremberg, was only too pleased to help, visiting Landsberg often, and at length, and toting with him works of some seminal Machiavellian thinkers. Haushofer brought Adolf Hitler Clausewitz's book on the art of making war, and Friedrich Ratzel's treatise on geopolitics.[49] He also brought his own theories on how geopolitical notions applied to Germany and her recovery.

Hitler was a good student, although he was also a creative one. He took Haushofer's notion that Germany's future may lie in the East and fused that, over the years, with his own racial obsessions. The land in the East that geopolitics demanded Germany possess was conveniently owned by the Bolsheviks, the despised spearheads of international Jewry, a race determined to extinguish all things right and German.

Hitler also assimilated Haushofer's ideas about Great Britain. But where Haushofer always saw two ways to view England—as an ally, in which case Germany would expand east, or as an enemy, which would force Germany to become a sea power—Adolf Hitler saw it only one way. England would somehow become Germany's mighty friend. She would drop her Bismarckian ways and see merit in a German expansion, never so much as to threaten England, to the East. In exchange for not creating a two-front war, Germany would forever assure England that no power would rise in Europe to threaten her.

Again, it was a concept wedded to Hitler's racial obsessions. As Hitler saw it, those Tommys who so tenaciously fought on the Western Front were not foreign or alien in any way. They were Ger-

manic, forced by vagaries of history and an unfortunate habit of listening to Jews onto a different path. The more stubborn British resistance became on the Western Front, the more ingrained in Hitler
became the notion that these were not inferior people. A psychologist might see it as something of a defense: if the British were really Germanic, then the Germanic people of whom Hitler counted
himself a member didn't really lose the war.

Whatever its origins, Hitler was obsessed with the notion.
Haushofer's idea of a possible Anglo-German alliance synergisti-
cally added to this passion of Hitler's, and also gave it structure,
logic and seemingly intellectual respectability. Hitler became the
Continent's greatest Anglophile. Years later, when the then German Führer first spoke to his generals about the reasons for Hess's
flight to England, he told them, honestly, that the Hess mission involved the "attempted unification of the Germanic races."[50]

Though it was little known at the time—and, in fact, mainly
known to this day only among historians of the Second World War,
with even some of them still confused—this obsession with the
English was a race-based concept of equal power to Hitler's de-
generate hatred of the Jews. It would determine Nazi foreign policy as much as any other factor. If an enemy ever came to
understand this, he would have a great advantage over Adolf Hitler.

Hess and Hitler, shoehorned in a Bavarian prison, were not so
concerned about enemies learning of the plan as they were about
getting it down. As they wrote *Mein Kampf*—Haushofer said that
Hess actually wrote large parts of it[51]—Hitler and Hess probably
didn't think it would be so bad if the British would someday read it.
Until the last days of his life, Adolf Hitler figured that if the British
ever *understood* what he was really after, they would surely come
around.

Hitler was right, in part. Across the Channel at least one person
would become a student of the book. But in Landsberg Prison in
1923, Adolf Hitler never envisioned that he would ever face an
Englishman like Winston Churchill. As for Stalin and Roosevelt,
the two other world leaders who would eventually share his stage,
there is little evidence that they read *Mein Kampf* or, having read it,
understood it.

If they had, they would have been treated to a full display of

Hitler's obsessions and plans, Haushofer's geopolitics wedded to Hitler's special brand of racism.

Hitler and Hess, in their roles as analyzers of history, would dissect past mistakes of German statesmanship. They wrote that the German leadership should have seen that "if land was desired in Europe, it could be obtained by and large only at the expense of Russia. . . . For such a policy there was but one ally in Europe: England."[52] And, of course, land was desired, for Hess and Hitler had learned that only through living space—Haushofer's Lebensraum—could Germany ever become great.

Hitler and Hess put so much weight on this notion that, in reflecting on the Kaiser's mistake in the Great European War, he wrote: "No sacrifice should have been too great for winning England's willingness. We should have renounced colonies and sea power, and spared English industry our competition."[53] Such sacrifice would have entailed "momentary limitation, but a great and mighty future."[54]

The colonial road, wrote the two top Nazis, was wrong: "If we chose this road, England would some day inevitably become our enemy. It was more than senseless—but quite in keeping with our own innocence—to wax indignant over the fact that England should one day take the liberty to oppose our peaceful activity with the brutality of a violent egoist."[55] Professor Haushofer could not have written it any better. Geopolitics was the controlling logic of great nations. If Germany pursued foreign colonies, it would need sea power, and sea power would invite England's iron wrath.

Hitler also told anyone who would listen—those who could see past the vile racism of the book—that he did not begrudge England its great victory, though that victory had plunged Germany into a near abyss. In a line worthy of Machiavelli, Hitler pronounced: "An alliance policy is not conducted from the standpoint of retrospective grudges, but is fructified by the knowledge of retrospective experience. . . . If we look about us for European allies from this standpoint, there remain only two states: England and Italy."[56] In case anyone hadn't heard, he reiterated: "In the predictable future there can be only two allies for Germany in Europe: England and Italy."[57]

Hitler and Hess also toyed with another geopolitical theme, one that survived nearly intact until the end of the war. Since Britain found her strength in sea power, she should also find her enemies there. One of those was surely the upstart Americans. "No ties of kinship," wrote Hitler, "can prevent a certain feeling of envious concern in England toward the growth of the American Union in all fields of international economic and power politics. The former colonial country, child of the great mother, seems to be growing into a new master of the world. It is understandable that England today re-examines her old alliances with anxious concern and British statesmen gaze with trepidation toward a period in which it will no longer be said:

" 'Britannia rules the waves!' but instead: 'The seas for the Union!' "[58]

It is, in fact, hard to thumb through too many pages in *Mein Kampf* without evidence of Hitler's obsession about the British. Hitler, the champion of iron will and brute force, said this of his racial colleagues on the Isles: "No people has ever with greater brutality better prepared its economic conquests with the sword, and later ruthlessly defended them, than the English nation."[59] Or: Britain "fought with mercenaries as long as mercenaries sufficed; but she reached down into the precious blood of the whole nation when only such a sacrifice could bring victory; but the determination for victory, the tenacity and ruthless pursuit of this struggle, remained unchanged."[60]

So it was all there, and clearly stated. Germany's interests were in the East, and to go in that direction Germany first needed to win over the British. Such a marriage of Anglo-German interests would only follow after a difficult courtship. The same qualities that made the British good partners would try the patience of any suitor. The British were not used to sharing power.

Hitler understood this, and he understood the historical obstacles in front of him. England, geopolitically, had sought to secure its rear by dividing Europe. With Europe divided and "balanced," she was free to pursue the world. For Hitler's strategy to work, he would have to convince England that a Europe, with Germany the dominant power, albeit mostly sequestered in the East, could also insure Great Britain's interests. The English leadership would have to be made to understand that Germany was a friend and would remain so. It would have to understand Hitler's racial obsessions.

Hitler and Hess wrote about this challenge in *Mein Kampf:* "For three hundred years the history of our continent has been basically determined by the attempt of England to obtain the necessary protection in the rear for Great British aims in world politics, indirectly through balanced, mutually interlocking relations of power."[61]

It would take a new worldview—a shift in geopolitical conceptions—for England to unload the baggage of Bismarck.

5 ⦂ *Toward War*

FROM MY PERSONAL MEETINGS WITH HITLER I LEARNED
ABOUT HIS BASIC BELIEF THAT THE ONLY HOPE FOR AN
ORDERED WORLD WAS THAT IT SHOULD BE RULED BY
THREE SUPER POWERS, THE BRITISH EMPIRE, THE
GREATER AMERICAS AND THE NEW GERMAN REICH. HE
GAVE ME ASSURANCE THAT THE GERMANS THEMSELVES
WOULD DESTROY THE COMMUNISTS BY THE CONQUEST OF
RUSSIA.

—*F. W. Winterbotham*

On December 20, 1924, a cold and overcast day, Adolf Hitler
emerged from Landsberg Prison, health improved, goals refined,
university education showing. Just outside the prison's portal, a car
had arrived to take him away. Hitler grabbed the passenger's side
door with his right hand, held a glove stiffly down with his left, and,
while looking twenty pounds heavier than when he entered, turned
to a photographer and struck an I-have-returned pose. The prison
had not given Hitler long pants for his leaving, so the picture exposed his bare legs below his trench coat. His fierceness made that
seem more ominous than silly. Hitler was taut, intense, hair parted
slightly toward the right, with a short cropped mustache. He had
the look of a fighter at the bell. The world be damned. *Mein Kampf*
would be real.

Though officially banned, the Nazi Party had survived his ab-

sence, but lately not well. In the December elections, votes for the
National Socialist bloc had fallen to 907,000 votes from 1,900,000
in the past election. Still, that was considerably more support than
Hitler had at the time of the Putsch. The Putsch had polarized the
Germans, forcing sides. And the trial of Hitler had made him a folk
hero and martyr. His oratory even read well in the papers, and the
Nazis had benefited. But with their magnet eventually muted and
behind bars, support was quickly falling off.

Hitler resolved to put an end to that as well as an end to the fac-
tional bickering that had naturally followed his absence. On February 24, 1925, Bavarian officials legalized the Nazi Party. Three
days later, Hitler returned to the politics of the beer hall, giving a
talk to a party convention in the same hall from where he had
launched his Putsch. The four thousand members who crowded
into the hall—one thousand had to be turned away because of
space—wanted to see if the master still had his touch. They would
not be disappointed.

Hitler hit the old themes—the Jews, the November Criminals,
the Bolsheviks—to the delight of the audience, but his main emphasis was on the party. If the nation was to regenerate itself, then
the party must do the same. Internecine battles must end. At one
point during the speech, Hitler turned to the party leaders in the
front tables. There was no doubting how this end to conflict was to
be done. He, Adolf Hitler, was to be the sole authority. "After a
year you can judge, my party comrades, if I have acted correctly and
that it is good; if I have not acted correctly, then I will place my office back in your hands. Until that moment, however, I alone lead
the movement and no one makes conditions for me so long as I personally assume all responsibility."[1] He didn't leave them much
choice, but suddenly, under his persuasive aura, they didn't seem
to want it; where only minutes earlier there had been sharp divisions between the socialist wing and the nationalist wing of the
party, there was now harmony. It took a political magician to
arrange a wedding of these divergent forces, and Hitler held the
wand. There was frenzy in the hall; many cried; listeners clam-
bered up on chairs to witness a rebirth; old enemies embraced.

The electric Second Coming of the Nazis so alarmed Bavarian

leaders that they banned Hitler from speaking, lest he create a second Putsch. That was, in a way, a benefit. Not able to speak in beer halls, Hitler went to one small Nazi cell after another, speaking even more intimately to most Nazi members.

Though Hitler had been released from Landsberg, Hess had been left behind. The absence of his friend emphasized to Hanfstaengl the "emotional quality of the friendship that [Hitler] had developed with Hess." Hitler would say: "Ach, mein Rudi. . . . Isn't it appalling to think he's still there?"[2] Hanfstaengl, ever the amateur psychologist, suspected a physical attraction between the two.

Soon, as Hitler began making his rounds to Nazi cells, Rudi was freed. Though Hitler would surely have spawned a personality cult regardless of what anyone else did, Hess began to craft a particularly successful one. Up to this time, Hitler had been addressed by the formal though customary salutation: "Herr Hitler." Hess found that entirely too commonplace. He first began calling Hitler "der Chef," but that was not quite up to the task. Finally, he settled upon the word "Führer" in imitation of Mussolini's appellation "Duce."[3] From hence forward, Adolf Hitler would be "der Führer." Hess also developed what became the customary Nazi greeting and departure line: "Heil Hitler."

Hess and der Führer would frequently retire to a pension on the Obersalzberg above the small town of Berchtesgaden, to work on the final draft of *Mein Kampf.* The book was published in July 1925 and was a moderate success, though it would, of course, become a raging best-seller in Germany as Hitler's fortunes rose. It was severely criticized in academic circles as a hodgepodge of variant wild ideas. Even Hanfstaengl had nothing good to say of it after the war, but, then again, after the war no one from the inner circle profited from saying anything in defense of Adolf Hitler.

The book was certainly a peculiar work, hateful and ugly. But the snobbish response was unfortunate. The European petite bourgeoisie would pay a heavy price for ignoring it.

Hitler faced a problem in the mid-1920s that was deeper than the annoying speaking ban. The forces that had imposed the ban, the same ones that were overseeing his parole, could at any time destroy the party by sending Hitler packing back to Austria. He was an Austrian citizen, not a German. As long as Hitler appeared to be a threat to the public order, that was always a possibility. So he undertook a course of action that was not his second nature: he would become Adolf Hitler, democrat. If he was ever to take power in Germany, Hitler resolved, it would have to be through the ballot box.

To be sure, Hitler always kept his hand close to the sword, as thousands of Brown Shirts could attest. Those Brown Shirts were not accustomed to the dirty democratic process of the Weimar Republic; in fact, they were mostly pledged against it. It was not easy to explain Hitler's changes of direction to a group of ruffians who were not used to subtle political dialogue. They were a constant problem for Hitler. If he disassembled them, he would lose his strongest supporters and the useful threat they posed to those in power. If he let them do what they wanted, he risked intervention by the government and its army, which would spell the end to his ambitions. Hitler would not be able to solve this dilemma fully until after coming to power. Until then, he played for time.

As Hitler, the democrat, did what he did best—persuade and lead—more and more of the day-to-day functions of the Nazi Party fell on his assistant. By the end of the 1920s, Rudolf Hess was the undisputed head of the party apparatus. It was also clear to others in the party that Hess was the one man Hitler talked to unofficially, as a friend. Hitler never talked this way to others. Even his boyhood friend Kubizek heard Hitler mostly through an orator's veneer. As such an intimate, Hess was very powerful in the party. Yet Hess, unlike the others that spun around Hitler, never seemed to exploit the power for himself. Everything was for Hitler.

From tiny conferences at Obersalzberg, to party rallies in Munich, and increasingly to the harder-sell regions of northern Germany, Hitler was building his party. Whether he would succeed in his ultimate goals was always a question. His main enemy was not Bolshevism. It was the economy. The relative prosperity of the 1920s assuaged some of the Versailles hurt and, therefore, much of the nationalistic passion from which the Nazi Party drew its sustenance.

At the end of 1926, Nazi Party membership stood at approximately fifty thousand. In March of 1927, the ban on Hitler's speaking was lifted. Predictably, he drew new adherents, and membership nearly doubled in the next year and a half. But the general public, which typically did not get its information at beer halls, was not on board. In the May 1928 elections for Reichstag deputies, the Nazis garnered only 810,000 votes, losing two of their thirteen seats. It was a miserable performance, and the Nazis were even more considered a fringe movement.

But Hitler's luck was soon to change. The next year, 1929, brought on Wall Street's crash and a worldwide economic crisis. Old fears and prejudices were aroused, particularly in a nation saddled with ruinous reparations it neither felt responsible for nor could afford. In Germany, most politicians did not sense the sea change that was taking place in the electorate. They would soon. In the Reichstag elections in 1930, to almost everybody's disbelief, the strange party that thought it could be both nationalist and socialist won 6,371,000 votes, 18 percent of all those cast in Germany. Hitler's deputies rose from 11 to 107, suddenly becoming an important force in one of the world's major industrialized countries.

This election marked the beginning of a marathon of elections, as Hitler tried to get enough votes to convince President Paul von Hindenburg, the former field marshal of the Great European War, that he should name Hitler Germany's Chancellor. Hindenburg was not an easy sell. He distrusted Hitler not only because of his lowly rank during the war, but because Hitler had such a hard time reining in the SA, about which Hindenburg complained bitterly.

Patchwork governments were formed with the main idea of keeping Hitler out of the chancellorship. The problem, though, was that not one of the other parties, even with alliances, had the political mass to deny Hitler for long. The instability resulted in numerous elections being called, and the Nazis tended to improve their standing as these came and went.

In the July 1932 Reichstag elections Hitler campaigned in what became the modern style, flying to fifty cities in the last two weeks alone. The effort paid off. The Nazis won 13,732,000 votes, 37.3 percent of the total, more than the combined count of the two closest vote-getters. The Nazis were suddenly the leading party in Germany. Hindenburg would not yet loosen the keys to the chancellery, but keeping them from the audacious Austrian was quickly becoming impractical.

Lost Chance

In April 1932, as Adolf Hitler's star shot up through the German political universe, an English visitor arrived in Munich with an unusual proposition. Winston Churchill checked into the Hotel Munich knowing full well that the politician who officed in that town might soon become the Chancellor of Germany.

Churchill was out of power, but he was certainly not out of politics. Unlike many world leaders, Churchill had read *Mein Kampf*, later declaring that "there was no book which deserved more careful study from the rulers, political and military, of the Allied Powers."[4] Churchill knew Hitler to be pro-British and anti-Bolshevik.

Churchill was, within limits, a kindred spirit. In 1920, he had refused to meet a Soviet trade representative because he said he didn't want to "shake hands with the hairy baboon."[5] Even after the war, Churchill said that "in the conflict between Fascism and Bolshevism there was no doubt where my sympathies and convictions lay."[6]

There was an unusual association already between Hitler and Churchill. It had begun with Hanfstaengl, the erudite follower of Hitler. Hanfstaengl, known among friends as Putzi, had formed an acquaintance with Churchill's son, Randolph. Somehow—the story has never fully been explored—Hanfstaengl says that Randolph Churchill was invited "to travel once or twice in the plane with us" while the Nazi leadership crisscrossed Germany in search of votes.[7] The image of Winston Churchill's son hopscotching around with the eventual German Führer does not appear in Churchill's later account of the affair.[8]

The day the Churchills checked into their Munich suite, Hanfstaengl and Hitler also arrived in Munich by plane. At the airport, there was a message for Hanfstaengl from Randolph. The Churchills, Randolph wrote, would very much like Hanfstaengl to join them for dinner that evening. Politely, Churchill asked, could Hanfstaengl also bring along his boss, Adolf Hitler?

Churchill was the very type of Englishman an Anglophile like Hitler should have cherished meeting: indomitable foe, incarnation of British resolve, no-man's-land enemy. Hitler, whose life's goal was a reunion of the "Nordic races," could not, of course, pass up a chance to talk directly about geopolitics with one of the fiercest leaders of the great but prodigal nation. Hanfstaengl was elated.

Hitler balked. "What on earth would I talk to him about?" he asked Hanfstaengl. Hanfstaengl was amazed. "But, Herr Hitler," he pleaded, "this is the easiest man to talk to in the world—art, politics, architecture, anything you choose. This is one of the most influential men in England; you must meet him."[9]

Hitler fidgeted and looked for other things to do, remaining adamant on one score: he would not meet Churchill. Writing about it twenty-five years later, Hanfstaengl said that in Hitler, "with a figure whom he knew to be his equal in political ability, the uncertain bourgeois re-emerged again. . . ." Meeting a man like Churchill was too much for Hitler, "the man who would not go to a dancing-class for fear of making a fool of himself, the man who only acquired confidence in his manipulation of a yelling audience."[10]

Hitler, the man who supposedly had no fear, was afraid of Winston Churchill and uncertain of his own powers in such high British company. A psychologist might just bring out the term "inferiority complex." Whatever the label, the emotion was real. Hitler was missing his best chance ever to talk directly to his eventual nemesis. Years later he would try to recapture the opportunity only to be rebuffed.

Hanfstaengl, confused by Hitler's response, nevertheless attended the dinner. Afterward, as was the custom, the women departed and Churchill, Hanfstaengl and a few other guests lit their cigars, poured some brandy, pushed back their chairs and began to chat. At one point Churchill, with a brandy glass held to his lips "so that his words reached my ears alone," whispered to Hanfstaengl a startling question: "Tell me, how does your chief feel about an alliance between your country, France and England?"

Hanfstaengl could hardly keep from spilling his drink. "I was transfixed," he later wrote. "I could feel my toes growing through my shoes into the carpet. Damn Hitler, I thought, here is the one

thing which would have him prestige and keep him within bounds
and he does not even have the social guts to be here to talk about
it."[11]

Sputtering a bit and trying to get back to the ground, Hanfstaengl
asked whether Italy should not be included in the arrangements.
"No, no," Churchill said, "we would have to leave them out for the
time being. You cannot have everybody joining a club at once."

Knowing that the only raison d'être of a Franco-German-Anglo
alliance was to produce a military combine against the Soviet
Union, Hanfstaengl decided he must immediately contact Hitler.
This was not idle chat. It was, instead, Hitler's dream. Hanfstaengl
fumbled for an excuse to leave, something about a phone call, and
darted out of the hotel and over to the Brown House in search of
Adolf Hitler. No one knew where the Führer was and calls around
didn't locate him. Just when Hanfstaengl was giving up, Hitler
strolled in, wearing a dirty white overcoat and a green hat.

Hanfstaengl cornered him and pleaded with Hitler to come at
once to Churchill's hotel. If Hitler refused, Hanfstaengl warned,
the Churchills "will think this is a deliberate insult."[12] Hanfstaengl
unfortunately neglected to tell the Führer what it was exactly that
Winston Churchill had in mind to talk about, later making the weak
excuse that he didn't want others to overhear him. Had Hitler
known that Churchill wanted to discuss an Anglo-German alliance
with France also a partner, perhaps he would have gone. But the
uninformed Hitler, unnaturally shy, said he was much too busy, and
went about his affairs.

Winston Churchill could not have viewed Hitler's stance as anything else than a rebuff by an upstart politician, one that believed
himself too self-important to talk to the descendant of Marlbor-
ough. Nevertheless, Churchill was patient, idling away in Munich
for two more days. Hitler never showed.

If Hanfstaengl had been just a bit more candid with Hitler or if
Hitler had been a little less shy, it is possible that subsequent
events could have taken an altogether different course. These two
men, so different in their background and education, nevertheless
had more than a few things in common. Both were out of power in
their countries, but were scheming for ways to take control. Both

had firm nationalist policies that were expansive; Hitler wanted to reunite the Reich and then expand toward the Ukraine; Churchill wanted to regain the nineteenth-century grandeur of the Empire, shoring up its imperialism in the Near and Far East. Both were at their core militarists. And Hitler and Churchill were also the two best orators on earth. Though no one could outdo Hitler's rabid anti-Bolshevism, Churchill could at least give him a run.

Churchill's suggestion of a possible alliance certainly doesn't mean that he had thought it through or, in the end, would have settled on it as a matter of policy. But it does indicate that he was not instinctively opposed to the notion of an alliance, even with a Nazi.

Power

Hitler's drive for power was creating chaos in Germany. The coalitions formed to deny the Nazis power had not enough power in themselves to hold together. Governments continued to form and collapse. In November 1932, though, the Nazi momentum appeared to flag. In an election on November 6 the Nazis lost two million votes and thirty-four seats. Although still the largest party, the Nazis appeared vulnerable.

That could have stiffened Hindenburg's resolve to keep Hitler out of power. The old gentleman did not trust Hitler, did not seem to like him, but his alternatives were not many. Someone had to run the government. A minor regional election in Lippe on January 15, 1933, would finally prove decisive. The Nazis sought to recover from their November setback by pouring resources and prestige— at a great deal of risk to Hitler—into the election. It worked. The Nazis won 39.6 percent of the vote, an increase of 17 percent over the November showing. The momentum they had seemed to have lost was back and the storm troopers once again were menacing. Fifteen days later, on January 30, 1933, Hindenburg named Adolf Hitler, a forty-three-year-old Austrian high school dropout, Chancellor of Germany.

Hitler wasted no time doing exactly what he said he would do in *Mein Kampf*. On one hand, he set about the rebuilding of Germany, first economically, then, on a mostly parallel course, militarily and finally with new territory. He implemented some of the most radically left-leaning programs that could be found anywhere outside the Soviet Union. Like the Soviet Union, the Nazis tried to convince the workers that their labor not only benefited them personally, but that it was patriotic and benefited the "community"; unlike the Bolsheviks, the Nazis succeeded. The real magic was likely far more monetarist than idealistic: deficit spending was the vehicle through which the Nazis primed the engine.[13]

Depending on one's point of view, the workers either profited from, or were swindled by programs that guaranteed holidays, access to formerly exclusive perks such as sea cruises, and the new autobahns where workers could drive their suddenly affordable Volkswagens. There was an explosion of free concerts, operas, films and sporting events, all geared to endear the state to the worker. There was health and unemployment insurance. In return, they gave up many labor organizations and the right to strike.

The results, however cynical the intent of those behind the program, were spectacular. When Hitler took office in January of 1933, German unemployment stood at 6,013,612. A year later, it had fallen to 3,772,792. By the time the Second World War began in September 1939, the unemployed ranks measured a mere 72,600.[14] The declining unemployment rolls were not due to make-work jobs. In the first year the Nazis were in office, Germany's total industrial production increased 30.8 percent, with a healthy 14.2 percent increase in consumer goods.[15] Total investments in Germany increased rapidly, from 6.8 billion deutsch marks in 1933 to 29.8 billion in 1938. Military investment, of course, led the way.[16] In the midst of a worldwide depression, it appeared to most Germans that the Nazi plans had much to offer.

Economic prosperity brought political dividends, which were always Hitler's ultimate aim. No longer would he rule with a mere plurality of the votes. He soon established such a stranglehold on the majority—most observers agreed that he won fairly over 90 percent of the votes in the later 1930s—that he safely dispensed with elections altogether. It was and still remains a hard concept for those outside of Germany to understand, but to the Germans of the mid-to-late 1930s, Adolf Hitler seemed more the ultimate democrat than the ultimate dictator.

The rebuilding of Germany's economy and military was only one side of Hitler's *Mein Kampf* equation. The other, always at or near the fore, was to win over Great Britain for the main territorial battles ahead. Upon assuming power, Hitler wasted no time implementing his grand Haushofer-inspired policy. He would make peace with Britain, then grab his precious living space in the East.

Shortly after taking power, Hitler spelled this formula out to his naval commander in chief, Admiral Erich Raeder. "It would be the tent pole of his future foreign policy," Raeder recalled, "to coexist peacefully with Britain, and he proposed to give practical expression to this by trying to sign a Naval Agreement with her. He would like to keep the German navy relatively small, as he wanted to recognize Britain's right to naval supremacy on account of her status as a world power."[17] It was the *Mein Kampf* formula: the best way to win over the British was to appear unthreatening, and the surest way to do that was to leave the Royal Navy alone.

Obtaining a German-British naval agreement while Germany otherwise embarked on a massive military buildup would be the material proof of his intentions. But Hitler knew that German restraint on naval matters would not be enough to allay British doubts about a strong, unified and expansion-minded Germany in Central Europe. To do that, Hitler would need to convince the British that such a Germany would never pose a threat to Britain, not by land, not by air and certainly not by sea.

One method would be to convince the British of the nostrums of *Mein Kampf:* an understanding between Germany and Great Britain, two great nations of the same race, would clearly be far more durable than one between more distant partners. The first was based on family, the latter on convenience. But Hitler would not leave this most important job to theory alone. If the British still had doubts, he would dash them through candor, or at least as much candor as the Nazis could muster. He intended to tell the British—just in case they didn't understand *Mein Kampf*—exactly what he intended to do. Certainly, the British would then appreciate his goodwill.

Frederick Winterbotham, head of air intelligence for MI6, the British foreign intelligence service, got a thorough dose of this crazy-quilt Nazi openness in the mid-1930s when he traveled to Germany on the off chance that he could glean the intention of the new Hitler government. He soon discovered just how easy the life of a spy could be in Nazi Germany.

"By 1934," Winterbotham later wrote, "I had obtained personal contact with the Head of State, Hitler, and with Alfred Rosenberg, the official Nationalist Party philosopher and Foreign Affairs expert, Rudolf Hess, Hitler's Deputy, Erich Koch and some of the senior serving officers of the Army and Air Force, and by working on their intense desire to keep Britain out of their coming wars of expansion and a belief that the RAF would respond both to persuasion and threats, I got them to disgorge from the 'horse's mouth' much of what we wanted to know.

"From my personal meetings with Hitler I learned about his basic belief that the only hope for an ordered world was that it should be ruled by three super powers, the British Empire, the Greater Americas and the new German Reich. He gave me assurance that the Germans themselves would destroy the Communists by the conquest of Russia."[18] It was as if the British agent had been given a seat on the Reich Defense Council.

Perhaps as odd as being told what the Germans planned to do, the Nazis told him how they were going to do it. Wrote Winterbotham: "From General Walter von Reichenau, Hitler's favorite general, I learned, in 1934, details of the German plans against Russia, and the strategy of the blitzkrieg, the massive tank spearheads supported by their mobile artillery, the dive bomber. . . .

"From Eric Koch, who showed me all over the great concrete preparations in East Prussia for Operation Otto, I found out the approximate date of the operation against Russia."[19] Otto was the first designation for the Russian invasion. It was later renamed Barbarossa.

In an intelligence understatement of the first order, Winterbotham declared: "The weeks I spent each year from 1934–8 travelling freely about Germany with Rosenberg, Rudolf Hess, Erich Koch or the ADC Rosenberg supplied me with an almost unique insight into the Nazi plans for the future and perhaps more important into the mentalities of these men, including Hitler."[20]

Winterbotham soon divined why exactly the Nazis were treating him to all their secrets. "In my case as a 'supposed' admirer of the regime," Winterbotham wrote, "they believed I could influence my friends in high places in London in their favor and achieve the neutrality of Britain in their coming wars."[21]

Winterbotham was only one of many Englishmen to be treated specially by the Germans during the 1930s, but he was clearly one of the shrewdest. He had noted the Nazi obsession. Hitler perhaps never realized how damaging it could be to arm the British SIS with such information.

Others followed Winterbotham into the warm kinship arms of the Nazis. These Britons, later called appeasers, produced scenes that only a few years later would seem insane.

There was this:

Lord Londonderry, the British air minister, made frequent trips to Hermann Göring's lakeside log lodge about forty miles from Berlin. He'd arrive on his private plane and then retire with his German counterpart for discussions, hunting and relaxation. Once, in 1936, interpreter Paul Schmidt came along and was generally quite surprised by how well these two competitors got along.

The atmosphere was rustic, for Göring's cabin, called Karinhall, was not yet the huge expanse it would soon become. Nestled in the Schorfheide Forest, it was a perfect setting for these two sportsmen. On this occasion, Londonderry had been embarrassed by recent German claims that the Reich had achieved air parity, and told Göring his own careful investigations showed this could simply not be the case. Göring, in turn, was frank, revealing to Schmidt's surprise much technical information about the Luftwaffe.

There was no mistaking how Göring viewed the British: just like the Führer did. "When Anglo-German relations were discussed," Schmidt later recalled, "Göring conveyed with remarkable skill the impression that Germany desired nothing more ardently than to be on friendly terms with England. 'If Germany and England stand together,' Göring emphasized more than once, 'there is no combination of Powers in the whole world that can oppose us.'"[22]

Londonderry, more reserved, but not much more, conveyed the impression that "he, too, was a devotee of Anglo-German friendship. More than once he emphasized the close kinship between the two peoples, the many characteristics they had in common, and the favorable conditions thereby provided for common political action."[23] Of course, there were no sweeter words for a Nazi to hear, or more damaging to misinterpret.

Schmidt was smitten by the British lord. "Listening to the tall, spare Englishman, who faintly resembled the King of Sweden, as he somewhat hesitatingly sought for the right words, one knew at once that this man sincerely desired an understanding with Germany. Göring must also have had this impression, for I have seldom heard him speak with less reserve than in his conversations with Lord Londonderry."[24]

Usually gregarious and sometimes bombastic, Göring absolutely outdid himself in the presence of the understanding Englishman and his family. To everybody's delight, Göring strutted about outside the lodge "in a huge hunter's hat, wielding a sort of old Germanic spear, clad in a white-sleeved leather jerkin, accompanied by the English Lord and his Lady, and sometimes their daughter. At the bison enclosure he would blow his horn. At the sound all the huge beasts came up, giving the impression that they knew Göring personally." The lord and his family loved the spectacle, having "obviously not seen anything of the kind in England" and "laughed freely," though, Schmidt noted, with "no condescension or contempt in the laughter."[25]

Hitler himself welcomed the lord at the Reichchancellory, where he strummed his favorite refrain: "How often, during the [First World] war when I was opposite British troops, did I say to myself that it was absolute madness to be fighting against these men who might well have belonged to our own people! That must never happen again."[26]

Londonderry produced only a few scenes in the odd montage of Hitler's courtship of the British. Other contributors seemed endless. David Lloyd George added his touch:

Lloyd George was an immense figure in Hitler's mind: the man who was Prime Minister of Great Britain while Hitler was an unknown soldier dodging bullets in the trenches on the Western Front. As was his nature, Hitler came to love his fiercest enemy. Lloyd George, he thought, was a genius, a great statesman, a man of honor, a worthy victor. Hitler had been emotionally drained when he was first brought, as an aspiring Chancellor, into the presence of Hindenburg, and had emerged under the old man's spell. But Lloyd George was almost godlike, superior to even Hindenburg.

Hitler finally met him in September of 1936. The Führer walked down to the foot of the steps leading to the Berghof—an honor he usually afforded only to the most important heads of state—and declared with outstretched arm, "I am exceptionally pleased to be able to welcome to my house the man whom we in Germany have always regarded as the actual victor of the World War."[27]

"And I deem myself lucky," replied an impressed Lloyd George, "to meet the man who, after defeat, has united the whole German people behind him and led them to recovery." Then the man who had brought on German defeat in 1918 looked out at the Obersalzberg landscape and said, "What a splendid place you have found up here."[28] Schmidt said: "It was one of Hitler's best days." He could have said more. This was probably the happiest day of Adolf Hitler's unhappy life.

This was not the shrinking Hitler who had avoided Winston Churchill in 1932. And this was certainly not the domineering Hitler who often extracted concessions from foreign leaders in the thin air of Obersalzberg. This was a Hitler too powerful to hide and too awed to dominate. Tanned from a few days at the Berghof, Hitler looked younger, more energized. Of course, he talked of the Great War, which was the common glue. He praised the British and their leader and absolutely impressed the former Prime Minister with his savant-like memory of precise dates and happenings of the war.

Lloyd George, wise as he no doubt was, fell victim to heartfelt flattery. He said that multinational alliances had helped create the Great War, which complemented Hitler's aversion of such alliances in favor of bilateral agreements instead. And Lloyd George said that current German peace initiatives were being frustrated at the staff level, something Hitler always suspected.

Lloyd George could not truly contain himself. He spoke, Schmidt said, "with eloquent enthusiasm . . . of the German measures for abolishing unemployment, of health insurance, social welfare and holidays. He had already investigated much of what was being done on the labour front, and seemed to be deeply impressed by what he had seen."[29]

Flattery worked both ways. Hitler was entranced. Years later, shortly after the Hess mission, Hitler would even predict that Churchill would be overthrown and replaced by Lloyd George and Samuel Hoare.

After leaving Hitler, Schmidt and Lloyd George rode back to his hotel at Berchtesgaden. They exchanged anecdotes of the Great European War. When they got to his hotel, Lloyd George's daughter laughingly greeted him with an outstretched arm and the words: "Heil Hitler." Lloyd George appeared to become even more serious. He said quietly: "Certainly, Heil Hitler. I say it too, for this is really a great man."[30]

No account of the Nazi courtship is complete without mention of the Duke of Windsor.

The Duke, formerly King Edward VIII, was to Fleet Street the very center of the universe. He had abdicated to marry his love, the American divorcee Mrs. Simpson. There had never been anything like that before in the history of the Crown; traditionally British kings would rather execute their wives than abdicate, so wherever he and the Duchess went, they were pursued. The image of a royal affair so passionate as to cause abdication piqued the imagination of most Europeans, Hitler included.

The abdication was considered unfortunate by the Nazis. The Duke had always been considered the leading German sympathizer in the Empire. From the abdication onward, the Nazis schemed to have the Duke return to the Crown, where they thought he could bring about the final rapprochement. Predictably, a court of spies of every national stripe attended Windsor and his wife.

As did others, the Duke traveled to Germany. On one stay, he and his wife visited Göring's country home, which had undergone a great expansion. Though rustic still in its setting, everything else

was different. No longer a cabin, it was an estate. The Reichsmarschall was soon enough in his element. The former King of
England and the German Luftwaffe commander scrambled up into
Göring's attic where there was an immense toy train set that covered the entire floor. The two were soon engrossed with the con-
traption, sending freight trains moving, whistles blowing. Göring
had a toy airplane hooked up to an overhead wire. Naturally, after
the Reichsmarschall sent the plane flying across the room, little toy
bombs dropped from its fuselage and pelted the railway.[31]

Two days later, the Duke and Duchess met Hitler at the Berghof.
The Führer was on his best behavior, gracious and warm. It was
clear, Schmidt said, that Hitler considered the Duke a key German
friend, though the two apparently did not discuss politics.[32]

The Windsors, during this vetting process, also dined with
Rudolf Hess and Ilse. Ernst Bohle, who would later translate a
Hess letter to the Duke of Hamilton, said Hess and the Duke
talked warmly of the basic identity of the German and English peo-
ples. Eventually, the Duke again ascended to an attic of a Nazi
leader, only this time he was not greeted to a toy train set. Instead,
Hess showed him toy models of the ships that fought the battle of
Jutland, and the two men discussed their nations' naval tactics.

Hitler did not depend alone on personal contacts to rope the
British into his master plan. He used speeches and the press as
well. In 1933 he told a British reporter that the Great European War
had been a misfortune of "these two great Germanic nations. . . . I
should be very happy if this unnatural state of things came to an
end and our two kindred peoples found their way back to their old
relations of friendship."33 A year later he told another British in-
terviewer that "Germanic nations such as ours ought to be friends
by sheer force of natural instinct. The Nazi Movement would regard war between Germany and England as a racial crime."34

The *Daily Mail* in 1937 reprinted a letter Hitler had sent to its
owner, Lord Rothermere. It read:

> All hope for the future is dead, so far as human eye can see,
> unless it comes from England and Germany.

I am no new advocate of an Anglo-German understanding. In
Germany I have made between four and five thousand speeches
to small, large, and mammoth audiences, yet there is no single
speech of mine, nor any line that I have written, in which I have
expressed anything contrary to this concept or against an Anglo-
German understanding.

Such an agreement between England and Germany would
represent the weight of influence for peace and common sense
of 120,000,000 of the most valuable people in the world. The
historically unique colonial aptitude and the naval power of
Britain would be combined with one of the first military nations
of the world. If this understanding could be still further enlarged
by the adhesion of the American nation, it would be absolutely
impossible to see who in the world could disturb a combination
for peace which would never, of set purpose or intent, neglect
the interest of the white people.[35]

Though many listened, not all were convinced. With Germany
rearming and threatening to break what few covenants of Versailles
remained, some in the British ruling class saw little optimism in
Anglo-German relations. Winston Churchill certainly didn't, and
his voice of caution was increasingly being heard, though not as
clearly as he wanted. There was no doubt that Churchill sensed
generally Hitler's aims. In 1935, Churchill declared that "if his
[Hitler's] proposal means that we should come to an understanding
with Germany to dominate Europe, I think this would be contrary
to the whole of our history."[36]

For his part, Hitler worried that he might die before he accomplished his goals. He said that members of his family died young,
and he expected to do the same. If so, Hitler felt Hess alone knew
the master plan, but perhaps did not have the political ability to see
it through. A sense of urgency came over Hitler. He would have to
do more. He would have to deal with his stoutest opponent.

Hitler asked Winston Churchill to come over to Germany for a
talk. Two such experienced politicians could work out the issue of
German *Lebensraum*, the Führer thought. This time, however, it
was Churchill's chance to snub Hitler. He refused to come, explaining that "as a private individual I could have placed myself
and my country at a disadvantage."[37]

Hitler, however, had set upon a course and, having done so, he was not easily dissuaded. Hitler ordered Ribbentrop to lay out for Churchill in the clearest terms possible the proposed Nazi program. On May 21, 1937, Ribbentrop asked Churchill to drop by the German embassy in London, ostensibly to talk about an article Churchill, by profession a journalist, had written. For two hours the two men talked, at first very affably. As Churchill later recalled, Ribbentrop said he had come to London to make a full case for "an Anglo-German entente or even alliance. Germany would stand guard for the British Empire in all its greatness and extent." What was needed was an agreement on the need for German Lebensraum in Europe. Germany, in turn, would guarantee Great Britain's interests in Europe, freeing Great Britain to repair its Empire.[38]

The notion was probably not all that far from the concept Churchill had in mind when he made his suggestion to Hanfstaengl five years earlier, but this time it was rejected out of hand. The Royal Navy, Churchill said, had proven quite capable of protecting British interests. No help from Germany was required. Ribbentrop, however, pushed on. He walked over to a large wall map and *pointed out the planned German Lebensraum in Poland, White Russia and the Ukraine.* Churchill, it seems, also had an honorary seat on the Reich Defense Council. The Germans had begun their courting by showing their plan to presumed British friends. Now they were delineating them to her enemies as well.

The session was both remarkable and strange and only got more so. Churchill explained to Ribbentrop that while "it was true we were on bad terms with Soviet Russia and that we hated Communism as much as Hitler did . . . Great Britain would never disinterest herself in the fortunes of the Continent to an extent which would enable Germany to gain the domination of Central and Eastern Europe."[39] England had no interest in a Germany three times her present size.

"In that case," Ribbentrop said, "war is inevitable. There is no way out. The Führer is resolved." The two men left the map and sat down. After some reflection, Churchill turned to Ribbentrop and warned: "Do not underrate England. She is very clever. If you plunge us all into another Great War, she will bring the whole world against you like the last time."

If Hitler had been patient perhaps Germany would have been by 1960 master of a United States of Europe. But he was not patient, and grew increasingly less so each month. He began to balance the idea that he was a man of destiny with the idea that he was mortal. He began to hurry.

In November 1937, he told his generals to prepare for war, and he told them why. Germany was not large enough agriculturally to feed itself, therefore it needed living space. If Germany sought this land overseas, she would "face sea lanes which are ruled by Britain," which "explains the great weakness in our food supply."[40] Instead Germany would seek its Lebensraum in Europe, by "conquering agriculturally useful space." He predicted war by the mid-1940s.

Lord Halifax, at this time the British foreign secretary, visited Germany, officially to partake in Hermann Göring's international hunting exhibition. Of course, the real intention was to get a current reading on German intentions. Hitler invited the Englishman to the Berghof. It was not time for idle chat or banter. Europe was facing a possible crisis over Hitler's designs on Austria. Halifax wanted to know what he had in mind there. Hitler did what he had been doing throughout: he revealed his plans, or at least those he thought he could achieve in his lifetime. There must be a "close union" between Austria and Germany, the problem with the Sudeten Germans must be addressed, German economic interests in southeastern Europe must be acknowledged, and the Germans had a dispute with the Poles over Danzig and the Polish Corridor.[41] The Führer was obviously frustrated that this simple formula didn't seem to be working. He complained to Halifax: "Obstacles are repeatedly being put in my way in South-East Europe by the Western Powers, and political ambitions which I have never entertained are attributed to me."[42]

The formula was now quite clear to the British. Sir Robert Vansittart, chief diplomatic advisor to His Majesty's Government and a close Churchill associate, said Germany was seeking "hegemony" in Central Europe, meaning "the conquest of Austria and Czechoslovakia, and the reconquest of Danzig and Memel; followed by the reduction of the other States to the condition of satellites—military satellites when required. This is a quite clear and comprehensible programme, but it is quite incompatible with our interests. We fought the last war to prevent this."[43]

Anschluss

While Adolf Hitler was romancing the British ruling class, he was not neglecting other planks in the *Mein Kampf* platform. To regain its position as a great power, Germany had first to establish sovereignty over its own territory. Only then could it reunite lands of the Greater Germany that had been stripped from it in Europe's internecine wars. In late 1937, Lord Halifax and others were about to witness the culmination of that plan.

Hitler had actually made the first big step in 1936, when he dealt the tattered Treaty of Versailles a fatal blow by marching a small number of troops into the Rhineland, which the hated treaty had declared demilitarized. His generals had been nearly apoplectic. There was no way Germany could enforce this decision through arms. It was still a crippled nation. But Hitler sent them anyway, with prudent orders that they should march directly back again at the first sign of trouble. But despite loud protestations and veiled threats from the British and the French, there was no trouble of a military kind. The world had not seen such a stone-cold gambler since Robert E. Lee. And each time Hitler won a bet, he grew more confident that he could do it again, with higher stakes.

With German sovereignty restored, Hitler took the second step toward Lebensraum—the reuniting of German lands sundered from Germany by politicians or the vagaries of history. When he looked at the map, he saw three such territories: his home country of Austria, the Sudeten area of the new state of Czechoslovakia, and a small strip of land in Poland called the Corridor. Hitler went about his tasks methodically, with each territory handled in succession, beginning with Austria. But what had changed was his tempo. Never a man known for great patience, Hitler was suddenly quickening the pace to the point that his generals and others doubted his sanity. Plots to overthrow Hitler were hatched in the High Command that would exist, unfulfilled, for the remainder of the war.

Just as Hitler was to embark on his conquests, he finally got welcome news from Great Britain. Neville Chamberlain became Prime Minister just as Hitler began his peaceful conquests, ushering in the period of appeasement. Chamberlain wanted nothing more than to avoid a new European war, and he took a charitable view toward Hitler's desire to unite Germany, as long as—and he underlined the point—Hitler did so peaceably. In this, Chamberlain was not far different from many of the other Englishmen who had visited Hitler in the mid-1930s, but unlike them, he was in a position to hand over to Hitler what he wanted. To Hitler, Chamberlain was a symptom of British willingness to deal favorably with Germany, evidence that his long years of working on the British were paying off.

Austria would be his biggest prize, and his easiest.

It was already filled with National Socialists, the nation thought of itself as German, and there were six hundred thousand Austrians out of work, while Germany was somehow avoiding the worldwide depression. After a browbeating—at the Berghof, of course—the Austrian leader, Kurt von Schuschnigg, agreed to make a Nazi the interior minister and head of the police; the rest was relatively easy. After several pretexts—one being that they had been invited in—German troops marched into Austria on March 12, 1938. No shots were fired. However ambivalent the Austrians had been before this happened, they now mostly appeared overjoyed. Hitler was hailed as a returning hero.

No sooner had Hitler won Anschluss, as the union with Austria became known, than he turned his attention to the next spot on the map, Czechoslovakia. Hitler saw that nation as a dagger aimed at the heart of the Reich, and he was right. If he had ever sent German armies to the Ukraine while a strong Czechoslovakia was still firmly embedded along Germany's flank, he would be taking an incalculable risk. That's at least one of the things the Allies had in mind when they created the state after the end of the First World War.

The area of western Czechoslovakia was predominately German, and from the way he looked at it, these Germans were being treated unfairly. It was a convenient excuse, largely unfounded, but like many successful politicians, Hitler managed to convince himself of the Czech outrages. The Czech government viewed things far differently, of course. Though the area was small, it was vital. It contained defense works that rivaled the Maginot Line. Without these, Czechoslovakia would be largely indefensible, as Hitler would soon prove.

The Czechs thought they were in a favorable position. They had an alliance with the Soviet Union, a friendship with France and great hope for England. They also had a military; though not as strong as Germany's, it was formidable, particularly when encased in its defense works. But as 1938 progressed, Czech President Eduard Benes began to develop a feeling that all the reassuring words from London, Paris and Moscow were not the same words being uttered privately.

Hitler was working himself into a war fury. He ordered the General Staff to draw up plans for an invasion. When they came, he couldn't believe it: the General Staff proposed an attack at the strongest point of the Czech defensive line—right where they expected it. Ever the believer in a flanking attack, Hitler ordered the generals to rethink their approach, while telling them that "I will decide to take action against Czechoslovakia only if I am firmly convinced . . . that France will not march, and that therefore England will not intervene."[44]

As the crisis intensified, Neville Chamberlain stepped in as the champion of peace. In a series of meetings in Germany, Chamberlain sought a formula that would satisfy the Führer while preserving British honor. He managed to do the former but not the latter. In a final face-to-face meeting in Munich in September 1938, Chamberlain agreed that the Sudetenland should be returned to the Reich. Back in London, Chamberlain—declaring that he had found "peace in our time"—was hailed as a great statesman in the cause of peace, though eventually the Munich sellout became the very symbol of appeasement.

Below the surface, there may have been other issues on Chamberlain's mind. Before agreeing to cede Sudeten Czechoslovakia to Hitler, Chamberlain reportedly received a report from the SIS entitled *What Should We Do?* It noted all of Germany's short-term goals, saying that Germany proposed the disintegration of the

USSR. Germany, the report observed, wanted a "deal" involving the recognition of Britain's supremacy overseas. Under certain circumstances, says an author who has summarized this document, the report concluded that a deal "might not prove to be uncongenial."[45]

While the SIS was reflecting on subterranean options, those above ground took the center. Hitler, who had assured Chamberlain that the Sudetenland was his last territorial ambition in Europe, soon remembered a couple more. Hitler bullied another Czech leader into signing over the rest of the nation. Chamberlain appeared deathly offended, and appeasement came to a sudden end.

With Czechoslovakia out of the way, Hitler finally turned his attention to the smallest parcel of all—the Polish Corridor. But this time he got something very different from the British. Something he could not believe.

6 :: *War*

I WOULD HAVE TO BE A COMPLETE IDIOT IF, ON ACCOUNT
OF THE MEASLY CORRIDOR QUESTION, I SHOULD SLIDE
INTO A WAR LIKE THE INCAPABLE NITWITS DID IN 1914.

—*Adolf Hitler*

The Polish Corridor was created at the conclusion of the First
World War—a thin stretch of land running from Germany, through
the former German city of Danzig, to a rump German territory that
was East Prussia. Until the Versailles treaty, it had been German.
Hitler wanted it back.

In October 1938, Hitler's foreign minister asked the Polish government to negotiate the return of Danzig, a League of Nations
Free City under Polish administration. He also wanted road and rail
links to East Prussia, and special rights for Germans in the Corridor. Poland demurred. The Poles had seen what happened to Austria and Czechoslovakia when they bargained with Adolf Hitler,
and they did not intend to let any part of their country fall into the
Reich's bosom, even if that territory was populated by Germans.
"Apart from the national character of the majority of the population," Poland declared, "everything in Danzig is definitely bound
up with Poland."[1] That was not a very ingenious argument to use on
Adolf Hitler.

As relations worsened in the spring of 1939, Hitler began claiming the Poles were systematically abusing the German population

in the Corridor, while Poland told Hitler to mind his own business. There was no doubting there was some truth to Hitler's claim. The Poles had been daring, perhaps even arrogant, in their dealings with the Reich. For once, there really was a German population suffering some mistreatment.

Even when Hitler only imagined mistreatment he could bring himself to fury. When he actually believed the reports, he could seem uncontrollable. Poland was such a case. Unlike the Austrians or Czechs, Hitler began looking upon the Poles with true hatred.

The Poles were not alone in facing down Hitler's hate. After Hitler occupied that part of Czechoslovakia about which he had earlier disclaimed interest, new starch shot into British collars. On March 31, 1939, Chamberlain guaranteed Poland's borders. Four days later the German Wehrmacht began planning for a late-summer campaign against the Polish state.[2]

The British-Polish understanding was a nightmare for Hitler. It was the first direct British pledge to a nation whose territory Hitler coveted. Throughout the spring and summer, Hitler vacillated about a planned war against Poland. At times he seemed to be spoiling for a fight; other times he seemed to dread testing British resolve. He was confident, then he wasn't.

In May, Hitler told his commanders that the era of easy victory was over. "Further successes," said the Führer, "cannot be obtained without the shedding of blood."[3] He did not say how much blood or whose blood. When he considered that the blood opposing him might be both British and Russian he shrank quickly away. Germany could not win a general war, at least not in 1939. Hitler had the tools to fight Poland, but hardly more. His navy was tiny, his air force and army untested. On paper, he was no match for the powers that surrounded him. Nor was German industry mobilized for war.

In early August 1939, as the Polish crisis was about to explode into world war, a British citizen whom the Nazis took quite seriously gave Nazi ideology chief Alfred Rosenberg a supposed insider's look into British thinking. In that it mirrored Hitler's prejudices, Rosenberg quickly dispatched a detailed memorandum to Hitler, with incalculable results. Baron William de Ropp claimed to be affiliated with the Royal Air Force, where, in the event of war, he would become chief of intelligence. Officers in the air corps, de Ropp said, were of the same mind as the German Führer, believing that it "was absurd for Germany and Britain to engage in a life and death combat on account of the Poles. As things were, the result could only be the destruction of the whole of European civilization, leaving Russia with her forces intact as the only beneficiary."[4]

The world had become so confused that logic was not prevailing. If Germany attacked Poland, France and England would be officially forced into the conflict. The hope, advised de Ropp, was for a quick and decisive demise of Poland, a total liquidation. Afterward, logic would return, for "the British Empire and Germany could not stake their whole existence for a State which would then have practically ceased to exist in its previous form." As far as Germany's long-term goals, the British officer class not only understood them, but approved. Germany's Lebensraum was for Britain's future "not only no harm but an advantage." "Germany," the officers realized, "had no subsequent designs on the British Empire."

Hitler liked that idea. When added to everything else—the ease of his rearmament, the Rhineland occupation, Anschluss, Munich—Hitler in early August was developing a belief that he would get out of this crisis with his dreams alive. Hitler told Halder "a number of times that it was beyond doubt that England and France were merely bluffing."[5] A week after the de Ropp memo, Hitler advised his generals that "England and France have undertaken obligations which neither is in a position to fulfill. . . . Little has been done on land. England will be able to send at most three divisions to the Continent. A little has been done for the Air Force, but it is only a beginning."[6] The worst that could be expected was something Hitler was willing to pay: "I am expecting an embargo on trade, not a blockade, and furthermore that relations will be broken off."[7]

Unthinkable

All the same, Hitler took no chances. With France and England pledged to come to Poland's aid, Hitler did the unthinkable: in

August, as a self-imposed deadline for solving the Polish question loomed and the situation with the British was getting nowhere, Hitler ordered his foreign minister to see if an understanding could be reached with Josef Stalin.

Whatever else might result from his planned Polish solution, Adolf Hitler did not dare invite a two-front war. One side or the other had to be neutralized. The depth of his aversion to fighting both Russia and the Western powers was evidenced by what Hitler was willing to give up to avoid it. A pact with Russia would mean German Lebensraum stopped at Poland, not at the Russian oil fields. It would contradict a decade of rabid Nazi anti-Communism. It would annul Hitler's anti-Semitism. If Hitler embraced the Soviet Union—which to him was the singular creation of the Jews—he would, in effect, become a Jewish ally. The bottom line of all this was quite clear: as long as Adolf Hitler was the Chancellor of Germany, Germany would not again fight the whole world alone. All else was secondary.

On August 14, 1939, Joachim von Ribbentrop—the man who had once pointed out the planned German conquest of the Ukraine to Winston Churchill—asked the German ambassador in Moscow to read to V. M. Molotov, the Soviet foreign minister, a proclamation. Saying that the Nazi and Bolshevik philosophies "do not prohibit a reasonable relationship between the two states" the communiqué suggested that the "period of opposition in foreign policy" could end, opening the "way to a new future for both countries." Declared the communiqué: "The Reich Government and the Soviet Government must, judging from past experience, take into account that the capitalistic Western democracies are the implacable enemies of both National Socialist Germany and Soviet Russia."[8]

It was a daring and brazen move from the Führer. But there could be no doubt about how this would play in Moscow. Stalin had seen Germany as a country whose every thrust had been to the south and east—in other words, toward Moscow's sphere of influence. Now Germany was willing to deal.

Stalin did not have to guess at the reasons for Hitler's volte-face. Hitler spelled them out: "The crisis which has been produced in German-Polish relations by English policy, as well as English agitation for war and the attempts at an alliance which are bound up with that policy, make a speedy clarification of German-Russian relations necessary."[9]

Two days after receiving Ribbentrop's suggestion—a blinding pace by Moscow standards—the Soviets responded. The German ambassador reported to Berlin that "Molotov received with greatest interest the information I had been instructed to convey, designated it as extremely important, and declared that he would report it to his Government at once and give me an answer shortly."[10] But that was not all. Molotov also broached what had before been unimaginable. He said he was "interested in the question of how the German Government were disposed towards the idea of concluding a non-aggression pact with the Soviet Union. . . ."[11]

It was the first time the words "non-aggression pact" had been uttered. Only one person in Soviet Russia would have ever dared say them. It wasn't Molotov. Stalin and Hitler were communicating.

In Berlin, Hitler learned from the Reich's Polish ambassador news that incensed him. "The position of the Reich Germans in Poland becomes daily more difficult," the ambassador reported. "Surrounded by hatred and Germanophobia, they see themselves being robbed of the essentials of their livelihood to an ever-increasing degree. Deportations and arrests are daily occurrences."[12] Though Hitler's regime would eventually redefine the words "deportations" and "arrests," in 1939 these words to Hitler meant insult and disrespect.

Hitler became more impatient. Even a minor delay in setting the date for Ribbentrop's visit sent the German Foreign Ministry into a frenzy. Worse, there was evidence that the British were also in Moscow, trying to entice Stalin.

On August 20, Moscow sent Hitler a copy of the proposed accord, containing everything Hitler wanted, plus some. The Soviets were suggesting a proviso to the pact: "The present Pact shall be valid only if a special Protocol is signed simultaneously, concerning the points in which the Contracting Parties are interested in the field of foreign policy."[13] The German contracting party did not yet know exactly what this special protocol would entail, but Hitler surely must have had a good idea.

Ribbentrop lost no time, arriving in Moscow on the twenty-third, as Russia and Germany announced the pact. The impossible had happened. Germany and Russia, while not formal allies, were nevertheless pledged to peaceful relations. "The sinister news," Churchill wrote later, "broke upon the world like an explosion."[14]

Not part of the announcement, of course, was the side agreement the Soviets had proposed—designated the "Secret Additional Protocol." So callous was the understanding that the Soviets didn't admit to its existence for over fifty years. Stalin won a sphere of influence throughout the Baltic states running from Finland to the "northern frontier of Lithuania," a provision Stalin would soon read, to Hitler's consternation, as the "southern frontier of Lithuania." In southeast Europe, Stalin's sphere included all of Bessarabia. The most heinous crime, of course, concerned Poland. The secret pact said that "in the event of a territorial and political transformation of the territories belonging to the Polish State, the spheres of interest of both Germany and the USSR shall be bounded approximately by the line of the rivers Narev, Vistula, and San."[15] The meaning was obvious, since everyone knew that the whole reason for the Nazi-Soviet agreement was to allow Hitler to commence the "territorial and political transformation" of Poland. Hitler had agreed to consume western Poland, and no more, while the massive Red Army would nourish itself on the eastern half. It was Stalin's price, paid for by Germany, using the currency of other people's blood.

Before the ink was dry on the Secret Protocol, Stalin lifted a glass and gave a toast to Adolf Hitler: "I know how much the German people loves its Führer. I would therefore like to drink his health."[16]

Hitler set the invasion of Poland to begin at dawn, August 26.

Anvil

England had boxed itself into a corner with Poland and knew no good way out. Arguments made to the Poles that they should negotiate went nowhere. The hope of roping Stalin into an anti-German alliance was gone. Chamberlain, back to the wall, was left with a last attempt to reason with the man who had just achieved the greatest diplomatic triumph of his life. On August 24, he delivered to Hitler one of the most famous documents of the war. It was either a last desperate effort to prevent calamity, or a document written mostly for the historians who would later ascribe war guilt. Perhaps it was a bit of both. Its points were clearly laid out. "Apparently the announcement of a German-Soviet Agreement is taken in some quarters in Berlin to indicate that intervention by Great Britain on behalf of Poland is no longer a contingency that need be reckoned with. No greater mistake could be made. Whatever may prove to be the nature of the German-Soviet Agreement, it cannot alter Great Britain's obligation to Poland, which His Majesty's Government have stated in public repeatedly and plainly and which they are determined to fulfil.

"It is alleged that, if His Majesty's Government had made their position clear in 1914, the great catastrophe would have been avoided. Whether or no there is any force in that allegation, His Majesty's Government are resolved that on this occasion there shall be no such tragic misunderstanding.

"If the case should arise, they are resolved and prepared to employ without delay all the forces at their command, and it is impossible to foresee the end of hostilities once engaged."[17]

Chamberlain then, again, offered to mediate the dispute.

Perhaps invigorated by his Moscow coup, Adolf Hitler received this message, hand-delivered by British Ambassador Neville Henderson, by indifferently proclaiming that "if you have given a blank check, you must also meet it."[18] He then launched into his own war-guilt message. England had poked its nose into affairs in which it had no national interests: Czechoslovakia and Poland. The treatment of Germans in those lands was an issue for Berlin, not London. Citing alleged Polish atrocities, Hitler declared that he "could not allow tens of thousands of fellow-Germans to be slaughtered for the sake of one of England's whims," namely its agreement with Poland.

Then he returned to his old obsession, telling Henderson that "England had made an enemy of the man who had wished to become her greatest friend. England would now make the acquaintance of a Germany very different from that which she had imagined for so many years."[19]

In the afternoon session, Hitler turned reflective. He told Henderson that he "was now 50, therefore if war had to come, it was better that it should come now than when he was 55 or even 60 years old." Then, as was the case this day, Hitler mixed reflection with threats: "England would do well to realize that as a front-line soldier he knew what war was and would utilize every means available. It was surely quite clear to everyone that the World War would not have been lost if he had been Chancellor at the time. . . .

"At the next instance of Polish provocation," the Führer threatened, "I shall act."[20]

On the morning of the twenty-fifth, Hitler received translations of speeches Chamberlain and Lord Halifax had given before Parliament. These men certainly didn't sound like they were bluffing. Interpreter Schmidt said the Führer turned "pensive."[21] At 1 P.M. he called Henderson into the chancellery. No longer swaggering, Hitler explained that after a night's reflection he had decided to "make a move towards England which should be as decisive as the move towards Russia. . . ."[22] He was short on specifics, and gave no reassuring news on the Polish question. He did, however, say that once the Polish question was settled he would pledge himself personally to the continued existence of the British Empire[23]—the same formula laid out to Churchill two years earlier.

The day had no end of bad news for Hitler. He soon learned that Great Britain had added to its existing agreements with Poland by signing a formal treaty. Hearing this, he sat "brooding at his desk until the French Ambassador, [Robert] Coulondre, was announced."[24] Coulondre would not lighten the Führer's mood. After Hitler fumed a bit about the Polish provocations, Coulondre declared: "I give you my word of honour as a French officer that the French army will fight by the side of Poland if that country should be attacked."[25] The messages arriving at the chancellery were consistent and clear. German aggression meant war. Short of that, the Allies were ready to deal. The French ambassador put it this way: "Right up to the last" the French would work for "moderation in Warsaw."[26]

Coulondre's appearance before Hitler was followed by the Italian ambassador, who delivered this from Hitler's ally, Mussolini: "In one of the most painful moments of my life I have to inform you that Italy is not ready for war."[27]

That was enough. Europe would not face war in twelve hours' time. Hitler called off the attack. The next day, Hitler told Göring that he had stopped the Polish invasion to give himself time to "eliminate British intervention."[28]

Hitler was cornered. It was increasingly clear that the Western powers were willing to try to force Poland to solve the Corridor problem much to Germany's benefit. But whether he gained this "territorial transformation" of Poland through Western pressure or through war, there was the problem of the secret agreement with the Russians. Hitler had already agreed to partition Poland and Stalin had the map in hand. A peaceful solution of the Polish question would alter that. A peaceful solution could be viewed in Moscow as a betrayal.

The West was unaware of the Secret Protocol, and was, therefore, unaware of how tightly Hitler was trapped. Should he surrender his hard-fought Russian card? If so, what protection would he have, finally, against the Soviet Union? The Russian card had worked so well that the West was lined up, perhaps, to desert Poland on the Corridor issue. It was a Pyrrhic victory for Hitler. And he sensed it.

This was the most serious crisis Hitler had ever faced. As he tried to work out a solution with the British during the next few days, Hitler bypassed his Foreign Ministry, choosing to deal directly and unconventionally with the British. Though diplomats would meet, the main negotiations with England would be conducted behind Ribbentrop's back. The conduit would also defy convention. A little-known Swedish businessman named Birger Dahlerus would be the instrument the Nazis and British used to try to avoid the Second World War.

Dahlerus not only ferried messages between heads of state, but was called upon to interpret the meaning of events, to suggest solutions, to—at times—negotiate. Hitler and the British Prime Minister were placing the fate of the world in the hands of an amateur. It almost worked. But when it didn't, Hitler proposed something stranger still.

Dahlerus

Birger Dahlerus had lived twelve years in England, giving him a perspective of that country that no top Nazi had. He also considered himself a friend of Germany, having made the acquaintance of Göring. He was appalled by the prospect of bloodshed between two countries he admired. While in London in July Dahlerus visited the Constitutional Club, where he and some of his British businessmen friends discussed the Third Reich. The British attitude was both chilled and resolute. While Hitler was seeing the appeasers at Munich, Dahlerus was seeing the stronger stalk that Hitler had met at Verdun. The British had grown tired of compromise. More important, they had developed a deep aversion to the Nazi leader.

Dahlerus jotted down some notes of his conversations. "Great Britain from now on has obligations which did not exist at [the] time of the Berchtesgaden meeting. . . . Great Britain will be involved automatically as a consequence of its obligations."[29]

"Germany," Dahlerus wrote, "will certainly be defeated again and will accomplish far less by war than by peaceful negotiation. England and her friends will likewise have to suffer much; possibly it will mean the end of civilization."[30]

The end of civilization was clearly something Dahlerus did not countenance. So this most self-confident of men, believing that German leaders did not know the real British attitude, took upon himself the task of setting Germany straight. He flew to Germany and met with Göring at Karinhall. The real problem, explained Dahlerus, was that the two sides not only spoke in different languages, but in different concepts as well. The British did not understand Hitler, and he did not understand them. To bridge this chasm, Dahlerus suggested that representatives of the two countries meet face-to-face in a neutral setting.

Göring was receptive. War threatened everything, not the least of which was Göring's growing personal empire. The Luftwaffe chief decided to broach with Hitler the concept of a face-to-face meeting with the British, a meeting not encumbered by diplomatic conventions, one where cards fell clearly on the table. Hitler immediately agreed.

Dahlerus flew to London to discuss the unusual peace bid. This time, he was not relegated to the Constitutional Club. Instead, he was in Whitehall meeting with Halifax and others. Halifax told Dahlerus that a meeting with Göring was acceptable, but the British delegation would not include any members of His Majesty's government or Parliament. However, Halifax said that "His Majesty's Government would await the results of the meeting with the greatest interest."[31] Hitler agreed to the British conditions.

On August 7, as the Polish crisis intensified, Hermann Göring sat down with seven Englishmen at a house owned by Dahlerus's wife at Schleswig-Holstein, near the Danish border. Discussions lasted from ten in the morning to late into the night. Dahlerus recalled during postwar testimony that the Englishmen "made it perfectly clear that in case Germany should try with force to occupy a foreign territory, the British Empire, in accordance with its obligations to Poland, would stand at the side of Poland."[32] For his part, the Reichsmarschall pledged to do "everything in his power" to avoid the conflict.

The Englishmen said that a conference on a more official level, with actual British leaders present, could help calm the situation. Göring passed this suggestion on to Hitler, and, again, the Führer agreed.

On August 23, as Dahlerus was packing for another trip—this time to Paris to pick up the British response to the conference suggestion—Göring, knowing that a war deadline was only seventy-two hours away, called Dahlerus and asked him to come instead immediately to Berlin. "Göring stated that the situation had . . . become very serious," Dahlerus recalled. No matter how fast an international conference might be arranged, it could not come fast enough. Göring implored Dahlerus to explain the situation—that there had been a sharp deterioration in German-Polish relations—to the British leaders. He was to underscore that "Germany wanted to come to an understanding with England."[33] It was the beginning of some of the most hectic and portentous negotiations this century.

When Dahlerus entered the Foreign Office, the tall, gaunt Halifax was decidedly optimistic. He took great pleasure that Hitler was not presently at war with Poland—Britain knew Hitler's deadline had come and passed without bloodshed. He thanked Dahlerus for his assistance, assuring him that he did not think negotiating through Dahlerus "would be required any longer."[34]

Dahlerus called Göring from the Foreign Office that evening and learned that the situation had again darkened ominously and that "war might break out at any moment."[35] He asked to impress upon his hosts that time was not an ally.

The next morning, the Swede met again with Halifax. "I told him that I had learned the German Government was trying to bring about a decision with all haste. And I stressed the importance of such an attempt in order to make it clear to him that in such a serious situation it was necessary to proceed with the greatest responsibility and care; I asked him to emphasize to the German Government that the British Government wanted an understanding."[36]

Dahlerus suggested that Halifax write to Göring about the British desires for an understanding. The foreign secretary huddled with Neville Chamberlain, emerging with a letter that might have defused the crisis. Dahlerus was soon on a plane headed for Germany. He was ferried to Göring's personal train, where he informed the Reichsmarschall that, from all his conversations in London, he believed there was no "doubt that, if the German Government proceeded against Danzig, it would immediately be at war with England."[37] He then handed Göring the letter.

The letter expressed a sincere desire for an Anglo-German understanding and a willingness to discuss all issues involving Poland should that conflict not result in German military aggression. The British asked for time—a few days. Göring read the letter, which was in English. He then asked the Swede to translate it into German. Once assured of its content, Hermann Göring ordered his train to stop at the next station. He had to reach the Führer. Motor cars took Göring and Dahlerus to a midnight rendezvous with Hitler.

Hitler was in a rare element when Dahlerus and Göring appeared at his study, agitated, pacing up and down, pontificating. If England wanted war he would counter by building "U-boats, U-boats, U-boats," and if that wasn't enough, he would build "aeroplanes, aeroplanes and still more aeroplanes." War, he said, "doesn't frighten me. Encirclement of Germany is an impossibility."[38] Just as suddenly as Hitler got himself into a lather, he calmed, asking Dahlerus a simple question: "Herr Dahlerus, tell me please, why I have not been able to arrive at an agreement with the British Government. You seem really to know England so well. Perhaps you can solve the riddle for me?"

"I hesitated at first," Dahlerus later recalled, "but then I told him that, with my intimate knowledge of the English people, I was personally of the opinion that their lack of confidence in him and his Government was the reason."[39] Few people were ever as blunt to Hitler as Birger Dahlerus. But if he took offense, Hitler didn't show it. Instead, he repeated German positions, and asked Dahlerus to travel back to London to explain them once again. Dahlerus pressed his luck. How could he return to London with nothing more than that? He asked for specifics. What territorial solution, for instance, did Hitler propose for the Polish Corridor?

"Well," Hitler said, "Henderson never asked about that!" Göring tore out a page of a map book and outlined the proposed German claim, and for the next hour and a half, Hitler explained his proposal in detail to the lone amateur diplomat. The proposal was as unusual as it was significant. Germany was prepared to sign a treaty with Britain covering all political and economic disputes. In exchange for England's help in resolving the Corridor question, Germany would guarantee Poland's boundaries. Hitler wanted an agreement on German colonies that had been stripped from her during the First World War. Finally, Germany proposed to give Great Britain military assistance wherever she should be attacked.[40]

Hitler had just won a nonaggression pact with the Soviet Union by proposing, among other things, the partition of Poland. Now he was proposing to *guarantee* borders that he had already redrawn in Stalin's favor. If he was serious, he was prepared to betray the Soviets.

Off flew Dahlerus. On the twenty-seventh, he met with Chamberlain, Halifax and Cadogan at 10 Downing Street. They were amazed at the German proposals, so different were they from those conveyed to Henderson. The game had changed. Different ideas were before the British, and some of them held clear promise. Hen-

derson, in London but not at these meetings, was scheduled to return to Berlin the next day with an official response to the official
German positions. Dahlerus suggested that Henderson should wait
an extra day to return to Berlin. That would give Dahlerus time to
give Hitler the British "unofficial" response to the "unofficial"
German initiative. Dahlerus would then gauge Hitler's reaction,
passing it on to the British embassy. Thereby the British could tai-
lor their final position in a way that was most likely to win Hitler's
approval. If this arrangement was not already unusual enough, all
these steps would be done with the full knowledge of the Germans.
The British agreed.

Dahlerus called Göring to see if the Germans would also find
this reasonable. They did.[41] Dahlerus left immediately for Berlin.
The British response he carried in his pocket was significant. While
saying that England did not need German military help around the
globe, it shredded what little remained of the Treaty of Versailles
by proclaiming that England would not negotiate with the Germans on colonies *while Germany was mobilized*. In other words, the
treaty that separated Germany from the colonies was negotiable. As
for Polish boundaries, British proposed having them guaranteed by
Russia, Germany, England, France and Italy, instead of by Germany alone. On the all-important Corridor question, the British
said it should be settled by Germany and Poland alone. Finally,
England had no problem in creating an overall agreement with
Germany.

Dahlerus was back in Berlin before midnight and rushed to
Göring's city home. The Reichsmarschall "did not consider the reply very favorable. I told him, however, that in view of the events
of the past year he could hardly expect the English to be satisfied
with the guarantees of Poland's boundaries by Germany only. In
reference to the colonial question, I made it clear to him that any
British Government that tried to force this point in Parliament as
long as Germany's forces were mobilized would be overthrown at
once."[42]

Göring left to brief Hitler while Dahlerus went to his hotel. He
would not sleep. Göring called at 1:30 A.M. with the news that
Hitler welcomed the British proposal, appreciated the suggestion

of internationally guaranteed Polish boundaries, and was delighted
with the willingness to form an Anglo-German agreement. If these
provisions were agreed upon, there would be no war.

Dahlerus took the news to the British embassy. Staff there cabled
London, and the British government crafted its "official" proposals
for the Führer. When His Majesty's official ambassador, fortified
with half a bottle of champagne,[43] came to Hitler he brought better
terms than even those already delivered by Dahlerus. The official
British reply didn't mention German colonies, opening that door
even further. And it was silent on military cooperation. On the question of guaranteeing Polish borders, the official response said only
that it should be guaranteed by "other Powers." It repeated that the
current crisis had to be settled by negotiations between Poland and
Germany. Most important, it revealed that England was already
pressuring its ally Poland to begin negotiations at the highest level
with Germany—exactly what Hitler wanted. In fact, it revealed that
this initiative had already borne fruit, with England having received
"a definite assurance from the Polish Government that they are prepared to enter into discussion on this basis, and His Majesty's Government hope the German Government would for their part also be
willing to agree to this course." Moreover, the British government
was "anxious to use all [its] influence to assist the achievement of a
solution which may commend itself both to Germany and to
Poland."[44]

Amid all the hopeful language, there was a warning. Failure to
reach a peaceful resolution with Poland "would ruin the hopes of
better understanding between Germany and Great Britain, would
bring the two countries into conflict, and might well plunge the
whole world into war. Such an outcome would be a calamity without parallel in history."[45]

On paper, here was a reasonable plan to avoid war. But if the actual discussion between Hitler and Ambassador Henderson was
any indication, there were more hurdles ahead. The ambassador
did not satisfy himself with delivering the note and carefully as-
sessing Hitler's reply. He chose, instead, to argue. Hitler had repeated a litany of alleged Polish provocations in the Corridor,
ending by saying that these were apparently "a matter of indiffer-

ence to Britain."[46] Henderson, perhaps it was the champagne, took this as a personal insult and reacted angrily and with hurt pride. It was he, Sir Neville Henderson, who had worked day and night trying to protect the peace, saying, according to the German version of this affair, that "the choice between war and peace now lay with the Führer."[47]

Hitler, at least outwardly, remained calm. He repeated that he wanted an alliance with England. "England," he said, "had repulsed him again and again and had thus forced him against his will into alliances with others, which had not been in keeping with his original intentions. Even now he still wanted friendship with England and he expressed the . . . hope that England would not let this last chance slip."[48]

After Henderson left, Göring, Hess and Himmler joined Hitler. He explained to them the British proposal, and—according to Himmler's diary—said that he was going to prepare a document aimed at the British "that is little less than a masterpiece of diplomacy. He wants to spend tonight thinking it over; because he always gets most of his best ideas in the small hours between 5 and 6 A.M."[49] Göring called Dahlerus, saying that Hitler considered the British proposal "highly satisfactory."[50]

Whatever ran through Hitler's mind at 5 A.M. on August 29, 1939, it was definitely not a masterpiece of diplomacy. He took the British up on their willingness to press the Poles into negotiations, but came up with a timetable that was impossible. He demanded that a fully empowered Polish representative arrive in Berlin within twenty-four hours. That was a schedule set more to meet the needs of his military—he had just set September 1 as the invasion date and would need lead time to countermand that order—than any possible diplomatic reason. Further, the document spelled out minimum German demands: when the representative did appear, he must be fully empowered to sign over the Corridor and Danzig.[51]

Henderson said that this "sounded like an ultimatum," though Hitler insisted that it "was only intended to stress the urgency of the moment—when the two fully mobilized armies were standing face to face."[52]

The diplomats were again making reverse progress. It was time again for the back door. Göring called Dahlerus. Events, he said, had taken an unsatisfactory course. He wanted Dahlerus to go to London and try to fix matters. At 5 A.M., August 30, Dahlerus headed across the Channel. He met with Chamberlain, Halifax, and Cadogan. It was obvious that "the British Government had become highly mistrustful. . . . They explained to me at the same time that it was hardly fair to expect the Polish Government to send delegates to Berlin to negotiate, after it was known what experience other countries had had in the past years when they had been in Berlin on [a] similar mission."[53] Searching for some hope, Dahlerus told the group that Hitler might propose to solve the Polish question by a plebiscite.[54]

The world war was little more than a day away.

The evening of August 30 was catastrophic. Henderson, who had grown cantankerous, went to Bismarck's former office to see the Nazi foreign minister. Ribbentrop "greeted Henderson with an icy expression and stiff formality," recalled German translator Schmidt. "The conversation was conducted partly in German, for Henderson liked to speak our language although he was not exactly a master of it."[55]

Henderson explained the obvious absence of a Polish representative by declaring that it had been "unreasonable" to insist on a deadline. "The time is up," Ribbentrop said. At the suggestion that the Germans could approach the Poles through their embassy, the normal way governments spoke, Ribbentrop boomed: "That's out of the question after what has happened. We demand that a negotiator empowered by his Government with full authority should come here to Berlin."[56]

His face reddening, his hands beginning to tremble, Henderson began to review the British reply to Hitler's strange communiqué. It was filled with optimistic words, but said that—while the British understood the need for speedy negotiations—it was impossible to begin them in but a single day. When Henderson had finished, Ribbentrop said mockingly: "Have you anything more to say?"[57] Henderson did. He said that the British government had information about German sabotage in Poland.

"That's a damned lie of the Polish Government's," bellowed

Ribbentrop. "I can only tell you, Herr Henderson, that the position is damned serious."[58] With a finger pointed toward the German foreign minister, Henderson shouted: "You have just said 'damned.' That's no word for a statesman to use in so grave a situation."

Shocked, Ribbentrop leaped to his feet, roaring, "What did you say?" Henderson had risen, too, and both men's eyes locked on. Translator Schmidt later said that "according to diplomatic convention I too should have risen; but to be frank I did not quite know how an interpreter should behave when speakers passed from words to deeds—and I really feared they might do so now. I therefore remained quietly seated and pretended to be writing in my notebook. Above me, I heard the two fighting cocks, breathing heavily."[59]

The first blows of the Second World War were not to be struck quite yet, and the men returned to their seats. Per instructions from Hitler, Ribbentrop then read to Henderson the Reich's sixteen-point proposal for solving the Polish question, the one that maybe could have worked had not Hitler had his early-morning brainstorm. Again, the Germans demanded concessions on Danzig and the Corridor. However, Hitler—as Dahlerus had already informed the British—intended to soften the blow by allowing the people of the Corridor and Danzig to vote on this measure in a plebiscite. Germany would also guarantee Poland access to the sea.[60]

In some respects, Hitler's offer was more reasonable than that offered to Austria and Czechoslovakia, two countries whose very sovereignty was challenged. But this was no sincere offer by a reborn democrat. It was posturing for posterity. Hitler had already issued the invasion orders, although his resolve was not yet one hundred percent. At the conclusion of Ribbentrop's presentation, Henderson asked for a copy of the proposal, as is the norm in such exchanges. Ribbentrop refused, on Hitler's orders. Henderson protested, but got nowhere. Schmidt saw through the scheme.

"Now I, in my turn, became agitated. I suddenly saw the game Hitler and Ribbentrop were playing. At that moment I understood that Hitler's high-sounding proposals had been produced only for show, and were never intended to be put into effect. The refusal to hand the document over to Henderson was made for fear that the

British Government would pass on the proposals to the Poles, who might well have accepted them."[61]

Ribbentrop had delivered the proposals at "top speed" in German. Henderson, even though his German was marginal, did not ask Schmidt for a translation. Schmidt could not believe the bungling. If Henderson had asked for one, it was pro forma that Schmidt would have obliged. Yet Henderson sat mute, missing the chance.

War appeared inevitable to everybody but Birger Dahlerus. As Ribbentrop and Henderson did battle, Dahlerus once again got into a plane headed to Berlin for a midnight session with Göring. Göring told him what had just happened, including Ribbentrop's refusal to give Henderson a copy of the proposal on Poland. Dahlerus said it was "impossible to treat the Ambassador of an Empire like Great Britain in this way."[62] He said Göring should get a copy of the proposal and read it to him in translation. Dahlerus, thereby, asked still another question that had escaped the grasp of the trained British ambassador. Göring got a copy and gave it to Dahlerus, who then took it to Henderson at 10 A.M., August 31. The world was eighteen hours away from war.

Delighted to get the proposals, Henderson asked Dahlerus to deliver a copy to Polish ambassador Josef Lipski. Dahlerus dutifully headed out with another British diplomat to the Polish embassy. If there was any possibility that Hitler's war was to be thwarted, the last chance was now. But the Poles could not have been more unimpressed with the sixteen-point plan. Facing imminent war with Germany, Lipski declared that "he had no reason to negotiate with the German Government. If it came to war between Poland and Germany, he knew—since he had lived five and a half years in Germany—that a revolution would break out in Germany and that they would march on Berlin."[63]

Desperate, Dahlerus arranged a meeting between Göring and Henderson that afternoon, but Henderson was in a suspicious mood and the meeting produced no results. Finally, Dahlerus suggested that Göring meet with British representatives directly in Holland, but it was too late. For months Hitler had favored this war. Now he would have it.

The Second World War began in the early-morning hours of September 1, 1939. On paper, it should not have been a walkover. Germany had 1.5 million men on the frontier. Poland had 1.3 million. Considering the military axiom that an attacker needs a two-to-one advantage over the attacked, it should not have been an easy fight. The difference, though, came with tanks and aircraft. Hitler had fourteen mechanized divisions. Poland had one tank brigade. And Hitler held the requisite two-to-one advantage in aircraft.[64]

There was no revolution in Germany. Yet there was no joy either. Germans knew the cost of war. And they had grown used to bloodless victories. Now this.

The Poles had to get adjusted to the idea that they were not soon to be marching on Berlin. German civilians in the Corridor paid heavily for Hitler's decision to attack. Poles murdered over 5,400 Germans[65]—a small enough number by Second World War standards, but the war was just getting started. It was an omen for how this conflict would play out.

There were still some who searched for peace. Dahlerus called Cadogan after talking with Göring *and* Hitler, with news that Hitler had a matter he wanted to discuss with the British. He proposed bringing it to London. With the fighting already under way, the British could only say no.[66]

Hitler, obviously, wanted to keep his trusted back door open. Despite the warnings from the British—clear, distinct and oft-repeated—Hitler had finally brought himself to believe that a general war was impossible. His effort now was to get the Polish question answered on the battlefield, and then enter *real* negotiations with the British. General Halder most recalled this comment from Hitler just before the war: "I would have to be a complete idiot if, on account of the measly Corridor question, I should slide into a war like the incapable nitwits did in 1914."[67] Only a day before the war, Hitler explained this optimism to his generals. It "was a reasonable assumption," he said, "that the Nazi-Soviet pact of August 1939 would rule out the possibility of Allied intervention in support of Poland, particularly in view of their behaviour on previous occasions."[68] And on the morning of the attack, Hitler expounded: "I will not attack England. Why should England attack me?"[69]

He was, in part, right. There was nothing France and England were willing to do militarily to come to the rescue of Poland. They could only watch. But they did one thing that unnerved the Führer. They declared war.

Just after midnight on September 3, 1939, the British embassy called the German Foreign Ministry to say a communication from London was to be delivered to the German government at 9 A.M. Sensing that this could contain "nothing agreeable," Ribbentrop made sure he was nowhere near the Foreign Ministry. He would not receive Henderson; Schmidt, only a translator, would. Though this was the most important single assignment of his life, Schmidt overslept, arriving outside the Foreign Ministry just in time to see Henderson already entering. Schmidt slipped in a side entrance and managed to get to Ribbentrop's office ahead of the British ambassador.

Henderson entered solemnly, shook Schmidt's hand but declined his invitation to sit. "I regret that on the instructions of my Government I have to hand you an ultimatum for the German Government," he said. Then he read it: "If His Majesty's Government has not received satisfactory assurances of the cessation of all aggressive action against Poland, and the withdrawal of German troops from the country, by 11 o'clock British Summer Time, from that time a state of war will exist between Great Britain and Germany."[70]

Henderson handed Schmidt a copy of the ultimatum. They exchanged a few words that Schmidt said were heartfelt. Then Schmidt rushed to Reichschancellory, where Hitler, Hess, Göring and Ribbentrop were waiting.

"When I entered the next room Hitler was sitting at his desk and Ribbentrop stood by the window. Both looked up expectantly as I came in. I stopped at some distance from Hitler's desk, and then slowly translated the British Government's ultimatum. When I finished, there was complete silence.

"Hitler sat immobile, gazing before him. He was at a loss. . . . He sat completely silent and unmoving." Hitler was like a gambler who had signed over the deed to his house and placed it on the table, only to have the better gambler opposite him call the bluff.

"After an interval which seemed an age, he turned to Ribbentrop, who had remained standing by the window. 'What now?' asked Hitler. . . ." Ribbentrop had a subdued answer: "I assume that the French will hand in a similar ultimatum within the hour."

His duty over, Schmidt left through an anteroom where various top Nazis had gathered. He told them the news. There was again a hush. "Goebbels stood in a corner, downcast and self-absorbed." Others milled, quietly. Göring turned to Schmidt and said: "If we lose this war, then God have mercy on us!"[71]

Hitler and Hess left to board a train to take them to the front. The Führer was pale, subdued and pensive. One of his secretaries had never before seen him quite like this. As the train headed east, Hitler turned to Hess to say: "Now, all my work crumbles. I wrote my book for nothing."[72]

Yet the beginning of the Second World War was not complete without its interlocutor, Dahlerus. Dahlerus met Göring and "appealed to him to try at least to arrange for a reasonable reply to the ultimatum. I had the impression that certain members of the German Government were in favour of war, and I was afraid if a written reply was given it would not be so worded as to avoid war with England."

Dahlerus proposed a unique solution. He said that "Göring should declare himself prepared to go to England, at once, before the 11 o'clock deadline, to negotiate there."[73] There was, of course, no way that Göring could have arrived in London before the expiration of the ultimatum. He couldn't have even taken off. In other words, Dahlerus was proffering that the number two man in Germany fly away to Great Britain at a time the countries were sure to be at war.

There was no way the Nazi Führer, after brazenly committing his troops to war, could send Göring to Great Britain to negotiate a way out. He would be inviting all sorts of risks, not the least of which would be that of appearing weak. Also, once in England, Göring could become the source of immense propaganda value, or worse.

Yet Hitler agreed to the plan. Göring, Hitler said, should go immediately to London and settle this exasperating problem as quickly as possible. Not only did this confirm again that Hitler preferred sending plenipotentiaries to settle major problems, but that he was willing to take risks, perhaps even extreme risks, in doing so.

Before the Reichsmarschall could fly away, Dahlerus tried to make sure he was still welcome. Sir Alexander Cadogan wrote in his diary that "Dahlerus rang up at 10:50 to say German reply on its way. Only hope was to ask Göring to fly over. I said 'Rats.' "[74] Ten-fifty A.M. was exactly ten minutes before the British would enter the Second World War.

The British Foreign Office nixed the idea. The British government could not, at least not officially, sanction a visit by Hitler's representative just after the English ultimatum expired.

Though the proposal that Göring jump in a plane and fly west was perhaps one extraordinary event in the prewar weeks, two others were also now clear to the British: Hitler's inclination to encapsulate secret negotiations so that only two or three others in the Reich knew what was really happening, and his willingness to isolate Ribbentrop and the standard foreign diplomatic machinery in dealing with England. Ribbentrop only knew that "something" was happening concerning a Swedish businessman named Dahlerus. He was never told what.[75]

After the war, prosecutors asked Göring what he wanted to accomplish by thwarting the Foreign Office. "At this time," Göring explained, "it was clear to me that it was not a question of accomplishing something. If I wanted to influence the Führer, that was possible only if I had something in my hand, that is, could say to him: On my own responsibility, but with your knowledge and without committing you and your Reich policies, I am conducting negotiations, in order, circumstances permitting, to create an atmosphere which will be able to facilitate the official negotiations in a direction of a peaceful solution."[76]

It was a labyrinthine logic, but one that made sense to Hitler. In fact, it was the paradigm of the Rudolf Hess mission—"On my own responsibility, but with your knowledge and without committing you and your Reich policies, I am conducting negotiations. . . ." The two had much in common: a peace endeavor by one of Hitler's closest confidants, but ostensibly without Hitler's official sanction, undertaken to bring peace with England. Third-party intermediaries were used to insulate Hitler. In Göring's case the intermediary was Dahlerus, in Hess's case Albrecht Haushofer and the Duke of Hamilton played the role, until, of course, Hess assumed it himself. The two events even had the common final element: a proposed flight to Britain during war.

The British were learning something else in the prewar weeks of 1939. Göring was not the only back-channel route to Adolf Hitler, nor, perhaps, was he the best. There was another candidate of equal stature: Hess.

Just before the guns started firing over the Polish border, the British secret services tried to get an intelligence agent in contact with Adolf Hitler, an endeavor revealed after the war by foreign intelligence chief, Walter Schellenberg. Exactly what was intended by such a meeting was either not revealed by Schellenberg, or was not discussed in a lengthy report the Americans filed about their interrogations.[77]

Whatever the intentions, it was the way the SIS went about securing the link that is intriguing. German intelligence during the war was a collage that was not only confusing at its time, but is to this day as well. The army, Gestapo, SS and Nazi Party had intelligence services, often duplicating, sometimes intermingled, and unusually ineffective. A most bizarre intelligence agency was the Jahnkeburo, run by a mysterious man named, of course, Kurt Jahnke. It was a quasi-independent service that hired out to the others, but was most closely connected to the Nazi Party and Hess, its leader. It was this obscure agency that the British and the Nazis tapped, indicating that even this early the SIS had a sophisticated understanding of German intelligence.

True to form, both the British and the Nazis kept to a minimum knowledge about this clandestine mission. Also true to form, Ribbentrop sensed that they were treading on his turf. Schellenberg said that "Ribbentrop was mortally offended when, during the Polish crisis, at the outbreak of war, Janke [sic] had wanted to avert the war with England, and had used every conceivable means to bring an English Intelligence man to Hitler through Hess and Himmler."[78]

Schellenberg—who was paying Jahnke two thousand marks a month, plus expenses, for his help with the Gestapo—had hardly a clue about his agent's intelligence unit. Schellenberg knew Jahnke had contacts in Switzerland and England, though he didn't know their names.

Jahnke had something else that made his work for Hess's party apparatus curious: he was likely a British agent. Schellenberg said that "Jahnke was of the opinion that the full value of a Secret Service always depended on the number and the standard of Double Agents. He hated Hitler and nearly all Nazis."[79]

It was British access to just such well-placed people as Jahnke that they would tap later when a visit from Rudolf Hess became necessary.

7 ∞ *En Finir*

I FELT A SERENITY OF MIND AND WAS CONSCIOUS OF A
KIND OF UPLIFTED DETACHMENT FROM HUMAN AND PER-
SONAL AFFAIRS.

—*Winston Churchill describing his feeling at the
beginning of the Second World War*

Berlin's streets were quiet, its people somber. But for a few strag-
glers, the square in front of the Reichschancellory was empty. Frustrated newsboys couldn't even sell out extras describing alleged
Polish atrocities.[1] Germans were going about their business, heads
down. Even the skies were overcast.

War was not welcomed in Hitler's Third Reich.

It had been different in the last war. Germany was then peopled
by idealists and romantics, eager for their country to win its right-
ful place among great nations. Upon hearing the war declaration,
women and children and would-be heroes clogged the streets and
beer halls and squares to watch parades or simply to shout support
for the great German Kaiser. Eventually, Wilhelm II appeared on
the balcony of his palace, amid falling flower petals that Americans
would describe as confetti, to acknowledge the love of his subjects.
War then was heroic and good.

Now war was not.

Germans had learned the cost of modern battle and no amount of hype from Joseph Goebbels could change that. German mothers and their sons were worried. Would there be a general European war? Would there be a world war?

Germans looked to one man for the answer, the same man who had faced down so many grave and ominous situations before. Surely Adolf Hitler could find a way out. To Germans, even now, Hitler was not so much a cause of war as a chance for peace. The Führer would find a way. To an outsider, the Germans seemed mechanical, going about their lives seeking neither war nor peace. William Shirer, one of the war's first historians, said they seemed "apathetic."

Shirer missed the correct word. The Germans were worried, though determined, accepting fate, but not trusting entirely in it, either. Mostly they were fatalists. They were resigned.

Hitler was concerned. He was concerned about the war, about his citizens' obvious lack of enthusiasm for it, and about how he could extract himself from the predicament he had handcrafted. Though he told himself that the British were bluffing and would not really fight, he knew, also, that they might and, in that case, the French might fight, too. Though he resolved that Germany would never again wage a protracted war involving trenches and gas, he knew that his new tactics of the "lightning strike" were largely untested. In other words, things dark and unexpected might soon happen, things Germans were not prepared for. At the moment, Hitler was the most popular politician in German history. He resolved to expend some of that goodwill to make Germans anticipate the possible.

Hitler took the podium in the Reichstag, grim and resigned.

"If I called up the Wehrmacht and if I now demand sacrifices from the German people, and if necessary the supreme sacrifice, I have a right to do so," Hitler told the politicians, and, by radio, the whole country. "For I myself am just as prepared as I was before to make any personal sacrifice. I am not demanding of any German man anything more than what I myself was ready to do voluntarily for four years. There will be no privation in Germany which I myself will not share from the start. . . . I do not want to be anything other than the first soldier of the German Reich. . . ."

"I have once more put on the uniform which was once the most holy and precious to me. I shall only take it off after victory or I shall not live to see the end."[2]

Though no speech about war could be welcomed in Germany of 1939, this one at least could be appreciated. The Germans always liked their ascetic corporal.

Hitler was beside himself this day about his own mortality. Of his life, he said, "anyone could take it." And in case someone did, Hitler for the first time spelled out his line of succession.

"If anything happens to me in this struggle," Hitler told Germany, "my first successor will be party comrade Göring. If anything happens to party comrade Göring then the next successor will be party comrade Hess. You would then be bound to them as Führer in blind loyalty and obedience as much as to me. If anything happens to party comrade Hess then I shall summon the Senate by law which will choose the most worthy, i.e. the bravest, from the midst."[3]

Hitler had picked as his first replacement the military man, not the political disciple, to lead Germany during war. But in being named the second in line at this time of crisis, Rudolf Hess's stature was confirmed throughout Germany.

Across the English Channel, Winston Churchill listened on his radio for the final word from Neville Chamberlain that the deadline had passed and Great Britain was at war. At 11:15 A.M., September 3, 1939, the Prime Minister informed his countrymen that twenty-one years after the last war ended a new one had begun. As Chamberlain finished his speech "a strange, prolonged, wailing noise, afterwards to become familiar, broke upon the ear," Churchill later wrote.[4] Winston and wife Clementine headed to the roof to see what the commotion was all about. "Around us on every side, in the clear, cool September light, rose the roofs and spires of London. Above them were already slowly rising thirty or forty cylindrical balloons." Believing the sirens had given a fifteen-minute warning, the Churchills confidently headed down to the bomb shelter "armed with a bottle of brandy and other appropriate medical comforts."

So fortified, Churchill noticed that about one hundred others had been assigned to the shelter. "Everyone," he reported, "was cheerful and jocular, as is the English manner when about to encounter the unknown. As I gazed from the doorway along the empty street and at the crowded room below, my imagination drew pictures of ruin and carnage and vast explosions shaking the ground; of buildings clattering down in dust and rubble, of fire brigades and ambulances scurrying through the smoke, beneath the drone of hostile aeroplanes."

Instead, there was only quiet. The old bulldog's imagination about how this war would be fought was accurate, but his timing was off. Regardless, what for many was a day of deep despair was something quite different for Winston Churchill. After the all-clear sounded, he made his way to Parliament. It was as if the wailing of the air-raid sirens had finally set him free. "As I sat in my place," he would write, "listening to the speeches, a very strong sense of calm came over me, after the intense passions and excitements of the last few days. I felt a serenity of mind and was conscious of a kind of uplifted detachment from human and personal affairs." So good was England's entry into this war that it had already "thrilled my being and seemed to lift our fate to those spheres far removed from earthly facts and physical sensation." It was as if the grim picture Churchill had imagined only moments before had been somehow choreographed with a fine work of Wagner. Something beautiful, at least. And military. In war, Churchill found peace.

There was more good news today for Churchill. As he listened to his fellow MPs, a note was passed to Churchill from a messenger. In Neville Chamberlain's scrawl, Churchill was asked if he could please present himself to the Prime Minister's office. There was an important matter to discuss.

After years in the wilderness—an outsider, consummate nag, constant critic—Winston Churchill was asked back into His Majesty's Government. Chamberlain offered Churchill the office he had once held and in which his greatest failure lay. Churchill was offered, and, of course, accepted the post of First Lord of the Admiralty. In a nation whose existence was based on the power of its navy, the offer was irresistible.

Hitler's greatest foe began circling the center of power.

Phony War

For all of Hitler's premonitions of death, heroism and sacrifice, and all of Churchill's visions of bright bursting bombs, the war in Europe looked more like a parlor game than Armageddon. Though declaring war, France and England did little to advance it. Certainly not as much as Poland had expected. Poland was being crushed while her allies looked on, displeased but unhelpful. Neville Chamberlain did send two divisions to France on September 4, but certainly not to fire any shots. French leaders, who had nearly as many troops as Germany, and more tanks, did little more than wring their hands. In fact, the major powers appeared to be trying to do everything but fight.

Meanwhile, Hitler imposed strict restrictions on his submarine fleet, and ordered troops in the West not to initiate action. Both sides vacillated. Yet, while Hitler vacillated between going to war and staying on the defensive, the West mostly vacillated about different ways of doing nothing.

The war was different in the East. There, the Germans fought well and fought hard. On the fifth of September, German troops entered Kraków. Twenty-four hours later, the Wehrmacht took Danzig and was fighting in the suburbs of Warsaw. Through bravery alone the Poles slowed the German advance.

The world had never seen fighting like this. German armor became the modern cavalry, attacking often independently of the infantry, supported by a new type of artillery: the dive-bomber. Those who faced the Stukas and survived seemed to remember most their terrible shrieking even more than the exploding bombs.

The West waited to see how much of a fight the Poles had in them. The Poles could have had the fight of Ulysses S. Grant for all the good it would have done them after September 17. Citing changing political geography and new strategic threats at its borders, Stalin sent some forty divisions into an eastern Poland guarded by a mere twenty-five battalions. Even then, the Soviets didn't play fair. Many came carrying white flags, shouting for the Poles not to shoot because their Russian brothers were coming to help them fight the Germans.

The end came quickly. Russian and German troops made contact twenty-four hours after the Red Army invaded. A day later, thirty thousand Polish troops reached Warsaw, where they mounted a desperate stand. After a murderous aerial assault, the Poles surrendered on September 27. Though Poland's suffering had only begun, its army's toll was already staggering. In less than a month, 120,000 Poles were dead, a million more were prisoners, many of whom would also soon die. Stalin quickly ordered the deaths of eleven thousand Polish officers and leaders. Many were buried in the Katyn Forest. Hitler, more slowly though more deliberately, would by 1945 murder almost all of Poland's three million Jews. The German and Soviet cost for the Polish annexation was fairly modest by these standards. Germany lost eleven thousand dead; the Red Army, through cunning, only seven hundred.[5]

Stalin's thrust into Poland presented Great Britain with a dilemma, both moral and practical. The British had declared war on Germany because England guaranteed that she would defend Poland against armed aggression. Now whole divisions of armed aggressors wearing red stars on their helmets poured into Poland. By the letter of its agreements, and perhaps morally, the British were obligated to declare war on the Soviet Union.

Though many in Britain—mainly the press and working class—clamored for just such a solution, British statesmen of the realpolitik knew better. If Britian went to war with Russia and Germany, it would face a Continental bloc too powerful to defeat. There was no statesman in England better schooled in realpolitik than Winston Churchill, who had always maintained that England could defeat Germany *only* if Russia was England's ally. The victory that Churchill wanted would be impossible if Russia was England's enemy. So Churchill did what he could to allay his countrymen's outrage, at a certain cost of principle. "I was still convinced," Churchill later wrote, "of the profound, and as I believed quenchless antagonism between Russia and Germany, and I clung to the hope that the Soviets would be drawn to our side by the force of events."[6]

Churchill took to the air and offered a reluctant apology to the Soviet dictator. "Russia," he told his countrymen, "has pursued a cold policy of self-interest. We could have wished that the Russian armies should be standing on their present line as the friends and allies of Poland instead of as invaders. But that the Russian armies should stand on this line was clearly necessary for the safety of Russia against the Nazi menace."[7]

In a letter to his sister, Chamberlain said he took "the same view as Winston to whose excellent broadcast we have just been listening."[8]

However, taking this line on Russia unleashed other problems on the British, not the least of which was the question of why they were in the war at all. Twenty-three days into the Second World War, Alexander Cadogan, permanent under secretary in the Foreign Office, grappled with the problem. Foreign Secretary Halifax had asked him to come up with a rational set of "War Aims."

"I told him," Cadogan said, "I saw awful difficulties. We can no longer say 'evacuate Poland' without going to war with Russia, which we don't want to do! I suppose the cry is 'Abolish Hitlerism.' "[9]

And soon enough British leaders began adopting "abolish Hitlerism" as the moral basis for the war. It was probably a policy of convenience for some, for having brought their country into a war the British leaders now needed a moral-sounding reason for fighting it, or for at least pretending to fight it, and abolishing Hitlerism sounded a good deal better than abolishing a united Germany. But it was exactly that deeper goal that soon began slipping into British thinking. Germany, which had developed the bad manners of always trying to unite and compete with Great Britain, was the sickness, Hitler the symptom.

Robert Vansittart, Britain's chief diplomatic adviser, and a political ally of the new First Lord, understood this. Vansittart said that Hitler's policy of uniting the German-speaking peoples of Central Europe was "a quite clear and comprehensible program, but it is quite incompatible with our interests. We fought the last war to prevent this."[10]

Cadogan thought the same. He saw a beautiful utility in the insistence that "*We won't make peace with Hitler.*" Wrote Cadogan: "Get rid of Hitler: that is my *war* aim—not peace aim. . . . Remove him, and there will be such disunity in Germany that they *can't* win [emphasis in original]."[11] Removing Hitler was a tactic to help win the war, not a move to end it. Cadogan next tried to convince French Ambassador André Corbin of the sagacity of this plan. Machiavelli could not have written a colder account of that meeting than Cadogan: "He [Corbin] trotted out the silly French arguments against attacking *Hitler*. I said I quite saw these but, as an *immediate war* aim, I thought it would be invaluable to get rid of Hitler. The French say that it's not only Hitler, but the German nation—'Il faut en finir.' Yes: but how? The French are a logical race: oughtn't they to stop and ask themselves *how* to 'en finir'? They didn't know how at Versailles [emphasis in original]." [12]

Cadogan was just beginning to see what would become the truth of the war. It would not be fought over Poland, nor even over Nazi ideology. In the end, it would prove to be not a new war at all, but a continuation of the last, after an extended cease-fire called Versailles. [13] The First World War was fought over the threat of German hegemony in Central Europe. The peace of Versailles had almost settled the question, but not quite, as Hitler deftly demonstrated. Now the British would settle the issue once again. Ousting Hitler would not be enough. Any solution that left Germany with its territory and military intact was not acceptable, be that Germany democratic, monarchic, or National Socialist.

In a sense, the real treaty that would be argued out with tanks, and shells and fifty-two million lives was not Versailles, but the Peace of Westphalia, which three hundred years before had dismembered the Holy Roman Empire and left Central Europe fragmented and of small importance; left it en finir.

That was not the plan in the beginning, and was still now mostly submerged. But as odd as it seemed to Western journalists, as inept as was the Allies' response, as tepid as the mighty dictator seemed, the period that became known as the Phony War spawned the most decisive decision of the war: the British determined that it was more important to fight the new empire than the new emperor.

In late September and early October of 1939, no one in Germany, particularly Hitler, knew the change occurring in London. To Hitler, the war should have been over. The angst of September 3 had passed as the Poles collapsed and then surrendered. If the Allies were fighting to defend Poland, they had nothing left to defend. Poland was gone. Naturally, Hitler thought the war would now be gone as well. No great nation, he reasoned, fought for lost causes.

Count Ciano met with Hitler when the Führer was enveloped in this moment of peace. Ciano had never liked the Austrian upstart, feared he would mean nothing but trouble for his father-in-law, Benito Mussolini, and wanted to do all he could to prevent Germany from pulling Italy into another world war. But for once even Ciano was smitten with the Führer. "I found Hitler very serene," the Italian foreign minister wrote in his diary. "At Salzburg the inner struggle of this man, decided upon action but not yet sure of his means and of his calculations, was apparent. Now, on the other hand, he seems absolutely sure of himself. . . . He was wearing a green-grey jacket with his usual black trousers. His face bore traces of recent fatigue, but this was not reflected in the alertness of his mind. . . . What most impressed me is his confidence in ultimate victory. Either he is bewitched, or he really is a genius. He outlines plans of action and cites dates with an assurance that does not admit of contradiction. Will he be proved right?"[14]

Hitler's calm was not shared by his generals. They did not know whether Hitler could win the war, but they feared he would surely lose it if he carried the attack west. "I did not know one single comrade," General Franz Halder later testified, "who advocated the war or who agitated for war."[15]

For once, Hitler did little to add to the worries of his generals. He saw no need to attack the West, since the war would soon be over. As no preparations were necessary, none were made. Hitler wrote General Wilhelm Keitel, Chief of Staff of the Wehrmacht, explaining that the German-Allied war was nothing but the "rattling of sabres for the benefit of the world, certainly nothing worth taking too seriously."

And Hitler's optimism was catching. "Despite our grave doubts," Keitel continued, "it did seem almost as though even now Hitler's intuition was to prove right again, for the daily reports from the west brought only news of minor skirmishing with outlying French units in the zone between the Maginot Line and our West Wall."[16]

To make sure that nothing upset the balance, Hitler ordered the few divisions he had sent west to refrain from fighting. There was as yet no planning by the High Command for a western offensive.[17] German troops could fire only if fired upon. German overflights of Allied territory were restricted to reconnaissance. Even the war at sea was tightly restricted.

But there were few hopeful signals from Great Britain. Talk there was tough and uncompromising. Even Neville Chamberlain seemed to be developing backbone heretofore unknown. The simple reality of Germany's fait accompli in Poland did not seem to be appreciated by the British government. As such, Adolf Hitler slowly grew perplexed. The racial brethren across the Channel were not acting as he had predicted. What possible advantage, he kept asking, did Britain see in continuing the fight?

Hitler set about trying to find out. During the next eight months he would do everything he could think of to bring the British around, each step becoming more daring than the one before—from secret negotiations and kidnapping to toying with his own resignation—until finally Adolf Hitler would launch the war, not to defeat the enemy, but to force upon her a peace. It was certainly odd, probably crazy, but in keeping with Hitler's unflinching obsession, one shared in lesser doses by other Nazis and, in fact, by most Germans.

During the First World War, German arms industrialist Gustav Krupp first spelled out the logic. A German victory at Ypres, he said, was crucial because it would take Germany to the English Channel "at the very marrow of England's world power, a position—perhaps the only one—which would bring us England's friendship. For only if we are able to hurt her people badly at this moment will she really leave us unmolested, perhaps even become our friend, insofar as England is capable of friendship at all."[18]

Hitler would be more succinct. Of British intransigence, Hitler predicted: "When we get to the Channel the English may then change their minds."[19]

8 : *Often Only Losers*

Hitler began his search for a German-British peace as Warsaw was
falling. His first step was logical. Since the British insisted they
were fighting the war to save the no longer existent Poland, Hitler
would take them at their word. He would end the war by giving
Poland back. Not all of Poland, of course—Germany would retain
the Corridor and Russia the east—but enough of Poland to give
British politicians a face-saving gesture if that was what was needed.

The first real hint that Hitler would resurrect some sort of Poland
came on September 25, 1939, when the Führer told his commanders he had not decided what to do with Polish territory now under
the Wehrmacht's thumb. "No final decision," Hitler said, "has yet
been made regarding the political future of the erstwhile Polish territory between the line of demarcation [with the Russians] and the
German frontier."[1]

What became of this territory and what became of the Polish people, was in Hitler's view now in the hands of the British. If they
would make a peace, a rump state could house as many of the hated
Poles as Hitler could wedge inside. If not, then Poland and her peo-

ple would be items found in history books alone.

It was not a grand or magnanimous concession and even in its incipient form it came with enough conditions to invite Western skepticism, but Hitler was proud of it and wanted immediately to begin discussions with the British. Predictably, he completely disdained the services of his foreign minister. Instead, Hitler asked Birger Dahlerus, the Swede who had tried so hard to prevent the war, to find a way to end it.

Hitler and Göring briefed Dahlerus at the Reichschancellory. The Führer, who had just won a major campaign, was in one of his mercurial moods, mixing bombast, threat and hope in a way others found frightening, but never Dahlerus. A report of the meeting shows that Hitler began by claiming that Poland was now a justly won spoil of war, deserving in her fate because of her intransigence. "Germany had won a victory in Poland which was without precedent in history," Hitler said. "In 14 days [Hitler] had completely destroyed a country of 36 million inhabitants which had an army of 45 divisions, in part well equipped, and whose soldiers had fought bravely. In these circumstances, the Führer had no intention of allowing anyone to interfere in the solution of the Polish question."[2]

Then, almost as quickly as he had said it, he took it back. "If the British still wanted to salvage something of Poland," Hitler said, "he could only advise them to hasten the peace discussions." Moments later Hitler completed the transformation from boastful victor to plain supplicant, telling Dahlerus: "If the British desired peace in Europe they should make it clearly understood. Germany would in any case be prepared for it, for she needed peace in order to cultivate the newly acquired areas in the East that had formerly belonged to the German cultural sphere. This would require at least 50 years."[3]

Hitler proceeded to sketch for Dahlerus not only the vague outlines of a future Poland, but of a future Germany as well. It would be a Germany with much of its population moved to the east, away from the British nexus of power. Further east still, in the new semi-sovereign Polish rump state, Hitler he said was considering sending the Jews. With that potent observation out, Hitler's imagination irretrievably loosened. He soon imagined plenipotentiaries flying off to clandestine meetings in foreign lands. Hitler wondered whether a Briton could come to Berlin for more direct conversations, or, as Göring had suggested, whether both sides could meet in neutral Holland. Whatever, Hitler was firmly resolved on one point, the one that would prove so important in the Hess Affair. "Before an armistice could be concluded," Hitler said, "an unofficial exchange of views must first have taken place in order to examine the prospects of its conclusion."[4]

Shuttle diplomacy of the Nazi sort began again. Dahlerus headed for London on the twenty-seventh, carrying a headful of Hitler proposals for the beginning of negotiations. That Dahlerus was accepted into Whitehall, though not with any great enthusiasm, is all the proof necessary that London had not yet firmly closed its mind on dealing with Hitler. But the results showed it might as well have.

Halifax and other top British foreign policy makers met Dahlerus between September 27 and October 5.[5] They were not impressed. After the first meeting, Cadogan noted: "Terms are as to be expected: give us a free hand in Central and E. Europe and we will guarantee the British Empire."[6] At the second meeting, on September 29, they told Dahlerus that Hitler "must do some *deed* as evidence of good faith" before negotiations could begin (emphasis in original).[7] There was no doubt what that deed was. Britain wanted Germany to curtsy, pirouette and dance those Panzers back to Germany. Poland should be restored, and not in the rump status Hitler envisioned.

Even though this was impossible—neither Hitler nor the vast majority of Germans would favor giving back the Corridor once German blood had been spilled to possess it—Hitler's views on Poland did seem to be mellowing. There is no doubt that his original plan was truly Hitlerian. His first conception was of a Poland dominated and repressed by Germany, even to the point of forbidding all higher education. But on October 1, while Dahlerus was meeting with British officials, Hitler told Count Ciano that Germany intended now to meddle as little as possible in a residual Polish state.[8]

As Dahlerus shuttled between Berlin, The Hague and London, world leaders sought to broker some peace that would have, in large measure, betrayed Poland. On October 1, Italy, Holland and the United States offered to mediate.[9] The next day Belgium offered its services,[10] followed quickly by Spain.[11] Three days later, Norway and Finland both offered to mediate.[12] American oil broker William Rhodes Davis, in Germany at the behest of President Roosevelt, told Göring that the United States was "prepared to put pressure on the western powers to start peace talks," and let it be known that the American position on Poland would be to allow Germany to keep the Corridor.[13]

No one, it seemed, wanted this war to continue, particularly over a country that had vanished.

Sensing an advantage, Hitler decided to strike—not with Stukas, but with doves. If everyone else in the world wanted peace, then Hitler would offer it to them, publicly. That would surely budge the British. On October 3, Göring told Roosevelt's emissary that Hitler planned an important speech three days hence, and he assured the American that if a brokered peace was possible, Hitler would restore a Poland minus much territory but otherwise free. The formula Hitler had mentioned to Ciano in private—a Poland largely free of German meddling—was quickly becoming policy.

On October 6, Hitler slowly walked to the podium at the Kroll Opera House to address the Reichstag. For a time the hushed audience saw a side of Hitler they never knew existed, if in fact it ever did. Adolf Hitler appeared far more a statesman than a politician or a military dictator, more moderate than militant. The resonant voice he had so successfully used to stir old hatreds was now commissioned for a different task.

Of the European conflict, Hitler said simply: "It would be more sensible to tackle the solution before millions of men are first uselessly sent to their death. . . ."[14] Failing to do this would be tragic: "French artillery will fire at Frieburg, and the Germans at Kolmar or Schlettstadt. Long range guns will then be set up, and from both sides destruction will strike deeper and deeper, and whatever cannot be reached by the long distance guns, will be destroyed from the air. And that will be very interesting for certain international journalists, and very profitable for the aeroplane, arms and munition manufactures, etc., but appalling for the victims. . . .

"If, however," Hitler continued, "the opinions of Messrs. Churchill and followers should prevail, this statement will have been my last. Then we shall fight. Neither the force of arms nor the lapse of time will conquer Germany. There will never be another November, 1918, in German history. It is infantile to hope for the disintegration of our people. Mr. Churchill may be convinced that Great Britain will win. I do not doubt for a single moment that Germany will be victorious. Destiny will decide who is right.

"One thing only is certain. In the course of world history, there have never been two victors, but very often only losers."[15]

Hitler then revealed a six-point peace plan. It called for not only a solution of the current crisis, but for a resolution of the Lebensraum issues of all of Central Europe and the Balkans. As for Germany's Lebensraum, Hitler pledged that the Reich's frontier would be bound by its "historical, ethnographical, and economic conditions."

Hitler also disclosed to the world what he had already revealed to the British: he was willing to restore Poland, though not Poland as it existed before, and only a Poland "constituted and governed as to prevent its becoming once again either a hotbed of anti-German activity, or a centre of intrigue against Germany and Russia."[16] Exactly how this could be achieved he left to the imagination.

Hitler even appeared ready to compromise on a long-standing German demand for the return of German colonies lost in the Versailles treaty. To be sure, Hitler demanded the colonies, but not indignantly and not even seriously. He said the demand "does not take the form of an ultimatum, nor is it a demand which is backed by force."[17] A demand not backed by force is not a demand at all. Hitler was writing off the colonies even before negotiations started.

Lost to many in Hitler's speech was one point that may have had meaning beyond the mere words. Negotiations to end the war, Hitler said, would also "attempt to reach a solution and settlement of the Jewish problem." It isn't known exactly when Adolf Hitler decided to murder the Jews under the Reich's control, but it's clear it wasn't yet. He was toying with moving them to the new Poland or to Madagascar. But as vicious an anti-Semite as Hitler was, removing the fate of German Jews from his hands alone and putting it, instead, on the bargaining table was a concession. What it could have led to isn't known, but anything would have been preferable to what later happened.

Rejection

While waiting to see if this last almost desperate bid would be accepted, Hitler set about preparing his reluctant generals for the war that would start if it wasn't. Hitler's words were not welcomed: "If it should become apparent in the near future," Hitler said, "that England, and, under England's leadership, also France, are not willing to make an end of the war, I am determined to act vigorously and aggressively without great delay."[18] The purpose of the attack, Hitler said, was to "defeat as strong a part of the French operational army as possible, as well as allies fighting by its side, and at the same time to gain as large an area as possible in Holland, Belgium and Northern France as a base for conducting a promising air and sea war against England and as a protective zone for the vital Ruhr area."[19]

Hitler used none of the rhetoric that would later characterize his plans for the Soviets. He did not describe this plan as a war of annihilation. He did not call it total war. Instead, Hitler told his generals of a potent idea already forming in his mind. The war would not be fought to defeat Britain, but to force her to the peace table. Hitler was heading for the Channel. "The great successes of the first month of war could," Hitler said, "in the event of an immediate peace, serve to strengthen the Reich both psychologically and materially to such an extent that, from a German point of view, there could be no objection to concluding the war, provided the success won by our armies was not jeopardized by the peace treaty."[20]

While Hitler sought a peace brought on by negotiations or swift force, the British held out for total war. British leaders seemed more annoyed than interested in the German Chancellor's proposals. Chamberlain delayed his outright rejection of Hitler's peace offensive not because for a moment he considered agreeing to any part of it. The British were concerned with appearing thoughtful, and if a few days' delay in responding was required, a few days' delay there would be.

Churchill later reflected on the mood in England after Hitler's speech. The Führer, wrote Churchill, "felt sure His Majesty's Government would be very glad to accept the decision reached by him in Poland, and that a peace offer would enable Mr. Chamberlain and his old colleagues, having vindicated their honor by a declaration of war, to get out of the scrape into which they had been forced by the warmongering elements in Parliament. It never occurred to him for a moment that Mr. Chamberlain and the rest of the British Empire and Commonwealth of nations now meant to have his blood or perish in the attempt."[21]

Birger Dahlerus sensed that a British rejection was coming. He sought to salvage what he could. Whatever Chamberlain said, Dahlerus warned Cadogan, he must not appear to demand Hitler's removal as a precondition for peace.[22] If that Rubicon was crossed, all might be lost.

Dahlerus certainly did not say this because he favored Hitler. Even elements in the German opposition who wanted to depose the Führer counseled the British against demanding Hitler's removal.

The problem was German memory. When German armies sued for peace in 1918, they were still a strong military force. But after the field marshals appeared at the bargaining table, the Allies refused to negotiate with members of the Kaiser's government. The Germans relented, removed the Kaiser and thereby disbanded Germany's form of government. The move only accelerated an internal collapse, and made no real difference with the Allies, except perhaps to increase their demands. Every German schoolboy knew that the demand to remove the Kaiser was a trick that led to Versailles. If Germans now sensed that a precondition to peace was the removal of Hitler, whether they supported the Führer or not, the chance of peace would be crushed under the weight of symbolism alone.

The advice was largely ignored. The British, after all, could hardly say that they wanted far more from the Germans than the removal of the Führer. On October 12, Neville Chamberlain publicly rejected Hitler's proposals and, more important, rejected Hitler and his government. Hitler's peace plans, Chamberlain said, were lies upon which no one now could believe. "The peace which we are determined to secure, however," Chamberlain said, "must be a real and settled peace, not an uneasy truce interrupted by constant alarms and repeated threats. What stands in the way of such a peace? It is the German Government, and the German Government alone."[23]

German State Secretary Ernst von Weizsäcker, who was then involved in a conspiracy to topple Hitler, nevertheless noted the Führer's great disappointment. "Before these answers came," wrote Weizsäcker, "the Führer himself had indulged in great hopes of seeing his dream of working with Britain fulfilled. He had set his heart on peace."[24]

Instead, Hitler now mobilized for war, despite dogged resistance from his generals. Keitel recalled: "The strength of the War Office opposition to Hitler's idea of putting the Army on a war footing in the west as early as October 1939 was soon demonstrated by various incidents. The War Office, together with the vast majority of the Army's senior generals . . . had not only military but political reasons for its stand, and I shared them to the full."[25] What the generals didn't know was that Hitler had not yet given up on finding peace with his racial brothers. He had only adopted more radical means to get it.

Walter Schellenberg would play one part. Rudolf Hess would play the other.

Venlo

While Hitler and his generals prepared for the coming war, Hitler sought secretly to pursue a peace with Britain. But since the British seemed to reject Hitler, Hitler would have to do it in another manner, and he did not yet know exactly how. Before anything, he had to determine the British price for peace. Was it, in fact, his destruction? Was it the end of National Socialism? Or was it the end of Germany? Hitler needed quick answers. The British, unwittingly, provided them.

The British steps that would bring Hitler his answers began a month before Chamberlain's fateful speech. After the outbreak of war, Europe was awash with rumors—quite true—that powerful generals in Hitler's army wanted to overthrow the Führer. If indeed these generals existed, the British wanted to do everything possible to encourage them, for nothing could more quicken Germany's defeat than a coup. Vansittart wrote: "For the present we need to separate the German Army and the Nazi Party . . . and we should at least do nothing to lump or drive them together until we have got them both where we want them."[26]

The British Secret Intelligence Service sent word to its European chiefs to find a way to contact the rebellious German generals. Dozens of such contacts would eventually be made, including one through the Vatican that led directly to the inner cell of the conspiracy. But, unfortunately for the British, an illegitimate one was found as well, and that one led directly to Adolf Hitler.

That contact began at The Hague, where Captain Payne Best, a monocled agent of the SIS, was stationed. Learning of the directive to consult with the German generals, Best thought he knew immediately where to go. Inside his quiver of sources was a particularly gifted one named Dr. Franz Fischer, a German expatriate who wanted to bring down Hitler's government. If anyone could find these generals it would be Fischer, a man with solid ties to forces opposed to Hitler. And Fischer proved his worth. He told Best he knew of an opposition member named Solms, a major in the Luftwaffe, who might be willing to courier messages between the SIS and the plotting generals. Best told him to arrange a meeting.

Unfortunately for Best, he did not yet realize that Dr. Fischer was a versatile man who managed to wear more than one hat. In addition to being a trusted agent of the SIS, Fischer was an even more trusted agent of Hitler's SS. As such, the German opposition members he would introduce to Best were not opposed to Adolf Hitler at all. Instead, they worked for him. Before Fischer's double game was through some of the last chances for peace in Europe had been shredded.

And Hitler had his answers.

This operation began unpretentiously in a hotel in the Dutch border town of Venlo. Fischer brought along Major Solms, his "opposition" contact, and introduced him to Best. It was a flop. Solms came across as a big, bluff man endowed with Bavarian braggadocio, but a man lacking any real information.[27] Solms didn't talk of the conspiracy, the conspirators or even of war settlements. Though intimating that he knew much, Solms revealed little. Had London not been so insistent on contacting the German opposition, one meeting with Solms would have sufficed. But pressured for results, Best scheduled a second meeting and by so doing produced somewhat of a breakthrough.

The second Best-Solms meeting was held at the end of September, after Hitler had firmly resolved the Polish question. Solms had changed. He was more serious, less evasive. Though still skirting details, he came directly to the central point. Solms told Best that he was connected to "a big conspiracy to remove Hitler from power in which some of the highest ranking army officers were involved."[28] Solms, though, said he was not empowered to reveal more, as the conspirators wanted to deal with Best directly. To assure the German conspirators that Best was a man of standing, he was asked to arrange for a certain news item of a specific text to be broadcast by the BBC. It was, on October 11.[29]

The whole matter would have fizzled had not Chamberlain stoutly rejected Hitler's advances the very next day. After the speech, the Venlo meetings took on a different meaning. On the German side, the change was dramatic. For one, Hitler himself became directly involved. He saw the SIS contacts as perhaps the best way to determine exactly what the British wanted. If the British wouldn't negotiate a peace with him, then maybe they would negotiate with the "opposition," and by so doing reveal their ultimate position on peace with Germany.

Suddenly, a formerly backwater operation became so important that the Führer assigned one of the most enigmatic characters of the war—Walter Schellenberg, chief of German counterintelligence—to direct the case. A brilliant though hard-drinking twenty-nine-year-old, Schellenberg would before the war was over try almost everything, including assassination, to bring down Adolf Hitler. Now, however, he was at the Führer's call. He would direct Hitler's negotiations with the SIS.

The stakes were growing higher for the British as well. After Chamberlain's speech, Germany soon showed every sign that it was preparing for a massive and early attack. If the German generals could really overthrow the Führer, the British knew they had to act fast. The SIS assigned Best's supervisor, Major R. H. Stevens, to attend all future discussions,[30] and also disclosed the urgency of the affair to Dutch military intelligence, which quickly assigned one of its best operatives, Lieutenant Klop, to shepherd the operation in any way desired by the British. That decision would soon prove timely.

Solms did not attend the next meeting between the SIS and the German opposition. Instead, two top agents who worked directly for Schellenberg crossed the border to meet Best and Stevens. They met at a café in Dinxperlo. The Englishmen wanted to move the meeting to The Hague, but the Germans feared venturing that far into neutral country. The group went to another café to debate matters and finally settled upon a house located by Best. These erratic movements attracted the attention of Dutch soldiers who, in turn, informed the police about the strangely behaving Germans.[31] Someone in the police made the accurate deduction that they were German spies. Soon a small battalion of police surrounded the house and demanded the Germans' surrender. The Germans were unnerved and Dr. Fischer nearly fainted.[32] Hitler's attempt at penetrating the SIS would have ended right there but for the unfortunate efficiency of Lieutenant Klop, who from the shadows managed to convince the police to back down. The excitement, though, had ruined everything. There were no serious negotiations to overthrow the Führer.

The Germans had nearly lost two secret agents and there was no reason to think the Dutch police would be less vigilant the next time. It was time for the operation to end. But so intense was Hitler's interest in the negotiations that he not only decided that the meetings should go on, but that a much more important agent should conduct them—Schellenberg himself. It was a grave risk for Hitler. If he lost Schellenberg, which was likely, he could lose Schellenberg's secrets as well. Schellenberg knew every suspected British spy in the Reich. If he was captured, the cost to Germany would be incalculable.

Yet Hitler risked it.

• • •

With orders from Hitler to proceed, Schellenberg methodically tried
to reduce the obvious risk. If detained by anyone, he wanted iden-
tification papers that would remove him as far as possible from the
taint of the SS. In the High Command's transport department there
was a good candidate, Major Schaemmel, a man close to the center
of the High Command, but not someone on whom either the British
or the Dutch would have a dossier. Schellenberg sent the real
Schaemmel to unknown duties in the East, where he disappeared.
Schellenberg then became Schaemmel, learning all he could about
him.

At 6 P.M. on October 20, 1939, the British sent "Schaemmel" word
that they would meet the following day in Zützen, Holland.[33] Dutch
customs proved to be amicable, and soon Schellenberg climbed into
the back seat of Best's large lumbering Buick and headed for Arnhem to pick up Stevens.[34] As the Buick rolled through the Dutch
countryside, Best, Stevens and Schellenberg plotted the future history of the twentieth century.

Schellenberg said he represented forces intending to slay the
tyrant Hitler. The conspirators, he said, planned "the forcible removal of Hitler and the setting up of a new regime." Schellenberg
wrote later that his "purpose in these conversations was to explore
the attitude of the British Government towards a new government
controlled by the German Army and whether they would be willing
to enter into a secret agreement with our group which would lead
to a peace treaty once we were in power."[35]

The British were naturally delighted with Schaemmel. Yes, they
said, His Majesty's Government would indeed "welcome the removal of Hitler and his regime," and would do all in its power to aid
the conspirators. However, Best and Stevens said they were not yet
in a position to discuss the peace terms the British might offer a successor government. Those terms, though, might be disclosed at
subsequent meetings.[36]

To anyone on the outside, Walter Schellenberg/Schaemmel appeared steady and cool, a man in control. On the inside, he was not.
After returning from the first meeting, Schellenberg sought the advice of Dr. Max de Crinis, a noted psychiatrist.[37] De Crinis was intrigued, and decided to offer Schellenberg more than mere

psychiatric counseling. De Crinis said that if it might help, he would be happy to attend the next negotiating session, posing as a senior German officer.

To Schellenberg, it was a perfect solution. Among Nazis there were few who could assume the sophisticated air of the upper class that so impressed the British. De Crinis could. He was impeccable: erudite, cosmopolitan, finely finished—a clear member of the Prussian ruling class. He would make a perfect senior observer to the talks. Schellenberg quickly created a legend for the doctor. He was to be Colonel Martini, a right-hand man to the opposition.[38] It was impromptu, daring and in keeping with the Führer's unconventional tactics. Schellenberg radioed the plan to headquarters. It was approved almost immediately.

Schellenberg and de Crinis headed for the border. Soon it would be Schellenberg's turn to soothe the psychiatrist's nerves.[39]

They crossed the border on October 30. At Arnhem, where they were supposed to rendezvous with the big Buick, they found nothing: no Buick, no British spies. An hour passed. The British didn't show. De Crinis, suddenly finding that secret agent work had its drawbacks, was anxious and growing more so.[40] He had good reason to be.

Dutch police spotted the lone Germans, questioned them, examined their papers and took them to headquarters. The Germans were thoroughly searched. Schellenberg only later realized that this search had been orchestrated by Lieutenant Klop in an effort to make sure the Germans were who they said they were and not agents of the SS.

As their possessions were spread out, Schellenberg was startled. He noticed a small packet of aspirin encased in an SS wrapper. If the police saw that, it could be over for the improvising secret agents. Schellenberg edged forward clumsily and nudged a hairbrush, which fell to the ground with a racket. The police watched the brush and not Schellenberg, who simultaneously snatched the aspirin pack and swallowed it.[41] The police didn't notice.

Once released, with apologies, Schellenberg was not surprised to find Best and Stevens outside, offering a story about accidentally going to the wrong rendezvous point.

Best and Stevens took the Germans to SIS offices in The Hague.

There Schellenberg/Schaemmel told the English agents that conditions in the Wehrmacht were intolerable, losses in Poland had been great and current conditions made an immediate peace imperative. The trouble was with the Führer. He listened to no one. Schaemmel ended his convincing preamble with a direct thrust: "We are Germans and have to think of the interests of our own country first. Before we take any steps against Hitler we want to know whether England and France are ready to grant us a peace which is both just and honorable."[42] Hitler's agent had cut to the marrow. What was it that the British really wanted from the war?

It turned out they wanted a lot. Best said the two sides "hammered out a protocol which could be submitted by us to a higher level."[43] He made no mention about what that protocol contained. Schellenberg, though, did. He said the British wanted the German generals to arrange "the political overthrow of Hitler and his closest assistants . . . to be followed immediately by the conclusion of peace with the Western Powers. The terms were to be the restoration of Austria, Czechoslovakia and Poland to the former status; the renunciation of Germany's economic policies and her return to the gold standard."[44]

The renunciation of Hitler's foreign triumphs together with the end of Hitler and his regime and submission of Germany to London's economic dictates were proposals about which London might rightly have felt positive. But not everyone in London would be satisfied with even this.

To go any further with the German generals, Chamberlain knew he and Halifax would have to let the other members of the War Cabinet in on the discussions. On November 1, he told the cabinet that there had been a series of secret meetings with representatives of coup-minded German generals. He proposed that the discussions proceed until a possible resolution was won. Almost immediately after he stopped speaking, he was hit by a typhoon of protest from the man who was now the second most powerful political figure in Great Britain. Winston Churchill didn't like anything he had heard. He had not been informed about the negotiations and he certainly didn't agree with them. What business did the British government have in negotiating with any German? Germany must be defeated and a peace imposed.[45]

Chamberlain and Halifax were stunned. They both already bore the label of appeasers and wanted no more of that, though there was no appeasement at all in the present package. It did everything but mandate a German surrender.

Cadogan sought to calm things. He told Halifax that "the first impact was bound to be unfavorable." Britain, he wrote in his diary, "must not listen too much to Winston on the subject of 'beating Germany.' We must try every means of helping G[ermany] to beat herself."[46]

After the cabinet session, Chamberlain and Halifax knew that politically they could not take the plotting with the German generals any further without Churchill's assent, and so they stalled for six days. They wrote and rewrote a response until, on November 6, they had a draft that Churchill accepted. The Germans were to be told that they must eliminate Hitler first. Only then would Britain entertain "political" discussions.[47] In other words, this was a repeat of 1918— the Germans were being asked to eliminate their government, without guarantees. Still, the British snub was not complete. That came when Best and Stevens were told that even this offer was to be handled as though it might be remanded. London said the agents were "authorized to impart the gist of this message to the Germans but [we] were instructed to give them nothing in writing."[48]

Best described the British offer as "a carefully worded and rather non-committal reply."[49]

There was nothing here for Hitler to think about for even a moment. The British not only wanted his destruction but an imposed peace that he and probably almost all Germans would have considered draconian. Still, the Führer waited days before replying, for what the world will never know. Alfred Rosenberg wrote in his diary: "The Führer mentioned several times that he still considered a German-English understanding to be desirable, particularly in the long term. He couldn't grasp what they [the British] were really after. Even if England secured a victory, the real winners would be the United States, Japan and Russia. England would come out of a war shattered in any case, let alone if it suffered a military *defeat* [emphasis in original]."[50]

The delay in hearing from Hitler frustrated Schellenberg. Believing that he was truly involved in important discussions that could somehow end the war, Schellenberg decided that if Berlin wouldn't act, he would have to do so on his own. He feared that an impasse could spook the British.

Dionysus

The focus of the Second World War turned improbably to the Café Backus, a Dutch brick-and-stone eatery named after the Roman version of the Greek god Dionysus, master of evil pleasures. With its well-kept shake shingles and oversized awnings, the Backus actually looked the very picture of rectitude. Outside the roofed veranda was a large garden and swings and teeter-totters for the children. But only two hundred yards away was the black-and-white-painted barrier marking the German frontier. Over that small distance would soon come one of the most startling espionage operations of the war.

Best and Stevens didn't like the idea of moving the meetings from Venlo—already but a few kilometers from the German border—to the Backus at the very edge. But Klop assured them that they would be safe. He would pay heavily for that mistake.

Best and Stevens first met Schellenberg there in early November, expecting him to be accompanied by one of the conspiring German generals. Schellenberg explained that the general had been called away for an important conference. The British accepted the excuse and proceeded to read for Schellenberg the British response. Best noted that it "did not seem to come quite up to their expectations."[51]

The two sides agreed to meet again at the Backus the next day, with the Germans bringing their chief. Schellenberg later recalled that he proposed a true Hitler-like gesture. He asked the British to have a plane stationed nearby so that the parties could, if needed, fly off to "where final discussions on the highest level could be held with the British Government."[52]

Back across the border, Schellenberg sent a report of the meeting to Berlin. Still there was no reply. Schellenberg surmised that the Führer was growing "uncomfortable" with "discussion about his overthrow."[53]

• • •

As Schellenberg prepared for further meetings, Adolf Hitler and Rudolf Hess—arm-in-arm as old warriors, companions and friends—ducked into a Munich beer hall for the annual reunion of the Old Fighters, veterans of the failed 1923 Putsch. These were Hitler's most ardent followers and pandemonium followed Hitler as he mounted the rostrum at 10:10 P.M., November 8, 1939. However much the Germans hated to be at war, they loved it just as well when Hitler explained it. But today, Hitler would cut his explanation short, and by so doing would save his life.

Fifty-seven minutes after he began the speech, Hitler ended it, leaving quickly with Hess through a side door. Eight minutes later, a bomb ripped apart the speaker's platform, killing seven and wounding sixty-three, including the father of Hitler's consort, Eva Braun. By the time of the explosion, Hitler had already reached his train, and was unaware of what had happened. Soon, though, Goebbels arrived with the news. Hitler reacted fiercely. There was no doubt in his mind who was behind the bombing—the same men who had been talking so easily about his elimination from power.

Schellenberg had just dozed off with the aid of a sleeping pill when his phone rang at midnight. It was Heinrich Himmler. "There's no doubt that the British Secret Service is behind it all," Himmler said. "The Führer and I were already on his train to Berlin when we got the news. He now says—and this is an order—when you meet the British agents for your conference tomorrow, you are to arrest them immediately and bring them to Germany."[54] There would be no flight to London.

Schellenberg met with the SS officer who had been assigned to watch over the Backus talks to prevent *Schellenberg* from being kidnapped. Instead, the two devised a plan to do the opposite, to kidnap the British agents. The target, they decided, would be Best's Buick. The moment it arrived, the SS detachment across the border would crash through the border barricades with automobiles, jump the British agents, and then literally throw the cars in reverse and depart, killing as few bystanders as possible.[55]

And it happened pretty much as planned. In the late afternoon of November 9, 1939, as Best's Buick roared toward the Backus and then sharply stopped, the SS crashed through wooden barricades, quickly consuming the two hundred meters that separated them. Their blazing guns unnerved the Dutch guards, who scurried about, firing not a shot. Resistance stiffened, though, in the final yards to the Buick.

Klop pulled out a heavy service revolver, jumped from the Buick, and, standing in the middle of the street, pumped round after round into the charging SS unit leader's car. Schellenberg was sure that the leader was dead, but instead he leapt from his car and Klop and the SS man commenced dueling in Wild West fashion, carefully firing at each other at close range. The German's aim was better and Klop slowly fell to his knees, mortally wounded. He was the operation's sole fatality.

Best and Stevens were hustled away to Germany to be interrogated. Neither gave Hitler what he wanted: proof that the British were behind the bombing. Best and Stevens insisted they had nothing to do with it. They would keep to the story through six years of German internment. They emerged from Dachau after the war, unharmed.

Days after the Backus incident, the real bomber, a diminutive artisan named Georg Elser, was captured at the Swiss border. Yes, he said, he had planted the bomb in an attempt to kill Hitler and end the war. No, he said, there were no accomplices.

Hitler was furious at what he considered an inept interrogation and demanded that the truth be extracted from Elser. Himmler, who would become notorious for his weak stomach in the physical presence of violence, nevertheless took on Elser with true Gestapo relish. Cursing and swearing at Elser, Himmler pummeled him with kicks and beat him with a whip. To no end. Elser stuck by his story. His intransigence saved his life. Himmler had him installed as a special prisoner to be treated well, apparently under the theory that only a live Elser could confirm that Himmler had done his best to get at the truth.[56]

Venlo was over and so too were Hitler's efforts to arrive at a peace with the present British government. He now felt clearly that only force of arms could bring about a revolution in the thinking of the British. It will never be known exactly how far Adolf Hitler would have gone to secure a peace in November 1939. It is hard enough to imagine Hitler agreeing to a Polish restoration, much less removing himself from power. Perhaps he only sought to fool the British into agreeing to a way to end the war while saving his hide. Indeed, one idea put forward by Schellenberg in the Best-Stevens talks was to leave Hitler in place as the titular head of government, but stripped of all real powers.[57]

But Hitler's pursuing the Venlo negotiations after it was clear that his departure was a precondition for peace suggests that the most radical figure of the twentieth century may have entertained some radical notions about how he could obtain for his countrymen the German-British alliance for which he had long dreamed and felt was absolutely necessary for long-term German success.[58] Days before the beer hall bomb there was a hint that he was prepared to go very far, indeed. German Prince Max Hohenlohe had spoken in Switzerland with representatives of Vansittart, returning to Germany to report to Göring that peace with England was possible, but only with Hitler and Ribbentrop removed from power. One observer recorded in his diary that Göring replied: "Hitler would agree to this."[59]

Whether he would have or not will never be known. After learning of England's ultimate demands—essentially a German surrender to England's will—Hitler prepared resolutely for the war he had wanted to avoid. Adolf Hitler turned his impressive capacity of innovation to devising a plan to get the Wehrmacht to the Channel and, by so doing, to finally win by force the British respect he had not won by stealth.

9 ∘ *Genius*

How, without changing Germany's tactical situation for the worse, could the generals get a
guarantee that a decent peace is still obtainable?

—*Ulrich von Hassell*

Perhaps because they so wanted to avoid war, Germany's generals
were extremely conservative at planning it. Even after their success
in Poland, the generals had not yet digested the new reality of modern warfare: mobility was as important as sheer mass, and, in some
cases, even more so. Instead, Hitler's generals tended to view the
future of this war as a head-on clash of infantry, a throwback to 1914.
German generals were preparing to refight the last war, and Hitler,
who had witnessed all of the last war he cared to, would have none
of it.

On October 19, Franz Halder, the Army's chief of staff, presented Hitler with the High Command's scheme for striking the
West. Code-named Case Yellow, the plan called for three army
groups to attack the West, the main thrust going through Holland
toward the Channel, then bending southerly into Belgium, heading for the French armies. It was essentially the Schlieffen plan of
the First World War, though with a more northern extension. And
it would have had about as good a chance for success now as it did
in 1914.

Hitler didn't say much as Halder made his presentation, but upon Halder's leaving the room he turned to General Keitel and issued an objection: "That is just the old Schlieffen plan, with a strong right flank along the Atlantic coast. You don't get away with an operation like that twice running. I have quite a different idea and I'll tell you about it in a day or two."[1]

Actually, six days passed before Hitler revealed the first part of his plan, and weeks would follow before he ordered his generals to change their old ideas. Yet even in the early stages, Hitler's idea was clear enough that his generals knew it was either the work of a genius or an idiot. Hitler intended to do as General Sherman would have done. He was ready to act with ruthless daring, ignoring military orthodoxy. Mobility was the key in modern war. Hitler's tanks would work like Sherman's cavalry, spearheading the infantry, and not where the enemy expected them, either.

If his generals were wedded to the past war, Hitler had every reason to believe the Allies would be also. In late October, Hitler suggested that his generals take advantage of this by attacking France directly. Hitler would attack from the north into Holland and northern Belgium, expending just enough strength there to be convincing. If Hitler was right, the Allies would quickly dispatch their best troops north to meet the Germans head-on—just as they had done in 1914. Hitler would then strike where the Allies could not afford to be struck. His main force would descend into France from Luxembourg, emerge from the Ardennes Forest, which the Allies thought to be impassable for motorized units, and cross the Meuse River near Sedan. From there, if all had worked as planned, the Germans would have little between them and the Channel, which they would march to as surely as Sherman had dissected Carolina. The Allies would be cut in two.

The problem with Hitler's plan was it had an equal potential for assuring an Allied victory. Field Marshal Keitel identified the flaw: "I had some misgivings, as this stroke of genius could go awry if the French tank army did not do us the favor of automatically driving through Belgium towards our northern flank."[2] Hitler was betting Germany's fate on his hunch that the Allies would be fooled by his strategic feint. If the Allies weren't accommodating, Hitler's plan would not seem to be brilliant at all. If the Allies concentrated their force on the German divisions emerging from the Ardennes, it would be the Germans who would be cut in half. Said Hitler: "I am staking my life's work on a gamble."[3]

Many German generals resisted Hitler's plans, believing them to be imprudently dangerous. It wasn't until January that Hitler's ideas actually became operational, and then only because fate intervened in Belgium and Hitler found allies among his military men. On January 10, a German plane carrying the entire operational plan still favored by the generals made a forced landing in bad weather in Belgium. Its crew was captured before all the secret documents could be destroyed. After that, even the advocates of the traditional stategy had to assume that the Allies knew their plan. If so, that plan could never work. It was at this point that Hitler learned that two of his brightest young generals—Heinz Guderian and Erich von Manstein—were also proposing alternatives to Case Yellow. Manstein maintained that the main attack should take place through the Ardennes, which he had determined were indeed passable. This was exactly what Hitler had suggested. Neither Hitler nor Manstein apparently knew of each other's thinking until after the Belgian plane incident. But when Hitler discovered that innovative general officers also shared his vision, he became set. Case Yellow was dead. Hitler's ideas would now command. From then on, Europe's history would depend on a feint.

Hitler immersed himself in planning the campaign. From the grand strategic deception, down to details about the size of field guns to be used, from what locations, and in what concentration, no detail was too small. Naturally, he became obsessed about a few matters. Hitler accepted on faith that his tanks could get through the thick forests around Sedan, so instead of fretting over that he spent most of his time worrying about the northern, and thus secondary, part of the plan.

Two matters bothered him most. Hitler was exceedingly anxious about the Belgian fortress of Eben Emael and the defenders' ability to destroy bridges needed for the northern part of the operation. If the attack in the north was blunted too easily, Hitler feared the enemy could focus on his main southern armies. Hitler sought to solve the problem the same way he had planned the Sedan offensive, with a mixture of creativity, gall and sheer gambler's instinct. The German would use gliders to land troops quietly at the fortress before other hostilities began, winning Eben Emael by surprise. The bridges would be secured in similar fashion. German trooops dressed as Dutch policemen would secure the bridges hours before the main assault.

Hitler's generals had never heard of such tactics, and were more than dubious. These plans were more like schoolyard fantasies than anything military men should seriously consider. Their anxiety was not lessened when the Führer complained that his generals should "have read more Karl May,"[4] a German writer of American-Indian tales.

From October to March, most ranking military men tried almost everything to convince Hitler not to strike. Though some respected his political finesse, few saw Hitler as a competent military man. He was a corporal and an artist who read too much Karl May, and too few military books. Army Commander in Chief Walther von Brauchitsch tried to convince Hitler that the German troops were not ready to face an enemy as skilled as the Allies. "During the Polish campaign the infantry had been shown to be over-cautious and insufficiently attack-minded," Brauchitsch told the Führer. "Discipline had unfortunately become very lax . . . there had been drunken orgies and bad behaviour in troop trains and on railway stations."[5] Hitler was furious, shouting at Brauchitsch that it was "incomprehensible" for a commander in chief to condemn his own army, and demanded proof. This was one of Hitler's first wild tirades directed against his generals, and it left Brauchitsch speechless. Hitler stormed from the room.[6]

The Führer could not be bluffed out of his war. "I can rely on the generals of the Air Force to the last. Member of the Party, Göring, will see to that," Hitler told his staff officers. "I can rely on the admirals of the Navy to the last. Admiral Raeder will see to that. But I cannot rely on the generals of the Army to the last."[7] A deep distrust between Hitler and his generals was settling in. It would eventually carry disastrous consequences.

For their part, the generals were becoming desperate. Hitler appeared ever more determined for war, and he was not being reasonable about it either.

If the generals wanted to avoid war, they would now have to do more than just talk about it.

Conspiracy

On October 11, Carl Gördeler, former mayor of Leipzig, and Ulrich von Hassell, former German ambassador to Rome, met over dinner at the Hotel Continental in Munich. These were two veterans of the most deadly game in the Third Reich—the conspiracy to topple Hitler, by murder, if necessary.

It was a day before Chamberlain was scheduled to respond to Hitler's peace proposal. Gördeler and Hassell knew they both must prepare the others for the worst: if Chamberlain rebuked the Führer, Hitler would likely retaliate with an attack on the West. It was time, Hassell said, to "apply the brakes to the runaway cart."[8] The two began sketching out a plan to eliminate Hitler and bring peace to Europe.

Hassell and Gördeler were not dreamers. Ever since the Munich crisis of 1938, the core of the conspiracy had been peopled with powerful military, intelligence and diplomatic men who had the means and power to act. They were united by a passionate hatred of Nazism, which was exceeded only by their hatred of Bolshevism. Largely ardent nationalists, they believed firmly in Hitler's goal of uniting Germany, though they disagreed with his method for doing so. They didn't want war, not because they were pacifists, but because they were realists. To them, there was no way Germany could win. The League of Nations, not war, would someday correctly address German grievances.

In the Abwehr, Germany's military intelligence agency, both its chief, the inscrutable Admiral Wilhelm Canaris, and his deputy, Colonel (later General) Hans Oster were deeply involved in betraying Hitler. Canaris played a role largely still a mystery, while Oster was a naked protagonist. In the Foreign Ministry, the German State Secretary Ernst von Weizsäcker was the leading opposition figure, though scores of others followed. One who would become the most important was Albrecht Haushofer, the true gray eminence of the war. Haushofer and Weizsäcker were in good company for the Foreign Ministry was saturated with anti-Hitlerites.

Influence in military intelligence and the foreign service was vital for the conspiracy, but not nearly as vital as influence in the High Command, and the general there that mattered most was the man presently refining Hitler's plan to crush the West. Hassell and Gördeler recalled that Franz Halder had been the firebrand during the Munich crisis. Then assistant to Chief of Staff Ludwig Beck, Halder had used his proximity to press Beck to topple Hitler. Hitler, Halder said, was a madman who would lead Germany to ruin. Stopping him was worth the risks to their own lives.

Beck thought much the same, but said it was not the role of the General Staff to alter German civilian leadership. An intellectual as comfortable discussing Kant as he was Gallipoli, Beck did what he considered to be the honorable thing: he resigned in protest over Hitler's policies. For appearances, Hitler asked him to stay on until the Munich crisis ended, during which time Beck saw that Halder had been right. It would have been more moral to rid Germany of Hitler than to retire with honor. As he turned over his command to Halder, Beck admitted his mistake: "I now realize that you were right at the time. Now all depends on you."[9]

By the autumn of 1939, Beck's and Halder's roles in the conspiracy had been reversed. It was now Beck from the outside urging his former protégé to eliminate Adolf Hitler. And it was Halder, now finally with the power to do it, who was hesitant. Beck, Hassell, Gördeler and a dozen others tried to work on Franz Halder's conscience. But the new chief of staff was troubled by more than his conscience. He was troubled by 1918.

Though he would say that "the German Army will do its duty for the Fatherland, even against the Hitler government, if and when the situation calls for it,"[10] Halder made clear that the situation would never call for it if the British planned to use Hitler's demise to destroy Germany.

Halder said that prewar 1938 had been different. Though a coup then would have surely sparked a civil war, Halder thought it could have quickly been contained. "After all," Halder explained, "that was peacetime, and we had our well-proven commanders everywhere in the country."[11] Now the commanders were busy facing off the British and the French. A civil war could not be contained unless the commanders left the front, a movement inviting attack. That attack would most certainly mean Germany's defeat and a return to the terms of Versailles, or worse.[12]

This Halder could not risk. If he were to destroy Adolf Hitler, Halder needed an agreement beforehand that the Allies would not strike while he couldn't defend.

The only way the conspirators could get this understanding was through the British.

That, everybody realized, could only come about if a secret solution was first worked out with the British beforehand. A solution was not capitulation. If Halder was to act, there must be guarantees that in exchange for eliminating Hitler and the Nazis, Britain would not press for the dismemberment of Germany.

General Georg Thomas, one of the most uncompromising opponents of Hitler's regime, agreed that there were two prerequisites for an end of Adolf Hitler. The Allies must agree to "a Germany that is intact, and above all, an intact Army so that our enemies would run a considerable risk if they persisted in continuing the war."[13]

Hassell and Gördeler understood the problem clearly. Hassell spelled out the essential question: "How, without changing Germany's tactical situation for the worse, could the generals get a guarantee that a decent peace is still obtainable?"[14] Neither man yet understood how unsettling the notion of a Germany left powerful would be to London. They thought optimistically that if the Chamberlain government had both peace and Hitler's downfall in its grasp it would surely be enough.

They decided to begin secretly making contacts with the British with the idea of arriving at a peace settlement acceptable to Halder. Gördeler sketched out an outline of what he thought would be the winning plan. Hassell wrote it down in his own shorthand in his diary. The plan had four points: "(1) moderate demands (German parts of Poland to us, the remainder to be independent, a new arrangement in Czechoslovakia); (2) the restitution of the rule of law in Germany; (3) general disarmament, with specific guarantees in the case of Germany (control of airplane and submarine production); and (4) the restoration of world commerce."[15] Of the four, the first point was by far the most important. Every conspirator knew that there would be only war if the British even hinted at dismembering Germany.

Armed with a plan, the Germans sought contacts with the British. Of the dozen contacts that were made, two took on the most importance for the conspirators. One involved a man code-named Mr. X. The other, improbably, involved the Pope.

Pius XII

Eugenio Pacelli—as Munich nuncio in 1917, nuncio in Berlin in the 1920s, and cardinal secretary of state from 1930 to 1939—had immersed himself in German issues. Now, as Pope Pius XII, he would use his knowledge of and empathy for the Germans to try to liberate them from Adolf Hitler.[16] The risks were extreme. Had Hitler uncovered the plot, the Catholic church in all of Europe, not to mention Pius, would have been endangered.

Former General Beck and the Abwehr's Oster started the initiative, knowing that the church had credibility, access to the British and over 1,500 years of experience in discretion. As an emissary, they settled on forty-one-year-old Josef Müller, an anti-Nazi Munich lawyer who had known Pacelli personally while performing pro bono work for the church in Germany. Unlike Beck or Oster, Müller had the advantage of being Catholic.

Müller had no idea what faced him as he accepted an official Abwehr invitation to visit its headquarters in Berlin. He expected trouble. Though he had not advertised his anti-Nazi views, a competent spy organization could have easily found them out. He was not heartened when Oster began the interview by informing him that "we know a great deal more about you than you do about us." Shortly, though, Oster said that what the Abwehr knew about Müller it liked. In fact, that was why he was there.

To an astonished Müller, Oster declared that "the Central Division of the Abwehr is also the central directorate of the German military Opposition under General Beck. . . . For us the wishes of General Beck are equivalent to orders." Müller was asked if he would be enlisted into the cause of defeating Adolf Hitler. And he was warned of the consequences if he agreed. "In war," Oster said, "many must stake their lives. We are staking ours for the cause of peace." If he was caught, Oster said, Müller should go quietly to his death.

The Munich lawyer somehow agreed on the spot to join a conspiracy about which he had known nothing an hour earlier. Oster immediately made him a reserve officer in military intelligence. Müller left for Rome.

His contact there was with Father Robert Leiber, a principal aide to Pius XII. The Pope, knowing that there was little time left for peace in Europe, agreed to be an honest broker between the conspirators and the British. The British, too, accepted the arrangement. They would at least listen to the Germans. Their ambassador would also use Father Leiber as their middleman.

The discussions dragged on from October to January, with little being accomplished. The conspirators grew increasingly nervous. The simple formula sketched out by Gördeler apparently was not making a fast impression on the British. Events at the Café Backus in November didn't help, making the British even more cautious. Meanwhile, Hitler was constantly cocking and uncocking the trigger on his invasion. The conspirators were nervous.

X
—

In January, with the Vatican meetings still producing no results, Hassell met J. Lonsdale Bryans, a friend of Hassell's future son-in-law and a man who would become known to the conspirators as Mr. X. Telling Hassell that he had special access to British Foreign Secretary Halifax, Lonsdale Bryans agreed that the war would be a calamity without parallel. Hassell asked him if he could deliver to Halifax a question: if German generals toppled Hitler, would Great Britain hold its fire?

1

Hitler's father, Alois Hitler.

Hitler's mother, Klara, shortly before her marriage. Her death left Adolf Hitler with inconsolable grief.

2

Hitler as a baby. 3

Professor Karl Haushofer: Hitler used 4
Haushofer's geopolitical theories to justify
German expansion in the east.

Hitler meets the Duke and Duchess of Windsor at Obersalzberg. Hitler
thought the Duke could regain the throne and make a pact with Germany.

5

Hitler's greatest gift was oratory. Here he addresses a party rally at Potsdam shortly before the outbreak of the war.

7

Hitler and his deputy Hess at a Munich beerhall shortly after the Second World War began.

Hess and Hitler at the Reichstag where Hitler gave his "last warning" before the start of the Battle of Britain. Josef Goebbels is in the background.

8

9

Pope Pius XII. He plotted with the Resistance to overthrow Hitler.

Churchill and Roosevelt. The Prime Minister had convinced the President that Hitler aimed to conquer the Western Hemisphere.

Churchill in the House of Commons. His deception led to Hitler's defeat, though at the price of millions of lives.

12

London firefighters battle the inferno left by German bombers on May 10, 1941, the day Hess arrived in Scotland. It was the worst — and last —day of the Blitz.

Churchill meets with Stalin. The Soviet leader was convinced that elements in Britain had plotted with the Nazis to destroy Russia.

Locals inspect the wreckage of Hess's plane. The Deputy Führer parachuted after failing to locate a landing strip next to the Duke of Hamilton's estate.

14

Hess or a double? Many at Nuremberg said his personality had sharply changed.

15

On January 8, 1940, Lonsdale Bryans met with Halifax. Halifax, speaking "personally," said that the British would not cross the Siegfried Line "if the revolution looked like being a genuine affair and producing a different regime in Germany, in which it might be possible to place some confidence in honest dealing."[17] That was a good start. But before the German generals would act against Hitler, they would need more than the personal ideas of the British foreign secretary. They would need guarantees that only governments can provide.

It wasn't until late February that Hassell and Lonsdale Bryans met again, this time in Arosa, a health spa in the Swiss Alps. Hassell was disappointed that Lonsdale Bryans brought along no certain guarantees, noting again that "the principal obstacle to any change in regime is the story of 1918, that is, German anxiety (above all on the part of the generals) lest things develop as they did then, after the Kaiser was sacrificed. . . . Unless there is some authoritative English statement on this point . . . there will be no prospect of a change in the German regime auspicious for the negotiated peace."[18] To get rid of Hitler, the generals must be confident that resulting civil strife "would in no way be exploited" by the British.[19] Lonsdale Bryans said he would try again.

This time, Hassell gave Lonsdale Bryans far more detailed peace positions drawn up by the conspirators. Perhaps if the British knew how different the new Germany would be from Hitler's, they would act. The new German rulers, Hassell said, would want a Europe ruled by "Christian ethics" and "justice and law as fundamental elements of public life." There would be "effective control of the executive power of state by the people" and "liberty of thought, conscience, and intellectual activity."[20] The conspirators wanted a reduction of armaments, economic cooperation and the restoration of an "independent Poland and of a Czech Republic."

But when he got to issues of territory, Hassell's position was no different from Hitler's; in fact, it could have been written by the Führer. "The union of Austria and the Sudeten with the Reich [would be kept] out of any discussion," the opposition's statement read. "In the same way there would be excluded a renewed discussion of occidental frontier-questions of the Reich. On the other hand, the German-Polish frontier will have to be more or less identical with the German frontier of 1914."[21] Hassell clearly did not yet realize that *the* issue for the British was the size of Germany, not the persona of her tyrant.

Lonsdale Bryans headed directly back to England, meeting with the Foreign Office on the twenty-eighth. The British were not impressed. Cadogan recorded succinctly in his diary this assessment: "Lonsdale Bryans, with his ridiculous stale story of a Germany opposition ready to overthrow Hitler, if we will guarantee we will not 'take advantage.' Let him talk, and then broke it to him that this was about the 100th time I had heard this story."[22]

Decentralization

Josef Müller and Father Leiber continued meeting, exactly how many times and under what conditions is not known. Except for one occasion, they kept no notes. Yet there were enough survivors of the war, and enough evidence in diaries and correspondence to know that in late February or early March,[23] Josef Müller returned to Germany believing that a breakthrough had been made. He had finally received some solid negotiating points from England. Greatly encouraged, the opposition asked him to write a report.

There is much disagreement about what was actually in the report, and no copy apparently survives. It is clear that there had finally been concrete discussion about postwar German borders. There the agreement stops. According to different versions, Polish partition was or was not agreed to. The Sudetenland was or was not to remain German. As for Austria, the British apparently did say it could remain with the Reich, after another plebiscite.[24]

All this was predicated upon there being an acceptable form of government in Germany. Ominously for any German remembering 1918, the British saw "decentralization of Germany"[25] as being the acceptable form. The Pope knew the Germans would not appreciate the possible connotations of the word "decentralization" and tried to soften them. Through Father Leiber he said that "such things as 'decentralization' and 'plebiscite in Austria' would certainly be no barriers to the peace if there was agreement on other points."[26] That would be easier for the Pope to say than for a German general to wager the life of his nation upon.

And there were other problems with the X report. It was a document not composed by the British, but was written from memory by an amateur diplomat who had taken no notes. Even then, it was not based on direct discussions with the British. Müller received his information from Father Leiber, who had received it orally from a British ambassador. And there was a final, critical problem. The British had not guaranteed that the Allies would refrain from staging an offensive during a possible German civil war.[27]

Whatever its shortcomings, the X report was the only thing in writing produced from the negotiations so far. It was on this thin reed that the opposition based its hopes.

Someone had to deliver the X report to Halder, and there was no more prestigious a choice than Hassell. Yet six to eight weeks passed between German receipt of the report and its transmittal to Halder, the man upon whom the question of peace or war hinged. There is no good explanation for the delay.

The report Halder saw in early April had apparently changed during its weeks in limbo. It contained all of the defects of the original, plus one. Halder recalled that when he finally got it, the X report said the British were offering to Germany dominion over Alsace-Lorraine. That suggestion satisfied Halder that the report was a fraud, an attempt to bribe foolish Germans with gifts the British didn't even possess. Alsace-Lorraine was French territory, and the French were showing no inclination to give it back.

Still, Halder gave the report to Walther von Brauchitsch, the German army's commander in chief. Brauchitsch, who had earlier indicated that he would not take part in a coup, but wouldn't resist it either, read the report and thought of making arrests. "You should not have shown this to me," he told Halder. "What we face here is pure national treason. That does not come into question for us under any conditions. We are at war. . . . That one in time of peace establishes contact with a foreign power may be considered. In war this is impossible for a soldier."[28]

Brauchitsch demanded that Halder reveal the report's author, but when his chief of staff refused, Brauchitsch dropped the matter. An investigation into the conspiracy would have decimated his officer corps, and probably would have implicated himself.

Though it was far too late, Hassell pressed on. He wanted to get from the British the assurance he thought could convince Halder to act against Hitler. Ten days after the report was rejected by Brauchitsch, Hassell again met Lonsdale Bryans in Arosa. Lonsdale Bryans said he had shown the opposition proposal to Halifax, who then passed it to Chamberlain. Eventually, Lonsdale Bryans said, Halifax returned and said "he was most grateful for the communication, valued it highly, and was in complete agreement with the principles set forth. He could not give a written assurance, such as Mr. X had suggested, because he had already done so through another channel just a week before."[29] What that channel was, if indeed it existed, was tapped far too late to make a difference.

The German opposition's peace bid had failed. And the British had lost their last cheap chance to rid Europe of Hitler.

Halder dismissed English overtures. "The peace assurances of England were all bluff," he said, "none of them were serious."[30] To another person, he said: "At bottom, England wants to destroy us anyway."[31]

Flank Attack

Blind to the plotting of the Abwehr, the Foreign Ministry and his General Staff, Hitler went about the business of making Germany ready for war. His military, he thought, was prepared and would fight well. But he was worried about strategic weaknesses his army could not easily cure. There were three: German oil came primarily from Romania, accessible by air from Britain's African possessions. Its iron came entirely from Sweden and could be cut off if the Royal Navy launched an attack through Norway. And German industry was concentrated in the Ruhr, reachable by Allied bombers, particularly if those bombers were based in France.

The issue of his southern flank, the oil fields, could not easily be addressed by the Germany of early 1940 if Germany tried to address it alone. Romania and North Africa were more in Italy's sphere of influence than Hitler's. If Italy was in the war, Britain would have to consider Italy's substantial navy before starting adventures in Greece and the Balkans. Hitler needed Italy, but Italy had not been the model of dependability. If she remained neutral, or worse, if she became a hostile power, Italy would so weaken the southern strategic flank that the Third Reich's oil would be in danger. And without that oil, the Reich could not survive.

Mussolini heightened Hitler's concerns when he wrote the Führer what Hitler considered an unpleasant letter. The Duce was not steeling himself for war. Instead, he was looking for an easy way out. He asked Hitler: "Is it worth while to risk all—including the regime—and sacrifice the flower of German generations in order to hasten the fall of a fruit which must of necessity fall and be harvested by us, who represent the new forces of Europe? The big democracies carry within themselves the seeds of their decadence."[32] Mussolini counseled Hitler to seek a compromise. Hitler was in no mood for that. He would have to change Mussolini's mind.

Hitler began the process on February 2 in a meeting with the Italian ambassador, Count Massimo Magistrati. German agents, Hitler said, had uncovered a document in the Far East proving beyond doubt that the "British war aim was the eventual destruction of Germany and Italy." Therefore, he said, he would "no longer consider a compromise."[33]

On March 18, Hitler took his argument directly to Mussolini. The Duce had agreed to meet the Führer at the 4,500 foot high Brenner Pass, only three hundred yards from the German frontier, determined either to avert war altogether, or, failing that, to assure that Italy remained out of the fight. He would fail on both counts.

Hitler stepped down onto the snow-swept tundra, and was greeted by a smiling Mussolini and Count Ciano. They retired immediately to the Italian train. Hitler consumed the meeting, as though the cold had given way to his raging fire. He talked fast, and nonstop and with a cadence that held Mussolini in its power, smothering the Duce with facts and numbers that Hitler recalled as easily as reciting the alphabet—troop strengths, reserves and technical details of guns, tanks and airplanes. Most who had seen him perform like this had been, as Mussolini was now, dazzled. German generals had long since stopped double-checking the Führer's facts. He was never wrong on issues of small detail. He told Mussolini that Germany had 205 army divisions, 160 of them first-class. Added to these were three SS divisions, twelve Death's Head regiments, and twenty-five police battalions. It was time to strike. Conditions had never been more favorable and could only worsen with time. Hitler hoped to have a victory by autumn.

Of course, Hitler said, all was not certain. Luck, he conceded, "was necessary for victory, but Moltke had said that in the long run luck was on the side of the able, and the Germans had been able and thorough in their preparations. The German people knew what they were fighting for. Either they would gain the victory over their enemies and prosper, or they would lose this way and perish."[34] The latter possibility came only because the British war aim was "the annihilation of Germany. . . ."[35] Paul Schmidt, who was at Brenner Pass as an interpreter, said Hitler was at his best, "able to smother Mussolini with facts and figures to such an extent that the Duce goggled in wonder like a child with a new toy."[36]

"Mussolini," Schmidt said, "used the few minutes left to him, to my surprise and, as I learned later, to the consternation of his associates, emphatically to reassert his intention of coming into the war."[37]

Mussolini, who had ventured to the Brenner Pass in order to tell Hitler no, ended the meeting by telling Hitler yes. Hitler's attempt to better secure his southern flank had succeeded. He would now turn to Germany's second strategic weakness.

Norway

The Soviet Union on November 30, 1939, attacked Finland, and though that campaign was being ineffectually prosecuted by the Red Army, it highlighted the importance of the region. Though Finland was not the key to German security, Sweden was. Without Swedish iron, Hitler's war machine could not produce machines at all. Norway was essential as well. If Germany controlled Norway, she could close the Baltic. English ships could not hazard the straits.

And if German troops were in Norway, British designs for landing on her western banks and marching to Sweden would also disappear. There was a third, nondefensive, reason for Germany to covet Norway: from Norway's deep-water ports, the German navy would be able to extend its reach significantly for operations against the British Isles.

Winston Churchill and Adolf Hitler both knew these facts, and both decided to act.

Hitler had ordered his staff to examine a limited operation against Norway in December after a meeting with Vidkun Quisling, head of a Norwegian copy of the National Socialists. Quisling had informed the Führer, incorrectly, that the Norwegian government had agreed with Britain to allow British troops to land, ostensibly on their way to help the Finns against the Soviets. The British, in fact, did have a plan, though the Norwegian government was not involved. And while the British were to say the plan, designed by Winston Churchill, was intended to thwart the Soviet Union, everyone knew that engaging a second major enemy was exactly the last thing Churchill or anyone else wanted to do. The British plan called for their troops to get to Finland by passing directly through Sweden's Kiruna-Gallivare ore fields. That was not an accident.

After ordering the study of British aims, Hitler mostly forgot about it, consumed by the details of the main western invasion. But on February 16, 1940, a British destroyer entered Norwegian waters to free three hundred British seamen who had been captured by the Germans and were being held on a tanker. Though he didn't know it, the destroyer captain had made an immense mistake. He had focused Adolf Hitler's creative capacities on his Swedish problem.

Hitler now figured that if the English knew they could cripple Germany by landing in Norway, they would do so. It wouldn't matter that Norway was neutral. The Britain he admired had always done anything it needed to do to prevail. By mid-March, Hitler learned through German spies that the British were loading troops on transports. They were headed for Norway.

Hitler set about to ruin their plans.

Churchill's operation was scheduled to begin on March 20. The British would land in Scandinavia to save Scandinavia from Russia.

Unfortunately for Churchill's real aims, the Finns and Russians settled their border dispute on March 12, depriving the British of any
moral high ground from which they could excuse their invasion of
Norway. That didn't matter to Churchill. He advised landing anyway. The war would have surely taken a different course if the
troops had landed immediately. But they didn't.

Prime Minister Chamberlain had sided with the First Lord. He
wanted the Norway invasion to continue, saying that Swedish iron
and Romanian oil were Germany's two greatest weaknesses.[38] The
British, after some delay, decided to proceed with a Royal Navy offensive action against Norway. It was scheduled to begin on April
8. Churchill later reported that Chamberlain was "so favorable to
my views at this juncture that we seemed almost to think as one."[39]

Berlin was aware in general of British intentions, and decided to
strike first. Hassell wrote in his diary: "I cannot conceive that the
English are neglecting to make their calculations accordingly. If, in
spite of this, they permit the action to succeed, they deserve to be
conquered."[40]

On April 3, the Germans began putting to sea. Seven slow-
moving transports camouflaged as coal vessels carried the heavy
equipment, large guns and ammunition stores that would be
needed for the operation. The initial 10,500 assault troops embarked four days later on fast warships. Practically the entire German Navy was committed.

Oblivious to the threat, the British began laying mines near
Narvik on Monday, April 8, preparing for their own invasion. The
next day, as the "coal vessels" and German warships approached six
Norwegian ports, German troops swept into Denmark, the southern strategic peninsula into the Baltic straits. The country capitulated by midday.

Churchill, meanwhile, believed that Hitler's navy was actually
trying a breakout into the Atlantic. He sent his warships north, convinced that German activity around the Norwegian ports was a di-
version. As such, most of Hitler's Trojan Horse forces made it
unmolested to their destinations, others came by air, and by April
10 it appeared that Hitler had won. Churchill, ignoring that he had
earlier planned a surprise invasion of Norway himself, wrote to

British Admiral Dudley Pound that the "Germans have succeeded in occupying all the ports on the Norwegian coast, including Narvik, and large-scale operations will be required to turn them out of any of them. Norwegian neutrality and our respect for it have made it impossible to prevent this ruthless coup."[41] Still, Churchill judged that Hitler had made a strategic blunder. He would not be able to hold Norway.

Churchill was at his most indecisive. He had misjudged German intentions and even more clearly misjudged their capabilities. Now he couldn't figure out how to react, where to land troops, or how many capital ships should go into the ever-increasing reach of the Luftwaffe, now operating from Scandinavia. In his recounting of the events, Churchill said he gladly welcomed it when Chamberlain took over his job of supervising the operation.[42] In fact, he did so because there was open rebellion against his fumbling of the affair.[43] Churchill was reduced to "giving guidance and direction"[44] to military men who wanted none of it.

Even with such shaky leadership, the British had resources. Their superiority at sea extracted serious German losses in ship tonnage, though the Royal Navy itself suffered from attacks from the air. British troops were landed at Narvik and near Trondheim and for several days the result of the contest appeared uncertain. Keen to avoid British disaster, Churchill even proposed leveling Narvik, regardless of the thousands of Norwegian lives that such an action would have cost.[45]

In the end, Hitler won. Churchill had lost one of the most strategically important battles of the war. Hitler's was an operation undertaken against the recommendation of most of his generals, at the risk of losing the entire German fleet, and against naval doctrine that warships should not range inside the perimeter of coastal guns.

Germany's execution had been nearly perfect. Great Britain's had been erratic. The strategic consequences almost guaranteed a long and deadly war. Hitler had closed the Baltic. His supply of iron was assured for the duration. Sweden, prudently, delivered the ore, but otherwise swore to remain neutral. Hitler wrote to Mussolini: "Duce, I believe I have never in all my life had greater luck than this time."[46]

Had these been other times, Winston Churchill—who was responsible for England's worst military defeat during the First World War and now was responsible for this—would have been tossed from the Cabinet in disgrace. The defeat, however, attached itself instead to Chamberlain, who had actually tried to rescue England from Churchill's errors. Hitler wasn't the only lucky leader in Europe. Churchill survived and pressure built instead on Chamberlain to resign.

Rubicon

German victory in Norway changed perceptions in the Army and Wehrmacht High Command. Once again the Führer's gambles had succeeded, and against an enemy far more powerful than the Poles. German general Friedrich Fromm, who had been cautious and clearheaded, was now drunk with victory, predicting that a massive offensive against the West would be quickly successful. After this, he said, the "Führer will make a very moderate, statesmanlike peace."[47]

Halder, who was never drunk with victory, was nevertheless grudgingly optimistic. Hitler did seem to be a lucky man. Halder wrote in his diary: "Allies: Atmosphere is pessimistic. In the event of serious military reverses, we may expect either a complete changeover or extensive alterations. Chamberlain's Cabinet will not be overthrown at the present moment. Only when Britain will have to bear the brunt of the war set off by him, will an antiwar party rise in the country."[48]

With his strategic northern flank covered, Hitler's attention turned with added confidence to the western invasion, which could secure the Ruhr. No one now doubted that he would launch it. What Hitler demanded were five straight days of good weather, and for some time German skies had not cooperated. Göring had even once been moved to hire a rainmaker, though this was as likely an attempt to deprive the Führer of his five days than to provide them.[49] Anyway, until the blue skies arrived, all anyone could do in Germany was wait.

It was at this point—May Day, 1940—that the British lost an ally that just possibly could have averted the disaster that was coming. The ally was not a powerful country, but in the long run would prove as valuable. For several months the British had been intercepting German military Enigma messages, though that ability had obviously not yet been decisive. On May 1, the Germans changed their encryption ciphers, and for twenty-one days the British were deaf.[50]

During this window, word came from the meteorologists. Keitel recounted: "On 8th May, as all the expert opinion was that a period of fine weather seemed to be in the offing, the order to launch the attack was issued for the 10th." Chief of Operations General Alfred Jodl and Keitel arrived at Führer headquarters near Aachen at 3 A.M., May 9. It was still dark, and Keitel took in the last sight of peace he would have for years, remarking on the "beautiful canopy of stars." He tried to get some sleep in a squat concrete cell, but couldn't. He heard Hitler in the next cell, reading a newspaper to himself.

Hitler jotted out a letter to Mussolini. It began: "Duce, When you receive this letter I shall already have crossed the Rubicon."[51]

In Berlin at 5:45 A.M. on the tenth, Ribbentrop handed the Dutch ambassador a memorandum explaining why his country was presently being invaded. It was no more deceitful than usual. The principal reason for the invasion of the Low Countries was to ward off French and British plans to do the same. Further, it said, the Netherlands were not a true neutral, but had in fact conspired with the British. Holland, the Germans maintained, had helped Best and Stevens in a plan for "the removal of the Führer and the German Government, by all and every means, and the setting up of a government in Germany willing to bring about the dissolution of the unity of the Reich and to assent to the formation of a powerless federal German state."[52]

At 6 A.M. a courier was to deliver to the Queen of the Netherlands a personal message from Germany explaining why her country was being at that hour invaded. The couriers never arrived. German tanks did.

The Phony War was over.

10: *Wrought by Criminals*

WEIZSACKER THOUGHT THERE WAS SOME CONSOLATION
IN THE KNOWLEDGE THAT VERY OFTEN IN HISTORY GREAT
TRANSFORMATIONS HAVE BEEN WROUGHT BY CRIMINALS.

—*Ulrich von Hassell*

It was a gambler's gamble; audacious, close to reckless. On paper, this was a battle Germany should not have fought. Into the breach Germany threw 141 divisions, equipped with 7,378 artillery pieces, 2,445 tanks and 5,446 aircraft. The Allies were stronger in all categories but air power. They had ready 144 divisions, with 13,974 artillery guns, 3,383 tanks and 3,099 planes.[1] The Allies were also the defenders, and thus, according to the military book, held the advantage—Germany did not have twice the military mass of the Allies.

Hitler treated that military book just as Sherman would have. He decided to outsmart it. For one, he thought the numbers deceived. Most of the Allied force was French, and whatever their numbers, Hitler usually discounted them. The British were the important enemy, and their numbers were small.

Still, there was that pit of doubt that every gambler feels when all the money is on the table. Keitel said the headquarters "atmosphere was electric with tension: among us there was nobody who was not exercised by the question of whether we had succeeded in taking the enemy tactically by surprise or not. Hitler himself was waiting feverishly for the first reports on special operations he had mounted against the Belgians' strong modern brick-fortifications. . . ."[2]

Hitler's plans for taking fortress Eben Emael with troops brought in by gliders worked perfectly. Using specially designed explosives, one hundred Germans totally disabled the fortress. Some other Hitler conceptions only partially worked. The German soldiers disguised as Dutch police preserved some bridges, but not all. The intact bridges, though, proved vital. German troops poured through the breaks, and despite spirited Dutch resistance the Germans were on time, the enemy falling back from the onslaught. The Germans in the north certainly appeared to be executing an improved version of the old 1914 plan.

Across the Channel, there was almost a sense of relief. The wait was over. Hitler was committed. Churchill breakfasted with Sam Hoare, who found him nonchalant as he dove into some bacon and eggs. The two men had once been bitter antagonists, and Churchill had lumped Hoare, unjustly, with the appeasers. But today, the most important one in Churchill's life, it was time for rapprochement. Sam Hoare had much to contribute.

At 11 A.M. Chamberlain summoned Churchill and Halifax to 10 Downing Street. Everyone knew that the Prime Minister's reign was over. So harmed was he by innumerable political injuries—by Munich, by Norway, by his clear failure to find a solution to Hitler— that he couldn't have lasted much longer anyway. Now with the main thrust of the German war finally started, it was important that a new leader be chosen quickly. Chamberlain didn't know that when the day began. He believed that the start of a war was a poor time to change leaders. A battle, he said, was beginning that would reshape civilization. He thought he should remain, but that was a lonely idea. Labour wouldn't join a new government, and his fellow Tories said Chamberlain could not stay.

Churchill and Halifax arrived at 10 Downing Street and sat together at a table opposite Chamberlain. Both knew what was coming.

Chamberlain was dispassionate, detached. He said he could not form a national government; negative reaction from the Labour

Party left him in no doubt of that. The only question remaining, therefore, was whom he should recommend as his replacement.[3] Since the only two people he could really consider for the job were sitting in front of him, the question should have drawn a lively discussion. Instead, it drew something even more compelling.

Churchill, as close to his dream as he had ever been, sat and said nothing. "I have had many important interviews in my public life," he later recalled, "and this was certainly the most important. Usually I talk a great deal, but on this occasion I was silent."[4]

And not only was Churchill silent. All three men sat mute, contemplative, for over two minutes. Chamberlain would have preferred Halifax, a loyal, clear-headed statesman, over the tempestuous Churchill, who had been Chamberlain's critic for much of the past few years. But there were many reasons why the choice could not be Halifax. His association with Chamberlain's failed policies would have alone sufficed.

Finally, Halifax broke the silence. No, he said, he was a Peer and not a member of the House of Commons, the body that must make crucial war decisions. The only choice left was Churchill, but Chamberlain still hesitated.

It wasn't until 6 P.M. that King George summoned Churchill. "He looked at me searchingly and quizzically for some moments," Churchill recounted, "and then said: 'I suppose you don't know why I have sent for you?' Adopting his mood, I replied: 'Sir, I simply couldn't imagine why.' " The King laughed heartily.[5]

Winston Spencer Churchill was Prime Minister of the United Kingdom.

Recalled Churchill: "As I went to bed at about 3 A.M., I was conscious of a profound sense of relief. . . . I felt as if I were walking with Destiny, and that all my past life had been but a preparation for this hour and for this trial."[6]

He immediately began implementing one of his two primary strategic plans—bringing America into the war. He took William Stephenson, a Canadian businessman, millionaire and spy, aside and gave him orders to travel to America and devise a plan to "bring the United States into the war."[7] Churchill made sure that Stephenson, later known best by his code name Intrepid, would not be hindered by normal conventions of behavior between two allies. Stephenson was empowered to do whatever was necessary, including murder, to lure America into the war.[8] It appears that Stephenson quickly began spreading rumors among Americans that the Nazis were arming Mexican Fascists for an attack on the United States.[9] Eventually, that tack would have great success.

A secret postwar report written by the SIS said Stephenson's agents manipulated American newspapers, radio stations and wire services, compromised famous correspondents, harassed and destroyed unfriendly U.S. politicians, and helped get a man the SIS controlled named as head of the Office of Strategic Services. The Americans were so easily controlled that the SIS concluded they were simply and embarrassingly naive. In seeking out reasons, it found these: "In planning its campaign, it was necessary for [the British] to remember . . . the simple truth that the United States, a sovereign entity of comparatively recent birth, is inhabited by people of many conflicting races, interests and creeds. These people, though fully conscious of their wealth and power in the aggregate, are still unsure of themselves individually, still basically on the defensive and still striving, as yet unavailingly but very defiantly, after national unity and indeed after some logical grounds for considering themselves a nation in the racial sense.

"It is their frustrated passion to achieve a genuine nationalism which leads them to such extravagances . . . as the annual 'I am American' day and to such absurdities of expression—often heard—as Wishing you a real American Christmas."[10]

If Stephenson and his army of thusly trained operatives were to be the agents for America's entry into the war, Churchill would be the motive force. He began almost immediately by playing on Franklin Roosevelt's worst fear: Adolf Hitler in possession of the British fleet. That Hitler never aimed at this was not important.

Churchill told Roosevelt: "You must not be blind to the fact that the whole remaining bargaining counter with Germany would be the fleet, and if this country was left by the United States to its fate no one would have the right to blame those then responsible if they made the best terms they could for the surviving inhabitants. Excuse me, Mr. President, putting this nightmare bluntly. Evidently

I could not answer for my successors who in utter despair and help-lessness might well have to accommodate themselves to the German will."[11]

In tandem with the American deception, Churchill began sculpturing for Hitler a British Peace Party. It was first done from necessity, to slow Hitler. Later it would be used to craft Churchill's other great plan, the one that would end with the Hess mission: convincing Hitler to turn his wrath elsewhere.

Perhaps neither the Americas nor the Peace Party would be necessary if the British military men did their jobs. London and Paris both knew the German Chancellor had taken an enormous risk in undertaking an offensive. At first it looked as if Hitler was doing exactly as expected. General Fedor von Bock attacked in the north, from the Netherlands and toward Liège in Belgium. The attack had all the appearance of the main German thrust. It was pushing the neutral's armies back on their heels at almost all points. "It seemed [like] the old Schlieffen plan, brought up to date with its Dutch extension," Churchill conceded.[12]

The French and British armies—the British Expeditionary Force had but ten divisions—hurried to check the Wehrmacht with their strongest and best forces. Other crack units peopled the Maginot Line, which only a fool would attack. The weakest units, recently called up reservists, defended the area around the supposedly impassable Ardennes Forest near Sedan.

Adolf Hitler could not believe his good fortune. The main Allied forces were surging to meet Bock. If they continued, he would soon charge into their flank and kill them. He later reflected: "When the news came that the enemy was advancing [to meet Bock] . . . I could have wept for joy! They'd fallen right into my trap!"[13]

General Gerd von Rundstedt pierced the impassable Ardennes in a little over twenty-four hours. By nightfall of the eleventh, General Heinz Guderian was a few miles from Sedan, his Panzers pointed toward the strategic Meuse River. German troops led by General Erwin Rommel crossed it on the thirteenth, and suddenly the Germans were set for a blitzkrieg toward the Channel ports, a move that would decapitate the Allies.

Those Allies did not fully realize their peril. Their units continued streaming north to attack Bock while an overwhelming mass of German steel coalesced in northern France, only a few miles from the terminus of the Maginot Line. Churchill told his countrymen on the thirteenth that all he could offer was "blood, toil, tears and sweat," having no idea yet how many tears would shortly flow from the Allies' fatal miscalculation about the Ardennes Forest and the flexibility of the German Wehrmacht.

On the fourteenth the full force of the catastrophe began to show. French General Charles Huntziger noticed with alarm the German bridgehead across the Meuse and ordered a counterattack. It was brushed off by Guderian. On the morning of the fifteenth, German reinforcements poured across the Meuse on a pontoon bridge, and the French panicked. French Premier Paul Reynaud awoke Churchill at 7:30 in the morning with this disquieting assessment: "We have been defeated."

Believing "the break-through at Sedan serious, but not mortal,"[14] Churchill flew the next day to Paris. It was even worse than he had imagined. If the fissure was at Sedan, "we should plug it," was Churchill's simple solution. He asked: "Where is the strategic reserve?" General Maurice Gamelin softly said: "Aucune."[15] There is none. Churchill sent his cabinet a telegram, saying, "Situation grave in the last degree."[16] Cadogan had this to say in his diary entry for May 16: "The blackest days I have ever lived through."[17]

By May 17 there was no more debate. Hitler's potentially catastrophic gamble had been vindicated. The Netherlands had fallen and Belgium was about to. Rundstedt's Army Group A was positioned to apply the coup de grace. The German breakthrough was going better than planned. On almost every front, the Wehrmacht was rolling ahead of schedule.

The Allies tried to regroup and challenge the Germans, and it is possible they could still have put up a fight if they had united their forces, north or south. But national gravity bent the shape of the battle. The French, concerned with France and Paris, seemed to unconsciously make decisions that favored a shift of forces to the south. The British, just as unconsciously, favored a more northerly strategy where the Channel ports—and in them, escape routes—were.

The German armies as yet suffered from no such split identity. They had a plan, and its overall thrust had not wavered. While the French feared the breakout was intended to capture Paris, Hitler had no intention of capturing enemy cities when enemy armies were in the field. He was headed, as always, for the English Channel.

By the eighteenth, German armor took Saint-Quentin, halfway from Sedan to the goal. On the nineteenth, the Germans were but forty miles from the coast. Twenty-four hours later Army Group A took Abbeville. German troops could smell the salt water they would see the next day. In eleven days, the Germans had pushed 240 miles into France. Churchill lamented that the Germans had such an easy time of it. "They had passed through scores of towns and hundreds of villages without the slightest opposition," Churchill said, "their officers looking out of the open cupolas and waving jauntily to the inhabitants."[18]

The British tried to make matters worse for the Germans the next day by attacking from the south, near Arras. It was a tough fight, but Rommel turned them back. After that, there was no chance left. If the Germans chose to do it, they could kill the British and French armies in the north, the cream of Allied armed forces.

German generals chose to do it. Hitler did not.

For several days, Hitler had been complaining that the rout was happening too *fast*, a sentiment that troubled Halder. The chief of staff worried that the Führer was losing his aggressive spirit, becoming "frightened by his own success," and wanting somehow "to pull the reins on us."[19] On the evening of the twenty-third, General von Rundstedt ordered that most of Army Group A's tanks closing in on Dunkirk should pause until Dunkirk's defenses were clarified and other troops could close with the armor. It was a routine and practical order that would not be routine or practical for long.

Hitler arrived at headquarters the next morning. By then, the German army was poised to press its advantage. The Army General Staff wanted now to finish things. Within a day, perhaps two, the British Expeditionary Force would be eliminated, its troops captured and unimportant. Instead, Hitler extended the Rundstedt order beyond all logical bounds.

At 11:42 A.M., May 24, Hitler ordered the entire advance to stay in place. The reins were pulled.

It was not an order understandable to German generals. Within their grasp was total victory, and they did not want to let it go. Hitler's order risked losing victory to some lesser result. Hitler had forever gambled against long odds, and won. Now, when the odds were small, perhaps nonexistent, he chose caution.

However much he disliked Hitler, General Halder appreciated victories. He tried to convince Hitler that now was the time to strike. Germany could win one of the greatest battles in history. He might as well have complained about the thunder. Hitler could not be swayed. "The left wing," Halder lamented in his diary, "consisting of armor and motorized forces, which has no enemy before it, will so be stopped dead in its tracks upon direct orders of the Führer!"[20]

Hitler offered excuses. None were persuasive. He said the Flanders terrain was not conducive to tank movement—there was too much water all around. He said the infantry was too far back. He said there might be another attack like Arras. He said other things.

Halder thought he saw through the Führer. For unknown reasons, Hitler had decided that "the battle of decision" must not be won against the forces collapsing into Dunkirk. It should be directed against the forces in northern France. "To camouflage this political move," Halder wrote, "the assertion is made that Flanders, crisscrossed by a multitude of waterways, is unsuited for tank warfare."[21]

Halder did not have to say what was politically different about the two enemy forces: those at Dunkirk were primarily British while those to the south were mostly French.

The halt of what had until then been a ruthless, unbending juggernaut mystified the world as well as Hitler's generals. Everywhere people had expected news that the British army had been defeated in Flanders, and that the German machine was pivoting toward Paris to finish matters. Instead, no one knew what was going on. The machine had simply stopped running. Into this vacuum of facts came journalists, postulating that the Wehrmacht's sudden halt was evidence of a slackening of German resolve, or dissension in the High Command, or some other calamity.

That was not the type of speculation that Hitler welcomed. He could take care of his generals, but he could not afford to allow his sole ally to begin questioning the Führer's will.

Hitler wrote to Mussolini, warning him not to believe the "dilettantes of the press of our Western Powers." This time Hitler chose not to excuse the halt order on canals and waterways; instead he said the German army was in need of some road maintenance. "I was of the opinion," Hitler wrote, "that even at the risk of the evacuation or withdrawal of some Anglo-French forces there would nevertheless have to be a lull in our advance. In the 2 days thus gained, we succeeded in repairing the roads, which were in part terribly devastated. . . ."[22] With roads improved, there would be no reason to fear supply shortages.

The pause lasted for fifty hours. Finally, at 1:30 P.M. on May 26, Hitler ordered the advance resumed. Whatever fears he had about the waterways of Flanders had vanished. As for the roads, Hitler would never again bring up the subject.

If those fifty hours were of little importance to Hitler, as he had told Mussolini, they made for one of the most calculable differences in the war for the Allies. Their troops had not yet escaped, but they were positioned to. A defense perimeter had been established. On May 27, 7,669 troops left Dunkirk; a day later, 17,804. The rate climbed steadily until May 31 when 68,014 troops made it out of Dunkirk alive. From there, the numbers slowly declined. By the time Dunkirk was over on June 6, over a third of a million troops had slipped away from the Germans, including over 130,000 Frenchmen.[23]

Hitler did not express one regret. Privately, he said it was exactly what he had wanted. He was now at the Channel, the point, Gustav Krupp had said, where Germany might finally win the respect of the British. Perhaps the only point.

Though at the time it was a complete mystery, and for many today it remains so, the halt order at Dunkirk was not to Hitler's closest confederates any mystery at all. To those, like Hess, it was merely a rational extension of his peculiar obsession, the one he bore ever since 1923 when Karl Haushofer was ushered into Landsberg Prison. It was elementary. Hitler wanted to preserve, not destroy, Great Britain. He was fighting this paradoxical war for that purpose.

Waterways or roadways or fear of his southern flank all could have legitimately entered into Hitler's reasoning in halting the tanks. But finally nothing could excuse the military madness of his action. Hitler had let an enemy, ready to be defeated with little effort, escape. If there's logic to be found it must come in a simpler formulation.

However he excused or rationalized it, Hitler let the British forces go because he did not, when all else was discounted, see them yet as the enemy at all. In fact, he would not and perhaps could not *ever* view them as the enemy. They were Nordic. They would be allies.

This was much on Hess's mind the day the French surrendered. Asked whether peace with England was possible, Hess said it was inevitable. "We'll make peace with England in the same way as with France," he said. "Only a few weeks back the Führer again spoke of the great value of the British Empire in the world order. Germany and France must stand together with England against the enemy of Europe, Bolshevism. That was the reason why the Führer allowed the English Army to escape at Dunkirk. He did not want to upset the possibility of an understanding. The British must see that and seize their chance. I can't imagine that cool, calculating England will run her neck into the Soviet noose, instead of saving it by coming to an understanding with us."[24]

Hess was right. This was exactly what Hitler was telling his friends. Explaining Dunkirk, Hitler told Gerdy Troost that "the blood of every single Englishman is too valuable to shed. Our two people belong together, racially and traditionally—that is and always has been my aim, even if our generals can't grasp it."[25] Other close associates heard similar reasoning expressed in different words. "The army is England's backbone," Hitler said. "If we destroy it, there goes the British Empire. We would not, nor could not inherit it. . . . My generals did not understand this."[26]

Even after the passage of nearly five years, near the very moment of Germany's defeat, Hitler reflected fondly of Dunkirk, if not the eventual response from the British government. It was as if nothing had changed in Hitler's mind since 1923. And, in fact, little had. *Mein Kampf* proved to be a marker in time. "Churchill was quite unable to appreciate the sporting spirit of which I had given proof by refraining from creating an irreparable breach between the British and ourselves," Hitler explained in casual table talk. "We did, indeed, refrain from annihilating them at Dunkirk. We ought to have been able to make them realize that their acceptance of the German hegemony in Europe, a state of affairs to the implementation of which they had always been opposed, but which I had implemented without any trouble, would bring them inestimable advantage."[27]

Winston Churchill, a student of *Mein Kampf* and of people, the man who had suggested to Putzi Hanfstaengl a decade earlier a German-English confederation against Stalin, a man who mixed romanticism and realism much as did Hitler, could certainly not have missed Hitler's most telling signal about the meaning of Dunkirk. Throughout the western campaign, Hitler's armies used sophisticated encoding machines they believed to be impenetrable. They sent all important communications in code, with High Command orders the most heavily enciphered of all. The British listened anyway, to coded messages and to others sent totally uncoded. Studying where radio signals emerged from and in what quantity supplied key intelligence about what sectors were active or about to become so.

On May 24, at 11:42 A.M., a British serviceman monitoring Wehrmacht radio traffic picked up something the British had never heard before: a direct, uncoded, Führerorder. It read: "BY ORDER OF THE FÜHRER . . . THE ATTACK NORTHWEST OF ARRAS IS TO BE LIMITED TO THE GENERAL LINE LENS-BETHUNE-AIRE-ST. OMER-GRAVELINES THE CANAL LINE WILL NOT BE CROSSED."[28]

It was Hitler's halt order. And it was meant for all to hear. The Führer did not want the British to misunderstand his "sporting spirit."[29]

Officers rushed the Führerorder to Winston Churchill, who marveled at his good luck. Hitler had granted Churchill the two days needed for the British to have their "miracle at Dunkirk."[30]

The temporary good fortune at Dunkirk could never, though, obscure the reality of what had happened. Europe had changed in ways that were fundamental. It would never again be as it was. Ulrich von Hassell, the German ambassador involved in the conspiracy to overthrow Hitler, reflected on the change. "The skepticism of most of the generals, above all Beck's, is proved wrong. . . . The credit due Hitler and Göring for producing these weapons and Hitler's personal success in directing the campaign are undeniable facts. . . . One must now reckon with a new structure for Europe, in Hitler's image, achieved through a peace supporting his wide aims. They are preparing to wipe out the peace of Westphalia."[31]

There would come, Hassell prophesied, the "ascendancy of Hitler's brand of socialism, the destruction of the upper class, the transformation of the churches into meaningless sects. . . . We shall get a godless nature, a dehumanized, cultureless Germany, and perhaps a Europe, conscienceless and brutal.

"Weizsäcker thought there was some consolation in the knowledge that very often in history great transformations have been wrought by criminals."[32]

Facts

Churchill also knew the facts. The Germans' advantage was overwhelming. The rout had been so quick and decisive that many of Hitler's best divisions had yet to be in battle.[33] German troops were fresh, well armed and in high spirits. The British had escaped with little more than their clothes. The island was as close to being disarmed as at any time in seven hundred years, its soldiers worn by a battle that had seen little but retreat, until there was no place left to go but the sea. England, Churchill said, was "alone, almost disarmed, with triumphant Germany and Italy at our throats, with the whole of Europe in Hitler's power. . . ."[34]

"All that stood between us and total surrender," wrote F. W. Winterbotham, the British head of air intelligence, "was the disarmed remains of the British Army evacuated from Dunkirk, and the Royal Air Force, pitifully small compared with the vast air fleets of the Luftwaffe."[35]

While speeches could begin to repair shattered morale, they could not affect the equation of military power. If he chose to,

Hitler could now destroy Great Britain. British leaders would have to face that fact as well. They had to deal with a new Europe and its new emperor.

And they were prepared to do so, even the new Prime Minister. In late May and June, Winston Churchill oscillated between asking Hitler for terms and waiting to see if other miracles might happen.

As the Germans swung from Abbeville to Dunkirk, Churchill's thoughts turned to Sam Hoare, Chamberlain's air minister with whom Churchill had breakfasted the day he assumed power. His aides thought Hoare would be the last man Churchill would think of in this crisis. Hoare was associated with the appeasers, and it was thought that the nonappeasing Churchill would have none of them. But on May 19, Churchill became intent with having Hoare sent to Madrid as British ambassador to Spain. Hoare came to Cadogan with the news that a Churchill deputy "had come to him with [an] urgent message from W. S. C. [Winston Spencer Churchill] that he must go to Spain *at once* [emphasis in original]."[36]

Cadogan didn't believe it and others denied it. Madrid was the focal point of Nazi intrigue; German spies were everywhere. It was the last place a Prime Minister should post a man associated with appeasing Adolf Hitler. India would have been better. As far as Cadogan was concerned, Outer Mongolia or the like was more suitable. But rumors that Churchill wanted Hoare in Madrid persisted and two days later the man who had once been Churchill's enemy flew to Spain as His Majesty's special representative.[37] A person identified by the Germans as a British Peace Party member was now stationed at the Second World War's communications hub for spies.

Coincidentally, Halder made an entry into his diary that day that has never been explained. He wrote: "We are seeking to arrive at an understanding with Britain on the basis of a division of the world."[38] Whatever Halder meant by this was apparently lost to the crush of events. Nothing the British did could slow the Wehrmacht. A division of the world would have to await a judgment at Flanders.

Roosevelt thought Hitler was near total victory. And, recalling what Churchill had cabled him, the President grew horrified of the idea of British leaders offering Hitler the fleet in return for easier surrender terms. Little during the first two years of the war would bother Roosevelt more than the image of Nazis manning British battleships. On the twenty-fourth, the President asked that the Dominions pressure London to dispatch the British fleet to North America. The fleet, though, stayed at Scapa Flow in northern Scotland.

On May 25—halfway through Hitler's pause—the British began to consider seriously a formula of surrender. Halifax, wondering in general about Mussolini's attitude, met with Italian ambassador Giuseppe Bastiani: could the Duce broker a peace between the two nations?

By the twenty-sixth, as German panzers resumed their attack on Dunkirk, Halifax in the War Cabinet said that British war aims had been changed by events. Destroying Germany was now only a dream. Saving England was the reality. "We had to face the fact," Halifax said, "that it was not so much now a question of imposing a complete defeat upon Germany but of safeguarding the independence of our Empire. . . . We should naturally be prepared to consider any proposals which might lead to this, provided our liberty and independence were assured."[39]

He put the question directly to Winston Churchill. If England could get out of the war with British sovereignty assured, and only that, would the new Prime Minister agree? Churchill's answer shows how truly desperate the situation was. Yes, said Winston Churchill, he "would be thankful to get out of our present difficulties on such terms, provided we retain the essentials and the elements of our vital strength, even at the loss of some territory."[40] He doubted, though, that Hitler would be so considerate.

The issue turned again to whether the British should appeal to Mussolini to mediate a peace. Halifax said if the Duce "could obtain terms which did not postulate the destruction of our independence, we would be foolish if we did not accept them."[41] In spirit, Churchill seemed to agree. But Churchill maintained that Hitler would not give England easy terms unless England had put up a strong fight somewhere, which she had not done so far. He hedged for time. "My own feeling," he later explained, "was that the pitch in which our affairs lay, we have nothing to offer which Mussolini could not take for himself or be given by Hitler if we were defeated."[42] Churchill said he would prefer to know how the Dunkirk evacuations went before deciding what terms to offer Hitler.

The issue was now one of timing. The British leadership—and that very much included Winston Churchill—was prepared to deal with a victorious Adolf Hitler if there was hope Hitler would be reasonable. Instead of division in the cabinet, there were merely differences in a continuum. The only issue was saving Britain. Anything else was so remote as to be invisible.

Hitler's next move was the one that mattered most. The cabinet knew England would almost certainly be defeated if Hitler came. Some thought logically that it might be better to settle the issue before that happened. Not only would lives be saved, but England was in a better position to bargain now than it would be with German tanks in London. In that case, Hitler wouldn't have to bargain at all.

Churchill was in less of a hurry than the others, less sure that Hitler would do now what was necessary, less convinced that he would press his advantage. It was partly due to Churchill's character. His reading of history convinced him that wars were fought between personalities as well as armies. Maybe there was something in Hitler that was not as practical as Bismarck or Frederick the Great. Neither of them would have halted the tanks in Flanders. But Hitler did, and that was worth considering.

Churchill certainly wouldn't risk the British Empire on any hazy hunch about the German dictator. He had to be prepared for a Führer who would eventually act more like his practical predecessors, a leader who would push his advantage. On the twenty-seventh, twenty-four hours after the Dunkirk evacuations began, Churchill asked his generals what chance England had of surviving if Hitler *did not* offer terms that preserved British sovereignty. He asked: "In the event of terms being offered to Britain which would place her entirely at the mercy of Germany through disarmament, cession of naval bases in the Orkneys, etc.; what are the prospects of our continuing the war alone against Germany and probably Italy?"[43]

The implicit understanding was clear enough. As on the twenty-sixth, Churchill would have accepted a peace if it was reasonably offered. He now only wanted to know what would happen if it was not.

The next day found Winston Churchill more inclined to accommodate Adolf Hitler than at any time of the war. He said he would give the Führer what the Führer had wanted when the war began if by doing so it would now end. Said Churchill: "If Herr Hitler was prepared to make peace on the terms of the restoration of the German colonies and the overlordship of Central Europe, that was one thing. But it was quite unlikely that he would make such an offer."[44]

If he had heard these words, Adolf Hitler would have been amazed and accommodating. The "overlordship of Central Europe" would in Hitler's dictionary translate as "Lebensraum."

Pliant as he appeared, Churchill still hedged for time. Believing that the crushing defeat in Belgium and France made it "impossible . . . for Germany to put forward any terms likely to be acceptable," Churchill asked French Premier Paul Reynaud to delay asking Mussolini to mediate an armistice. "You will ask, then, how is the situation to be improved? My reply is that by showing that after the loss of our two armies and the support of our Belgian ally we still have stout hearts and confidence in ourselves, we shall at once *strengthen our hands in negotiations* and draw the admiration and perhaps the material help of the U.S.A. . . .

"It would indeed be a tragedy if by too hasty an acceptance of defeat we threw away a chance that was almost within our grasp of securing an honourable issue from the struggle [emphasis added]."[45]

There was little in Churchill's approach to Germany at the end of May that is consistent with his subsequent image as one who would never deal with the devil. Churchill would have dealt with anyone and done anything to save Great Britain, as he would prove many times during the war. That is as it should have been. The first task of a statesman is to preserve the state.

But the legend that grants Churchill the power to look into Hitler's mind, and from that perspective to guide England to victory, neglects certain advantages available to the Prime Minister. On May 22, the British broke into the German Luftwaffe's code.[46] Though the break was not complete and the code could only be partially read, from then on Winston Churchill's wisdom and genius were guided by facts. If Herman Göring was planning anything major, Churchill would be informed, not so much because he was a great psychoanalyst, but because he employed great mathematicians at Bletchley Park.

That others around him appeared less sure of Hitler's plans is probably because they were not as well informed. One account, endorsed by Churchill's personal spy, William Stephenson, even maintains that while Neville Chamberlain was in power, Churchill received the Bletchley decrypts, but Chamberlain didn't. The then Prime Minister purposely was not told that Great Britain had broken the German code, and thus was kept from the most important intelligence in the United Kingdom.[47] This is hard to accept, because, if true, it would mean that Churchill may have come close to treason. Whatever the truth, it seems clear that Enigma, the German code, was Churchill's special secret.

The twenty-eighth would not pass without still more surprises from Winston Churchill.

Just as he had plucked Samuel Hoare, supposedly Germany's friend, out of his expected oblivion to instead become ambassador to Spain, he now sought to elevate to the cabinet the Englishman Adolf Hitler respected more than any other.

One of Adolf Hitler's best days before the advent of the Second World War had been when the British leader of the First World War came to visit him in 1936. Then as now Hitler saw Lloyd George as the hero and true winner of the World War, a man who embodied what was best in the English. Lloyd George didn't hurt his standing in the Führer's eyes when he said that Adolf Hitler was "the greatest living German."[48] A month and a half into the war, stenographers recorded that Hitler told Swedish explorer Sven Hedin that he "could not say this publicly, but the only man in England that he would care to call a genius was Lloyd George. . . . Of all the British to whom he had spoken to date, Lloyd George had made the greatest impression upon him."[49] And two weeks later—on November 1, 1939—Hitler told Alfred Rosenberg that it was with Lloyd George that he would most prefer to bargain for peace.[50] Much later, when peace with Britain appeared remote, Hitler lamented that if "Lloyd George had the necessary power, he would certainly have been the architect of a German-English understanding."[51]

Though the pattern was not obvious at the time, in inviting Hoare and Lloyd George into his government, Winston Churchill was fostering Hitler's greatest illusion: there was a shadow government in Britain, one not controlled by Jews and capitalists, and one with which he could eventually reach his goal.[52] When Lloyd George turned down Churchill, it only increased his stature in Adolf Hitler's eyes. In the months ahead, Lloyd George, Hoare and other Peace Party members, including the Duke of Windsor, would assume great significance in Hitler's planning.

If England needed a strategic deception, Churchill had the power to provide it. Parliament made Churchill the virtual dictator of Great Britain. As Churchill described it, he had "practically unlimited power over life, liberty and property of all His Majesty's subjects." He was empowered to "direct anyone to perform any service required."[53] His secretary, John Colville, wrote in his diary that "in a totalitarian war even a democracy must surrender its liberties. But what a precedent for future peacetime Governments; and will state control, once instituted, ever be abandoned."[54] As days passed, Colville grew more concerned, watching how Churchill took to the new role. The English were imitating the Nazis: "complete governmental powers, internment camps and now Storm Troopers."[55] Churchill began one meeting by simply asking: "Home Secretary: Let me see a list of prominent persons you have arrested."[56]

If Churchill was listening to Enigma or to the German conspirators inside the Abwehr, he may have known he had time as well as power to perfect a deception. On May 28, the dictator on the other side of the Channel began planning to disband thirty-five divisions—approximately a million troops. Within weeks, he would make the plan an order.[57]

Hitler, once again, was hoping for an early finish to the Second World War before it became a world war. And he was willing to pay for it. On June 2, he told aides that he would make peace with England even if England would not agree to the restoration of German colonies.[58]

Count Ciano, in another rare concession to Hitler, said that "Hitler is now the gambler who has made a big scoop and would like to get up from the table risking nothing more. Today he speaks with a reserve and a perspicacity which, after such a victory, are really astonishing. I cannot be accused of excessive tenderness towards him, but today I truly admire him."[59]

Ciano asked Ribbentrop the essential question: "Do you prefer the continuation of the war, or peace." Without a moment's hesitation, Ribbentrop replied: "Peace."[60]

"Without Delay"

The world did not know this. Peace was the last thing Adolf Hitler was supposed to be now considering. Instead, the world feared he would soon do to the Isles what he was doing to France. He would invade and conquer. And there was little the British could have done to stop him.

The Royal Navy could have tried, but only if Winston Churchill cared to risk the end of the Royal Navy. In the few miles between Calais and Dover, capital ships would be largely in range of German coastal guns, and those that weren't would be welcomed by Stuka dive-bombers. Operating within these straits would be suicidal. Though some Germans would not make it to shore, many more would, and those who could not make it by sea would make it by air. Hitler had already pioneered the airdrop to the rear.

No one wanted to do this more than the German High Command. The time to strike was now. England was in full, chaotic retreat. That's how German General Erhard Milch and others saw it. He urged "the immediate transfer to the Channel coast of all available Luftwaffe forces. . . . The invasion of Great Britain should begin without delay."[61] Wrote Keitel: "Nobody was in the dark about the risk we would be running; everybody was well aware that its [the invasion's] success would demand a maximum effort by army, navy and air force, but everybody realized that the longer the invasion was postponed, the stronger the British defenses would become."[62] The War Office, he said, was "strongly in favor of risking the operation and made every possible effort to promote its execution."

Hitler, Keitel conceded, had been far more used to generals who didn't want to fight than to those who would actually take risks. Now, however, "Hitler found himself under considerable pressure from that quarter, a circumstance to which he was totally unaccustomed."[63]

Keitel said it took some months before he realized what was

likely motivating Hitler. Hitler, he said, held back because "he was reluctant to accept the inevitable loss of his last chance of settling the war with Britain by diplomatic means, something which I am convinced he was at that time still hoping to achieve."[64]

General Gunther Blumentritt, Rundstedt's operational planner, realized what was happening earlier than did Keitel. He visited Hitler's headquarters at the height of the Dunkirk crisis and was stunned to find Hitler "in very good humor. . . .

"He then astonished us by speaking with admiration of the British Empire, of the necessity for its existence, and of the civilization that Britain had brought into the world. . . . He compared the British Empire with the Catholic church—saying they were both essential elements of stability in the world. He said that all he wanted from Britain was that she should acknowledge Germany's position on the Continent. . . . He would even offer to support Britain with troops if she should be involved in any difficulties anywhere. . . .

"He concluded by saying that his aim was to make peace with Britain on a basis that she would regard as compatible with her honor to accept."[65]

"We Shall Never Surrender"

The last Allied troops, 26,175 of them, left Dunkirk on June 6. Strewn behind them were 7,000 tons of ammunition, 90,000 rifles, 2,300 field guns, 8,000 smaller guns and 120,000 vehicles.[66] They were to be replaced by words.

That same day, Churchill delivered a fiery speech in Commons that—either because he was too busy or, by one account, because he was too inebriated—was later delivered over the radio to the nation by an impersonator. The thirty-seven-year-old actor said, "It was just another job."[67] It was more than that. It became part of Churchill's legend. And surely that was deserved. Whether from himself or from an impersonator, no other words could connote such resolve: "We shall not flag or fail. We shall go on to the end. . . . We shall fight on the beaches, we shall fight on the landing grounds, we shall fight in the fields and in the streets, we shall fight in the hills. We shall never surrender."[68]

British radio listeners were enthralled by these words and heartened. At the helm it appeared there was a fighter.

The only man in Europe who could outspeak Winston Churchill was also impressed. In Churchill's words, Hitler saw his ideal of an English warrior—tenacious, uncompromising, solid. That he also thought of Churchill as a fat, undisciplined alcoholic was ancillary.

Hitler did not invade England the following day. Instead he turned the Wehrmacht on France. The French fought better than many generally accord them, but there was really no stopping the Germans. By June 9, the French Tenth Army was surrounded near the Somme River. The following day, Mussolini finally entered the war, assured, he thought, that Italy was on the winning side. The Italians, however, would not have any more success against the French than they would have against any other force. Essentially, they went nowhere.

Churchill tried to bolster flagging French resolve, but words alone could do nothing. The French asked for air cover. The British could not help, at least not in the quantities that might have made some difference. Outside of Enigma, the RAF was the only weapon the British had left and they chose not to squander it over France. Hoping to save Paris from the Luftwaffe, Reynaud declared it an open city on the thirteenth. German troops occupied the city the next day. Verdun, which had withstood the Germans stoutly during the last war, fell next, and there was nothing left to do but sue for peace.

Hitler arranged for the surrender to take place at Compiègne, the exact spot where the Germans had surrendered to the Allies in 1918. On a monument erected to commemorate that occasion the Allies had emblazoned these words: "Here on the eleventh of November 1918 succumbed the criminal pride of the German people." Twenty-two years later, Adolf Hitler would erase those words. The train car in which Marshall Ferdinand Foch had dictated his terms in 1918 was retrieved from exhibition in Paris. Inside it there would be a new peace agreement, one that would not implicate the criminal pride of the German people. It was Hitler's turn to dictate peace. In some respects that diktat was to prove soft, better than the one Germany had received.

Germany would occupy northern and far-western France, territory it needed to control in order to further the fight against England if England chose still to fight. In the remaining territory, France would retain its sovereignty and, to Mussolini's dismay, its colonies. France would also retain its fleet, the one French instrument of war that most concerned the British. Marshal Henri Philippe Pétain replaced Reynaud, and the locus of unoccupied France became Vichy, not Paris.

Hitler did not give these terms because he had any great respect for the French. He gave them to impress the British with his reasonableness. If he made such terms with a country he occupied, the British should know he would make even better terms for them. "The British," Hitler told Jodl, "have lost the war, but they don't know it. One must give them time, and they will come round."[69]

Hitler ordered the monument at Compiègne dynamited by German troops, allowing only the statue of Foch to remain, a symbol of the Führer's respect.

11 :: *Conspiracies*

No one knew how much time Hitler would give the British. Most thought he would give them no time at all. But while the world waited for Germany to invade England, Germany's Luftwaffe sat on the ground, its army remained in camp and its dictator became something of a tourist, having his photograph taken against the backdrop of the Eiffel Tower. This was not the picture of an avenging tyrant most had come to fear. The Führer was acting strangely. Did he know something others did not?

He did. Long before this war began, Adolf Hitler had a special line to the British ruling class through which he could learn its feelings and intentions. He had learned from this source that Churchill was in trouble, and that reasonable men in England were ready to make peace. All that was necessary was for Germany to deliver to England a substantial blow and reasonable men in England would deliver Hitler his elusive peace. The blow had now been administered. Hitler awaited the reasonable men.

What he heard during the summer of 1940 reassured him. From throughout Europe and the United States came rumors of peace. British leaders unofficially told Germany that they would soon be ready to end the war. There was only one problem, and it would not last: Winston Churchill.

The campaign was so widespread in scope and so consistent in content that today there should be little room for doubt that it had a single architect and that its mission was to buy time. Either this, or much of upper class England was involved in a massive conspiracy against Winston Churchill. If so, Churchill should have honored the traitors. By creating in Hitler's mind the image of a huge and powerful British Peace Party, they caused Hitler to delay and, in the end, to cancel his invasion of the Isles.

The conspiracy, or the deception, had three parts. The oldest, and probably the most important, was embedded in the Secret Intelligence Service.

The Air Ministry Conspiracy

Perhaps Hitler's best secret source to the British aristocracy was Baron William de Ropp, the tall, blue-eyed displaced Balt, living in Switzerland and married to an Englishwoman. De Ropp had fought in the RAF during the First World War and had considerable connections in England. De Ropp befriended Nazi ideologist Alfred Rosenberg in 1930 and through him became a confidant of Hess and Hitler.[1] After the Nazis assumed power and Rosenberg went to work for Hess, de Ropp became a key Nazi advisor on British affairs. Throughout the 1930s, de Ropp told the Germans repeatedly that in Great Britain there was a strong pro-German, anti-Bolshevik party that understood the racial ties between their two peoples and shared Hitler's goal of a common alliance against the Soviet Union. Its base, de Ropp said, was in the Air Ministry.

That this was absurd did nothing to deter Hitler from believing it. He had predicted in his book that such people existed. He had since said as much to anyone who would listen. If de Ropp brought more proof, it was only to the good. Further, it was clear to Hitler that de Ropp was not a mere braggart. He did have high connections in Great Britain. De Ropp was even able to arrange for Rosenberg to travel to England to meet some of the Peace Party members.

Rosenberg was impressed. In a memo he sent to Hitler he said he had made "a number of contacts which worked out well for an Anglo-German understanding. In the forefront here was Squadron

Leader W., a member of the Air General Staff, who was entirely convinced that Germany and England must move together to ward off the Bolshevik danger. The outcome of the various discussions was the widening of the group amongst the Air General Staff, and the Royal Air Force Club became the center for fostering Anglo-German understanding."[2]

Of particular note, Rosenberg told Hitler, was ascendancy in the Foreign Office of former Minister of Aviation Samuel Hoare, "who still today maintains his old personal connections with the Ministry of Aviation. At his request a Memorandum inspired by us on the intellectual foundations of National Socialism, had been passed to him, as he wishes to try to understand our Movement more fully."[3]

Hitler would have had de Ropp arrested on the spot if he ever learned for whom it was that "Squadron Leader W." actually worked. Squadron Leader W. was F. W. Winterbotham, head of British air intelligence and the same man who had befriended Hess and Rosenberg during the 1930s. He was a spy. His mission was to destroy Adolf Hitler, not to march with him against the Reds. And William de Ropp was Winterbotham's man, and thus a British double agent. Unknown to the Führer, the SIS had for years manipulated his obsession about a Peace Party to influence him and divine his intentions.

Just before the war began, de Ropp prepared a way to use the deception if hostilities started. He told Rosenberg that in case of war he would be stationed in Geneva. When the Peace Party wanted to end the conflict, de Ropp would send a message, signed "George."[4] Twenty-three days into the war, de Ropp contacted the German Foreign Ministry with word that the Peace Party in the RAF wanted to meet secretly in Switzerland with German representatives to discuss a settlement.[5] Officials asked Hitler what they should do. Hitler's response has not been found, but it is nearly impossible that Hitler did not respond aggressively.

How aggressively was reflected two weeks later, when the Germans sent de Ropp a proposal, which has also been lost. But the German Foreign Ministry did record de Ropp's response, and that left little doubt that Hitler had a radical solution to force an end to the war: "Surprised by this far-reaching possibility, on which he [de Ropp] had not counted at all, de Ropp declared that in this extraordinary situation he must first make inquiry of his own Ministry. The Ministry informed him that in the present situation, it did not believe that in the interest of the matter it ought to sponsor such a journey with the reception which would be involved. . . . It requested, however, that the opportunity be postponed to a more suitable time [when] they could make use of an authoritative statement on Germany's intentions."[6]

From Switzerland, de Ropp arranged the help of Carl Jacob Burckhardt, a leading intellectual, head of the International Red Cross, and, judging from his actions, a de facto British agent. If a peace could be negotiated between Hitler and the Peace Party, de Ropp was to come to Berlin as a Red Cross official. De Ropp cautioned, however, that the Peace Party was not positioned to reverse British policy until after a major battle left no doubt about German military might.

This battle having now occurred, Hitler awaited to see if de Ropp had been right. Would the Peace Party emerge?

Peace Party Conspiracy

The Peace Party that emerged in 1940 knew practically no bounds. It extended throughout the diplomatic corps, the upper class, and even ensnared a former King. It was either the greatest unprosecuted crime in English history, or the second most successful deception of the war. The Hess mission, which would grow out of the Peace Party and be forever related to it, would be the most successful of them all.

In early June, Prince Max Hohenlohe—an agent mostly in the service of Germany but who saw himself as a disciple for peace—was briefed on German terms for a settlement. He left immediately to contact English diplomats and Carl Burckhardt in Switzerland. The terms are not known, but the British let it be known that they were appreciative. The day after Hohenlohe's meetings in Switzerland, Halifax's under secretary of state, R. A. Butler, told colleagues that the British were working with the Vatican to find a peace settlement with the Germans.[7]

By June 17, Butler, in what he claimed was a chance encounter,

met the Swedish Minister, Bjorn Prytz, on the street and asked him
to come to his office. Once there, Butler made comments that appeared to be from anything but chance. Instead, they appear to be
intended to have an effect in Berlin, and, if so, they succeeded. Butler told Prytz that "no opportunity would be neglected for concluding a compromise peace if the chance [was] offered on
reasonable conditions . . . the so-called die-hards would not be allowed to stand in the way of negotiations." There was little doubt
in Prytz's mind who Butler was alluding to by the term "die-hard."
There appeared to be a rift in the cabinet between the Foreign Office and Churchill.

As if to underscore the level of the British peace feelers, Butler
left the office to speak with Halifax. When he returned, he said that
the British foreign minister had a message for Sweden: "Common
sense and not bravado would dictate the British government's policy."[8]

Prytz rushed off a telegram to Stockholm reporting not only this
message but also his impression, from discussions with several
prominent Englishmen, that Halifax might replace Churchill within
ten days. The telegram went to King Gustav V, its import relayed
to the Italian ambassador, thence to Count Ciano in Rome and finally to Ribbentrop and Hitler. This all happened within hours.[9] Simultaneously with Prytz's message from Halifax came one from the
British ambassador to Sweden. The ambassador told the Swedish
foreign minister that "the British government is inclined to enter
into peace negotiations with Germany and Italy."[10]

On the nineteenth, the Swedes made sure the Germans knew
what the Swedish government thought was happening in London.
The Swedish Minister in Berlin told German State Secretary
Weizsäcker that the Swedish mission in London was reporting "a
return to sound common sense in authoritative circles in London."[11]

Two days later, Prince Hohenlohe, after conferring in Switzerland with Burckhardt, reported to the German Foreign Ministry
that there was a strong peace movement in England wanting to hold
discussions with Hitler's government.[12] The Peace Party was active
and not apparently shy at bucking the official government position.
Everywhere, Englishmen were committing treason.

All of this was having the effect on Hitler that they almost certainly intended it to have. On the day of Hohenlohe's latest message, Hitler met with his generals and learned that they were impatient. They saw no good reason to wait any longer before launching an invasion. But Hitler said he was in no hurry and, anyway, was considering whether an invasion would ever be necessary. If Britain did not make peace, he suggested that perhaps she could be defeated by air power.

The Führer was giving his generals the unmistakable impression that England was an enemy he had little heart for defeating, and one to whom he would offer almost any terms to end the war. Halder wrote on June 22 that "the near future will show whether Britain will do the reasonable thing in the light of our victories, or will try to carry on the war single-handedly."[13] Certainly Britain of late appeared very ready to do the reasonable thing. The same day Halder wrote those words, the German Foreign Ministry heard that Hitler's favorite Englishman, Lloyd George, could soon replace Churchill. The Swedish minister discouraged this idea, though he reaffirmed to the Germans that a powerful Peace Party was coalescing around Halifax.[14] Something definitely appeared to be happening in Great Britain.

Hitler naturally and logically concluded that the forces of peace were aligned with Halifax and those of war with Churchill. And he could not believe his good luck. Everything that was happening was very good for Germany. On June 24, the day France formally surrendered and Hitler erased the shame of Versailles, the Führer was in a paradoxical mood. He was master of Europe and could do about anything he wished to do. But instead he lost almost all ambition. He told his inner circle: "The war in the West is over. France has been defeated, and with England I shall reach an understanding very shortly."[15]

The Führer continued to spell out his goals. Had the session been broadcast, no one in the world, except perhaps Winston Churchill, would have believed it. It would have been written off as propaganda from Joseph Goebbels.

Not only was Hitler in no mood for world conquest, he was hardly even ready for the *Mein Kampf* dream of conquering the Ukraine.

"There will remain," Hitler told his close advisors, "our settling of our accounts with the East. But that is a task that opens global problems . . . perhaps I shall have to leave that to my successor. Now we'll have our hands full for years, to digest and consolidate what we have achieved in Europe."[16]

Sure of victory in the West and not yet planning an attack in the East, Hitler shifted several divisions, including an armored strike force, to the East, where they could watch over German strategic interests in the Romanian oil fields. He was more afraid of an attack by Stalin than he was prepared to launch one himself.

Britain soon learned of Hitler's mood. There was much to be happy with, and much to worry about. If Hitler became too pacific, he might actually be able to force a peace that would not suit ultimate British goals. When Information Minister Duff Cooper and his Parliamentary Secretary Harold Nicolson returned to the Information Ministry on the twenty-sixth they found a "flash to the effect that Hitler is going to offer us sensationally generous terms." Nicolson wrote: "I doubt whether our opinion is strong enough to resist this temptation."[17] It is still today unknown what that flash was and from whom it came, but it had its effect. After receiving the flash, the cabinet met, but an important part of the minutes "is not open for public inspection, and has not been filmed."[18]

Following the meeting, there was no letup in the secret peace contacts, but the official British government line hardened, its denunciation of anything involving Hitler became still more strident. Hitler was a liar. He could never be trusted. He sought to conquer the world and only a small island stood between the dictator and his goal. Churchill, who was so near to capitulation in May, was now becoming a legend: the British bulldog who would have nothing of Adolf Hitler.

It was at this point that Churchill said he had an insight. "To those who like myself had studied his moves," Churchill later wrote of Hitler, "it did not seem impossible that he would consent to leave Britain and her Empire and Fleet intact and make a peace which would have secured him that free hand in the East of which Ribbentrop had talked to me in 1937, and which was his heart's main desire."[19] On June 27, Churchill committed his expanding insight to writing. He told South African Prime Minister Jan Christiaan Smuts: "If Hitler fails to beat us here, he will probably recoil eastward. Indeed, he may do this even without trying invasion, to find employment for his Army, and take the edge off the winter strain upon him."[20,21]

Hitler, meanwhile, still patiently awaited the ascendance of the British Peace Party. Goebbels wrote in his diary on the twenty-eighth. "There are two [British] parties—a war-party and a peace-party. They struggle for power. Churchill's stock is not high. Through Sweden and Spain there already are feelers."[22]

By July 8, Winston Churchill appeared even more convinced that either through manipulation or sheer good luck, Adolf Hitler would leave Britain and fight the Soviets. He wrote to his minister of aircraft production: "When I look round to see how we can win the war, I see that there is only one sure path. We have no Continental army which can defeat the German military power. The blockade is broken and Hitler has Asia and probably Africa to draw from. Should he be repulsed here or not try invasion, he will recoil eastward, and we have nothing to stop him."[23] He told the minister that bombers would defeat Germany.

There was more behind Churchill's reasoning than insight, but even he could not legally reveal that at the time he wrote his war histories. Winterbotham, who not only handled de Ropp but also the British code breakers, was more forthright. He did not refer to "insight" when describing why the British started thinking Hitler would turn east. Instead, he said, *"From many secret sources* of information . . . it seemed certain that Hitler would attack Russia in the East in the spring of 1941 and if he wanted the Sea Lion [the planned invasion of England] affair mopped up in time to deploy his main forces in the East, he must start his invasion by around mid-September at the latest [emphasis added]."[24]

As soon as Churchill and his agents became convinced that they could plan a war strategy around Hitler recoiling east, Hitler—through his own insight—knew it, and set about, reluctantly, to hammer down a point: this would not be a two-front war. Halder recorded that the "Führer is most concerned about the question of why Britain will not yet make peace. He sees the answer, as we do, in the fact that Britain still has hopes of Russia. He reckons therefore that England will have to be compelled to make peace by force. But he does not like doing this. The reason is that if we crush England's military power the British Empire will collapse. That is of no use to Germany. German blood would be shed to accomplish something that would benefit only Japan, America and others."[25]

By July 15, with no British Peace Party yet in power, a confidential briefing by the German Propaganda Ministry now brought top German opinion makers up to date on the negotiations:

"New authentic information has clarified the recent political soundings which have taken place between Germany and Britain during the pause in hostilities. It is now certain that Germany's views have been passed on to Churchill directly via leading Swedish circles i.e. via Stockholm and that contact has been further sought with Halifax via the British ambassador in Madrid, Sir Samuel Hoare. About twelve or thirteen days ago, these soundings were broken off as a result of the hostile attitude of the British ruling class . . . .

"Until the soundings were broken off, the Führer was of the opinion that sooner or later Germany would have to work together with the healthy section of the British people and therefore that it was not appropriate to destroy the whole empire, since this would simply mean that the Russians, the Japanese and the Americans could secure an easy inheritance which is not in our interest.

"The Führer wants an early end to the war . . . [he] wants to consolidate the Reich in all spheres of life during the period in which he is in full possession of his energies . . . . Socialism will crown the Führer's work and these efforts too can only flourish in peace time."[26]

A day later Adolf Hitler, who considered himself Britain's greatest friend, issued Directive No. 16, the order to prepare for an invasion of the British Isles. His reluctance was evident in the very first paragraph: "Since England, despite her militarily hopeless situation still shows no sign of willingness to come to terms, I have decided to prepare a landing operation against England, and *if necessary to carry it out* [emphasis added]."[27] As always in his fight against Britain, even if he landed, Hitler still hoped not to destroy

her. He explained in the second paragraph: "The aim of this operation is to eliminate the English homeland as a base for the carrying on of the war against Germany, and *if it should become necessary*
to occupy it completely [emphasis added]."[28]

As a precondition to invasion, Hitler said that the "English Air
Force must be so beaten down in its morale and in fact, that it can
no longer display any appreciable aggressive force in opposition to
the German crossing."[29] Forty days after the last British troop departed Dunkirk, the German Führer had finally ordered the
Wehrmacht to begin *planning* an invasion of England, and even
then with the understanding that Hitler didn't really want to do
that at all.

The British no doubt had some more insights about this change
of heart and in the coming months they would do everything possible to confirm to Hitler that his heart was telling him the truth. He
did not need to invade. The Peace Party, so large in June but somewhat quiet since, would now grow to new heights. Even some historians who don't think that the earlier peace feelers had Churchill's
signature on them concede that the ones that now followed did. Historian John Luccas said that now Churchill "in all probability . . . did
not discourage a few careful and confidential attempts to throw some
bait to German agents—more precisely, to pretend to listen to them.
But on the larger and public level the impression of an unbreakable
British resolve to fight had to be maintained."[30]

Two days after Hitler had ordered an invasion prepared, much
more bait was thrown his way. Again it involved Carl Burckhardt:
scholar, former high commissioner of Danzig, head of the International Red Cross, contact man for the German opposition. Burckhardt persuaded Prince Max Hohenlohe to meet with the British
ambassador to Switzerland, Sir David Kelly, to talk of peace. Hohenlohe—and this is based mostly on his version, written at the
time—refused until a direct request came from Kelly himself. Met
at the ambassador's door by Kelly's wife, Hohenlohe knew exactly
what awaited him. Mrs. Kelly told him he must "lose no time" to
"discuss peace possibilities with her husband."[31] The ambassador
shortly took the Prince aside and said he was a messenger—and not
Churchill's. Instead he represented more accommodating officials:

Butler, Vansittart, Halifax and others. These men sought peace and were not stubborn or warmongers or anything else associated with the Prime Minister. They were, however, British and honorable and would fight to the end, if necessary, until "a reasonable peace could be made."

Hohenlohe was suspicious. Halifax and Butler were certainly now firmly encased in the Peace Party legend, but Vansittart was a bitter anti-appeaser. The Prince told the German Foreign Ministry that he did not discuss too deeply this peace feeler from Kelly because of "the suspicion that conversations are intended to gain time. . . ."[32]

Hohenlohe, and even Hitler, may have been suspicious of the torrent of peace feelers coming from Britain, but Hitler decided nevertheless to gamble again that strong British opponents of Churchill would rescue everyone from the war he had begun. On July 19, a day after Hohenlohe told the Foreign Ministry of his discussions with Kelly, Hitler again used the podium of the Reichstag to advocate an end to the war.

He was this time more personal about Churchill, surer that Churchill was at odds with the British people. He predicted that an air war would cause "incredible misery and misfortune. . . . Naturally this will not affect Mr. Churchill, for he will certainly be in Canada . . . but for millions of other people there will be great misery. And perhaps Mr. Churchill should believe me for once when I prophesy the following:

"A great empire will be destroyed. A world empire that I never intended to destroy or even damage. But it is clear to me that the continuation of this struggle will end with the complete destruction of one of the two opponents. Mr. Churchill may believe that this will be Germany. I know that it will be England.

"At this hour I feel compelled by conscience once more to appeal to reason in England. I believe I am in a position to do this because I am not the vanquished begging for favors. As victor, I am speaking in the name of reason.

"I can see no reason why this war should go on."[33]

Hitler warned against anyone believing, as some surely did, that this plea was caused by fear or indecision. "Mr. Churchill may reject this declaration of mine by shouting that it is only the product

of my fear and my doubts," Hitler said. "But at least I have relieved
my conscience before the events that threaten. . . ."[34]

Even as Hitler spoke, the British ambassador to the United
States, Lord Lothian, told his Foreign Office of back-door discussions with the German chargé d'affaires. In apparent direct contra-
vention of orders, Lothian said he had initiated the contact and
could report that Hitler would indeed grant favorable peace terms.[35]
Weizsäcker noted: "a curious peace feeler from the British Ambassador in Washington. Lord Lothian made advances . . . which, if he
were a normal British Ambassador, he must have been authorized."[36]

If Hitler appeared unnaturally compromising to the German people who listened to his speech, for a time he appeared to his generals to be briefly cavalier. He seemed ready to wait one last time for
the Peace Party, now again very prominent, to act. Two days after
his Reichstag speech, Hitler told the army commander in chief,
Brauchitsch, that he was not certain what his next move should be.
Halder recorded in his diary: "Führer—not clear what is going on
in England. The preparations for a decision through force of arms
must be completed as quickly as possible. . . . As soon as things become clear he will once more take the political and diplomatic initiative."[37] Hitler saw only two reasons for Britain's refusal to
conclude the war: "hope of a change in America" and "hope on
Russia."[38]

There was absolutely no doubt, though, that the allegedly illicit
peace offensive by Halifax, Kelly, Lothian and others had succeeded. Halder recorded these Führer thoughts: "Appraisal of the
effect of the peace feelers. . . . Lloyd George: letter to King and Parliament. Duke of Windsor: letter to King. [German chargé d'affaires
to the United States Hans] Thomsen: News from England. Situation considered hopeless. English ambassador in Washington [Loth-
ian]: England has lost the war. It should pay up. But not do anything
contrary to its honor. Possibility of a cabinet consisting of Lloyd
George, Chamberlain, Halifax. . . ."[39]

As he waited for the Peace Party, and prepared for the battle that
would come if it failed, Hitler's sanguine mood of June 24 began to
recede. He was again thinking of winning German Lebensraum in
his lifetime, not leaving it to a successor. Halder wrote in his diary:
"Political goal: Ukrainian empire."[40]

Yet it was too early to claim victory for the British stalling strategy. Although Hitler didn't want to destroy Britain, he also certainly didn't want a two-front war. That was how Germany lost the First World War and Hitler would not lightly decide to make that mistake again. He was clearly of two minds, and struggling.

The next few weeks would show Hitler's mind at its most baffling. He seemed intent at times to do nothing, waiting for the Peace Party. Then, as if in some disordered dream, he would plan his march on Russia, either as a way to convince England to settle, or as an end in itself. If the various diaries of the time appear confusing to historians, it is because they were reporting plans of a confused man. It was the struggle of a man possessed, a man finding that what had been the simple harmonic of a small orderly set of political beliefs was now a discord. He had based his career on the certainty that Germany and England would unite as allies. Now he was poised to crush that would-be friend.

He told his generals: "In the event of our being unable to force a decision against England and of the danger of England allying herself with Russia, the answer to the question of whether one should then launch a *two front war against Russia is that it is better to keep on friendly terms with Russia* [emphasis added]."[41]

No sooner had he said that than he adopted the exact opposite notion: he would first defeat Russia in order to convince his racial brethren on the Isle that there was no hope in fighting further. That this would violate his obsession with avoiding a two-front war momentarily didn't seem to matter.

On July 31, 1940, Hitler started to indoctrinate his generals in this strange idea. Meeting at his Obersalzberg retreat, Hitler and the High Command analyzed the cross-Channel invasion in the type of minute detail Hitler preferred. The commanders, as usual, were eager to begin, but not as eager as before. They thought an invasion could occur in September, but preferred to wait until spring. The Führer, as usual, was not as anxious to begin an invasion as to force a peace short of British destruction. He said he placed most of his hope on an air attack, believing it, alone, could decide matters. As for physically taking British territory, Hitler showed little stomach. Halder wrote that the Führer emphasized "his skepticism concerning technical possibilities."[42]

Everywhere, Hitler displayed an aversion to doing anything decisive against Great Britain. The German navy, he complained, did not compare to the Royal fleet. Time and weather were against him. By spring, the Wehrmacht might be ready, but so too might be the British army. Better to strike by September 15 than to wait too long, but a strike by then was improbable. Only with absolute air superiority would Hitler consider it.

Hitler appeared to be raising obstacles to invading Great Britain that even German generals could not surmount.

Then Hitler unveiled the incipient notion of beating England by beating Russia. The generals should have expected it. The Führer, after all, was the man who had staged the Phony War in order to make peace with Great Britain, the man who had invaded the West not to destroy England but to win her over, the man who was planning an invasion of England not to conquer her but to convince her. It made sense that Hitler might do even more radical ventures to win England's friendship.

Halder recorded the Führer's thoughts: "England's hope is Russia and America. If hope on Russia is eliminated, America also is eliminated . . . Russia the factor on which England is mainly betting. . . .

"Should Russia . . . be smashed, then England's last hope is extinguished. Germany is then master of Europe and the Balkans.

"Decision: In the course of this contest Russia must be disposed of. Spring '41."[43]

Hitler called for a quick crushing of Russia, in five months. Germany would gain the Ukraine, White Russia and the Baltic states. It would take 120 German divisions. Sixty divisions would control the West.

This was not, however, a simple demarcation. What Hitler's generals did not know was that Hitler could probably never launch this mad enterprise unless he was certain that there would be no second front. And dealing with the Peace Party was the only way he could get that certainty. If the Peace Party could not conclude the war outright, which Hitler still thought probable, it would have to prove it could at least restrain Winston Churchill.

If not, Hitler would be forced to do something he wanted to do least. He would destroy the British Empire.

In the late summer of 1940, Hitler's hopes turned toward two men: in Spain was the one man Hitler thought could most easily lead Britain to an understanding, even an alliance, with Germany— a friend of Germany who understood the racial calamity of the war. He was His Majesty the Duke of Windsor, the former Edward VIII, King of England.

Hitler would now try everything to have the very popular former King take the lead in the Peace Party. If that happened, a compromise peace would be certain.

Hitler, though, prepared himself for a failure of the mission. He authorized the man he trusted most in the world to begin making contact with the Peace Party itself. Rudolf Hess began preparing for a different mission.

Churchill, meanwhile, was also set on keeping peace contacts open, and not only to stall the Germans. Behind his public image as the bulldog, Churchill knew if Hitler pressed, Great Britain might have to come to terms. On August 1, Britain sent out a peace feeler to the King of Sweden. On August 3, Churchill criticized the effort, not because it had been made, but because of the language that was used, which Churchill thought demonstrated weakness. "A firm reply of the kind I have outlined," Churchill said, "is the only chance of extorting from Germany any offers that are not fantastic."[44]

Winston Churchill was still seeking offers.

The Royal Conspiracy

Hitler adulated the Duke of Windsor from the time he was Edward VIII, King of England. Both Hitler and Hess credited the King with avoiding a war after Germany reoccupied the Rhineland in 1936, a time when Germany was vulnerable and Britain was not. The Führer had faith that in the King there was a man who thought as he did. With him on the throne, Hitler knew his cherished alliance would come to be.

It was a black day in England when Edward abdicated on December 11, 1936, to marry Mrs. Wallis Simpson, an American. But it was a blacker day still in Germany. Hitler saw his best friend in Britain leave on a romantic whim. This was unthinkable, and so Hitler chose not to think of it. Instead, he believed Germany's opponents had somehow forced the King out to avoid a German-British understanding. And Hitler was not one to give up a notion once it had settled in. His belief in Edward, now the Duke of Windsor, held firm. He thought that Windsor could recapture the throne and end the unnecessary war.

The Duke had been in France working as the British military liaison to the French General Staff when the German Panzers raced out of the Ardennes. But as France collapsed, the Duke and Duchess had to flee. The British did not need the former King to land in German hands. The Windsors crossed the Spanish border on June 20 and headed for Madrid.

The Spanish knew of the German interest in Windsor, and tried to be helpful. The German ambassador to Madrid told Berlin on the twenty-third that "the [Spanish] Foreign Minister assumes . . . that we might perhaps be interested in detaining the Duke of Windsor here and possibly in establishing contact with him."[45]

There was nothing the Germans wanted more. Windsor was a capital asset that could not be lost. On the twenty-fourth, Ribbentrop asked his ambassador: "Is it possible in the first place to detain the Duke and Duchess of Windsor for a couple of weeks in Spain before they are granted an exit visa? It would be necessary at all events to be sure that it did not appear in any way that the suggestion came from Germany."[46] Spain promptly agreed "to do everything possible to detain Windsor here for a time."[47]

It was not penal detention. The Duke and Duchess settled in at the Ritz, where they naturally became the social focal point of Madrid. Far from distancing himself from the controversial couple, British Ambassador Sam Hoare held a reception for them at the embassy, one well attended by Madrid's society.

If there were doubts about the Duke's supposed attitude toward Germany and peace, he dispelled them at the reception. American Ambassador Alexander Weddell got close enough to Windsor to hear him issue some fairly significant opinions. In a cable to Washington, Weddell reported that Windsor thought "the most important thing now was to end the war before thousands more were killed or maimed to save the faces of a few politicians."[48]

He went on to elaborate: "In the past ten years Germany has totally reorganized the order of its society in preparation for this war. Countries which were unwilling to accept such a reorganization of society and concomitant sacrifices should direct their policies accordingly and thereby avoid dangerous adventures.

"The Duchess put the same thing more directly," Weddell continued, "by declaring that France had lost because it was internally diseased and that a country which was not in a condition to fight a war should never have declared war."

Weddell concluded that Windsor's sentiments represented an element in England, "possibly a growing one, who would find in Windsor and his circle of friends a group who are realists in world politics and who hope to come into their own in the event of peace."[49]

Hitler had long before drawn the same conclusion.

During his stay in Madrid, Windsor met several times with Spanish Foreign Minister Atienza Beigbeder, who, naturally, passed on what he said to German Ambassador Eberhard Stohrer. On July 3, that connection brought Berlin suggestive information. The foreign minister told Stohrer that the Windsors were preparing a short trip to Portugal. He also said the Duke had been talking freely again. "Windsor has expressed himself to the Foreign Minister and other acquaintances in strong terms against Churchill and against this war."[50] Stohrer passed this on to Berlin before Berlin could say that the Duke must stay in Spain, not venture to the less friendly Lisbon.

It was too late. The Duke and Duchess had already left for Portugal.

The German information was clearly right in one respect. The Duke and Churchill had been feuding, though not about the war or world politics. The Duke wanted to return to England with an important position. His younger brother, the new King, had resisted, and, because of that, there was little Churchill could do. He insisted that Windsor return to England whether a new position was available or not, reminding Windsor that he was a military officer, who, if the request was made into an order, would have to return.

Churchill wanted Windsor off the Iberian Peninsula, even if he had to be forced. He knew what Windsor didn't. A thicket of German agents was intriguing to move Windsor from Churchill's control to their own.

On July 3, the Duke accepted the inevitable. He agreed to return to London. Less than twenty-four hours later, Churchill reversed plans. He named Windsor governor of the Bahamas, a British territory. The Bahamas were more important than the Americans or Germans ever realized. They served as the outpost from which William Stephenson and scores of others conducted the massive covert campaign to force America into the war. At the time, the Bahamas were probably the most tightly secured British acreage on earth. In the Bahamas, the Duke of Windsor would be well surrounded by Churchill's agents. He would, if Churchill chose, be controlled by them.

The Germans, who wanted to keep Windsor close at hand, were not pleased with developments. They wanted Windsor in some friendly country, not Portugal, certainly not England and definitely not the remote Bahamas. Their mood was not improved by a July 11 telegram from the German ambassador in Lisbon. Spaniards traveling with Windsor, the ambassador reported, claimed that the Duke's appointment to the Bahamas was "intended to keep him far away from England, since his return would bring with it very strong encouragement to English friends of peace. . . . He [Windsor] is convinced that if he had remained on the throne war would have been avoided, and he characterizes himself as a firm supporter of a peaceful arrangement with Germany."[51]

Hitler and Ribbentrop were alarmed. The ultimate leader of the Peace Party was to be sequestered in the Bahamas, completely out of the reach of Germany. Ribbentrop sent an emergency message to the embassy in Madrid: "We are especially interested in having the Duke return to Spain at all events." Windsor, Ribbentrop said, was surrounded by British agents who wanted to remove him "if necessary by force." Therefore, the German foreign minister said, "haste is accordingly required."[52] Ribbentrop, believing that the British might actually be going to kill the Duke, wanted German agents to determine posthaste how to get the Duke to Spain. Germany's involvement, Ribbentrop said, must never be known. Perhaps the ever helpful Spanish could find a way to bring back the Duke.

"For your personal information," Ribbentrop wrote, "I would like to add: After their return to Spain the Duke and his wife must be persuaded or compelled to remain on Spanish territory. . . .

"At any rate, at a suitable occasion in Spain the Duke must be informed that Germany wants peace with the English people, that the Churchill clique stands in the way of it, and that it would be a good thing if the Duke would hold himself in readiness for further developments. Germany is determined to force England to peace by every means of power and upon this happening would be prepared to accommodate any desire expressed by the Duke, especially with a view to the assumption of the English throne by the Duke and Duchess." If he did not want back the throne, the Reich would nevertheless guarantee him a "life suitable for a king."[53]

However nicely put, the Germans were preparing, if need be, a friendly kidnapping of the former King of England. One German versed in the art of kidnapping foreign nationals was Walter Schellenberg, who had performed the service on Best and Stevens at Venlo. Hitler and Ribbentrop turned to the Nazi counterintelligence chief to once more risk his life in a peculiar mission outside of Germany. Schellenberg, who had since Venlo turned thirty, was to travel to Portugal to reason with the Duke of Windsor, code-named Willi by the Germans.

Hitler, Schellenberg recalled in his memoirs, authorized him to offer Windsor fifty million Swiss francs, deposited secretly in a Swiss bank, if the Duke disassociated himself from English policy. It was not so much a bribe as a guarantee that if Windsor risked his status in England, and thereby his property, by advocating peace, he would not suffer a financial loss if Churchill prevailed against him.

Hitler imagined the Duke of Windsor waiting in the wings in a neutral country, not conscripted but not totally free either. "The Führer would, of course, prefer him to live in Switzerland," Schellenberg recalled hearing from Ribbentrop, "though any other neutral country would do so long as it's not outside the economic or the political or military influence of the German Reich."

It was, Ribbentrop thought, a good plan, though it had an obvious peril: the SIS. Ribbentrop told Schellenberg that if "the British Secret Service should try to frustrate the Duke in some such arrangement, then the Führer orders that you are to circumvent the British plans, even at the risk of your life, and, if need be, by the use of force. Whatever happens, the Duke of Windsor must be brought safely to the country of his choice. Hitler attaches the greatest importance to this operation, and he has come to the conclusion after serious consideration that if the Duke should prove hesitant, he himself would have no objection to you helping the Duke to reach the right decision by coercion—even by threats or force if the circumstances make it advisable."[54]

Ribbentrop, Schellenberg said, made it clear that the force would not be intended to hurt the Duke, and that once Windsor was in a neutral country—and away from the British Secret Service—he would be free to make his own decisions.

What the Germans did not know and what some historians have unwisely ignored is that the German radio traffic directing initiatives against the Duke was highly susceptible to British decoding. If the English knew early of German interest in Windsor, they would have moved quickly to exploit their knowledge. Intimations that Windsor wanted to lead the peace movement could have as easily come from British disinformation as from the Duke, and for purposes far different than Hitler ever expected. Perhaps, even, Windsor's loose talk at Sam Hoare's reception was not so loose after all.

In fact, the British cryptoanalysts had detected the Windsor conspiracy. Winterbotham, master of the Enigma intercepts, said after the war that the Windsor traffic was intercepted.[55] The historian who asked him that question apparently didn't determine if the traffic had been decoded as well, but the implication was that it had been. If so, ever since the first German telegram expressed interest in keeping Windsor in Spain, the SIS likely knew of it.

The Germans conceived a plan to have the Duke accept a hunting invitation that took him close to the Spanish border, or to repair for a vacation in the same easterly direction. In either case, the Duke would find himself in Spain. That this did not take place is probably owing to SIS finesse, not Windsor's indecision.

The Duke met with the British ambassador and emerged far more agreeable about his proposed posting. An intermediary sent by the Germans to persuade him to return to Spain was rebuffed. The Duke said he was going to the Bahamas, but held out the possibility that eventually the role of peacemaker might befall him. He simply "should not now, by negotiations carried on contrary to the orders of his Government, let loose against himself the propaganda of his English opponents, which might deprive him of all prestige at the period when he might possibly take action." Then the courier curiously added this: "He [Windsor] could, if the occasion arose, take action even from the Bahamas."[56]

The Duke then tried to deceive the Germans about the time of his departure. He said it would come in a week. It was scheduled, in fact, for the next day. By now, the Duke was definitely playing his government's game, which he had perhaps been doing for some time. The Germans, though, were hard to outsmart. They had efficiently examined the shipping schedules and deduced that the Duke was trying, for reasons unknown, to slip away. This would not do. From the Bahamas, the Germans were certain, the Duke would never "be free to intervene" on their behalf.[57] Ribbentrop sent the detailed proposal to the Duke, which he had earlier intended only to submit when the Duke was back in Spain. There was now no time for that. Plans to abduct the Duke were faltering.[58] In the message delivered by an intermediary, Ribbentrop told Windsor that Churchill was sending him to the Bahamas to block all communication with the Germans. He might as well be under arrest.

But Windsor seemed not to be in the least worried about that. According to the intermediary, Windsor assured the Germans he would be "in continuing communication with his previous host and had agreed with him upon a code word, which upon receiving he would immediately return to Europe. He insisted that this would be possible at any time, since he had foreseen all eventualities and had already initiated the necessary arrangements."[59] Windsor told his friend to relay to Germany, confidentially, his "admiration and sympathy for the Führer."[60]

Something had fundamentally changed, for there was in Windsor a total transformation. Windsor had gone from a man around whom spies intrigued to being an intriguer himself, one equipped with code words, safe houses and secret means of transatlantic flight. He had also gone from talking peace to talking treason.

The Duke and Duchess left Lisbon for the Bahamas aboard the *Excalibur* at twilight, August 1, 1940. The Germans were confident it was the last they would hear from him. If they had known what awaited the Duke in Nassau, that confidence would have been unlimited. The island was teaming with British secret agents whose job it was in part to keep care of the Duke.

Communication was not possible.

Directive No. 17

As the Duke and Duchess of Windsor sailed from Lisbon, Hitler lost his last hope that the British Peace Party could avert the war Hitler did not want to fight. While Hess now began planning his mission in detail, Hitler knew he would now have to press Britain. It was time for bombs. Goebbels noted in his diary entry of August 1, 1940: "Our feelers to England without results . . . the Führer now too sees no other possibility but war."[61]

Hitler issued Directive No. 17, calling for an attack on England directed "primarily against the planes themselves, their ground organization, and their supply installations, also against the aircraft industry, including plants producing antiaircraft material."[62] Hitler did not authorize bombing civilian populations, even if Great Britain attacked German civilians. "I reserve for myself," he said, "the decision on terror attacks as a means of reprisal."[63] Some 2,669 war planes—1,015 bombers, 346 dive-bombers and 933 fighters—were set aside for the attack. Opposing them were some 675 British fighters. The attack was to begin on the fifth.

Finally, on August 13, 1940, came an operation the Germans called Eagle Day: 1,485 Luftwaffe war planes appeared over England, mostly in the southeast, raiding the forward airfields of Lympne, Hawkinge and Manston, strafing and bombing radar stations, announcing to the world that Hitler's pause had ended. At Detling airfield, 186 German war planes caught the British by surprise, destroying twenty-two aircraft on the ground and suffering no losses themselves. Thirteen precious RAF fighters were shot down in the air. The Germans lost forty-five planes.

Two days later—August 15, 1940—came the greatest air battle of the war as 1,786 German raiders descended on England. With radar and advance warnings from Enigma, the British avoided disaster, shooting down seventy-five German planes. Britain, though, lost thirty-five more fighters, and that was thirty-five more than she could afford. What the English would call the Battle of Britain had begun.

On August 15 a telegram arrived in Portugal. The Duke of Windsor's secret line to Portugal had been activated. The Duke, who said he would send this signal when it was time for his return to Europe, sought instructions. The German ambassador was told immediately about the telegram, and quickly cabled Ribbentrop: "The confidant has just received a telegram from the Duke from Bermuda asking him to send a communication as soon as action was advisable."[64]

To the Germans, the telegram had to mean one thing: the British Peace Party and the Duke of Windsor were finally prepared to act. They didn't know that the only way the Duke could have penetrated the massive security that surrounded him was if the security services were themselves behind it. If they had known, they would have surely been cautious.

Records on what happened next with the Duke of Windsor are lost or unavailable. But one thing is clear: Rudolf Hess suddenly became immersed in the planning for a highly secret mission.

The Battle of Britain continued, but would only once again reach the ferocity of August 15: the day Rudolf Hess completed it.

A war of attrition favored Hitler because he had more to attrit. The ratio of losses began to narrow, and the ratio of fighter losses actually favored Germany. By the end of August the British had lost 338 Hurricanes and Spitfires outright. Another 107 had been badly damaged. Germany had lost 177 of its top-line Messerschmidt-109s, the deadliest fighter then in existence. Another twenty-four were greatly damaged.[65]

The Battle of Britain soon began to change the character and face of the war. On August 24, ten Luftwaffe bombers that were supposed to hit oil storage facilities, mistakenly dropped bombs on central London, killing nine civilians. On August 25, eigthy-one British bombers dropped bombs on mostly civilian areas of Berlin. They returned three more times until Hitler, on September 4, threatened to retaliate, but did not. If goaded into changing his attacks from military targets to suburbs, German bombs and lives would be wasted.

Still, the specter of what this war might become had appeared to Hitler. With the machines and passions of war unbridled, a war of extermination could ensue, one that would obliterate either Britain or Germany, not with the signing of a document in a railway car, but with the reduction of the loser to rubble, to nonexistence. The crescendo of blinding bombs that Winston Churchill had expected on September 3, 1939, now, more than a year later, was expected, too, by Hitler.

It was not what he wanted. But if he had to, he might do it. He did not intend to lose. On September 7, Hitler allowed Hermann Göring to bomb military targets in London: arsenals, docks, warehouses, petroleum facilities. The term "surgical strike" had not yet been coined, but that's what was intended. It was not the result. On the first day, 448 Londoners lost their lives. The bombers returned again and again and the term "Blitz" came to describe the onslaught.

Though the Blitz would continue until the day that Rudolf Hess departed for Dungavel House, the Battle of Britain ended on September 17, 1940, thirty-six days after it had begun. Only a tiny few knew it at the time. Frederick Winterbotham, the air intelligence chief who controlled the Air Ministry conspiracy and Baron de Ropp, was the first official to learn of the victory. In the morning, Winterbotham was told from intercepted signals that Hitler had personally ordered the dismantling of air-loading equipment at Dutch airbases. Much as the halt order at Dunkirk had told the British that they would survive to fight again, the September 17 Führer-order invigorated Winterbotham. He knew immediately that "if the loading equipment was being dismantled, the invasion could not take place. . . ."[66] Winterbotham sent word immediately to Winston Churchill that their efforts had succeeded. Hitler would not land soon in England.

Winterbotham was called to 10 Downing Street to deliver the verdict:

> There was already intermittent bombing and anti-aircraft fire as we left in Stewart's car for Storey's Gate; it was drizzling, and ghostly forms moved about in the darkening streets.
>
> Underground, in Churchill's war room, Hastings Ismay was already welcoming the chiefs of staff and setting the conference in place. They had been briefed by their directors of Intelligence. Winston arrived.
>
> I was struck by the extraordinary change that had come over these men in the last few hours. It was as if someone had suddenly cut all the strings of the violins in the middle of a dreary concerto. There were controlled smiles on the faces of these men.
>
> Churchill read out the signal, his face beaming, then he rightly asked the Chief of Air Staff Sir Cyril Newall to explain its significance. Cyril Newall had been well briefed; he gave it as his considered opinion that this marked the end of Sea Lion, at least for this year. . . . The conference knew that the dismantling of the air-loading equipment meant the end of the threat, and so it was accepted.
>
> There was a very broad smile on Churchill's face now as he lit up his massive cigar and suggested that we should all take a little fresh air.
>
> It was a wild scene. Standing with our backs to the concrete were ranged the three chiefs of staff, then General Ismay, Stewart and myself. Winston stood alone in front, his dark blue boiler suit undone at the neck, a tin hat on his head, his hands folded on his stout stick in front of him, his chin thrust out, the long cigar in his mouth, and just across the other side of St. James's Park, Carlton House Terrace was ablaze: the boom of bombs exploding to the south, the crack and rattle of the AA guns and exploding shells, the red white glow of the fires silhouetting the black trunks of the great trees in the park.
>
> It was a moment in history to remember, and above the noise came the angry voice of Winston Churchill: "By God, we will get the B's for this."[67]

12 : *The Hess Mission*

Though Churchill thought he was now safe, he would soon learn he was wrong. Hitler would continue to conduct this war as he always had, with bravado and instinct mixed inseparably with obsession. He wanted a peace with England and he wanted the Ukraine and he wasn't going to give those two up without some serious fighting.

The Führer was being patient. Although he was toying with the mad idea of fighting Russia in order to win Great Britain, he was not yet committed to that course. By mid-November, he warned his army commanders that in addition to their planning for war on Russia, they must also plan for something quite different. "Because, with changes in the over-all situation," Hitler said, "the possibility or necessity may arise to return in the spring of 1941 to Operation Sea Lion, the three branches of the armed forces must earnestly try in every way to improve the groundwork for such an operation."[1]

The generals were again confused. Did Hitler want a one-front war or a two-front war? When spring came, which enemy would it be that Germany invaded, England or Russia? Hitler had once told Halder that his generals would never know exactly what he was thinking, and he seemed to be making good on that claim now. Halder would complain after the war that the "sources of information of this mysterious man were a puzzle."[2]

As the Battle of Britain began, Hitler was indeed keeping much from his generals. They did not know that the former King of England was back in touch with the Führer through a contact in Portugal. Nor did they know that through Portugal Hitler was to begin his most singular, most subterranean and most important peace feeler of the war. His Deputy Führer was to find a peace that so far had eluded him. Unfortunately for Hitler, he enlisted the help of a man sworn to destroy him, and who, tens of millions of deaths later, would succeed.

Cold Passion

Rudolf Hess had always tried to protect Albrecht Haushofer. In the 1930s, Hess had exempted the part-Jewish Haushofer from anti-Jewish laws, and found a place for him in the Nazi Party's foreign department working with Ribbentrop. And when Ribbentrop eventually capped his career by winning the job as foreign minister, Haushofer went with him, at least in part to keep Hess informed about Ribbentrop's activities. Haushofer had described himself as "not completely without passion, but it is a different passion of coldness, of stillness, of abstraction."[3] But he was more than this. He was a brooding, depressed yet brilliant man, torn inside by the company he kept; a German elitist who looked down upon all Nazis as inferiors.

Tall, square-jawed and handsome, Haushofer lived a life that on the surface was as ascetic as Hitler's, the man he despised the most. As he settled into his service for the Nazis, he saw no hope for a happy end. Of himself, he wrote to his mother, there were four alternatives:

"A violent end from outside by chance or by intention;

"Economic decline to a point where life stops;

"Internal destruction through permanent time-serving;

"A voluntary exit."[4]

Still, Haushofer was in the service of Hess, a man for whom he had more than mere cold passion. To Haushofer, Hess meant well. Though not as brilliant as himself, conversations with the Deputy Führer were at least tolerable. In corresponding with each other,

Haushofer and his father, Karl, adopted the nickname Tomo for Hess, a word derived from the Japanese word for friend.

His thoughts of death did not disable Haushofer. On one level, he served his masters well. The Nazis actively consulted with him on Czech problems before Munich, and he traveled to Japan, China and North America to gauge for the Germans the world situation. But it was his contacts with and understanding of the British that most impressed the Nazis. Those contacts expanded even more after Ribbentrop was made German ambassador to the Court of St. James. Haushofer made many trips to London, on Hess missions and for Ribbentrop.

But some of Haushofer's best contacts with the British did not take place in London, but in Berlin. Germany hosted the 1936 Berlin Olympic Games, and many curious Britons used it as an excuse to view firsthand the country that was making such a stir. Haushofer met many of them, but by far his most portentous new acquaintance was the Marquis of Clydesdale.

The Oxford-educated Clydesdale was many things that Haushofer was not. He was a titled member of the aristocracy, not a mixed-blood academic. He was a risk-taker, not a sufferer of existential angst. He was, in the language of the time, a man's man. Clydesdale had in 1933 set about to pilot a plane over Mount Everest. People warned that no plane could do it and it was suicide to try. Clydesdale disregarded this and risked his life and succeeded, becoming the first human to pilot a plane over the world's tallest mountain. Clydesdale's feats were not restricted to the air, but included blood sports. He had won Scotland's middleweight amateur boxing championship.

Further, unlike Haushofer, Clydesdale was a military man. He was posted not at headquarters, but near the front, should a front ever develop. Clydesdale was the commander of an RAF squadron in Scotland. Baron de Ropp had told Hitler that high in the RAF command there were such people as Clydesdale. Now there was proof.

Clydesdale was also a member of Parliament, and went to Germany not only to see the Games, but to see the Nazis. His younger brother, David, was the one who reported meeting a most interesting German, a Ribbentrop aide named Albrecht Haushofer.

Haushofer was not an unknown name. It was associated with German geopolitics, and so it was natural that Clydesdale and other Parliament members met Haushofer at a dinner to discuss the European political situation. Albrecht Haushofer was clearly not a Nazi. When someone asked him about Goebbels, Haushofer lowered his voice and said: "Goebbels is a poisonous little man, who will give you dinner one night and sign your death warrant the next morning."[5] Such talk had not been expected of a German official who briefed both Hess and Hitler. Someone asked Haushofer about the odd importance the Nazis placed on being Nordic. Haushofer lightheartedly tapped his nose, remarking that it was not exactly Nordic.[6]

The British seemed to enjoy this unusual German intellectual, and he had seemed to enjoy them. Later, Clydesdale asked Haushofer if he could, out of curiosity, meet with Göring, whom Clydesdale knew both as a hero of the First World War and as the present chief of the Luftwaffe. Göring always loved meetings with the British upper class, and could not resist meeting the daring young man who had conquered Everest.

As had happened with secret agent Winterbotham, Göring saw no need to hide anything from Clydesdale. Instead, he gave the Englishman free rein to visit German air bases, not because he was naive, but because he was determined to cultivate English friends for the main battle ahead. Göring's chief of staff told the Marquis that "I feel we have a common enemy in Bolshevism."[7] Of course, Göring held a huge reception for the Marquis at Karinhall.

Whatever their differences in style and background, Albrecht Haushofer and the Marquis of Clydesdale were drawn to each other. They met in Munich in January of 1937 as the Marquis was returning from a ski trip to the Alps, and both ventured to the home of Albrecht's father. They talked of Clydesdale's exploits, instead of war, peace or politics, and the Marquis arranged to send the old geopolitician a copy of his book, *The Pilot's Book of Everest*. Soon after this, Clydesdale invited Albrecht to England to speak to the Royal Institute of International Affairs at Chatham House on Germany's economic position.[8]

During that visit, Albrecht stayed with Clydesdale at his country residence. Soon after that, Albrecht, who had originally addressed the Marquis in letters as "Dear Lord Clydesdale," started them instead with "My dear Douglo," a most friendly shortening of Clydesdale's common name, Douglas. Albrecht now ended his letters with "Yours forever," instead of the earlier "Yours sincerely." Their relationship was clearly warm, and getting more so.

Haushofer would stay again with Clydesdale at his estate in Dungavel, Scotland, in April 1938. By then he was near to crossing the line, near to becoming a German traitor. At one point he grabbed Clydesdale's atlas and drew lines, without any authority, denoting Hitler's claims on Czechoslovakia.

No one knows exactly how many times Haushofer and Clydesdale met, or the true extent of their correspondence. But theirs was a relationship that would change the war. The Marquis of Clydesdale was soon due to assume a new honorific title and it would become synonymous with the Deputy Führer of Germany. The Marquis was to become the Duke of Hamilton, and his Scottish estate—Dungavel House—would be Rudolf Hess's target.

The glue uniting them was Albrecht Haushofer.

While Haushofer increased his attachment to Hamilton, his estrangement from the Nazis grew. He considered fleeing Germany, but the protection afforded by Hess made that less imperative. Besides, he was a fatalist. He told his mother that he "must . . . make the effort to carry on life until it is taken from me by external forces. . . . I know exactly that I could survive a war in the attitude demanded from me only on one condition; that my own life has become completely indifferent to me, that no event, be it the most atrocious, could produce in me a spark of emotion."[9]

It perhaps would take such a fatalist to take the risks Albrecht now took. In a letter addressed to the Duke forty-seven days before the Second World War began, Albrecht's cold passion crossed the line separating secret opposition to Adolf Hitler from treason.

He had lost hope that "the great man of the regime would be prepared to slow down," he wrote. Now that it was clear that he could not, by working on the inside, tame Hitler, Haushofer decided to do what he could to assure that Hitler had no easy victory. Through Hess, Haushofer was familiar with Hitler's plans. He decided to make England aware of them as well. "I want to send you a word of warning," Haushofer wrote to Hamilton. "To the best of my knowledge there is not yet a definite time-table for the actual explosion, but any date after the middle of August may prove to be the fatal one." He called upon Hamilton to do what he could to avoid the war. As with most in the opposition, he considered Hitler's territorial ambitions acceptable; in fact, he found them inevitable. But he wanted a solution short of war. He cautioned Hamilton: "I cannot imagine even a short-range settlement without a change in the status of Danzig and without some sort of change in the Corridor."[10] Haushofer recommended that the British seek out Mussolini to help pressure Hitler to let time, not arms, settle Germany's problems.

Haushofer knew he had undertaken a dangerous mission. He told Hamilton: "I know that you realize the risk I should be running if the existence of this letter should become known. . . . Therefore, I wanted to add what may seem very curious to you: please destroy this letter after reading it—and destroy it most carefully. But perhaps this is unfair: so I give you freedom for your own discretion to show this letter personally either to Lord H[alifax] or to his Under Secretary Mr. B[utler]—if you see fit of course—under the condition: that no notes should be taken, my name never mentioned, and the letter be destroyed immediately afterwards."[11]

The first person Hamilton showed the letter to was not Halifax or Butler. Hamilton's son, James Douglas-Hamilton, reported in 1971 that his father approached Winston Churchill in the House of Commons and asked to see him that evening. Churchill later met him, draped in a towel after a bath, at his home. He studied the letter very carefully, then uttered: "There is going to be war very soon."[12] Hamilton's son does not explain why his father took the letter to Churchill, who was then a backbencher, out of power and in the wilderness. Whatever the reason, Churchill had learned that there was a traitor in Germany with close ties to the highest Nazis, and to Hamilton. That was not the type of information Churchill easily forgot.

Double Game

By early 1940, Albrecht Haushofer joined the main body of the conspiracy against Hitler. He became a member of the Wednesday Society, supposedly an intellectual discussion group, but in reality a group of about a dozen hard-core members of the resistance, men such as Beck, Hassell, Gördeler and Oster.

By the summer of 1940 the group decided to make another attempt to reach an understanding with British peace interests. Now that Hitler had bloodied British noses and was threatening to do much more, it might be that the British were ready to reason. Haushofer drew up peace proposals: Germany would leave the western territories it had just occupied—France, Denmark, Belgium, Holland and Norway. Further, Germany would recognize Great Britain's special interests in the Mediterranean, the Middle East and India and would use its navy to protect those interests. Britain, in turn, would recognize German special interests in southeast Europe. Poland was covered under this wording: "The regulation of her [Germany's] eastern frontier is regarded by Germany as a special problem which should be settled by the directly concerned states alone, without the participation of the other nations."[13]

The most amazing thing about this proposal is how closely it approximated a formula Hitler was willing to accept.[14] It was so close, in fact, to Hitler's position that by the time it reached the British it may have had something of his blessing. Yet that was weeks away, time enough for Albrecht Haushofer to play another double game.

As the German opposition composed its peace plan, the versatile Albrecht Haushofer began a similar venture on behalf of the Nazis. As the Battle of Britain was set to begin, Hitler and Hess worried that their attack might really harm the British Empire. Hess called in Albrecht Haushofer in early August and asked if there were not among his many British acquaintances someone with whom to reason. Then on August 15—the day the Duke of Windsor miraculously signaled the Germans that he was ready to assume the role as leader of the United Kingdom—Hess ordered Haushofer to begin preparing for a "special task." What that was isn't known.

While Albrecht took on his special task, Hess contacted Albrecht's father. They met at Karl Haushofer's country estate on August 31, and busied themselves with the intractable question of peace. For nine hours Hess and his mentor tried to figure out what the Germans had been missing in their attempts to talk the British into stopping the war. Both knew the Peace Party existed. Neither knew why it did not act. Nothing seemed to move the man at the center. How to bypass Churchill, or eliminate him, was the question.

The two men retired to the night air of the Grunwalder Forest. For three hours they walked in the woods, seeking the right formula, debating options. Suddenly, Haushofer hit upon an idea. There was, he said, a friend of his son—a certain Duke of Hamilton—who could be a vital contact with British peace interests.

Exactly what Haushofer told Hess about this British aristocrat isn't known. Nor is it known why he mentioned his son's close friend at all. But the suggestion wasn't idle. It came instead with a detailed scheme to contact Hamilton. Haushofer said an "old lady" friend, a Mrs. Roberts, lived in Portugal and for some reason would be the perfect conduit to the Duke.[15]

Hess and Haushofer discussed their plans until 2 A.M. September 1, almost a year to the hour since the beginning of the Second World War. Whatever it was that the senior Haushofer had told Hess, it had an immediate effect. The Deputy Führer was suddenly optimistic, his attention galvanized, his idea simple: through Mrs. Roberts was the path to the Duke of Hamilton, and through the Duke of Hamilton was the path that would answer the British Sphinx.

It's not hard to speculate what must have partially attracted Hess to Hamilton. Hess had been told that Hamilton had access to the King and Churchill,[16] and was a high ranking member of the RAF—either a general, an officer controlling "the air defense of an important part of Scotland" or in the Air Ministry itself.[17] Those positions were highly significant. Hess knew of the Air Ministry conspiracy.

Two days later, Karl Haushofer wrote to his son, describing the meeting with Hess. The letter was in the type of code two relatives or friends use when they want to talk secretly. Hess was referred to as "Tomo" and Hitler as "the highest ranking person," and there was much indecipherable talk that would mean nothing to outsiders. Despite the language, the essentials seem clear.

Haushofer told his son that Tomo left the forest walk with an agenda on his mind. "As you know," Haushofer paraphrased Hess as saying, "everything is so prepared for a very hard and severe attack on the island in question that the highest ranking person only has to press a button to set it off. But before this decision, which is perhaps inevitable, the thought once more occurs as to whether there is really no way of stopping something which would have such infinitely momentous consequences. There is a line of reasoning in connection with this which I must absolutely pass on to you because it was obviously communicated to me with this intention. Do you, too, see no way in which such possibilities could be discussed at a third place with a middle man, possibly the old Ian Hamilton [a British general] or the other [Duke of] Hamilton?"

Haushofer said he "replied to these suggestions that there would perhaps have been an excellent opportunity for this in Lisbon at the Centennial, if, instead of harmless figureheads, it had been possible to send well-disguised political persons there."[18]

Then Haushofer turned to the proposed conduit. It was, he said, "a stroke of fate that our old friend, Mrs. V.R. . . . finally found a way of sending a note with cordial and gracious words of good wishes not only for your mother, but also for Heinz [Albrecht's brother] and me, and added the address. Address your reply to: Miss V. Roberts, c/o Postbox 506, Lisbon, Portugal. I have the feeling that no good possibility should be overlooked; at least it should be well considered.

"That the larger stage has suddenly called for you again does not astonish me. Indeed, Tomo, too, on Saturday and Sunday almost expressed a wish to the same effect and was personally delightfully cordial."[19]

There could not have been a more important mission. Two weeks into the Battle of Britain, Hess said that Hitler was prepared for "a very hard and severe attack" on England and had only "to press a button to set it off." This did not refer to the air assault, because that was already well under way. It had to refer to the next stage—

the land invasion of England. Hess had been given the responsibility of finding a way to avoid that.

What was particularly odd about this new peace feeler was the conduit—Mrs. Mary Violet Roberts, a nondescript British expatriate. With all the connections possessed by the Nazis, a hitherto unknown Mrs. Roberts would seem the most unlikely person to whom the Nazis would turn. Yet it was Mrs. Roberts, a woman who remains as anonymous today as she was fifty-four years ago, that the Nazis asked to handle the peace feeler they considered their most important.

And their interest in Mrs. Roberts was not at all passive. "Under no condition must we disregard the contact or allow it to die aborning," Hess told Karl Haushofer. "I consider it best that you or Albrecht write to the old lady, who is a friend of your family, suggesting that she try to ask Albrecht's friend [Hamilton] whether he would be prepared if necessary to come to the neutral territory in which she resides, or at any rate *has an address through which she can be reached*, just to talk to Albrecht [emphasis added]."[20] Clearly, Mrs. Roberts was more than a simple courier. The meeting Hess wanted should either be in Portugal or at some other location where Mrs. Roberts could remain available. Her position was clear. With Haushofer and Hamilton already together, the only logical reason to keep in touch with Mrs. Roberts was if she, in turn, was in contact with some other, important, participant. Mrs. Roberts was not only handling mail.

Karl Haushofer's coded letter to his son might have contained the key to understanding Mrs. Roberts's unusual role. The elder Haushofer had mentioned a "larger stage" that called on Albrecht "again." Had Albrecht Haushofer been involved in an earlier and related effort for the Nazis?

Perhaps he had. Two days before the Duke of Windsor sailed from Portugal, the Duke's would-be abductor, Schellenberg, sent a telegram to someone in Germany initialed "A.H." It read: "Just a note to keep you informed. Our friend 'Tomo' met with 'C' and 'Willi' this morning. Seven points plan was discussed in detail. Meeting again on 29.7 Urgent you contact the old lady as soon as possible. S."[21] Willi was the code name the Germans used for Windsor. Tomo, of course, was to the Haushofers, Rudolf Hess. And A.H. could stand for many people, including Hitler. But Hitler presumably would not be taking orders from Schellenberg to contact the "old lady." A.H. was also the way Albrecht Haushofer signed his correspondence. And since Albrecht Haushofer, Karl Haushofer and Rudolf Hess all referred to Mrs. Roberts as the "old lady," it is not unreasonable to posit that the "old lady" in Schellenberg's telegram was also Rudolf Hess's "old lady." Violet Roberts, after all, was in Lisbon, in contact with top Nazis, and a bridge to the British. If so, then there's no mystery why Hess settled on her. She was, to the Nazis, connected to the most important person of all—the future leader of the United Kingdom, the Duke of Windsor.

Reluctance

Whatever intrigues were taking place in Portugal, Albrecht Haushofer did not seem anxious to have his new friend Hamilton involved. Pressed by Hess for contacts with British peace interests, Albrecht suggested Hamilton last. Better contacts, he told Hess, would be Sam Hoare or Lord Lothian.[22] They were qualified peace party candidates, and professionals at negotiations. Hamilton was an innocent. Besides, Albrecht argued, a letter to Hamilton would probably never arrive. Once it left Mrs. Roberts, anything could happen. Certainly if it suggested German-British negotiations the British censors would snatch it and cause no end of trouble. And even if it did arrive, the Duke could not fly off surreptitiously to a neutral country to meet German agents. He would at least need clearance from Halifax.

It was a credible try to avoid the Deputy Führer's wishes, but it could not succeed. Hess was set on Hamilton and was not to be denied. Besides, there was more than Hess behind the effort. Albrecht had told his father that he had "the strong impression" Hess was operating with "the prior knowledge of the Fuhrer."[23] If Hitler and his deputy wanted Hamilton contacted, Albrecht Haushofer would have to do so, whatever his personal feelings toward the Duke.

Albrecht conceded the inevitable on September 19. He would

write the needed letter to Hamilton. To do so, he said, he would have to take precautions. The British censor must not recognize the letter for what it was. It would have to be extremely circumspect. "In view of my close personal relations and intimate acquaintance with Douglas H[amilton] I can write a few lines to him . . . in such a way that *he alone* will recognize that behind my wish to see him in Lisbon there is something more serious than a personal whim [emphasis in original]."[24] Doing anything else would threaten Hamilton, and Albrecht asked Hess to imagine if the roles were reversed. If a high officer of the Luftwaffe received a letter that directly suggested a foreign rendezvous, the German security services would not be amused. "I do not think that you need much imagination to picture yourself the faces that Canaris or [SD chief Reinhard] Heydrich would make," Haushofer said. "And they would not merely make faces, you may be certain!"[25]

Albrecht had determined to help his Nazi patrons, but in such a way—he apparently thought—that protected his friend Hamilton.

Having met as adults and then only sporadically, it is hard to explain the depth of Albrecht's attachment to the Duke. The words Albrecht used when the subject was Hamilton border on the romantic. That certainly seemed to be the case in the September 23 letter Albrecht sent, through Mrs. Roberts, to Hamilton. In it, Albrecht said: "I am sure you know that my attachment to you remains unaltered and unalterable, whatever the circumstances may be."[26]

Those were warm words in a letter whose subject was deadly serious. Deeper in the letter, Albrecht told the Duke: "If you remember some of my last communications in July 1939, you—and your friends in high places—may find some significance in the fact that I am able to ask you whether you could find time to have a talk with me somewhere on the outskirts of Europe, perhaps in Portugal. I could reach Lisbon any time (and without any kind of difficulties) within a few days after receiving news from you. Of course I do not know whether you can make your authorities understand so much, that they give you leave.

"But at least you may be able to answer my question. Letters will reach me (fairly quickly; they would take some four or five days from Lisbon on the utmost) in the following way: double closed envelope: inside address; 'Dr. A. H.' Nothing more! Outside address: Minero Silricola Ltd., Rau do Cais de Santarem 32/1, Lisbon, Portugal." [27]

If Haushofer actually thought this wording was too clever for the British Secret Intelligence Service, he was being highly naive. The letter was intercepted by British authorities a few days after it was sent along by Mrs. Roberts, if, in fact, she didn't send it directly to them in the first place. From there it descended into the shadow world, not to reappear for five months when the British master of the Double Cross System would make a certain proposition to the Duke of Hamilton.

How many other letters were sent through Mrs. Roberts, and how many came back through her to the Nazis isn't known. There were, however, several. Karl Haushofer said after the war that the Haushofers sent many Hess-inspired letters through Portugal, and that Hess had received replies. [28] Since the Duke of Hamilton had not received the letters, it was someone else who was replying. The SIS appeared to be in direct contact with the Deputy Führer.

Albrecht Haushofer soon lost his unwanted monopoly on connections to the Duke of Hamilton. By October, only weeks after the first message to Hamilton was sent, Hess himself began composing letters to the Duke. [29] For this, he used his close associate, Ernst Bohle. Bohle was a senior Nazi official who headed the NSDAP organization, which maintained contacts with Germans living abroad. He had been born in England, lived as a youth in South Africa and maintained British citizenship until renouncing it in 1937. English was his first language.

Hess, whose knowledge of English was itself excellent, nevertheless wrote his letters in German and had Bohle translate them into English. Bohle made the translation and typed a letter, which was revised and added to until early January 1941. [30] There may have been several letters translated and sent, for Bohle referred to them in the plural.

To Bohle, the contents of these letters "seemed sensible and clear." He said after the war that nowhere in the translations was there talk of Hess meeting Hamilton in Great Britain. There was, however, a suggestion of a Hess-Hamilton rendezvous in Switzerland. And when he learned of that Bohle "suggested that he would like to accompany Hess, in view of his own British background, and Hess replied that if he took anyone it would, of course, be Bohle."[31]

Bohle thought the enterprise had the feel of a grand and exciting secret mission. He felt there were only three people in Germany who knew the high-stakes game being played: Hitler, Hess and himself. He did not know of Albrecht Haushofer's involvement, or that of Albrecht's father.

While Hitler and Hess went out in search of the perfect link to the Peace Party, the Peace Party continued to offer encouragement. On October 23, Hitler learned via Sweden that the British ambassador was again sending unmistakable peace signals. The British, he told an intermediary, were ready for behind-the-scenes discussions on German terms. The Nazi security service cabled Berlin that "England would be satisfied with as little as cultural autonomy for Poland." Further: "England is attempting to create for herself a similar retreat with respect to the other European countries . . . by intimating that here, too, she might accept concessions on the part of Germany in the cultural field as a solution." And finally there came a name that Hitler had not heard mentioned lately in the cause of peace: "To all appearances, Churchill wishes to achieve a peace, which would save the face of the British Empire as much as possible."[32]

Hitler's agents learned in Geneva on December 4 that a "highly respected" member of the Conservative Party, and a boyhood friend of Churchill, was saying that the British cabinet was split, and that some of its members were required to make "warlike speeches which are not quite in accordance with their views."[33]

Other peace feelers came to Berlin. But they all continued to have the same fault—they never produced results. Hess and Hitler were now set on proactive approaches to Hamilton and Windsor. They didn't want to just talk of peace. They planned to force it.

Albrecht Haushofer, while appearing to be reluctant to involve his friend Hamilton, showed no reluctance when it came to himself.

He, too, was being proactive. And as always, he was versatile. While officially working with Hess to find Hamilton, he searched for other British contacts for the German resistance. In fact, he may even have managed to combine both jobs.

After composing the peace plan for the resistance, Haushofer needed to get it to someone in Britain who could negotiate with them. In September 1940, he met with a former student of his— Heinrich Stahmer, a secretary to the German mission in Madrid— and convinced him to give the proposal to a man whom Albrecht had mentioned frequently: Samuel Hoare.

Stahmer was most impressed when Haushofer showed him some letters to Hamilton and to Hess. It was obvious the Deputy Führer knew about the mission, Stahmer thought, and so he agreed to go ahead. During subsequent negotiations, the talks with Hoare took on an official, and at times, amazing tone. After the war, Stahmer said the German side proposed holding an informal meeting in Spain or Portugal with Hoare and Halifax on one side and Hess and Albrecht Haushofer on the other.[34] Since there is no way the loyal Hess would have been operating without Hitler's knowledge, Hitler must have known of the Hoare contact.

What is even more remarkable was a proposal made by the German side and agreed to by Hoare and whoever he represented. If Stahmer's memory is correct, Hess and Hitler were prepared for a move so dramatic that if it was suggested by anyone other than a strange and obsessed Austrian artist turned dictator, it would have to be rejected out of hand. Stahmer said that a peace settlement would force both Hitler and Churchill from power.

Whether Hitler—who had previously allowed discussion of this possibility to take place at Venlo and had returned to it occasionally—would have stepped aside is impossible to say. Common sense would argue against it, but Hitler was peculiar and obsessed. If by stepping aside he could win his cherished alliance with England and retire as a German hero, he may have been at least willing to consider it.

For Churchill, though, there was no possibility of leaving. He was playing a game he thought he could win. The best interpretation seems to be that this was a move in the shadow war meant to prove the Peace Party was not only serious, but powerful. If Hoare felt free to talk of the removal of the Prime Minister, he was clearly both.

Training

While Albrecht Haushofer played his double game, Rudolf Hess began painstaking preparations for some special and highly secret project. It all involved a flight he might take, somewhere. Publicly, Hitler had forbidden Rudolf Hess to fly—fearing, he said, the accidental loss of his deputy. Privately, things were different. Hitler's personal pilot, Hans Baur, trained Hess on a Messerschmidt aircraft, which Willy Messerschmidt personally altered with reserve fuel tanks to give the plane range enough to reach Dungavel House, or some other distant destination.[35] And from the Wehrmacht's High Command, Hess began receiving weather and tactical maps of Europe. Hess was clearly not trying to hide his flying from the Führer.

Though Hess was preparing for a flight, his training did not presage a trip to Switzerland, as Bohle thought. If that's where Hess was heading, he would have been better served by a train or a car than a Messerschmidt-110. He certainly wouldn't have needed extra fuel tanks if, for some odd reason, he did intend to fly there. Hess was planning a long-distance flight. A high British official later told the American military attaché in London that the original plan was for Hess to travel to Lisbon to meet Hamilton.[36] That confirms Stahmer's story at one point, at least: Albrecht Haushofer was arranging a meeting between the Duke of Hamilton and the Deputy Führer on neutral ground.

Still, already nascent in Hess's mind might have been an even more unlikely destination. Hess may have needed extra fuel tanks to get to Lisbon, but he would have hardly had to travel there alone. Just as Schellenberg had no trouble getting to Lisbon to try to negotiate with Windsor, the SS could certainly have arranged for Hess to go to Portugal—incognito as Karl Haushofer had suggested— without the risks attendant with a solo flight.

By one account, since October 1940 Adolf Hitler and Rudolf Hess had settled upon Scotland as the target, a grand gesture to bring on a German-English peace so that Hitler could invade the Soviet

Union. The two had even prepared a cover story if the mission went awry. "In such an unlikely event," Hess reportedly said, "you could declare publicly you had no knowledge of my intentions and could denounce me as a traitor to the cause of National Socialism."[37]

By whatever measure, Hess prepared in detail. Hess's wife, Ilse, recalled that her husband traveled to an airport near Augsburg once or twice a week for training flights. Messerschmidt estimated that Hess made some twenty or so such training flights. Whatever the count, Hess was fastidious. The Nazis even provided him with the spectacularly tailored black-leather flying suit he would wear on the eventual mission. He also began using a radio set, operated from a back room in his home.[38] Hess was in contact with someone.

Ilse recalled Hess's preparation as a time of great mystery. Once, while waiting in her husband's office, Ilse picked up the telephone. "A voice filled with matter-of-fact conviction," she said, "and evidently conveying some expected message, gave me a weather report for some mysterious places referred to as X and Y. Rather astonished, I jotted down this, to me, quite incomprehensible message. But I noticed from the confused manner of the secretary, who had just come in, that this was something I was not supposed to know anything about!"[39]

How many times, if any, Hess actually began his flight only to turn back isn't known. Some who were close to him believe Hess made at least two false starts. The first known time he actually seemed to prepare for something other than a training flight was on January 11, 1941, two days after Hitler reaffirmed his decision to attack the Soviet Union in a conference with his generals.[40] The next alleged attempt came March or April; accounts vary. Whether real or not, these extended flights left a permanent impression on Hess's aides.

One reason his aides thought these two attempts were real was the letter Hess gave them before the flights with the demand that should he not return to Augsburg after four hours, they were to open it and take it to Hitler. One of his flights lasted four and a half hours and Hess's adjutant, Karl-Heinz Pintsch, opened the letter and to his horror discovered that Hess was flying to Great Britain. When two of Hess's bodyguards asked what the letter said, Pintsch simply handed them the letter.

But Hess had not gone to Great Britain. The roar of his plane was heard overhead and soon Hess was on the ground again, with some explaining to do. He swore Pintsch to silence, but the bodyguards were a different matter. They reported to Reinhard Heydrich and had made daily reports to the SD chief about Hess's training. According to the account of Journalist Wulf Schwarzwäller, this time was no exception. They told Heydrich of the flight, the letter and the plan to go to Britain.

If there was any doubt about the level of clearance Hess's training had, it was resolved by Heydrich's reply. He told the guards: "As usual, continue to report."[41]

As usual, Hitler's generals did not know precisely what was happening. In late November 1940, Halder wrote: "It is heartening to see that the Führer is again taking an interest in Sea Lion."[42] On December 5, it was Operation Otto, shortly to be renamed Barbarossa, that was foremost. Sea Lion, Hitler instructed his generals, could "be left out of our consideration."[43] On the thirteenth, Halder underlined this passage in his diary after hearing from the Führer: "*We do not seek conflict with Russia.*"[44] Five days later, Hitler issued Directive No. 21, which specified that the coming conflict would be with Russia. However, on the same day, he mixed that decision with an overreaching need for peace with Britain. Wrote Halder: "He [Hitler] is always thinking of making peace with England at the expense of France."[45]

For the next few months, Hitler acted very much like a man trying hard and unsuccessfully to persuade his generals that there was logic to attacking Russia while leaving Britain in the war. What the generals didn't know was how hard Hitler was now working to remove Britain from the war. It was the same carrot and stick operation as before, only this time the carrot would be carried by the Deputy Führer himself. And the stick would seem as ominous as ever.

Was There Time?

No matter how many tracks the British were using to convince Hitler it was safe to turn east, he was not turning there fast enough.

Nor did British hopes on America seem to be working. Ultra may have been telling London the Wehrmacht was pointing toward Moscow, but Hitler's reply so far to a shower of peace feelers was a shower of iron. As air raid sirens sounded at night, Britons knew that the Luftwaffe was not decreasing, but increasing, its bombings. If Göring was trying to husband ordnance for the great drive east, he was doing so in a most peculiar way.

Hitler had been prepared to invade the West twenty-seven times during the Phony War until the day he finally did so. And even then the way he did it was a surprise. The man was unpredictable.

The question for the British leadership was simple. If, for some reason, Hitler did not invade Russia or substantially delayed, could Great Britain survive?

By early 1941, hopes on America were fading. The United States did send Britain fifty old American destroyers, but little else. America was not mobilized, and, in the absence of some dramatic provocation, might not be mobilized for five years, if even then.

Churchill's agent in America, William Stephenson, had done his best. He had planted false stories about Germany, bought journalists, entrapped politicians, blackmailed opponents of U.S. involvement. He had even helped to place a person the British Secret Intelligence Service called "our man"—William "Wild Bill" Donovan—as head of the OSS, America's wartime spy agency.[46] Yet none of this, so far, had pushed America to war.

British plans to woo America were stalled not because the President was unconvinced, but because the public was. Churchill had Roosevelt firmly in hand. Long after the Prime Minister learned that Sea Lion had been called off, he continued to tell Roosevelt the opposite: England was about to be invaded, and the fleet was in danger. The President believed it.

On January 17, Secretary of the Navy Frank Knox told the House Foreign Affairs Committee that the only thing standing between the Americas and the Germans was the British fleet, and if Hitler got that, his sea power would be seven times more than that of the United States.[47] William Bullitt, American ambassador at large, followed that up the next week by testifying that an invasion of the Isles was imminent, and the consequences particularly terrifying. "Should the British Navy be eliminated," he testified, "and should the Panama Canal be blocked before we are prepared, invasion of the Western Hemisphere here would be almost certain."[48] Churchill sent Roosevelt a private letter three days later with this prevarication: "All my information shows that the Germans are persevering in their preparations to invade this country and we are getting ready to give them a reception worthy of the occasion."[49] George Marshall, chairman of the Joint Chiefs of Staff, wasted no time disseminating Churchill's propaganda. He called a news conference to reveal that Germany would invade Great Britain that spring. Knox followed with a declaration that if Britain was defeated he was "positive" the Americas would be invaded, in which case, he said, "the odds are against us."[50]

The effort to distort Hitler's real goals was working well at the highest levels, but hardly anywhere else. The country was isolationist, and the picture of the Huns marching through Mexico still seemed rather silly, which it was. Two thirds of Americans were against any military intervention at all. Churchill had misjudged.

There were more immediate problems for the British than American reluctance to fight their war. On February 6, 1941, Erwin Rommel took over two fledgling German divisions and with this token force soon made clear that, even outnumbered, German troops could have their way with the British. The first of Rommel's troops landed at Tripoli on the fourteenth. Two weeks later, he was pushing the British back.

Rommel was in North Africa because the British were in North Africa. And the British were there because of oil. North Africa was the route to Iraq and the Persian Gulf. And the oil from Iraq and the Persian Gulf was the only thing that kept the British fleet afloat. General Friedrich Paulus observed that an invasion was not Britain's primary worry. "England's foremost concern is the eastern Mediterranean and the land route to India."[51]

Hitler continued to send Rommel troops, though not in the quantity Rommel wanted. Would Hitler's ever creative military imagination hit upon the strategy that would win the war? Britain's position was not yet desperate, but it was certainly not improving. It was time to accelerate the shadow war.

On January 30, the British did something they had not done since

Venlo. Either in response to Albrecht Haushofer's approach to Sam
Hoare, or his letters to Hamilton, or both, the British now chose to
hand the Germans specific proposals for peace.

Carl Burckhardt contacted Ulrich von Hassell in Geneva. He said
he had news from the British government, delivered to him by a
trusted intermediary. The intermediary, Burckhardt said, told him
that "a reasonable peace could still be concluded."[52] The terms were
better than any Albrecht Haushofer or even Adolf Hitler had so far
advanced. Holland and Belgium were to be restored, but Denmark
would "remain in the German sphere of influence." Additionally,
"some kind of Poland (minus the former German provinces) to be
resurrected for reasons of prestige. Otherwise no special interest in
the East (not even for Czechoslovakia)." Though this was astonishing enough, what followed was stunning: "Former German
colonies to Germany. The British Empire to remain otherwise un-
shorn. England had no special passion for France."[53]

The British now appeared not only to offer terms, but generous
ones. They would be clearly acceptable to Hitler, who would not
have missed the significance of England's lack of "special interest
in the East." There was, though, an old problem: would the British
make this peace with Hitler? Hassell said he learned that "one was
highly reluctant to make peace with Hitler. The main reason, one
simply can't believe a word he says. The English Counsel General
also told Carl Burckhardt recently that in no event would peace be
made with Hitler."[54]

Instead of taking this critical new information to Halder or other
military members of the resistance, Hassell sought out Hess's ally,
Albrecht Haushofer. Haushofer relayed the peace feeler to Hess,
who in turn told Hitler.[55] On March 10, 1941, Albrecht told Hassell:
"There is an urgent desire for peace in high quarters."[56]

Hassell tried to find a way to get Haushofer to Burckhardt so that
he could "come home with an authentic confirmation" that a peace
treaty would automatically follow a change of regime. The main
step was taken in April, when Burckhardt wrote to Albrecht that he
had "greetings to pass on to me from someone in my old circle of
English friends."[57] He suggested that Albrecht come to see him directly. There was little question in Albrecht's mind but the "old cir-

cle" meant Hamilton.[58] He took the letter to Hess, and Hess authorized his mission to Geneva. Before he left, the German resistance warned Burckhardt that Haushofer "was coming with two faces"—for the resistance and for Hess.[59]

Actually, Albrecht probably wore three faces. His father recalled that Albrecht was also supposed to either meet or communicate with Sam Hoare,[60] with whom Albrecht had been discussing a change of regime in Germany.

By this point, talk of such a change was clearly being considered. While waiting for Albrecht Haushofer to arrive, Burckhardt was visited by an agent of Heinrich Himmler's. The agent asked if the British would accept the SS chief as an acceptable substitute for Hitler.[61]

Double Cross

Across the Channel, the Duke of Hamilton was quietly informed that his government had a great deal of interest in his friend Albrecht Haushofer. British air intelligence—the same organization running William de Ropp and his contacts with Alfred Rosenberg—had in February asked Hamilton to visit the office of Group Captain F. G. Stammers. When the meeting finally took place in mid-March, Hamilton was put on the defensive. "What," he was asked, "had [he] done with the letter which Albrecht Haushofer had written to him?"[62] A photo copy of the September 23 letter was passed to him. Hamilton had never seen it, but the implication was clear. British intelligence had a copy of a letter that involved the Duke in possible treason. A member of the German Foreign Ministry had sought a secret rendezvous with the Duke in Portugal.

Albrecht had been right. His innocent friend could be destroyed by the whole affair. Hamilton was left to ponder his fate for a month. In mid-April, as Haushofer was planning his meeting with Burckhardt, Hamilton was ordered to appear before Group Captain D. L. Blackford, who worked with Winterbotham in the Air Ministry's intelligence office.[63] When the Duke appeared at 11:30 A.M. April 25, he was met not only by Blackford but also by one of the Second

World War's deadliest practitioners of deceit. T. A. Robertson, of British Counter Intelligence, was the man in charge of capturing German officers and agents and forcing them to report back to the Third Reich information he and his superiors scripted. Those that agreed lived, at least for a time. Those that refused were often executed. It was called the Double Cross System.[64]

Robertson asked Hamilton to do something only a man fearing public humiliation or worse would ever do. He asked Hamilton to betray his friend. They wanted Hamilton to go to Portugal to meet Haushofer and perhaps others, acting outwardly as a friend and secretly as a British agent. What exactly he was to do with Haushofer isn't known. Given Stahmer's testimony that the Germans had proposed a meeting between Hamilton and Halifax on one side and Hess and Haushofer on the other, this trip was likely only a step toward accomplishing some even deeper goal.

Albrecht Haushofer had resisted involving his friend Hamilton in a deadly game, but had done so when Adolf Hitler said he must. Hamilton also tried to protect his special friend, but would bow to pressure as well. Having been braced with the possible accusation of treason by Blackford and then intimidated even more by Robertson, Hamilton was still honorable. On April 28, Hamilton agreed to undertake the mission, but he tried to make conditions. Fearful that somehow his trip could be confused as a real attempt by him to negotiate with the Nazis, Hamilton asked that Sam Hoare be informed beforehand of the mission. Further, he tried to protect Haushofer. He told these hard men that "it would be dangerous to allow him to believe that the authorities had withheld his letter from me last autumn and had now released it and had asked me to answer it."[65] He must, Hamilton argued, be told why the letter had been intercepted.[66]

To Churchill's men, what the Duke of Hamilton wanted or didn't want was unimportant. He would go if they needed him to go. But April 28 was also the day that Albrecht Haushofer met in Switzerland with Burckhardt and that seemed to change matters. Hamilton would not be meeting Hess or Haushofer in Portugal. Instead, the Deputy Führer would be coming to him.

Soon there was word that Rudolf Hess was planning a flight to a peace meeting. In mid-month, British intelligence sources reported to London that Hess had actually flown to Madrid for peace talks.[67] The plan that had taken so long to mature appeared finally to be ready. And the leaks were coming not from Germany, but elsewhere.

If so, it may have been just in time for England. Her position seemed everywhere to be crumbling, the situation was desperate. If Hitler did not push east soon, England could face defeat anyway. Rommel won Benghazi on April 4; two days later, German forces swept into Greece, relentlessly pushing the British back. On the ninth, as Rommel's forces overran Bardia, the German Second Panzer Division smashed Salonika in Greece. The Allies tried a new defensive position around Mount Olympus, but were forced to retreat. The Germans were relentlessly eliminating the British from Continental Europe.

Britain dispatched troops to Iraq on the nineteenth to try to put down a rebellion that threatened Britain's lifeline to oil. Within a day, the Iraqi leader said he would allow no more British troops in his country. Britain's oil lifeline was in mortal danger.

Greece capitulated on the twentieth, and the British headed for another ignominious evacuation, managing to extricate forty thousand men. As with Dunkirk, they left without their equipment. Three days before Haushofer met Burckhardt, Rommel took the Halfaya Pass in Egypt. If he made it to Suez, Churchill's government could have fallen.

Events were quickly outpacing any British plans. Nothing the British had done so far gave them any reason to hope that they could stop Rommel, or, indeed, any German general. They hadn't managed to do so anywhere. Wrote Churchill years later: "Looking back upon the unceasing tumult of the war, I cannot recall any period when its stresses and the onset of so many problems all at once or in rapid succession bore more directly on me and my colleagues than the first half of 1941."[68] If there was a contingency plan, it was time to launch it.

By then Haushofer returned from his Geneva talks and told Hassell that "England still wants peace on a rational basis, but (1) not with our present rulers, and (2) perhaps not for much longer."[69]

There was urgency on both sides. If Hitler was to gain his dream, it's possible he too felt there may be no better moment.

Flight

On May 5, 1941, Albrecht Haushofer composed at Hitler's mountain chalet a memorandum for the Führer concerning his discussions in Geneva.[70] The same day in Berlin, Hitler had one of the longest meetings he held during this part of the war. For four hours he and Rudolf Hess met in the Reichschancellory—alone, without secretaries or aides. One person, outside the doors, later reported hearing snippets of the discussions.[71] Adjutant Alfred Leitgen said none of it made sense, but he did recall hearing someone mention the names: "Albrecht Haushofer" and "Hamilton." He also recalled this odd phrase: "No problems at all with the airplane." And from Hess he heard the fragment: "simply declared insane!"[72]

After the marathon session the Führer and his deputy emerged, appearing particularly affectionate. Leitgen said that Hitler "held Hess's hand in his for minutes. They silently looked into each other's eyes." Another account is similar. It says that as the two emerged, Hitler put his arm around Rudolf Hess as though the two were taking leave. "Hess," Hitler gibed, "you are and always were thoroughly pig-headed."[73]

Hess went to Augsburg and summoned Albrecht for a briefing. The news from Geneva was very favorable—whatever that news was—and Hess told Albrecht to recontact Burckhardt.[74]

On Friday, May 9, Hess telephoned Alfred Rosenberg, who was in Berlin. Rosenberg, Hess said, must come immediately to Munich. Hess had already arranged for a plane to ferry Rosenberg across Germany. Rosenberg's most important job in the Nazi Party had been to keep in contact with William de Ropp, the Balt that air intelligence had used to convince the Nazis that an anti-Churchill revolution would take place inside the Air Ministry. Rosenberg would be just the man to contact if Rudolf Hess decided to fly away to Britain to meet these revolutionaries. Why this should be done suddenly is not known. But it did appear that Hess was making a change of plans. On the same day he summoned Rosenberg, Hess tried repeatedly to reach a colleague to cancel a meeting scheduled for later in May.[75]

Rosenberg finally arrived at Hess's home in Harlaching in the late morning of Saturday, May 10. He and Hess dined alone. The Deputy Führer made sure that no one overheard what was said, asking his wife, Ilse, to keep the servants away.[76] The meeting ended at 1 P.M. and Rosenberg left immediately to see Adolf Hitler at Obersalzberg, some 110 miles away.[77] There are no records or notes concerning what Hess and Rosenberg discussed or of what Rosenberg later told to Hitler. But it was clear extreme security was involved. If not, Hess could have simply told Rosenberg on the telephone what he had in mind, instead of sending a plane to bring him to Munich. For his part, Rosenberg could have also called the Führer instead of speeding away to meet him in person. Yet with people such as Himmler already vying to replace him, perhaps the Führer and his deputy were merely being prudent.

After Rosenberg left to see Hitler, Hess seemed relaxed. In fact, he took a nap, awaking at 2:30 P.M. to take tea with his wife. Ilse Hess suspected that something significant was happening but did not know what. Ilse gave her version of her last hours with her husband in a book she published in 1954: Rudolf "arrived for his tea, having changed his clothes and, much to my surprise, was wearing bluish-grey breeches and high airman's boots, most unusual! Casually he remarked that he had received a call from Berlin in the meantime and would be making a short detour to Augsburg on his way to headquarters. . . .

"When I asked him the meaning of the blue shirt, he smiled and gave the charming explanation: 'To give you a pleasant surprise!' What, I wonder, did he *really* think and feel a couple hours before he took off on his flight to England? We can only conjecture. I can see my husband standing there before me as if it were yesterday. And I remember so clearly how doubtfully I received this surprising piece of matrimonial gallantry. Tea over, he kissed my hand and stood at the door of the nursery, grown suddenly very grave, with the air of one deep in thought and almost hesitating [emphasis in original]."

Ilse asked her husband: "When will you be coming back?"

He responded: "I am not quite certain, perhaps tomorrow; but I should certainly be home by Monday evening."[78]

Pintsch and the two bodyguards picked up Hess at his home and left for Augsburg. But just outside the city and into the forest, Hess asked the driver to stop. He gathered about him some weather maps and began walking through the woods, apparently studying the maps, but soon losing interest. He looked about and strolled alone. This was not a man in a rush, certainly not a man concerned about what Rosenberg might be telling Adolf Hitler. Perhaps this was even a man who knew he had time enough to wait for Hitler's response. Whatever, Hess meandered, taking in the feel of Germany during his last day as a free man.[79]

He eventually returned and the group made its way to the airport where Hess's ME-110 awaited.

The reason for Hess's blue shirt, which had seemed out of character to Ilse, was soon apparent. From his black suitcase Hess took out his leather Luftwaffe flying jacket. Rudolf Hess was becoming Captain Alfred Horn, an unknown man with a lengthy letter for the Duke of Hamilton.

At 6 P.M., May 10, 1941, Rudolf Hess fired up the twin engines of his Messerschmidt and flew west.

13 : *Deal*

"Zenchen" thinks that it is not yet time for peace talks. As the war develops, however, Hess could become the center of intrigue for the conclusion of a compromise peace and could be useful to both the Peace Party in Britain and Hitler.

—*A secret report to Stalin concerning espionage from Russian spy Zenchen (Kim Philby)*

Since German border incursions on April 5, Josef Stalin believed that war with Germany was inevitable. But he was determined to postpone it for a year, believing Hitler would be accommodating. Certainly, Stalin felt, Hitler would not attack before eliminating Great Britain. Instead he would do the logical thing: he would land his troops in Iraq and Syria and allow Rommel to checkmate Egypt. That done, Britain would be without oil or gas and would crumble.[1] Then, Hitler would come to Russia.

However, Stalin was not naive. He thought that the British leadership would see the same game, and would try to do everything possible to turn Hitler away from the Middle East and toward Moscow, or conversely try to get Stalin to strike first. Therefore, the warnings he was receiving about a German invasion he interpreted as provocations—British attempts to move him to war. It simply would make no sense for Hitler to attack. Stalin increased military readiness, but did not order full mobilization. Instead, he decided to placate the German dictator, and increased deliveries of raw materials to Germany.[2] Then came Hess.

Stalin thought from the start that the mission was part of the larger British attempt to shift the direction of the war. But he could not understand why the British had allowed the affair to be made public. There was danger here, and Stalin needed answers.

The issue of what Hess was doing in Scotland was suddenly the central focus of Soviet intelligence. On May 14, the Soviet NKVD (predecessor to the KGB) resident in London cabled Moscow that Soviet mole Kim Philby, code-named Zenchen, was attempting to find out more about the Deputy Führer's mission. Released by the KGB in 1991, the cable, the Russians say, read:

Top Secret
Memo

Vadim reporting from London:

1. According to "Zenchen," Hess said on arrival in Britain that first of all he wanted to contact Hamilton whom he had met in 1934 when they both participated in aviation competitions. Hamilton belongs to the so-called Cliveden clique. Hess landed near Hamilton's estate;

2. Hess told Kirkpatrick, the first Back Street employee who recognized him, that he had brought peace proposals. We do not know yet what these proposals are. (Kirkpatrick is a former employee of the British Embassy in Berlin.)

May 14, 1941. No. 376.[3]

On the bottom of the cable, the NKDV ordered agent Boris Rybukin: "Forward this cable to Berlin, London, Stockholm, America and Rome. Request: Try to find out the details of these proposals."[4]

Reports poured into Moscow Center. An agent code-named Git reported from America that "Hess arrived in England to start negotiations on a truce, and it had been fully agreed to by Hitler. Since it was impossible for Hitler to openly propose a truce without losses to German morale, he chose Hess as his secret emissary."[5] From Berlin, agent Yun cabled that "Hess is in excellent condition and flew to England on the German government's assignment." Another agent, with supposed connections with the Wehrmacht's High

Command confirmed that "the action taken by Hess is not a defection, but a mission of proposing peace to England, approved by Hitler." Another agent called Extern told Moscow that "Hess was sent by Hitler to negotiate peace, and in the case England agrees, Germany will immediately attack the USSR."[6]

Still there was no confirmation from London that Hess had brought word of an invasion of Russia. But Philby reported on the eighteenth, however, that he had learned from Tom Dupree, deputy head of the Foreign Office's press department, that high government officials were indeed meeting with Hess. Further, it was clear that Hess had come to Scotland to meet with the Peace Party that had been carefully created by the SIS, and that the British were going to preserve him for possible later negotiations with Adolf Hitler. A mere eight days into the Hess Affair, Stalin had good insight that it was somehow more important than the press reported. A cable to Moscow read: "[Lord] Beaverbrook and [Anthony] Eden visited Hess. However, this is officially denied.

"Hess said in a conversation with [Ivone] Kirkpatrick that a war between the two northern peoples was a crime. He thinks that there is a strong anti-Churchill party in Britain which stands for peace. His arrival, he contends, will give it a powerful impetus in the struggle for peace.

"When asked by 'Zenchen' whether he thought a British-German alliance against the USSR would be acceptable for Hess, Tom Dupree said this was precisely Hess's aim. . . .

" 'Zenchen' thinks that it is not yet time for peace talks. As the war develops, however, Hess could become the center of intrigue for the conclusion of a compromise peace and could be useful to both the Peace Party in Britain and Hitler."[7]

If the secret documents are accurate, Stalin now knew why the British had decided to keep so mum on Hess and were refusing to use him for propaganda purposes. Hess was too important to waste. If he was discredited or used to issue anti-Hitler propaganda, he would never be able to negotiate on behalf of Adolf Hitler if Britain wanted a separate peace. What Stalin didn't know, but probably could have guessed, was whether the British had lured Hess to Scotland in the first place, and whether he brought word of the coming invasion.

America, which in May was stonewalled by the British when its President sought the truth about the Hess mission, would learn half of the answer in November. A year later, Stalin would learn the other half, and it would change the history of the twentieth century.

On October 31, Captain Raymond Lee, military attaché in the American embassy in London, was met by a breathless reporter named Laird who had just been given a detailed memo on the Hess affair by someone "intimately associated" with Churchill.[8] Lee later revealed in his diary that the source was Churchill's intelligence liaison Desmond Morton, whom he called "one of the discreet and shadowy figures who surround the Prime Minister."[9] The information was sensational. Lee called it the "story of the year," which the unfortunate newsman couldn't publish for security reasons.[10] Lee showed the information to Ambassador Winant on November 4, then cabled a memo to Brigadier General Sherman Miles, assistant chief of staff of army intelligence. For the first time, official Washington learned that Hess "gave warning of Hitler's intentions to invade Russia."[11] The explosiveness of that one fact was appreciated by Lee, who asked the general not to "duplicate this memorandum and show it only to such individuals as are really entitled to read it, as it would be a pity if it were traced back, through me, to my informant."[12] (For the full text of Lee's cable, see Chapter Two.)

Cold Revelations

As Washington was learning more about the Hess mission, so was Stalin. One of Moscow's spies, whose identity has not been disclosed, sent the Soviet leader almost identical information as that which had gone to General Miles. Stalin learned that Hess had said upon arrival: "If Britain continued to fight in the west, we would have to eliminate it after we had eliminated Russia."[13] Almost instantly, Stalin's suspicions about England grew. There was nothing in the cable that indicated that Hess had any prior contact with England, save a lone letter to the Duke of Hamilton. Nor was there anything indicating that Hess had brought with him detailed proposals for a settlement. Still, there was enough to raise two simple questions: Why, if Churchill knew of Hess's statements, did he not tell Stalin? And did the silence that followed Hess's mission indicate tacit approval of Hitler's designs?[14] Stalin could not have been pleased to read that Morton—Churchill's intelligence man—had "visited Hess several times."[15]

Captain Lee noticed a sudden change in Soviet perspective. He wrote in his diary: "There is extremely bad news from [British Ambassador] Sir Stafford Cripps who, in his cable to the Foreign Office, said that popular opinion in Moscow is now beginning to be aroused over the lack of British activity and there are accusations becoming audible that the British are letting the Russians down by not opening up a second front anywhere."[16]

However, with no evidence that the British were actually colluding with Hess, Stalin turned his attention to the more pressing issue of survival. Hitler was at his throat and defeat was possible. It would not be for another year—in October 1942—that Stalin would learn the truth of the Hess Affair. By then, a lot of what had happened during the first part of the year would seem to him more understandable, more defined. And that knowledge would have deep consequences for the war and the peace that followed.

Nineteen forty-two had been terrible for the Russian dictator. The Americans promised help. The British mostly continued to refuse. The U.S. Joint Chiefs of Staff and their President had planned a second front in Europe, primarily to deflect enough of the Wehrmacht, which was grinding down the Red Army. In March, Roosevelt told Churchill that he was "becoming more and more interested in the establishment of this new front . . . this summer." He said he knew there would be losses but said they were worth taking. "Such losses will be compensated by at least equal German losses and by compelling Germans to divert large forces of all kinds from Russian fronts."[17] Churchill was not impressed and paid only lip service to the President's plea. In April, Roosevelt complained to Churchill that "the Russians are today killing more Germans and destroying more equipment than you and I put together." And said of the second front: "Go to it!"[18] Roosevelt also went further and told Soviet Foreign Minister Molotov of his attitude, pledging a second front as soon as possible in 1942. Naturally the Soviets were pleased. The sooner it could start, the better.

Winston Churchill had no intention of creating a second front in 1942, as he would have no intention of doing so in 1943, or indeed even 1944. Never once did Churchill advocate a direct assault on Hitler's Europe. In 1942, Churchill would not only block the second front, but he was growingly unwilling to protect convoys of American supplies headed for the Russian ports of Murmansk and Archangel. Hearing in April that the convoys would be deferred, Roosevelt told Churchill he was "greatly disturbed" and feared the "political repercussions in Russia."[19] Churchill replied: "With very great respect, what you suggest is beyond our power to fulfil."[20] Instead, Churchill lobbied hard for more supplies for Great Britain, even on May 20 making a not so veiled threat to settle with Hitler unless this happened. He told the American President that unless more planes were delivered in quantity "an entirely new view of the war would have to be taken."[21]

Molotov went to London to press for both the second front and the aid. He asked the British the critical question: "Supposing the Soviet Army failed to hold out against the maximum effort which Hitler would undoubtedly exert during 1942, how would the British Government view the position in which they would be placed?"[22] Churchill still refused all suggestions of a second front, and soon some in the American High Command suspected that British war policy now had considerably less to do with beating Hitler than with extending Britain's colonial empire.[23]

Churchill traveled to Moscow to try to placate Stalin in August, but the Russian bear was hard to placate. He wanted deeds, not words, and Churchill's plan for the Allies to land in North Africa seemed to Stalin not only ineffective but no help at all to the Red Army. And he was right. The landing in North Africa took away from Europe the British Eighth Air Force, which was assigned the job of heavy bombing of Germany. The bombing was not resumed until September 1944.[24] Torch, as the operation was called, also took so many British warships that it effectively stopped the northern convoys upon which Stalin depended.

But Churchill did more than force the North African operation. He suggested another aimed at Norway. Roosevelt was alarmed. In a September message, which he decided not to send, Roosevelt told

Churchill: "Unless we analyze every implication of present and pro-
jected operations, we will find ourselves committed to the unfor-
givable military blunder of dispersion to the point where decisive
action against a concentrated enemy becomes impossible."[25]

By early October, Churchill sent Roosevelt a message that even
Adolf Hitler would have seconded. He suggested that America reduce its production of tanks and bullets, saying "it would appear
that we are making provision on a scale which is altogether too lavish."[26] Instead, Churchill wanted more planes and ships. Tanks
fought on continents. Planes and ships could operate elsewhere.
Churchill had no intention of creating a second front or fighting
Adolf Hitler anywhere where it would hurt the Führer.

Stalin had a great capacity for suspicion, but in this case his suspicion was reasonable. He was fighting Hitler alone and his allies
were doing anything but. He had complained and argued and done
what he could, but nothing seemed to help. He told the Associated
Press on October 4, 1942, that what the Allies had done so far was
of little military value, while what the Russians were doing at Stal-
ingrad was significant. He said his hopes rested upon more aid. "In
order to amplify and improve this aid one thing is required: that the
Allies fulfill their obligations fully and on time."[27] Yet even in going
to the press, Stalin stayed civil, and his suspicions had not yet irretrievably shattered the implicit trust necessary among allies. The
Americans, who for the most part shared Stalin's opinion, agreed
three days later to a massive increase in aid.

But that was not to produce the result desired. Later in the month
the last vestige of Stalin's trust evaporated. The world didn't know
exactly why, but the Soviet dictator, who had endured to now the
inadequacies of his allies, suddenly became strident in a way that
would never fully leave him. And the shift had something to do with
Rudolf Hess, who had been out of the news and the public's mind
for over a year. Suddenly Stalin believed that the peculiar way the
Western Allies were fighting the war had something to do with Hess.
Stalin demanded that Hess be brought to trial immediately. Soviet
media said that the British Peace Party, which they called the Cliveden Set, was at the center of a conspiracy.[28]

Stalin refused to even respond to an offer to supply air support
to his army in the Caucasus. Instead, he simply replied to all mes-

sages with a cryptic "thank you." Churchill cabled Roosevelt on the twenty-fourth. "All this chatter about Hess may be another symptom. I am frankly perplexed and would be grateful for your thoughts at the earliest moment because time is passing."[29] Historian Warren Kimball, who more than anyone has followed the correspondence of the three Allied leaders of the war, says that Churchill's October 24 message to the President marked the beginning of the Cold War. Stalin would never again trust the West and the feeling, eventually, would become mutual.

In 1991, shortly before the Soviet Union dissolved, the KGB released the intelligence cable that began the Cold War. It did, in fact, concern the mission of Rudolf Hess. The report to Stalin in October 1942 originated with Colonel Moravec, head of Czech intelligence in exile, who cooperated with all sides trying to crush Adolf Hitler. It read:

Top Secret

No copy can be made without permission
from the Secretariat of the People's Commissariat
for Internal Affairs.

Copy No. 4

October 2

STATE DEFENSE COMMITTEE OF THE USSR
To: Comrade Stalin and
    Comrade Molotov

Col. Moravec, chief of the Czech military intelligence told the PCIA station chief in London the following:
The widely spread opinion that Hess flew to Britain unexpectedly is untrue. Long before that flight Hess corresponded on this question with Lord Hamilton discussing all the details of his forthcoming flight. Hamilton did not personally participate in the correspondence, however. All the letters addressed to Hamilton failed to reach him. They were received by the intelligence service. Hamilton's alleged answers were also written by the intelligence service. This is how the British managed to trick Hess into flying to Britain.

Col. Moravec also said that he saw the Hess-Hamilton correspondence with his own eyes. According to Moravec, in his letters Hess sufficiently clearly laid down the plans of the German government connected with the attack on the Soviet Union.

The letters also contained well argued proposals on the need to discontinue the war between Britain and Germany.

Col. Moravec said in conclusion that the British had written affidavits to the effect that Hess and other Nazi leaders were guilty of preparing an attack on the USSR.

[signed] L. Beria, People's Commissar for Internal Affairs of the USSR.[30]

There was no question why Stalin's cold heart froze further after receiving this message. This was far worse than even what he had learned a year earlier. Hess didn't first disclose the Soviet invasion plans when he arrived on May 10, as the Americans were eventually told, but had mentioned the overall German strategy in writing even beforehand. And the British had negotiated the point. Karl Haushofer told the Americans after the war that several letters passed back and forth between Hess and "friends" in Great Britain beginning in September 1940. Now Stalin was told that those messages which discussed the invasion of the Soviet Union were from the SIS. He concluded that some inside the British government were behind that invasion. And he was undoubtedly right.

When Hitler had his "insight" that he would not face a second front in Europe as he attacked the Soviet Union—the mad idea his generals never understood—it was at a time when Hess was negotiating that very point. The Cold War stemmed from Stalin's own insight that the British seemed to be holding fast to whatever deal had been struck. Wherever Stalin looked, he saw Winston Churchill resisting the kind of real military action that might defeat Hitler. Instead, Churchill, as George C. Marshall suspected, seemed to be exploiting the German-Soviet bloodbath to secure British colonial interests in the Middle East.

Oddly, however, Stalin did not blame Churchill, though he didn't trust him. He, like Hitler and Hess, believed that in the British government there was a powerful Peace Party that had commanded the Rudolf Hess Affair. He did, though, note how effective that party had been. It had saved Great Britain at the cost of mostly Russian blood.

Postscript

In a little-noted May 1943 article in the small but respected publication called the *American Mercury* there appeared an anonymously written article. The editors said, "The writer, a highly reputable observer, is known to us and we publish this article with full faith in its sources." The information reported may have seemed outlandish at the time. Now, it seems prescient.

The magazine reported that Ernst Bohle—who was writing the mysteriously missing letter from Hess to Hamilton—was at first to be the man to fly to Britain. Few knew Bohle in 1943. And no one but an insider knew he had anything to do with the Hess mission. Hitler, the magazine said, vetoed Bohle as the messenger for the cause of British-German peace. Instead, he selected his deputy for the mission. The Germans sent the British a letter explaining the change of plans, and finally, perhaps very late in the game, the British Peace Party agreed. Rudolf Hess could come to Great Britain.

The magazine said—again correctly—that for months the two sides had corresponded, with the Germans pushing "their proposal in the name of peace and Nordic friendship." One thing the magazine said the Germans didn't know was that the person responding to these letters was not the Duke of Hamilton, but the British SIS.

On the night of the actual flight, the magazine correctly noted that Göring administered the deadliest—and the last—Blitz of England. Hess, it said, was supposed to land at the airstrip at Dungavel House, where an "official reception committee composed of Military Intelligence officers and Secret Service agents was waiting." However, the magazine reported, Hess did not find the landing strip, bailed out of his plane ten miles away, and was soon incarcerated by "canny Scots" with an "instinctive distrust of aristocracy" who "became suspicious of the whole situation" and refused to cede their ward immediately to officialdom. By the time those who were supposed to have Hess finally managed to get him, word had slipped out to the world press.

As for Hess's mystery letter to the Duke of Hamilton, what the magazine reported was almost identical to what Karl Haushofer told the Americans after the war. Hitler would have evacuated all of his western conquests—totally and without condition. Britain, for its part, would display "benevolent neutrality" toward German affairs in the East. Plebiscites, not arms, would determine how European peoples were associated. The magazine had nearly every plank in the peace plan that Karl Haushofer revealed to the Americans. It may have been shy only one: the negotiations had typically been prefaced on the condition of Hitler's removal. Whether this was an issue isn't known. But it is probable.

Hitler told his inner circle on September 2, 1942: "When once the terms we offered to Great Britain are made public there will be an uproar throughout the Kingdom."[31]

That, somehow, the contacts with the Duke of Windsor were involved in setting up the Hess affair there is little doubt. And Windsor was not the passive victim as was Hamilton. A former King could not be treated as Hamilton had been.

On April 23, 1942—eleven months after Hess had flown away— J. Edgar Hoover told the State Department that "information has been received from a confidential source close to the Duke of Windsor at Nassau that the Duke is very much worried for fear of being kidnapped by the Germans and being traded for the release of Rudolph [sic] Hess."[32] That the Duke of Windsor, across the Atlantic and surrounded by hundreds of troops, somehow saw his fate tied with Hess's must have been because it was.

As for Hess, he almost immediately and miraculously resumed contact with Germany, sending seemingly innocuous letters to Göring, his wife and others. Not so innocuous was their routing. They were sent to Carl Burckhardt in Geneva, and retrieved by Walter Schellenberg. The Peace Party was still in contact with Hitler.

Meanwhile the Germans may have established a fund for Rudolf Hess while he was in English custody in anticipation of his return after the German victory. In a Swiss numbered account, the Luftwaffe deposited some 672,905 Swiss francs in the name of Edgar

Horn. Alfred Horn was the name Hess first used on British soil. Americans after the war, searching for laundered Nazi money, discovered the account and began searching for Edgar Horn, whom they described as the "brother-in-law of Rudolf Hess."[33] Edgar Horn did not exist. Rudolf Hess did.

As for the man who eventually died in Spandau Prison, logic says that no one would sacrifice his life to imitate another. He must have been Hess. Unfortunately, the medical evidence is irrefutable that he wasn't Hess. As Hugh Thomas and other surgeons have pointed out, only a reversal of the whole course of medical history and the basis of medical science would allow a finding that the Spandau prisoner was Rudolf Hess.

There is another kind of logic, though, and it is strong: if the British used Hess to negotiate a war that killed twenty million Russians, it would be important that Hess not be available afterward to tell of it. Not, in any case, when the war ended with but two superpowers, one headed by a man who already suspected dirty play, had the world's largest army and was aggressively expanding at the same time that American troops were heading home.

The man in Spandau Prison did not allow a member of the Hess family to see him for twenty-eight years. Perhaps there was a reason for that as well.

Finally, there is a question much larger than the identity of Prisoner No. 7. Namely: What did the whole Hess ruse accomplish? Did forcing the war east save Britain from defeat? It did, but only from a man intent on not defeating her. Hitler, as much as Churchill, saved Britain. Did Churchill's insistence on fighting Hitler advance the British Empire—Churchill's reason for fighting the war? No. The Empire disintegrated after the war as England emerged an enfeebled, almost irrelevant, country. Did Barbarossa check imperial Marxism? No again. It did the opposite. The war turned the Soviet Union into a superpower intent on doing something Hitler hadn't: gaining world hegemony.

At least it is true that Churchill stopped one of the most evil men to ever live. The problem, though, was that he stopped him too late, after the evil man had done his evil. This was not a war, for instance, to save the Jews, because it saved none. Instead, the German push east resulted in the Holocaust.

This should be considered: after his victory in the West, Hitler wanted to stop. He said it would take a hundred years to consolidate his victory. He proposed to free the countries he had captured in the West. He ordered thirty divisions decommissioned. Most of what Hitler said and did from September 1939 to sometime before the invasion of Russia was designed to end the war, not to prosecute it. If Britain had offered peace, Hitler would have taken it on terms favorable to the British Empire. The record leaves no doubt there.

Instead, Britain officially rejected peace while it covertly accepted it, and by doing so Britain emboldened Hitler. The Peace Party deception produced the worst of all possible results. It gave Hitler free rein in the East while resolving nothing in the West.

To be sure, a peace in the summer of 1940 would have ended at a high cost: except for a possible rump state, Poland would have ceased to exist. Czechoslovakia would have remained a German protectorate and much of the rest of non-Soviet Eastern Europe would have been encased in a German sphere of influence at least as tightly managed as the Western Hemisphere was by the Monroe Doctrine. Jews would most likely have been excluded from Central Europe.

Was stopping this worth fifty-two million deaths?

It is hard to answer yes since the Europe that emerged from the ashes found Poland, Czechoslovakia, and most of Eastern Europe enslaved anyway, perhaps even in harsher straits than the Hitler of 1940 had himself imagined. And six million Jews had been murdered.

It might be true that Hitler would have tired of an early peace and would have quickly resumed his aggression, especially in the East. That was certainly the plan in *Mein Kampf,* and Hitler if nothing else stuck to his old notions. We will never know if a real peace with Britain could have altered that.

Intelligence work in the twentieth century has been called by insiders the "great game." In the Hess case, though, that game produced only losers.

Notes

PREFACE

1. All descriptions derive from Hugh W. Thomas, *The Murder of Rudolf Hess* (New York: Harper & Row, 1979), and from personal conversations with Dr. Thomas in 1992.

CHAPTER 1: TYPHOON

1. *Facts on File: 1941*, Persons Index (New York: Facts on File), cite 1942, p. 91K.
2. John Colville, *The Fringes of Power: 10 Downing Street Diaries, 1939–1955* (New York: Norton, 1985), p. 144.
3. William L. Shirer, *The Nightmare Years* (Boston: Little, Brown, 1984), p. 407.
4. Winston S. Churchill, *The Grand Alliance* (Boston: Houghton Mifflin, 1950), p. 221.
5. Interview with Russian historian Alexander Orlov, May, 1991.
6. *The Halder War Diary: 1939–1942*, eds., Charles Burdick and Hans-Adolf Jacobsen (Novato, CA: Presidio Press, 1988), p. 227.
7. J. Noakes and G. Pridham, eds., *Nazism, A History in Documents and Eyewitness Accounts: The Nazi Party, State and Society* (New York: Schocken, 1983), p. 783. (Originally published in Great Britain by the Department of History and Archaeology, University of Exeter.) Hereinafter referred to as NAZ.
8. Ibid., p. 790.
9. Ibid., p. 797.
10. Ibid., p. 812.
11. Ibid., p. 812.
12. *Facts on File: 1941*, p. 161F.
13. Ibid., p. 176A.
14. Warren F. Kimball, ed., *Churchill and Roosevelt: The Complete Correspondence* (Princeton: Princeton University Press, 1984), R-38-X.

15. Ibid., Vol. 1, p. 177.

16. *The Diaries of Sir Alexander Cadogan*, ed., David Dilks (New York: Putnam, 1971), p. 373.

17. Ibid., p. 375.

18. *Churchill and Roosevelt*, C-84-X.

19. Ibid.

CHAPTER 2: QUIXOTIC

1. Churchill, *Grand Alliance*, p. 106.

2. *Churchill and Roosevelt*, R-39-X.

3. Churchill, *Grand Alliance*, p. 41. Also see Martin Gilbert, *The Second World War* (New York: Holt, 1989), p. 181.

4. J. Bernard Hutton, *Hess: The Man and His Mission* (New York: Macmillan, 1970), p. 43.

5. David Irving, *Hess: The Missing Years, 1941–1945* (London and New York: Macmillan, 1987), pp. 74–75.

6. Ilse Hess, *Prisoner of Peace* (London: Britons, 1954), p. 33.

7. Ibid.

8. Hess's words as recounted by Home Guardsmen Jack Paterson and Robert Gibson, *New York Times*, 14 May 1941.

9. Ibid.

10. Irving, *Hess*, p. 80.

11. *New York Times*, 15 May 1941, p. 1.

12. Irving, *Hess*, p. 80.

13. See the Albert Speer Interrogation, RG 226, XL 17234. National Archives.

14. *Trial of German Major War Criminals: Proceedings of the International Military Tribunal Sitting at Nuremberg, Germany*, Vol. 9 (London: H.M. Stationery Office, 1947), p. 363. Hereinafter referred to as IMT.

15. 862.00/4012, State Department Archives.

16. Ibid.

17. James Leasor, *The Uninvited Envoy* (New York, Toronto, and London: McGraw-Hill, 1963). The quotations in this section are from pp. 93–98 and 122–30.

18. Ibid., p. 126.

19. 862.00/4018, State Department Archives.

20. Ibid., 862.00/4019.

21. Ibid.

22. Ibid., 862.00/4014.

23. Ibid., 862.00/4016.

24. *New York Times*, 15 May 1941.

25. Ibid.

26. The Goebbels materials quoted in this chapter are from *The Goebbels Diaries: 1939–1941*, trans. and ed., Fred Taylor (New York: Putnam, 1983).

27. Ibid., p. 365.

28. Ibid., p. 367.

29. Ibid., p. 369.

30. *Ciano's Diary: 1939–1943*, ed., Malcolm Muggeridge (London: William Heinemann, 1947), p. 341.

31. Ibid., p. 342

32. Ibid., p. 343.

33. Ibid., p. 352.

34. *Churchill and Roosevelt*, C-11-X.

35. *New York Times*, 14 May 1941, p. 1.

36. Pre-encoded telegram, 740.0011, 10944 1/2, State Department Archives.

37. Churchill, *Grand Alliance*, p. 46.

38. 862.00/4036, State Department Archives.

39. *Churchill and Roosevelt*, p. 187.

40. 862.00/4033, State Department Archives.

41. Bryan I. Fugate, *Operation Barbarossa: Strategy and Tactics on the Eastern Front, 1941* (Novato, CA: Presidio Press, 1984), p. 53.

42. 740-0011 European War/1939/11348, State Department Archives.

43. Ibid., 740.0011/11032.

44. Ibid., 740.0011/11345.

45. Ibid., 862.00/4041.

46. War Department cablegram, May 13, 1941, Microfilm Roll 54, not separately numbered, National Archives.

47. All of the following Goebbels cites on RAF air activity are from the *Goebbels Diaries*, beginning on p. 369.

48. Ibid., p. 413.

49. Ibid., p. 431.

50. *Facts on File: 1941*, p. 236N.

51. Ibid., p. 237I.

52. 740.0011/11769, State Department Archives.

53. *Goebbels Diaries*, p. 399.

54. *Halder War Diary*, p. 411.

55. *Goebbels Diaries*, p. 424.

56. *Halder War Diary*, p. 234.

57. *New York Times*, 21 June 1941, p. 16.

58. *Churchill and Roosevelt*, p. 211.

59. *Halder War Diary*, p. 438.

60. *New York Times*, 29 June 1941, p. 6E.

61. Interviews with Alexander Orlov, Moscow 1991.

62. NAZ, p. 818.

63. John Toland, *Adolf Hitler* (Garden City, NY: Doubleday, 1976), p. 666.

64. *Secret Nuremberg Testimony of Heinz Guderian*, Sept. 11, 1945, National Archives.

65. *U.S. Strategic Bombing Survey APO 413*, July 6, 1945, RG 226, 137995, National Archives.

66. *Evaluation Report 53, Combined Intelligence Objectives Sub-Committee, Interrogation of Albert Speer*, p. 2.

67. Ibid.

68. RG 226, file 137995, National Archives.

69. November 5, 1941, letter from Raymond Lee to General Sherman Miles, RG 319, Box 83. National Archives.

CHAPTER 3: REVELATIONS

1. *Hitler's Secret Conversations*, compiled by Martin Bormann and translated by Norman Cameron and R. H. Stevens (New York: Farrar, Straus and Young, 1953), p. 555.

2. Secret OSS report on the interrogation of Karl Haushofer, RG 226, XL 22853, National Archives.

3. Combined Intelligence Objectives Sub-Committee Report on the Interrogation of Dr. Karl Haushofer, RG 226, XL 11080, National Archives.

4. RG 266, XL 22853, National Archives, from which the following descriptions and quotations are derived.

5. Irving, *Hess*, pp. 58–59.

6. Confidential File, 840.414/11-2745, State Department Archives.

7. Peter Padfield, *Hess: Flight for the Führer* (London: Weidenfeld and Nicolson, 1991), p. 185.

8. Wulf Schwarzwäller, *Rudolf Hess: The Last Nazi* (Bethesda, MD: National Press and Star Agency, 1988), p. 218.

9. All Halder quotations unless otherwise noted, come from the *U.S. Strategic Bombing Survey*, *APO 413*, RG 226, 137995, National Archives.

10. Churchill, *Grand Alliance*, p. 320.

11. Ibid., p. 321.

12. According to an account in *The Independent* on October 28, 1990, the files Sir Maurice Oldfield pinched suggest that either Rudolf Hess did not arrive in Great Britain at all, or that a switch was made shortly after he was captured and before he was interrogated in depth.

Chapter 4: Breath of Evil

1. Albrecht Haushofer, *Moabit Sonnets*, trans., M. D. Herter Norton (New York: Norton, 1978).

2. There are numerous accounts of the Free Corps movement. A succinct version can be found in George L. Moose, *The Crisis of German Ideology: Intellectual Origins of the Third Reich* (New York: Schocken, 1981).

3. Toland, *Hitler*, p. 72.

4. See Wolfe, p. 11, *The Weimar Republic and Nazi Germany* (Chicago: Warren Bayard Morris, Nelson-Hall, 1982).

5. OSS biographical report, RG 238, Box 180. National Archives. Also, the *New York Times* profile of May 13, 1941, p. 4, is illuminating.

6. RG 238, Entry 51, Box 180, National Archives.

7. *Biographies of Certain Potential War Criminals*, National Archives.

8. Interview with Dr. Hugh Thomas, confirmed in the previously cited documents at the National Archives in notes 5 and 7.

9. Louis L. Snyder, *Hitler's Elite* (New York: Hippocrene Books, 1989), p. 77; and Schwarzwäller, *Rudolf Hess*, p. 69.

10. Army General Staff Intelligence Report, RG 238, Entry 51, Box 180, National Archives.

11. October 5, 1945, testimony before Nuremberg court, National Archives.

12. OSS Secret File, 266 XL 22853, National Archives.

13. Toland, *Hitler*, p. 16.

14. Adolf Hitler, *Mein Kampf*, trans., Ralph Manheim (Boston: Houghton Mifflin, 1943), p. 9.

15. August Kubizek, *Young Hitler: The Story of Our Friendship* (London:

Allan Wingate, 1954), p. 17.

16. Ibid., p. 15.

17. Ibid., p. 166.

18. Ibid., p. 167.

19. Hitler, *Mein Kampf*, p. 19.

20. Toland, *Hitler*, p. 23.

21. Ibid., p. 27.

22. Hitler, *Mein Kampf*, p. 18.

23. Ibid., p. 27.

24. Toland, *Hitler*, p. 41.

25. Hitler, *Mein Kampf*, p. 21.

26. Toland, *Hitler*, p. 48.

27. Hitler, *Mein Kampf*, p. 126.

28. Toland, *Hitler*, p. 70.

29. Hitler, *Mein Kampf*, p. 202.

30. Toland, *Hitler*, p. xix.

31. Hitler, *Mein Kampf*, p. 206.

32. NAZ, p. 11.

33. Hutton, *Hess*, p. 14.

34. NAZ, p. 15.

35. Toland, *Hitler*, p. 27.

36. RG 238, Entry 51, Box 180, National Archives.

37. Ernst "Putzi" Hanfstaengl, *Hitler: The Missing Years* (London: Eyre & Spottiswoode, 1957), p. 35.

38. Ibid., p. 44.

39. Ibid.

40. NAZ, p. 20.

41. Ibid.

42. Ibid.

43. Ibid., p. 33.

44. Toland, *Hitler*, p. 182.

45. NAZ, p. 35.

46. Hanfstaengl, *Hitler*, p. 114.

47. Ibid.

48. Ibid., p. 115.

49. RG 226, XL 11080, National Archives.

50. *Halder War Diary*, p. 386.

51. Testimony of Karl Haushofer taken at Nuremberg, Germany, Oct. 5, 1945, National Archives.

52. Hitler, *Mein Kampf*, p. 140.
53. Ibid.
54. Ibid.
55. Ibid., p. 143.
56. Ibid., p. 620.
57. Ibid., p. 625.
58. Ibid., p. 638.
59. Ibid., p. 144.
60. Ibid.
61. Ibid., p. 613.

CHAPTER 5: TOWARD WAR

1. Toland, *Hitler*, p. 208.
2. Hanfstaengl, *Hitler*, p. 123.
3. Ibid., p. 131.
4. Winston S. Churchill, *The Gathering Storm* (Boston: Houghton Mifflin, 1948), p. 55.
5. Christopher Andrew and Oleg Gordievsky, *KGB: The Inside Story* (New York: HarperCollins, 1990), p. 73.
6. Winston S. Churchill, *Their Finest Hour* (Boston: Houghton Mifflin, 1949), p. 121.
7. Hanfstaengl, *Hitler*, p. 184.
8. Churchill, *Gathering Storm*, pp. 83–84.
9. Hanfstaengl, *Hitler*, p. 185.
10. Ibid.
11. Ibid., p. 186.
12. Ibid.
13. NAZ, p. 260.
14. Ibid., p. 359.
15. Ibid., p. 296
16. Ibid., p. 297.
17. David Irving, *Hitler's War* (New York: Avon, 1990), p. 42.
18. Frederick W. Winterbotham, *The Ultra Secret* (New York: Harper & Row, 1974), pp. 4–5.
19. Ibid., p. 5.
20. Ibid., p. 12.
21. Ibid.
22. Paul Schmidt, *Hitler's Interpreter* (London: William Heinemann, 1951), p. 53.

23. Ibid., pp. 53–54.

24. Ibid.

25. Ibid.

26. Ibid., p. 55.

27. Ibid., p. 56.

28. Ibid.

29. Ibid., p. 57.

30. Ibid., p. 59.

31. Ibid., p. 75.

32. Ibid.

33. *Speeches of Adolf Hitler,* Vol. 2, ed., Norman H. Baynes (London: Oxford University Press, 1942), p. 1105.

34. Ibid., p. 1185.

35. *Daily Mail,* 4 Sept. 1937.

36. John Lukacs, *The Duel, 10 May–31 July 1940: The Eighty-Day Struggle between Churchill and Hitler* (New York: Ticknor & Fields, 1991), p. 48.

37. Churchill, *Gathering Storm,* p. 250.

38. Ibid., pp. 222–34.

39. Ibid.

40. Annex "A" to C.I.C. Memorandum for Information to No. 76, RG 226, R 2, National Archives.

41. Schmidt, *Hitler's Interpreter,* pp. 76–77.

42. Ibid.

43. *Diaries of Sir Alexander Cadogan,* p. 15.

44. Churchill, *Gathering Storm,* p. 290.

45. Anthony Cave Brown, *"C:" The Secret Life of Sir Stewart Graham Menzies* (New York: Macmillan, 1987), pp. 190–91. Cave Brown cites no source for this document.

CHAPTER 6: WAR

1. IMT, Vol. 2, p. 137.

2. Ibid., p. 142.

3. IMT, Vol. 1, p. 167.

4. *Documents on German Foreign Policy, 1918–1945,* Series D, Vol. 7 (Washington: U.S. Government Printing Office, 1957–1964), No. 74. (Hereinafter referred to as DGFP.)

5. *U.S. Strategic Bombing Survey,* Interview 53, RG 226, 137995, National Archives.

6. NAZ, p. 741.
7. Ibid.
8. DGFP, Series D, Vol. 7, No. 56.
9. Ibid.
10. Ibid., No. 70.
11. Ibid.
12. Ibid., No. 82.
13. Ibid., No. 133.
14. Churchill, *Gathering Storm*, p. 394.
15. All "Secret Protocol" quotations are from DGFP, Series D, Vol. 10, No. 10.
16. Schmidt, *Hitler's Interpreter*, p. 138.
17. DGFP, Series D, Vol. 7, No. 200, enclosure.
18. Ibid.
19. Ibid., p. 212.
20. Ibid., No. 200/afternoon.
21. Schmidt, *Hitler's Interpreter*, p. 142.
22. DGFP, Series D, Vol. 7, No. 265.
23. Ibid.
24. Schmidt, *Hitler's Interpreter*, p. 144.
25. Ibid., p. 145.
26. Ibid.
27. Ibid., p. 146.
28. IMT, Vol. 9, p. 224.
29. Ibid., p. 210.
30. Ibid., p. 211.
31. Ibid., p. 212.
32. Ibid.
33. Ibid.
34. Ibid., p. 213.
35. Briger Dahlerus, *The Last Attempt* (London: Hutchinson, 1948), p. 53.
36. IMT, Vol. 9, p. 213.
37. Ibid., p. 214.
38. Dahlerus, *Last Attempt*, pp. 60–62.
39. IMT, Vol. 9, p. 214.
40. Dahlerus, *Last Attempt*, pp. 60–62.
41. *Diaries of Sir Alexander Cadogan*, p. 202.
42. IMT, Vol. 9, p. 216.

43. Toland, *Hitler,* p. 560.
44. DGFP, Series D, Vol. 7, No. 384/enclosure.
45. Ibid.
46. Ibid.
47. Schmidt, *Hitler's Interpreter,* p. 48.
48. DGFP, Series D, Vol. 7, No. 384.
49. Irving, *Hitler's War,* p. 207.
50. IMT, Vol. 9, p. 216.
51. DGFP, Vol. 7, No. 421.
52. IMT, Vol. 2, pp. 170–71.
53. IMT, Vol. 9, p. 217.
54. *Diaries of Sir Alexander Cadogan,* pp. 204–5.
55. Schmidt, *Hitler's Interpreter,* p. 150.
56. Ibid., p. 151.
57. Ibid.
58. Ibid., p. 152.
59. Ibid.
60. DGFP, Vol. 7, No. 458.
61. Schmidt, *Hitler's Interpreter,* p. 153.
62. IMT, Vol. 9, p. 217.
63. Ibid., p. 218.
64. NAZ, p. 757.
65. NAZ, p. 935.
66. *Diaries of Sir Alexander Cadogan,* pp. 212–13.
67. NAZ, p. 135.
68. NAZ, p. 753.
69. Schwarzwäller, *Hess,* p. 180.
70. Schmidt, *Hitler's Interpreter,* p. 157.
71. Ibid., p. 158.
72. Toland, *Hitler,* p. 578.
73. IMT, Vol. 9, p. 219.
74. *Diaries of Sir Alexander Cadogan,* pp. 212–13.
75. IMT, Vol. 9, p. 237.
76. Ibid., p. 234.
77. The 226 pages of the *Final Report on the Case of Walter Friedrich Schellenberg* reside in a file cabinet in the Captured German Records section of the National Archives. See archivist Robert Wolfe.
78. Appendix XV to the *Schellenberg Final Report,* p. 1.
79. Ibid., p. 2.

CHAPTER 7: EN FINIR

1. Shirer, *Nightmare Years*, pp. 444–45.
2. NAZ, p. 755.
3. Ibid., p. 756.
4. This and the following quotations are from Churchill, *Gathering Storm*, pp. 408–9.
5. NAZ, p. 758.
6. Churchill, *Gathering Storm*, p. 448.
7. Ibid., p. 449.
8. Ibid.
9. *Diaries of Sir Alexander Cadogan*, p. 219.
10. Ibid., p. 15.
11. Ibid., p. 221.
12. Ibid., pp. 222–23.
13. This notion was best argued by A. J. P. Taylor.
14. *Ciano Diaries*, p. 162.
15. IMT, Trials of War Criminals, the *High Command Case*, Vol. 10, p. 541.
16. Wilhelm Keitel, *The Memoirs of Field-Marshall Keitel*, trans., David Irving, ed., Walter Gorlitz (London: William Kimber, 1965), pp. 93–94.
17. The Halder testimony is from IMT, *High Command Case*, Vol. 10, p. 856.
18. Cave Brown, *"C,"* p. 75.
19. Lukacs, p. 81.

CHAPTER 8: OFTEN ONLY LOSERS

1. DGFP, Vol. 8, No. 135.
2. Ibid., No. 138.
3. Ibid.
4. Ibid.
5. Two meetings are recorded in Cadogan's diary, p. 200, and the third was mentioned by Gilbert, *Second World War*, p. 19.
6. *Diaries of Sir Alexander Cadogan*, p. 220.
7. Ibid.
8. DGFP, Series D, Vol. 8, No. 176.
9. Ibid., No. 242; note, p. 270.
10. Ibid., No. 179.
11. Ibid., No. 186.
12. Ibid., No. 242.

13. Irving, *Hitler's War*, p. 234.
14. *My New Order: A Collection of Speeches by Adolf Hitler*, ed., Raoul de Roussy de Sales (New York: Reynal & Hitchcock, 1941), pp. 755–56.
15. Ibid.
16. DGFP, Series D, Vol. 8. See ed. Note to No. 205.
17. Ibid.
18. Ibid., No. 224.
19. Ibid.
20. NAZ, p. 760.
21. Churchill, *Gathering Storm*, pp. 484–85.
22. *Diaries of Sir Alexander Cadogan*, p. 223.
23. Ibid.
24. Irving, *Hitler's War*, p. 236.
25. Keitel, *Memoirs*, pp. 99–100.
26. Callum A. MacDonald, *European Studies Review*, "The Venlo Affair," Oct. 1978, p. 445.
27. Payne S. Best, *The Venlo Incident* (London: Hutchinson, 1950), p. 8.
28. Ibid.
29. Ibid.
30. MacDonald, "Venlo Affair," p. 446.
31. Ibid., p. 452.
32. Ibid., p. 453.
33. Walter Schellenberg, *The Schellenberg Memoirs*, ed. and trans., Louis Hagen (London: Andre Deutsch, 1956), p. 84.
34. This meeting does not appear in Best's account, only in Schellenberg's.
35. Schellenberg, *Memoirs*, p. 85.
36. Ibid. The British account omits this meeting.
37. Ibid., p. 86.
38. Ibid.
39. The accounts of Best and Schellenberg differ on the number of times Schellenberg actually came across the border. Best said three times, Schellenberg four. The difference is of little consequence, though it appears that Best's memory combined two separate meetings into one. Best later wrote a book about the aftermath of the Venlo incident, but his account of the crucial meetings and negotiations is curiously truncated.

40. Schellenberg, *Memoirs*, p. 87.

41. Ibid.

42. Best, *Venlo Incident*, p. 12.

43. Ibid.

44. Schellenberg, *Memoirs*, p. 89.

45. MacDonald, *Venlo Affair*, p. 456.

46. *Diaries of Sir Alexander Cadogan*, p. 228.

47. Ibid., p. 229.

48. Best, *Venlo Incident*, p. 12.

49. Ibid.

50. NAZ, p. 758.

51. Best, *Venlo Incident*, p. 13.

52. Schellenberg, *Memoirs*, p. 92.

53. Ibid.

54. Ibid., p. 94.

55. By some accounts, Hitler had already decided on a kidnapping even before the bombing. If so, Himmler's call seems redundant, at best. It's more likely that the final decision to attempt an abduction was a direct result of the bombing—an event that would justify the extreme actions.

56. This account of the Elser affair is from Toland, *Hitler*, pp. 591–94.

57. Anthony Cave Brown, "*C*," p. 215.

58. Some have theorized Hitler had more subtle reasons for Venlo than merely learning about British ambitions. He may have wanted to infiltrate the SIS, or embarrass the SIS by kidnapping its agents, or learn the identities of German generals who may actually have been conspiring against him. All these explanations are unsatisfactory. Hitler wasn't trying to infiltrate the SIS at The Hague, because it was already infiltrated by Dr. Fischer. The brash kidnapping actually hurt German penetration, since it exposed Fischer. Nor do the risks involved in sending Schellenberg and violating a neutral's territory justify the hollow victory of embarrassing the SIS. And certainly there are more direct ways of finding the German opposition than asking the British, who were themselves groping about in search of the identities. No, if Hitler set up a deception to learn about the true British peace terms it was clearly because he wanted to know those terms.

59. Recorded in the diary of Helmuth Groscurth, translated in a note

by Harold Deutsch, *The Conspiracy against Hitler in the Twilight War* (Minneapolis: University of Minnesota Press, 1968), p. 163.

CHAPTER 9: GENIUS

1. Keitel, *Memoirs,* p. 102.
2. Ibid., pp. 102–3.
3. NAZ, p. 765.
4. Irving, *Hitler's War,* p. 243.
5. Keitel, *Memoirs,* p. 102.
6. Ibid.
7. *Secret Nuremberg Testimony of Heinz Guderian,* Sept. 11, 1945, pp. 12–13, National Archives.
8. *Hassell Diaries,* p. 74.
9. Deutsch, *Conspiracy against Hitler,* p. 31.
10. Klemens von Klemperer, *German Resistance against Hitler* (Oxford: Clarendon Press, 1992), p. 176.
11. IMT, *High Command Case,* Vol. 10, p. 545.
12. See Halder's testimony in ibid. He says that in 1939 and 1940 any "attempt of a forcible solution against the system in power was inseparably tied up with the danger of civil war, in the face of the enemy at the frontiers of the country."
13. *Hassell Diaries,* pp. 127–28.
14. Ibid., pp. 93–94.
15. Ibid., p. 76.
16. Unless otherwise noted, details in this subsection concerning the opposition's dealing with Pius XII are based largely upon the account of Harold Deutsch, cited above, pp. 102–48. Deutsch conducted over 119 interviews with the principals, including Halder, Gördeler, Müller, and Leiber. Since much British archival material is still sealed, Deutsch's account—based upon key interviews unavailable anywhere else—ranks nearly as high in importance as primary material. Although the current author disagrees with several of Deutsch's conclusions, there is no debating his careful and exhaustive historiography.
17. Klemperer, *Resistance,* p. 169.
18. *Hassell Diaries,* p. 117.
19. Ibid., p. 116.
20. Hassell's own note in English, in *Hassell Diaries,* p. 118.
21. Ibid., p. 118.

22. *Diaries of Sir Alexander Cadogan*, p. 256.

23. Klemperer, *German Resistance*, p. 173. Deutsch puts the date nearer to the first of February.

24. *Hassell Diaries*, p. 125.

25. Ibid.

26. Ibid.

27. Klemperer, *German Resistance*, p. 175.

28. Deutsch, *Conspiracy against Hitler*, p. 312.

29. *Hassell Diaries*, p. 133.

30. Deutsch translation of Helmuth Groscurth diary entry of January 13, in *Conspiracy against Hitler*, p. 285.

31. Deutsch, *Conspiracy against Hitler*, p. 269.

32. Toland, *Hitler*, p. 596.

33. DGFP, Series D, Vol. 8, No. 591.

34. DGFP, Series D, Vol. 9, No. 1.

35. Ibid.

36. Schmidt, *Hitler's Interpreter*, p. 172.

37. Ibid., p. 173.

38. Churchill, *Gathering Storm*, p. 577.

39. Ibid., p. 582.

40. *Hassell Diaries*, p. 131.

41. Churchill, *Gathering Storm*, p. 600.

42. In surrendering his powers, Churchill did not stop his plotting or blame-shifting. He wrote to Chamberlain: "I am very grateful to you for having at my request taken over the day-to-day management of the Military Co-ordination, etc. I think I ought, however, to let you know that I shall not be willing to receive that task back from you without the necessary powers. At present no one has the power. There are six Chiefs of the Staff, three Ministers, and General Ismay, who all have a voice in Norwegian operations." *Gathering Storm*, p. 642.

43. David Irving, *Churchill's War* (New York: Avon, 1991), pp. 247–88.

44. Churchill, *Gathering Storm*, p. 644.

45. Irving, *Churchill's War*, p. 251.

46. DGFP, Vol. 9, No. 138.

47. *Hassell Diaries*, p. 137.

48. *Halder War Diary*, p. 129.

49. Toland, *Hitler*, p. 598.

50. Cave Brown, *"C,"* p. 250.

51. DGFP, Vol. 9, No. 212.
52. DGFP, Ibid., No. 214.

CHAPTER 10: WROUGHT BY CRIMINALS

1. NAZ, p. 774.
2. Keitel, *Memoirs*, p. 110.
3. Churchill, *Gathering Storm*, p. 662.
4. Ibid., p. 663.
5. Ibid., p. 665.
6. Ibid., p. 667.
7. T. F. Troy, *Donovan and the CIA* (Washington, D.C.: CIA, 1981), p. 31.
8. See David Ignatius, "How Churchill's Agents Secretly Manipulated the U.S. Before Pearl Harbor," *Washington Post*, 17 September 1989, p. C-1.
9. Cave Brown, *"C,"* pp. 367–68.
10. On September 17, 1989, the *Washington Post* reported that journalist David Ignatius had been allowed to read and take notes from, but not to copy, the SIS's study, called *British Security Coordination (BSC): An Account of Secret Activities in the Western Hemisphere, 1940–45*. Former CIA agent Thomas Troy, who has seen one of the ten 423-page copies of the report, confirmed to this author its existence and the accuracy of the *Post*'s article.
11. *Churchill and Roosevelt*, C-11-X.
12. Churchill, *Gathering Storm*, p. 664.
13. Irving, *Hitler's War*, p. 114.
14. Churchill, *Finest Hour*, p. 48.
15. Ibid., p. 46.
16. Ibid., p. 50.
17. *Diaries of Sir Alexander Cadogan*, p. 284.
18. Churchill, *Finest Hour*, p. 60.
19. *Halder War Diary*, p. 148.
20. Ibid.
21. Ibid., p. 165.
22. DGFP, Vol. 9, No. 317.
23. NAZ, p. 777.
24. Felix Kersten, *The Kersten Memoirs: 1940–1945*, trans., Constantine Fitzgibbon and James Oliver (New York: Macmillan, 1957), p. 88.
25. Toland, *Hitler*, p. 611.

26. Lukacs, *The Duel*, p. 86.

27. *Hitler's Secret Conversations*, p. 90.

28. John Costello, *Ten Days to Destiny* (New York: William Morrow, 1991), p. 175.

29. Those who argue that it was Army Group A that made the decision to stop base much of their belief on a sentence in Jodl's war diary entry of May 25. The OKH asks on this date to resume the tank offensive. The diary entry says: "The Führer is against, leaves the decision to Army Group A." Procedurally, it would have been problematic for Army Group A to resume the offensive without going again to Hitler. It was Hitler's order that caused the halt and only another one could countermand it. When Hitler had had enough of the delay, he—not Army Group A—gave the order. Hitler could at times delegate much authority, but on matters concerning Great Britain he delegated very little. He certainly wouldn't have placed the critical issue of her survival in the hands of officers he did not entirely respect.

30. Churchill, *Finest Hour*, p. 76.

31. *Hassell Diaries*, p. 139.

32. Ibid.

33. DGFP, Series D, Vol. 9, No. 317.

34. Churchill, *Finest Hour*, p. 4.

35. Winterbotham, *Ultra Secret*, p. 24.

36. *Diaries of Sir Alexander Cadogan*, p. 286.

37. Ibid., p. 287.

38. *Halder Diaries*, p. 156.

39. CAB:65/13 wm(40), 139th conclusions, confidential annex, cited in Lukacs, *The Duel*, p. 92.

40. Ibid., p. 93.

41. Ibid., p. 94.

42. Churchill, *Finest Hour*, p. 124.

43. Ibid., p. 88.

44. CAB 65-13, WM (40) 142 conclusions, confidential annex, cited in Lukacs, *The Duel*, p. 97.

45. Churchill, *Finest Hour*, p. 125.

46. Cave Brown, *"C,"* p. 250.

47. William Stevenson, *A Man Called Intrepid* (New York and London: Harcourt Brace Jovanovich, 1976), p. 24.

48. See Chapter 5.

49. DGFP, Series D, Vol. 8, No. 263

50. NAZ, p. 759.

51. *Hitler's Secret Conversations,* p. 208.

52. NAZ, p. 758.

53. Churchill, *Finest Hour,* p. 63.

54. Colville, *Fringes of Power,* p. 139.

55. Ibid., p. 163.

56. Ibid., p. 173.

57. NAZ, p. 782.

58. Lukacs, *The Duel,* p. 109.

59. NAZ, p. 778.

60. NAZ, p. 777.

61. Robert Smith Thompson, *A Time for War* (New York: Prentice Hall, 1991), p. 250

62. Keitel, *Memoirs,* p. 116.

63. Ibid.

64. Ibid., p. 188.

65. B. H. Liddell Hart, *History of the Second World War* (London: Cassell & Company, 1970), p. 83.

66. Churchill, *Finest Hour,* p. 141.

67. Robert Goralski, *World War II Almanac: 1931–1945* (New York: Putnam, 1981), pp. 116–17.

68. Churchill, *Finest Hour,* p. 118.

69. Goralski, *World War II Almanac,* p. 122.

CHAPTER 11: CONSPIRACIES

1. F. W. Winterbotham, *Secret and Personal* (London: William Kimber, 1969), pp. 24–25.

2. Ibid., p. 79.

3. Ibid., p. 80.

4. DGFP, Series D, Vol. 7, No. 151.

5. DGFP, Series D, Vol. 8, No. 134.

6. DGFP, Series D, Vol. 8, No. 203.

7. Peter Padfield, *Hess: Flight for the Fuhrer* (London: Weidenfeld and Nicolson, 1991), p. 123.

8. Lukacs, *The Duel,* p. 132.

9. Ibid.

10. Clive Ponting, *1940: Myth and Reality* (London: Hamish Hamilton, 1990), p. 114.

11. DGFP, Series D, Vol. 9, p. 620.
12. Lukacs, *The Duel*, p. 133.
13. *Halder War Diaries*, p. 215.
14. DGFP, Series D, Vol. 9, No. 529.
15. Lukacs, *The Duel*, p. 149.
16. Ibid.
17. Ibid., pp. 139–40.
18. Ibid.
19. Churchill, *Finest Hour*, p. 226.
20. Ibid., p. 228.
21. Since many of the British records on the peace moves may be sealed, help might come from official German documents. Unfortunately, a main source for German documents, those published by a joint American-English committee, have produced very little on the German side. For instance, between March 17, 1940, and June 22, 1940, the Documents on German Foreign Policy contain forty relevant documents on German-American relations, but only five on German-British relations.
22. Lukacs, *The Duel*, p. 149.
23. Churchill, *Finest Hour*, p. 643.
24. Winterbotham, *Ultra Secret*, p. 69.
25. NAZ, p. 783.
26. Ibid., p. 780.
27. DGFP, Series D, Vol. 10, p. 226.
28. Ibid.
29. Ibid.
30. Lukacs, *The Duel*, p. 164.
31. DGFP, Series D, Vol. 10, pp. 245–46.
32. Ibid.
33. NAZ, p. 786.
34. Ibid., p. 787.
35. Padfield, p. 127.
36. Ibid.
37. NAZ, p. 787.
38. Ibid.
39. Ibid., p. 788.
40. *Halder War Diaries*, p. 231.
41. Ibid., p. 789.
42. DGFP, Series D, Vol. 10, No. 261. See ed. Note.

43. Ibid.
44. Lukacs, p. 205.
45. DGFP, Series D, Vol. 10, No. 2.
46. Ibid., Vol. 10, No. 9.
47. Ibid., note.
48. *Foreign Relations of the United States*. British Commonwealth, the Soviet Union, Near East, Africa, Vol. 3 (Washington: U.S. Government Printing Office, 1958), p. 41.
49. Ibid.
50. DGFP, Series D, Vol. 10, No. 86.
51. Ibid., No. 152.
52. Ibid.
53. Ibid.
54. Schellenberg, *Memoirs*, p. 120.
55. Peter Allen, *The Crown and the Swastika* (London: Robert Hale, 1983), p. 188.
56. DGFP, Series D, Vol. 10, No. 264.
57. Ibid.
58. Schellenberg, *Memoirs*, p. 139.
59. DGFP, Series D, Vol. 10, No. 276.
60. Ibid.
61. Lukacs, *The Duel*, p. 183.
62. DGFP, Series D, Vol. 10, No. 270.
63. Ibid.
64. DGFP, Series D, No. 276. See ed. Note.
65. Liddell Hart, *History of the Second World War*, p. 103.
66. Winterbotham, *Ultra Secret*, p. 58.
67. Ibid., pp. 59–60.

CHAPTER 12: THE HESS MISSION

1. DGFP, Series D, Vol. 11, No. 323.
2. Confidential File, *U.S. Strategic Bombing Survey, APO 413*, RG 226, 137995, p. 3, National Archives.
3. James Douglas-Hamilton, *Motive for a Mission* (London: Macmillan, and New York: St. Martin's, 1971), p. 42.
4. Ibid., p. 56.
5. Ibid., p. 70.
6. Ibid., p. 69.
7. Ibid., p. 70.

8. Ibid., p. 71.

9. Ibid., p. 81.

10. Ibid., p. 94.

11. Ibid.

12. Ibid., p. 96.

13. Ibid., Appendix I.

14. See Karl Haushofer's reference to the terms in Chapter 3.

15. See DGFP, Series D, Vol. 11, No. 46. Hess tells Karl Haushofer: "Should success be the fate of the enterprise, the oracle given to you with regard to the month of August would yet be fulfilled, since the name of the young friend and the old lady friend of your family occurred to you during our quiet walk on the last day of that month." The enterprise referred to was contacting Hamilton through Mrs. Roberts. The identities, then, of the "young friend" and the "old lady friend" seem obvious.

16. DGFP, Series D, Vol. 11, No. 61.

17. Ibid., No. 76. See enclosure.

18. Ibid., No. 12.

19. Ibid.

20. Ibid., No. 46.

21. Allen, *Crown and the Swastika*, p. 213. Allen was apparently the first historian to see the possible relationship between this telegram and Hess.

22. DGFP, Series D, Vol. 11, No. 61.

23. Ibid.

24. Ibid., No. 76.

25. Ibid.

26. Douglas-Hamilton, *Motive for a Mission*, p. 147.

27. Ibid. The letter contained in DGFP, Series D, Vol. 11, No. 76, enclosure two is slightly different and less compromising on the issue of the secret nature of this affair. That, however, was a mere draft. Hamilton says the letter as quoted was the one his father belatedly received in Great Britain.

28. See Haushofer interrogation in Chapter Three.

29. RG 226, XL 19614, Interview with Ernst Wilhelm Bohle, National Archives.

30. Wolf Rudiger Hess, *My Father Rudolf Hess*, trans. Frederick and Christine Crowley (London: W. H. Allen, 1987), pp. 58–59.

31. RG 226, XL 19614, National Archives.

32. DGFP, Series D, Vol. 11, No. 223.

33. Ibid., No. 453.

34. Hess archives, Note by W. H. Stahmer, "*Truth and Misunderstanding about Rudolf Hess,*" 1959, cited in Wolf Rudiger Hess, *My Father Rudolf Hess*, p. 81.

35. Ilse Hess, *Prisoner of Peace*, pp. 42–43.

36. Raymond Lee to General Sherman Miles, Nov. 5, 1941, RG 319, National Archives.

37. Hutton, *Hess*, p. 31.

38. Ilse Hess, *Prisoner of Peace*, pp. 12–13.

39. Ibid.

40. Roger Manvell and Heinrich Frankel, *Hess: A Biography* (London: MacGibbon and Kee, 1973), p. 92.

41. Schwarzwäller, *Rudolf Hess*, p. 212.

42. *Halder War Diary*, p. 288.

43. Ibid., p. 292.

44. Ibid., p. 305.

45. Ibid., p. 307.

46. *Washington Post*, 17 Sept. 1989, p. C1.

47. *Facts on File: 1941*, p. 90A.

48. Ibid., p. 986.

49. *Churchill and Roosevelt*, C-58-X.

50. *Facts on File: 1941*, p. 106F.

51. *Halder War Diary*, p. 341.

52. *Hassell Diaries*, p. 170.

53. Ibid.

54. Ibid., p. 171.

55. See Haushofer's memorandum to Hitler, May 12, 1941, DGFP, Series D, Vol. 12, No. 500; *Hassell's Diaries*, May 10, 1941, pp. 137–38; Wolf Hess, *My Father Rudolf Hess*, p. 82; Padfield, *Hess*, p. 174.

56. *Hassell Diaries*, p. 174.

57. DGFP, Vol. 12, No. 500.

58. Haushofer later said: "Since the possibility existed that these greetings were in connection with my letter of last autumn, I thought I should again submit the matter to the Deputy of the Fuhrer. . . ." Ibid.

59. *Hassell Diaries*, p. 194.

60. See Chapter 3.

61. *Hassell Diaries*, p. 194.

62. Douglas-Hamilton, *Motive for a Mission*, p. 146.
63. Ibid., p. 148.
64. See J. C. Masterman, *The Double Cross System* (New Haven: Yale University Press, 1972).
65. Douglas-Hamilton, *Motive for a Mission*, p. 149.
66. Ibid.
67. Padfield, *Hess*, p. 147.
68. Churchill, *Grand Alliance*, p. 3.
69. *Hassell Diaries*, p. 194.
70. See Chapter 3.
71. See Padfield, *Hess*, p. 185.
72. Schwarzwäller, *Rudolf Hess*, p. 218.
73. Padfield, *Hess*, p. 186.
74. Ibid.
75. Ibid., p. 191.
76. Wolf Rudiger Hess, *My Father Rudolf Hess*, p. 146.
77. Padfield, *Hess*, p. 193.
78. Ilse Hess, *Prisoner of Peace*, pp. 20–21.
79. Manvell and Frankel, *Hess*, p. 96.

CHAPTER 13: DEAL

1. Interview with Russian military historian and archivist Alexander Orlov, May 1991.
2. Ibid.
3. Cable given to the author in May 1991 by the KGB. Translation by the Soviet press agency, Novosti.
4. Ibid.
5. Quoted from an article given to the author by KGB spokesman Oleg Tzarev. Translation by Vitaly Konzhukov, former senior editor of the Soviet press agency, Novosti. The translation differs somewhat from the one used by Costello, *Ten Days to Destiny*, p. 436.
6. Ibid.
7. Cable #338, KGB's Black Bertha File.
8. *The London Journal of Raymond E. Lee: 1940–1941* (Boston: Little, Brown, 1971), p. 437.
9. Ibid., p. 464.
10. Ibid., p. 437.
11. RG 319, Box 83, National Archives.

12. Ibid.

13. Novosti translation of Black Bertha cable dated Oct. 3, 1941.

14. Oleg Tzarev, a former KGB agent who researched the Black Bertha file, told the author that Stalin considered that last question with great seriousness.

15. Black Bertha cable dated Oct. 3, 1941.

16. Lee, *Journal,* p. 436.

17. *Churchill and Roosevelt,* R-115.

18. Ibid., R-131/1.

19. Ibid., R-140/1

20. Ibid., C-85.

21. Ibid., C-88.

22. Ibid., p. 492.

23. Ibid., p. 575.

24. Ibid., p. 596.

25. Ibid., R-186/3

26. Ibid., C-156.

27. *Facts on File; 1942,* p. 317F

28. Ibid., p. 636.

29. Ibid., C-172

30. Cable No. 450, KGB's Black Bertha file. Translation by Novosti. Translation varies some from that given to Costello, who first published extracts in 1991 in *Ten Days to Destiny.*

31. *Hitler's Secret Conversations,* p. 555.

32. Hand-delivered letter to Adolf A. Berle, Jr., declassified January 27, 1975, State Department Archives, National Achives.

33. Enclosure to Safehaven Report No. 25, March 27, 1946, from American embassy in Paris, National Archives.

Select Bibliography

Allen, Peter. *The Windsor Secret: New Revelations of the Nazi Connection.* New York: Stein and Day, 1984.

Andrew, Christopher. *The Making of the British Intelligence Community.* London: William Heinemann, 1985.

Andrew, Christopher, and Oleg Gordievsky. *KGB: The Inside Story.* New York: HarperCollins, 1990.

Benoist-Méchin, Jacques. *Sixty Days That Shook the West.* Edited by Cyril Falls. Translated by Peter Wiles. New York: Putnam, 1963.

Best, Payne S. *The Venlo Incident.* London: Hutchinson, 1950.

Bradley, John. *Churchill and the British.* New York: Gloucester Press, 1990.

Bullock, Alan. *Hitler: A Study in Tyranny.* New York: Harper & Row, 1964.

Cadogan, Alexander. *The Diaries of Sir Alexander Cadogan.* Edited by David Dilks. New York: Putnam, 1971.

Callahan, Raymond A. *Churchill: Retreat from Empire.* Wilmington, DE: Scholarly Resources, 1984.

Cave Brown, Anthony. *Bodyguard of Lies.* New York: Harper & Row, 1975.

———. *"C:" The Secret Life of Sir Stewart Graham Menzies.* New York: Macmillan, 1987.

Churchill, Winston S. *The Gathering Storm.* Boston: Houghton Mifflin, 1948.

———. *The Grand Alliance.* Boston: Houghton Mifflin, 1950.

———. *The Hinge of Fate.* Boston: Houghton Mifflin, 1950.

———. *Their Finest Hour.* Boston: Houghton Mifflin, 1949.

Ciano, Galeazzo. *The Ciano Diaries.* London: William Heinemann, 1946.

Clark, Alan. *Barbarossa.* New York: William Morrow, 1965.

Colville, John. *The Fringes of Power: 10 Downing Street Diaries,*

1939–1955. New York: Norton, 1985.

Conot, Robert E. *Justice at Nuremberg*. New York: Harper & Row, 1983.

Conquest, Robert. *The Great Terror*. New York: Oxford University Press, 1990.

Costello, John. *Ten Days to Destiny*. New York: William Morrow, 1991.

Deutsch, Harold. *The Conspiracy against Hitler in the Twilight War*. Minneapolis: University of Minnesota Press, 1968.

Documents on British Foreign Policy: 1919–1939. Series 2, Vols. 12–21, and Series 3, Vols. 1–10. London: H.M. Stationery Office, 1946–1976.

Documents on German Foreign Policy: 1918–1945. Series C, Vols. 1–6, and Series D, Vols. 1–13. Washington: U.S. Government Printing Office, 1957–1964.

Doenitz, Karl. *The Doenitz Memoirs*. Cleveland and New York: World Publishing, 1959.

Douglas-Hamilton, James. *Motive for a Mission*. London: Macmillan, and New York: St. Martin's, 1971.

Dunlop, Richard. *Donovan: America's Master Spy*. Chicago: Rand McNally, 1982.

Eden, Anthony. *Memoirs: The Reckoning*. Boston: Houghton Mifflin, 1965.

Foreign Relations of the United States: 1940. Washington: U.S. Government Printing Office, 1952.

Fugate, Bryan I. *Operation Barbarossa: Strategy and Tactics on the Eastern Front, 1941*. Novato, CA: Presidio Press, 1984.

Gardner, Brian. *Churchill in Power*. Boston: Houghton Mifflin, 1970.

Gilbert, Martin, *Churchill: A Life*. New York: Holt, 1991.

———. *The Second World War*. New York: Holt, 1989.

Gisevius, Hans Bernd. *To the Bitter End*. Oxford: Alden Press, 1948.

Goebbels, Joseph. *The Goebbels Diaries: 1939–1941*. Translated and edited by Fred Taylor. New York: Putnam, 1983.

Goralski, Robert, ed. *World War II Almanac: 1931–1945*. New York: Putnam, 1981.

Halder, Franz. *The Halder War Diary: 1939–1942*. Edited by Charles Burdick and Hans-Adolf Jacobsen. Novato, CA: Presidio Press, 1988.

Hanfstaengl, Ernst "Putzi." *Hitler: The Missing Years*. London: Eyre & Spottiswoode, 1957.

Hassell, Ulrich von. *The von Hassell Diaries*. Garden City, NY: Doubleday, 1947.

Haushofer, Albrecht. *Moabit Sonnets*. Translated by M. D. Herter Norton. New York: Norton, 1978.

Hess, Ilse. *Prisoner of Peace*. London: Britons, 1954.

Hess, Wolf Rudiger. *My Father Rudolf Hess*. Translated by Frederick and Christine Crowley. London: W. H. Allen, 1987.

Higgins, Trumbull. *Winston Churchill and the Second Front: 1940–1943*. New York: Oxford University Press, 1957.

Hilberg, Raul. *The Destruction of the European Jews*. New York: Octagon Books, 1978.

Hinsley, F. H. *British Intelligence in the Second World War*. Vol 1. London: H.M. Stationery Office, 1979.

Hitler, Adolf. *Hitler's Secret Conversations*. Compiled by Martin Bormann. Translated by Norman Cameron and R. H. Stevens. New York: Farrar, Straus and Young, 1953.

———. *Mein Kampf*. Translated by Ralph Manheim. Boston: Houghton Mifflin, 1943.

———. *My New Order:* Edited by Raoul de Roussy de Sales. New York: Reynal & Hitchcock, 1941.

———. *Speeches of Adolf Hitler: April 1922–August 1939*. Edited by Norman H. Baynes. New York: Howard Fertig, 1969.

Hoare, Samuel. *Nine Troubled Years*. London: Colling, 1953.

Hutton, J. Bernard. *Hess: The Man and His Mission*. New York: Macmillan, 1970.

Irving, David. *Churchill's War*. New York: Avon, 1991 (first published in 1987).

———. *Hess: The Missing Years, 1941–1945*. London and New York: Macmillan, 1987.

———. *Hitler's War*. New York: Avon, 1990 (a condensation of three previously published volumes).

Jackson, Robert. *Dunkirk: The British Evacuation, 1940*. New York: St. Martin's, 1976.

Keitel, Wilhelm. *The Memoirs of Field Marshal Keitel*. Translated by David Irving. Edited by Walter Gorlitz. London: William Kimber, 1965.

Kersten, Felix. *The Kersten Memoirs: 1940–1945*. Translated by Constantine Fitzgibbon and James Oliver. New York: Macmillan, 1957.

Kimball, Warren F., ed. *Churchill and Roosevelt: The Complete Correspondence*. Vols. 1 & 2. Princeton: Princeton University Press, 1984.

Klemperer, Klemens von. *German Resistance against Hitler*. Oxford:

Clarendon Press, 1992.

Kubizek, August. *Young Hitler: The Story of Our Friendship*. London: Alan Wingate, 1954.

Lee, Raymond E. *The London Journal of General Raymond E. Lee: 1940–1941*. Boston: Little, Brown, 1971.

Lessor, James. *The Uninvited Envoy*. New York, Toronto, and London: McGraw-Hill, 1963.

Liddell Hart, B. H. *History of the Second World War*. London: Cassell & Company, 1970.

Lukacs, John. *The Duel, 10 May–31 July 1940: The Eighty-Day Struggle between Churchill and Hitler*. New York: Ticknor & Fields, 1991.

Manchester, William, *The Last Lion, Winston Spencer Churchill: Visions of Glory, 1874–1932*. Boston: Little, Brown: 1983.

————. *The Last Lion, Winston Spencer Churchill: Alone, 1932–1940*. Boston: Little, Brown, 1988.

Manvell, Roger, and Heinrich Frankel. *Hess: A Biography*. London: MacGibbon and Kee, 1973.

Maser, Werner. *Hitler's Letters and Notes*. Translated by Arnold Pomerans. New York: Harper & Row, 1973.

Masterman, J. C. *The Double Cross System*. New Haven: Yale University Press, 1972.

Moravec, Frantisek. *Master of Spies*. London: Bodley Head, 1985.

Noakes, J., and G. Pridham. *Nazism, A History in Documents and Eyewitness Accounts: Foreign Policy, War and Racial Extermination*. New York: Schocken, 1988. (Originally published in Great Britain by the Department of History and Archaeology, University of Exeter.)

————. *Nazism, A History in Documents and Eyewitness Accounts: The Nazi Party, State and Society*. New York, Schocken, 1983. (Originally published in Great Britain by the Department of History and Archaeology, University of Exeter.)

Padfield, Peter. *Hess: Flight for the Fuhrer*. London: Weidenfeld and Nicolson, 1991.

Papen, Franz von. *Memoirs, Franz von Papen*. New York: Dutton, 1953.

Reithinger, Gerald. *The SS: Alibi of a Nation*. Englewood Cliffs, NJ: Prentice-Hall, 1981.

Ritter, Gerhard. *The German Resistance*. Translated by R. T. Clark. New York: Praeger, 1958.

Rosenberg, Alfred. *Memoirs of Alfred Rosenberg*. Translated by Eric Posselt. Chicago: Ziff-Davis, 1949.

Schellenberg, Walter. *The Schellenberg Memoirs*. Edited and translated by Louis Hagen. London: Andre Deutsch, 1956.

Schmidt, Paul. *Hitler's Interpreter*. London: William Heinemann, 1951.

Schwarzwäller, Wulf. *Rudolf Hess: The Last Nazi*. Bethesda, MD: National Press and Star Agency, 1988.

Shirer, William L. *The Nightmare Years*. Boston: Little, Brown, 1984.

———. *The Rise and Fall of the Third Reich*. New York: Simon and Schuster, 1960.

Snyder, Louis L. *Hitler's Elite*. New York: Hippocrene Books, 1989.

Speer, Albert. *Inside the Third Reich*. Translated by Richard and Clara Winston. New York: Macmillan, 1970.

———. *Spandau*. New York: Pocket Books, 1977.

Sweet-Escott, Bickham. *Baker Street Irregular*. London: Methuen, 1965.

Taylor, A. J. P. *The Origins of the Second World War*. New York: Atheneum, 1983 (first published in 1961).

Thomas, Hugh W. *The Murder of Rudolf Hess*. New York: Harper & Row, 1979.

Thompson, Robert Smith. *A Time for War*. New York: Prentice Hall, 1991.

Toland, John. *Adolf Hitler*. Garden City, NY: Doubleday, 1976.

Toynbee, Arnold, ed. *Survey of International Affairs: 1939–46*. Vols. 3–10. London: Oxford University Press, 1953–1958.

Trial of German Major War Criminals: Proceedings of the International Military Tribunal Sitting at Nuremberg, Germany. Vols. 1–23. London: H.M. Stationery Office, 1945–1951.

Wagener, Otto. *Hitler: Memoirs of a Confidant*. Edited by Henry Ashby Turner, Jr. Translated by Ruth Hein. New Haven: Yale University Press, 1985.

Watt, Donald Cameron. *How War Came: The Immediate Origins of the Second World War, 1938–1939*. London: William Heinemann, 1989.

Weitz, John. *Hitler's Diplomat: The Life and Times of Joachim von Ribbentrop*. New York: Ticknor & Fields, 1992.

Winterbotham, Frederick W. *The Nazi Connection*. New York: Harper & Row, 1978.

———. *Secret and Personal*. London: William Kimber, 1969.

———. *The Ultra Secret*. New York: Harper & Row, 1974.

Zhukov, G. K. *The Memoirs of Marshal Zhukov*. London: Jonathan Cape, 1971.

Index

Abwehr, anti-Hitlerites in, 188, 191–92, 196, 221
Academy of Fine Arts (Vienna), 86–87, 88
Air Ministry, British:
  conspiracy in, 227–29, 258
  see also Royal Air Force
Alsace-Lorraine, 195
American Mercury, 287
Anschluss, 125, 126, 127, 130, 132
anti-Bolshevism, 23, 74, 117, 124, 133
  as potential basis for Anglo-German solidarity, 25, 56, 61, 75, 114, 213, 227, 228, 254
  in Weimar Germany, 80, 83
anti-capitalism, 80, 83, 93
anti-Semitism:
  of German Workers' Party, 93
  of Hitler, 88, 90, 91, 95, 101, 102, 133
  in Weimar Germany, 80–81, 83, 84, 93
appeasement policy, 127, 128–29
appeasers, 179
  Hoare associated with, 205, 216
  Nazi Germany visited by, 118–22, 139
Associated Press, 284
Astor, William Waldorf, 52
Austria, 147
  disposition of, discussed in armistice negotiations, 178, 193, 194
  K. Haushofer's views on, 68

Hitler's designs on, 68, 125, 126, 127, 130, 132

Bahamas, Windsor named governor of, 243, 246, 247
Balkans, 197
Baltic Sea, Nazi control of, 198, 200, 201
Baltic states, 135, 239
Barbarossa (Nazi invasion of Soviet Union), 26, 51–59, 73, 74, 170, 251, 268–69
  Allied aid to Soviet Union in, 282, 283, 284
  Churchill's prediction of, 232–33
  Directive No. 18 and, 21
  early Soviet losses in, 57
  extermination of Jews in, 58
  Hess mission and, 13, 35, 41, 47–48, 54, 55–57, 60, 61, 62, 75, 76, 266–67, 279–82, 286, 289
  and Hitler's reluctance to wage two-front war, 22, 23, 133, 238, 239
  launching of, 53
  military strategy in, 53–54, 57, 58–59
  "neutralization" of England as precondition for, 22–23
  Soviet preparations for, 47–48
  Stalin's views on likelihood of, 22, 278–79
  Weizsäcker's briefing on, 52–53
  Winterbotham shown plans for, 117–18

Bastiani, Giuseppe, 217

Battle of Britain, 75, 247–49, 257

Bauer, Hans, 266

Beaverbrook, Robert Maxwell
  Aitken, Lord, 52, 280

Beck, Ludwig, 189, 191, 192, 215,
  257

Beigbeder, Atienza, 242

Belgium, 168, 170
  disposition of, discussed in
    armistice negotiations, 53, 257,
    271
  Nazi attack on, 184, 185, 186–87,
    205, 208–9, 219

Benes, Eduard, 128

Beria, Lavrenty P., 286

Bernhard, Georg, 55–57, 59, 63

Bessarabia, 135

Best, Payne:
  kidnapping of, 181–82, 244
  peace terms delineated by, 178
  talks between rebellious German
    generals and, 173–83, 203

Bismarck, Otto von, 218

Blackford, D. L., 272–73

Blitz, 21, 23–24, 26, 27–28, 50, 75,
  157–58, 247–49, 250, 257, 269,
  287

blitzkrieg ("lightning strike")
  tactics, 73, 117, 156

blitzkrieg toward English Channel,
  19, 208–25
  Churchill's response to success
    of, 215–21, 223–24
  French surrender in, 224–25
  launching of, 202–5
  pause at Dunkirk in, 210–14, 217,
    218
  planning of, 184–88

Bloch, Edward, 87, 88

Blumentritt, Gunther, 223

Bock, Fedor von, 208, 209

Bohle, Ernst, 122, 263–64, 266, 287

Bolshevism, 92, 101, 109, 111, 188
  see also anti-Bolshevism

Brauchitsch, Walther von, 187,
  195–96, 237

Braun, Eva, 181

British Empire, 54, 132, 239, 257
  British attempts at extension of,
    114, 283, 286
  disposition of, discussed in
    armistice negotiations, 167,
    218, 232, 264, 271
  Hitler's interest in preservation
    of, 23, 124, 137, 213, 223, 234,
    290
  postwar disintegration of, 289
  preservation of, as key British
    goal, 24, 82, 289
  Roosevelt's attitude toward, 24
  see also Great Britain

British Expeditionary Force, 208,
  209, 210–14
  evacuated from Dunkirk, 19, 58,
    73, 212, 213, 214, 215, 217, 223

British fleet, *see* Royal Navy

Brown Shirts (SA), 97, 98, 109, 110

Bryans, J. Lonsdale (Mr. X), 191,
  192–94, 196

Bullitt, William, 269

Burckhardt, Carl Jacob, 229, 230,
  235, 271–72, 273, 275, 288

Butler, R. A., 229–30, 236, 256

Cadogan, Sir Alexander, 24–25,
  179, 194, 209, 216
  Hitler's peace offensive and,
    167, 171
  Polish crisis and, 142, 146, 149,
    152
  war aims and, 161–62

Canaris, Wilhelm, 188

capitalism, opposition to, 80, 83, 93

Case Yellow, 184–86

Catholic church, 191–92, 223

Chamberlain, Neville, 159, 161,
  164, 220, 237
  appeasement policy of, 127,
    128–29
  Churchill offered Prime
    Ministership by, 158
  German opposition's peace bids
    and, 178–79, 190, 196
  Hitler's peace offensive rejected
    by, 170–72, 174, 175, 188
  Norway offensive and, 200, 201,
    202

ouster of, 202, 205–6
Polish crisis and, 131, 135–36,
    137, 141, 142, 146
war declared by, 157
China, 253
Churchill, Clementine, 157
Churchill, Randolph, 20, 21, 111
Churchill, Winston, 19–26, 48, 77,
    85, 102, 135, 137, 169, 236–37,
    239, 249, 258, 264, 274
  Allied military strategy and,
    282–84
  Anglo-Soviet alliance and,
    160–61
  appointed Prime Minister, 206
  assessment of, 289–90
  breaking of Nazi codes and,
    219–20, 221
  Chamberlain's resignation and,
    205–6
  German opposition's peace bids
    and, 178–79
  A. Haushofer's letter and, 256
  Hess mission and, 35, 40, 42,
    45–46, 47, 49, 51, 55, 56–57,
    61, 78, 281–82, 285, 289–90
  Hitler's desire for Anglo-German
    alliance and, 123–24
  Hitler's peace offensives and,
    171, 234, 235, 240
  Hoare sent to Madrid by, 70, 216,
    220–21
  Lloyd George invited into
    cabinet of, 220–21
  meeting with Hitler sought by
    (1932), 111–14, 120, 124
  Nazi invasion of France and, 209,
    210, 213–14, 215
  Nazi invasion of Soviet Union
    and, 26, 59, 76, 133, 232–33,
    286
  Norway offensive and, 199–201,
    202
  planned invasion of England
    and, 249–50
  possible overthrow of, 46, 52, 54–
    55, 56, 57, 121, 230, 231, 233,
    265–66
  radio addresses of, 223–24

response of, to start of war, 155,
    157–58
secret control of Peace Party
    ascribed to, 26, 235
stalling strategy ascribed to, 19–
    20, 23, 226–47
surrender considered by, 216,
    217–19
U.S. urged to enter war by,
    20–21, 23, 24–25, 27, 44–46,
    47, 54, 206–8, 219, 269–70
war powers of, 221
Windsor's feuding with, 242–43,
    246
Ciano, Count Galeazzo, 43, 163,
    167, 168, 197, 221–22, 230
Civil War, U.S., 53–54
Clausewitz, Carl von, 101
Cliveden Set, see Peace Party
Clydesdale, Marquis of, see
    Hamilton, Duke of
Cold War, 13, 62, 285, 286
Colville, John, 221
communism, see anti-Bolshevism;
    Bolshevism
Cooper, Duff, 43, 232
Corbin, André, 162
Coulondre, Robert, 137
crash of 1929, 110
Crete, 22, 24
Crinis, Max de, 176–77
Cripps, Sir Stafford, 76, 282
Czechoslovakia, 253, 255
  disposition of, discussed in
    armistice negotiations, 178,
    191, 193, 271, 290
  Nazi conquest of, 125, 126,
    127–29, 130, 131, 136, 147
  Sudeten area of, 68, 125, 126,
    128, 129, 193, 194

Dachau, 67
Dahlerus, Birger:
  in armistice negotiations,
    166–67, 171
  in negotiations over Polish
    crisis, 138–46, 147, 148
  outbreak of war and, 149, 151,
    152, 153

Daily Mail (London), 122–23
Danzig, 125, 130, 141, 145, 147,
    159, 256
Davis, William Rhodes, 168
Denmark:
    disposition of, discussed in
        armistice negotiations, 69, 257,
        271
    Nazi invasion of, 200
Directive No. 16, 234
Directive No. 17, 247
Directive No. 18, 21
Directive No. 21, 268
Donovan, William "Wild Bill," 269
Douglas-Hamilton, James, 256
Drexler, Anton, 91, 92, 96, 99
Dungavel House (near Glasgow,
    Scotland), as Hess's
    destination, 29, 32
Dunkirk:
    evacuations from, 19, 58, 73, 212,
        213, 214, 215, 217, 223
    pause in Nazi offensive at,
        210–14, 217, 218
Dupree, Tom, 280

Eagle Day (Aug. 13, 1940), 247
Eastern Europe, 82, 124, 290
    see also specific countries
East Prussia, 130
Eben Emael, battle of, 186–87, 205
Eden, Anthony, 24, 41, 280
Egypt, 22, 25, 274, 278
Einsatzgruppen, 58
Eisner, Kurt, 81, 83
Elser, Georg, 182
England, *see* Great Britain
English Channel, Nazi offensive
    toward, *see* blitzkrieg toward
    English Channel
Enigma, 203, 219–20, 221, 245, 248

Fascism, 111
Finland, 168
    Soviet attack on, 198, 199–200
Fischer, Franz, 173–74, 175
Foch, Ferdinand, 224, 225
Foreign Ministry, Nazi, anti-
    Hitlerites in, 188–89, 196

Foreign Office, British, 78
    anti-Hitlerite conspiracy and,
        192–94, 196
France, 128, 163, 178, 190, 196,
    268, 271
    disposition of, discussed in
        armistice negotiations, 69, 195,
        257
    and invasion of Low Countries,
        203, 204, 208–9
    Nazi attack on, 73, 74, 170, 184,
        185–88, 208–15, 217, 218, 219,
        222, 223, 224–25, 241, 242
    Polish crisis and, 132, 137, 143,
        150
    possibility of Anglo-German
        alliance with, 112–13
    Ruhr occupied by, 97, 98
    surrender of, 224–25
    war declared by, 150, 151, 156,
        159
Franz Ferdinand, archduke of
    Austria, 89
Frederick II (the Great), king of
    Prussia, 218
Free Corps, 80–81, 83, 91, 92
Fromm, Friedrich, 202
Fugate, Bryan, 47

Gallup, George, 24
Gamelin, Maurice, 209
Geopolitical Institute (Berlin), 69
geopolitics, 101–5
    K. Haushofer's theories on,
        81–82, 84, 94
    Hitler's racial obsessions wedded
        to, 101–2
George VI, king of England, 61,
    206, 237, 242, 258
German Workers' Party, 91–94
    see also National Socialist
        German Workers Party
Germany, imperial, 155
    collapse of, 171, 179
    defeat of, 79–82, 90, 102, 103
Germany, Nazi (Third Reich):
    air force of, *see* Luftwaffe
    Allied bombing of, 50–51, 283
    anti-Hitlerites in, 47, 172, 173–

183, 188–96, 203, 221, 257, 265
army of, *see* Wehrmacht
British shipping disrupted by,
    21, 27
British visitors to (appeasers),
    118–22, 139
divisions demobilized by, 59, 221
early victories of, 19–20, 21–22
England bombed by, 21, 23–24,
    26, 27–28, 50, 75, 157–58,
    247–49, 250, 257, 269, 287
expansionism of, 101, 114, 116,
    124, 125–53; *see also*
    Lebensraum
foreign policy of, 66, 67, 68, 71,
    81–82, 84, 101–5
Hitler named Chancellor of, 114
Hitler's rebuilding of, 114–15
intelligence services of, 153–54;
    see also Abwehr
iron supplies of, 196, 198–201
munitions production halted in,
    59
oil supplies of, 196–98, 200, 232
peace overtures of, 25–26, 69–75,
    77, 164–83, 221–22, 226–47,
    251, 257–68, 271–72, 290; *see
    also* Rudolf Hess Affair
Poland invaded by, 19, 68, 72, 73,
    131, 135, 138, 140–41, 145,
    147, 149, 159–60, 163, 164,
    166, 178, 187
possible change of regime in,
    265, 271, 272, 288
Soviet nonaggression pact with,
    48, 133–35, 136, 138, 142, 149
Soviet Union invaded by, 13, 21,
    22–23, 26, 35, 41, 47–48,
    51–62, 73, 74, 75, 76, 117, 170,
    232–33, 238, 239, 251, 266–69,
    278–82, 286, 289; *see also*
    Barbarossa
uniting of German peoples in,
    68, 161, 188, 193–94, 219, 221
war declared on, 73
see also Hitler, Adolf
Germany, Weimar, 79–114
    anti-Semitism in, 80–81, 83, 84,
    93

Free Corps in, 80–81, 83, 91, 92
Hitler's rise to power in, 107–11,
    114
Reds and leftists in, 79, 80–81,
    92, 97
reparation payments of, 80, 95,
    96, 110
Gestapo, 153, 154
Gibson, Robert, 31
Glasgow Daily Record, 36–38, 39
Goebbels, Joseph, 52, 151, 156,
    181, 231, 233, 247, 254
    on decline in Allied air raids,
    50–51
    Hess mission and, 42–43, 45
Gördeler, Carl, 188, 189, 190, 192,
    257
Göring, Hermann, 98, 187, 202,
    215, 219
    air raids on England carried out
    by, 23–24, 27–28, 50, 249, 269,
    287
    armistice negotiations and, 74,
    166, 167, 168, 183
    declarations of war and, 150,
    151–53
    Englishmen's meetings with,
    118–19, 121–22, 125, 254
    named Hitler's successor, 157
    Polish crisis and, 138, 139, 140–
    146, 148, 149, 153
Great Britain, 112–13, 128, 134,
    189, 197, 198
    alleged conspiracy of Nazi
    sympathizers in, 77–78
    appeasement period in, 127,
    128–29
    Churchill's war powers in, 221
    code breaking in, 203, 219–20,
    221, 245
    decentralization of Germany as
    goal of, 194
    early losses of, 19–20, 21–22, 27
    fleet of, *see* Royal Navy
    German anti-Hitlerites and, 173–
    183, 190–96, 257, 265, 271–72
    A. Haushofer's contacts in,
    253–55
    K. Haushofer's ideas about, 82,

Great Britain *(cont.)*
    101, 102
    Hitler's desire for alliance with,
        67, 74–75, 101–5, 116–26, 129,
        145, 212–13
    intelligence services of, *see*
        Secret Intelligence Service,
        British
    and invasion of Low Countries,
        203, 204, 205, 208–9
    Nazi air raids on, 21, 23–24, 26,
        27–28, 50, 75, 157–58, 247–49,
        250, 257, 269, 287
    and Nazi invasion of France,
        209–15
    and Nazi invasion of Soviet
        Union, 251, 268–69, 278
    Nazi peace overtures to, 25–26,
        69–75, 77, 164–83, 221–22,
        226–47, 251, 257–68, 271–72,
        290; *see also* Rudolf Hess Affair
    Nazi sympathizers in (appeasers),
        118–22, 139, 179, 205, 216
    Nazi territorial ambitions and,
        116, 124–29, 131–33, 135–53
    Norway offensive and, 196,
        198–202
    peace forces in, *see* Peace Party
    planned invasion of, 222–23, 231,
        233, 234–35, 239, 249–50, 251,
        259–60, 268, 269–70
    Polish crisis and, 73, 131–33,
        135–53
    sea power of, 82, 104, 116, 124,
        129
    Soviet alliance with, 160–61
    Soviet moles in, 49
    surrender considered by, 216,
        217–19
    vulnerable to Nazi attack, 19,
        215–16, 218, 222
    war aims of, 161–62, 171–83, 217
    war declared by, 150–53, 156,
        157, 159, 160
    see also British Empire
Greece, 24, 197, 274
Guderian, Heinz, 58, 186, 208, 209
Gustav V, king of Sweden, 230,
    240

Halder, Franz, 132, 149, 163, 202,
    251, 268, 271
    Allies' interview with, 72–76
    in conspiracy against Hitler,
        189–90, 195–96
    Eastern campaign and, 52, 57, 59,
        239
    possible Anglo-German accord
        and, 23, 53, 54–55, 216, 231,
        233–34
    strike against West and, 184–85,
        210, 211
Halifax, Edward F. L. Wood, Lord,
    46, 74, 126, 137, 161, 167, 234,
    256, 261, 273
    Chamberlain's resignation and,
        205–6
    German opposition's peace bids
        and, 178–79, 192–93, 196
    Germany visited by, 125
    Peace Party and, 230, 231, 236,
        237
    Polish crisis and, 140–41, 142,
        146
    surrender considered by, 217
Hamilton, Duke of (formerly
        Marquis of Clydesdale):
    forced to become British agent,
        272–73
    A. Haushofer betrayed by, 273
    A. Haushofer's letters to, 34, 61,
        255–56, 262–63, 265, 271, 272,
        273
    A. Haushofer's relationship with,
        253–55, 262
    Hess mission and, 28, 29, 32–33,
        34, 37, 38, 39, 48, 51, 60–61,
        72, 75, 77, 153, 266, 273, 275,
        277, 279, 281, 285
    Hess's letters to, 122, 263–64,
        285–86, 287, 288
    as link to Peace Party, 258–64
    Mrs. Roberts as conduit to, 258,
        259, 260–61, 262, 263
Hamilton, Ian, 259
Hanfstaengl, Ernst "Putzi," 95–96,
    100, 108, 214
    Churchill and, 111, 112–13, 124
Hassell, Ulrich von, 184, 200, 204,

214–15
  in conspiracy against Hitler, 188–
    196, 257
  in peace negotiations, 74, 190–94,
    271, 274
Haushofer, Albrecht, 67, 72, 79,
    153, 252–65
  betrayed by Hamilton, 273
  death of, 66, 69, 70–71
  diary of, 71
  in German opposition, 189, 252,
    255–57, 265
  Hamilton's relationship with,
    253–55, 262
  Hamilton written by, 34, 61,
    255–56, 262–63, 265, 271, 272,
    273
  Hess mission and, 32, 55, 61, 69,
    71, 72, 266
  Hess's relationship with, 252–53,
    255, 262
  peace feelers conveyed by, 34,
    35, 51, 55, 257–63, 264–65,
    271–72, 274–75
Haushofer, Heinz, 259
Haushofer, Karl, 32, 34, 212, 253,
    254, 266, 272
  diary of, 71
  Hess influenced by, 82, 83–84,
    94
  Hitler first encountered by,
    93–94
  Hitler influenced by, 66–68, 94,
    101–2, 103, 116, 212
  interrogated by U.S. agents,
    65–71, 73, 74, 75, 286, 288
  Lebensraum notion of, 81–82,
    103
  peace feelers and, 69–70, 71,
    258–61, 263, 264
Hedin, Sven, 220
"Heil Hitler," as customary Nazi
    salutation, 108
Henderson, Sir Neville:
  declaration of war and, 150
  Polish crisis and, 136–37, 142–43,
    144–45, 146–48
Hess, Ilse, 16, 122, 267, 276–77
Hess, Rudolf, 98, 117, 122, 123,

145, 150, 151, 154, 172, 181,
    227, 278
  as back-channel route to Hitler,
    153
  background of, 82–83
  British officials' interviews
    with, 46, 60–62
  fund established for, 288–89
  halt order at Dunkirk and, 212,
    213
  Hamilton written by, 263–64,
    285–86, 287, 288
  A. Haushofer's relationship with,
    252–53, 255, 262
  K. Haushofer's influence on, 82,
    83–84, 94
  K. Haushofer's relationship with,
    66–68
  Hitler first encountered by,
    93–94
  Hitler's relationship with, 100,
    108, 109
  impostor posing as, 16–17, 289
  in Landsberg Prison, 100–101,
    102, 108
  medical history of, 13–14, 16, 17,
    32, 83, 94, 289
  in mission to British Isles,
    12–13, 28–57, 59–76, 77, 78,
    102, 152–53, 208, 229, 240,
    247, 248, 255, 266–68, 275–77,
    279–80, 281–82, 284–90; *see
    also* Rudolf Hess Affair
  named second in line of
    succession, 157
  at Nuremberg trials, 12, 64–65
  peace feelers and, 257–62,
    263–64, 271, 272, 273–74
  physical examinations of, 13,
    14–16
  in Spandau Prison, 12–17, 289
  in Thule Society, 83, 92
  in World War I, 13–14, 16, 83
  in writing of *Mein Kampf*, 101,
    102, 103–4, 105, 108
Rudolf Hess Affair, 12–13, 28–57,
    59–63, 152–53, 208, 229, 240,
    255, 287–90
  accomplishments of, 289–90

Rudolf Hess Affair *(cont.)*
  airplane for, 266
  Bernhard's near-untangling of,
    55–57, 59, 63
  British statements on, 38–39,
    40–43, 45–46, 51, 54, 57, 77, 78
  capture of Hess in, 30–32
  decline of air raids and, 50–51
  false starts in, 267–68
  first newspaper story on, 36–38,
    39
  flight and bailout in, 28–30
  German propaganda on, 35–36,
    38, 40, 41–42, 43
  global response to, 39–40, 43
  Halder's information on, 72–76
  K. Haushofer's information on,
    65–71, 75
  Hess's identity revealed in, 32,
    60
  Hitler's advance knowledge of,
    266, 275, 279, 280
  Hitler's public response to,
    33–36, 71–72, 102, 267
  Lee's communiqué on, 60–62, 63
  messenger chosen in, 287
  motivation ascribed to Hess in,
    41, 42
  Nazi-Soviet conflict and, 13, 35,
    41, 47–48, 54, 55–57, 60, 61,
    62, 75, 76, 266–67, 279–82,
    286, 289
  as peace initiative, 33, 34–35,
    40, 46, 48–49, 50–51, 55–56,
    57, 61, 64, 69–70, 71–72,
    75–76, 279, 280, 288
  planning of, 34, 61, 247, 248,
    266–68, 275–77
  postwar reexamination of, 62–63,
    64–76, 77
  Soviet interpretation of, 47–48,
    279–80, 281–82, 284–87
  training flights for, 266, 267
  U.S. perception of, 44–47, 48–49,
    60–62, 281
Heydrich, Reinhard, 268
Himmler, Heinrich, 58, 66, 145,
    153, 181, 182, 272, 276
Hindenburg, Paul von, 79, 110–11,

114, 120, 184
Hitler, Adolf, 12, 57, 64, 70, 78,
    78, 84–154, 207, 289–90
  air raids on England and, 27–28,
    50, 247, 249, 257
  Anglo-German alliance as goal
    of, 67, 74–75, 101–5, 116–26,
    129, 145, 212–13
  anti-Semitism of, 88, 90, 91, 95,
    101, 102, 133
  asexuality of, 85–86, 96
  as aspiring artist, 84, 86–87, 88
  background of, 84
  banned from public speaking,
    108, 109–10
  beer hall Putsch of, 97–98, 107
  beer hall speeches of, 94–96, 107
  blindness of, 90–91
  British Peace Party and, 25–26,
    51, 52, 54–55, 208, 226–47, 264
  chancellorship sought by,
    110–11, 114
  Churchill as viewed by, 224
  Churchill's desire for meeting
    with (1932), 111–14, 120, 124
  declarations of war and, 150–53,
    156
  destitution experienced by,
    87–88, 93
  divisions disbanded by, 59, 221
  in early days of war, 159, 163–64
  economic programs of, 114–15
  electoral tactics of, 109–10, 114,
    115
  "der Führer" appellation of, 108
  generals' relationships with,
    187–88, 215, 251–52
  geopolitical thinking of, 101–5
  German opposition to, 47, 172,
    173–83, 188–96, 203, 221, 257,
    265
  global ambitions ascribed to,
    20–21, 44–46, 54
  K. Haushofer's influence on, 66–
    68, 94, 101–2, 103, 116, 212
  A. Haushofer's opposition to,
    252, 255–57
  Hess mission and, 13, 33–36, 41,
    43–44, 46, 49–50, 51, 55,

71–72, 77, 102, 266–67, 275,
    279, 280, 287
Hess's relationship with, 100,
    108, 109
impatience of, 123, 125, 134
incarcerated in Landsberg
    Prison, 99, 100–106
invasion of England planned by,
    251, 259–60, 268, 269
invasion of Soviet Union and,
    53–54, 57–59, 74, 75, 232–33,
    238, 239, 251, 266–67
Iron Cross won by, 89, 91, 94
Jews exterminated by, 160, 169
line of succession specified by,
    157
Lloyd George admired by,
    220–21
master plan of, 63, 74–75
military strategy of, 22–23,
    184–88, 202, 204, 222–23, 251,
    270
mother's death and, 87, 88
offensive against West and,
    184–88, 202–5, 208–20,
    222–23, 224–25
peace with England sought by,
    74–75, 164–83, 221–22,
    226–47, 251, 257–68, 271–72,
    288, 290
personality cult of, 108
physical appearance of, 85
Polish crisis and, 68, 73, 130–53
political career begun by, 92–93
portrayed as demon, 20
possible replacement of, 265,
    271, 272, 288
in post–World War I army, 91–92
public speaking manner of,
    94–96
radio address of, at start of war,
    156–57
removal of, as British war aim,
    161–62, 171–83
rise to power of, 107–11, 114
simple lifestyle of, 96
Stalin's nonaggression pact with,
    48, 133–35, 136, 138, 142, 149
standard foreign diplomatic

machinery bypassed by,
    152–53
strategic weaknesses combatted
    by, 196–202
surrender to, considered by
    British, 216, 217–19
treason charged against, 98–100
trial of, 99–100, 107
two-front war avoided by, 23,
    133, 238, 239
in Vienna, 84–88
vulnerable to Weimar authori-
    ties, 108–9
war preparations launched by,
    125
in World War I, 89–91
    see also Germany, Nazi
Hitler, Alois, 84, 87
Hitler, Klara, 84, 85, 87, 88
Hoare, Samuel, Lord Templewood,
    55, 205, 228
appointed ambassador to Spain,
    70, 216, 220–21
peace feelers and, 55, 69, 70,
    234, 261, 265–66, 271, 272, 273
as possible replacement for
    Churchill, 70, 121
Windsors feted by, 241, 245
Hohenlohe, Prince Max, 183, 229,
    230–31, 235–36
Holland, 168, 170
disposition of, discussed in
    armistice negotiations, 53, 257,
    271
meetings of German opposition
    in, 173–78, 180–83
Nazi attack on, 184, 185, 203–5,
    208–9
Holocaust, 58, 62, 73, 160, 169, 290
Home Guards, 31, 32
Hoover, J. Edgar, 48–49, 62, 63, 77,
    288
House Foreign Affairs Committee,
    20, 269
House of Commons, 51
Huntziger, Charles, 209

India, 257, 270
Iraq, 22, 24, 25, 26, 270, 274, 278

iron, Nazi supplies of, 196, 198–201
Ismay, Hastings, 250
Italy, 143, 168, 215, 218, 230
    entry into war of, 137, 163,
      197–98, 224
    Hess mission and, 43
    Nazi oil supplies and, 196–98
    as potential ally, 103, 113

Jahnke, Kurt, 153–54
Jahnkeburo, 153
Japan, 23, 82, 179, 234, 253
Jews:
    extermination of, 58, 62, 160,
      169, 290
    Hitler's peace offensive and,
      169–70
    of Poland, 160, 166
Jodl, Alfred, 203, 225
Joint Chiefs of Staff, U.S., 282

Kahr, Gustav Ritter von, 98
Katyn Forest massacre, 160
Keitel, Wilhelm, 163, 172, 185, 203,
    204–5, 222–23
Kelly, Sir David, 235–36, 237
Kennedy, Joseph, 20
KGB, 279, 285
Kimball, Warren, 285
Kirkpatrick, Ivone, 41, 60, 61, 279,
    280
Klop, Lieutenant, 175, 177, 180,
    182
Knox, Frank, 269, 270
Koch, Erich, 117
Krupp, Gustav, 164, 212
Kubizek, August, 85–86, 87, 109

Labour Party (British), 205–6
Laird (reporter), 281
League of Nations, 188
Lebensraum notion, 81–82, 103,
    123, 124, 125, 126, 132, 133,
    169, 219, 237
Lee, Raymond, 60–62, 63, 77, 281,
    282
Leiber, Father Robert, 192, 194–95
Leitgen, Alfred, 72, 275
Lenin, V. I., 56

Lindbergh, Charles, 24, 45
Lipski, Josef, 148
Livingstone, Clem, 37–38
Lloyd George, David, 55, 119–21,
    231, 237
    Hitler's admiration for, 220–21
    invited into Churchill's cabinet,
      220–21
Londonderry, Lord, 118–19
Lothian, Lord, 237, 261
Luccas, John, 235
Ludendorff, Erich, 56, 79, 98
Luftwaffe, 21, 118, 139, 187, 201,
    215, 222, 224, 226, 254
    code of, broken by British,
      219–20
    England bombed by, 27–28, 50,
      247–49, 250, 269
    fund established for Hess by,
      288–89
Luxembourg, 185

McAuslane, Max, 37
McCormick, Anne, 54
McLean, David, 30–31, 37, 38, 78
Maginot Line, 208
Magistrati, Count Massimo, 197
Manstein, Erich von, 186
Marshall, George C., 270, 286
Marxism, 289
May, Karl, 187
Mein Kampf (Hitler), 88–89, 100,
    101, 102–5, 106, 108, 111, 114,
    116, 126, 151, 213, 214, 227,
    231, 290
Messerschmidt, Willy, 266, 267
Mexico, 207, 270
Middle East, 24, 25, 257, 278, 286
    oil fields in, 21–22, 25
Milch, Erhard, 222
Miles, Sherman, 77, 281
    Lee's communiqué to, 60–62
Molotov, V. M., 48, 133, 134, 282,
    283
Moravec, Colonel, 285–86
Morton, Desmond, 281, 282
Moscow, Nazi offensive toward, 57,
    58–59
Muller (lawyer), 74

Müller, Josef, 191–92, 194–95
Munich pact (1938), 128–29, 188,
    189
Mussolini, Benito, 23, 43, 108, 201,
    203, 212, 225, 256
    armistice negotiations and, 217,
        219
    Hess misison and, 43
    Italy's entry into war and, 137,
        163, 197–98, 224

National Archives, U.S., 72
National Socialist German Workers
    Party (Nazi Party), 94–98,
    106–10, 114, 153, 173
    electoral politics and, 109–10,
        114
    German Workers' Party as
        predecessor of, 91–94
    Hitler's attempted Putsch and,
        97–98
    Hitler's control of, 96, 107
    Hitler's imprisonment and,
        106–7
    Hitler's speeches on behalf of,
        94–96
    membership in, 97, 109–10
    policing of rallies of, 97
Navy, German, 187, 239
    Norway offensive and, 199,
        200–201
Nazi Party, *see* National Socialist
    German Workers Party
Newall, Sir Cyril, 250
New York Times, 41, 42, 55–57
Nicolson, Harold, 232
NKVD, 279
North African campaign, 24, 59,
    283
    oil supplies and, 21–22, 25, 196–
        197, 270, 274, 278
Norway, 69, 74, 75, 168, 257, 283
    Nazi offensive for control of,
        196, 198–202
Nuremberg laws, 93
Nuremberg trials, 12, 64–65, 101

O'Connell, Archbishop William, 24
Office of Strategic Services (OSS),
    207, 269
oil:
    Nazi supplies of, 196–98, 200,
        232
    North African campaign and,
        21–22, 25, 196–97, 270, 274,
        278
    in Soviet Union, 54, 58, 133
Oldfield, Sir Maurice, 78
Olympic Games (1936), 32, 60, 253
Oster, Hans, 188, 191–92, 257
Otto (operation), 117

Panama Canal, 270
Pan-German movement, 80
Paris, German occupation of, 224
Parliament, British, 221
Paterson, Jack, 31
Paulus, Friedrich, 270
Peace Party (Cliveden Set), 25–26,
    27, 59, 216, 221, 290
    Air Ministry conspiracy and,
        227–29, 258
    as chimera, 26, 33
    in Churchill's stalling strategy,
        226–47
    control of, ascribed to Churchill,
        26, 208
    Duke of Windsor and, 240–47,
        248
    Hess mission and, 32–33, 34, 35,
        46, 48–49, 51, 61, 278, 280,
        286–87, 288
    Nazi contacts with, 55, 70, 71–72,
        258, 261, 264–65, 288
    and possible overthrow of
        Churchill, 46, 52, 54–55, 230,
        231, 233, 265–66
    as traitorous conspiracy, 77–78
Persian Gulf, 270
Pétain, Henri Philippe, 225
Philby, Kim, 278, 279, 280
Phony War period, 73, 159–203, 269
Pintsch, Karl-Heinz, 267–68, 277
Pius XII, Pope, 191–92, 194–95
Poland, 124, 130–53, 162, 257
    abuse of German population in,
        130–31, 134, 136, 149, 155
    British pledge to, 73, 131–33,

Poland *(cont.)*
135–48
British ultimatum on, 149–53
Dahlerus's diplomacy and,
138–53
disposition of, discussed in
armistice negotiations, 165–66,
167–68, 169, 182, 190, 193–94,
264, 271, 290
Hitler's hatred for, 131
Nazi invasion of, 19, 68, 72, 73,
131, 135, 138, 140–41, 145,
147, 149, 159–60, 163, 164,
166, 178, 187
Secret Protocol on, 135, 138, 142
Soviet invasion of, 135, 159–61,
165
Polish Corridor, 73, 125, 126, 129,
130–31, 138, 142, 143, 144–45,
147, 149, 165, 167, 168, 256
Pound, Dudley, 201
Prytz, Bjorn, 230
Putsch (1923), 97–98, 107
reunion of Old Fighters from,
181, 182

Quisling, Vidkun, 199

Raeder, Erich, 116, 187
Ratzel, Friedrich, 101
Red Army, 198
Nazi invasion and, 57, 58, 272,
283
Poland invaded by, 135, 159–61
Reich Defense Council, 124
Reichenau, Walter von, 117
Reynaud, Paul, 209, 219, 224
Rhineland, 126, 132
Ribbentrop, Joachim von, 43, 52,
183, 203, 221–22, 230, 232, 248
bypassed in secret negotiations,
138, 152, 153
Churchill's meeting with (1937),
124
declarations of war and, 150–51
A. Haushofer and, 252, 253
K. Haushofer's influence on, 68
Nazi-Soviet nonaggression pact
and, 133, 134–35

Polish crisis and, 138, 146–48
Windsor affair and, 241, 243–45,
246
Roberts, Mary Violet, 258, 259,
260–61, 262, 263
Robertson, T. A., 273
Romania, Nazi oil supplies and,
196–97, 200, 232
Rommel, Erwin, 21, 59, 208, 210,
270, 274, 278
Roosevelt, Franklin D., 77, 102–3,
168, 285
Allied military strategy and, 282,
283–84
Hess mission and, 44–47, 61, 62,
281
Nazi intentions as viewed by,
44–46, 54
security of British fleet as
concern of, 44–45, 207–8,
216–17
U.S. entry into war and, 20, 24–
25, 27, 44–46, 47, 54, 207–8,
269, 270
Ropp, Baron William de, 131–32,
227, 228–29, 233, 249, 253,
272, 275
Rosenberg, Alfred, 117, 131, 179,
220, 272
British Peace Party and, 227–28
Hess mission and, 275–76
Rothermere, Lord, 122–23
Royal Air Force (RAF), 28, 50–51,
117, 132, 215, 224, 227, 228,
235, 247–48, 253, 258, 283
Royal Air Force Club, 228
Royal College of Surgeons
(Edinburgh), 17
Royal Institute of International
Affairs, 254
Royal Navy, 124, 222, 232, 239,
269, 270
Norway offensive and, 196,
200–201
possible German control of,
44–45, 207–8, 216–17
Ruhr, 97, 98, 196, 202
Rundstedt, Gerd von, 208, 209,
210, 223

Rybukin, Boris, 279

Schaemmel, Major, 176
Schellenberg, Walter, 153–54, 172,
    260–61, 266, 288
    in secret negotiations with SIS,
    174–83
    Windsor kidnap plot and, 244–45
Schlieffen plan, 184, 185, 208
Schmidt, Paul, 118, 119, 120–21,
    137, 146, 147–48, 150–51, 198
Schofield, Eric, 36–37
Schuschnigg, Kurt von, 127
Schutzstaffel (SS), 66, 67, 97, 153,
    173, 176, 177, 181–82, 198,
    266, 272
Schwarzwäller, Wulf, 268
Sea Lion (planned invasion of
    England), 222–23, 231, 233,
    234–35, 239, 249–50, 251, 259–
    260, 268, 269–70
Secret Intelligence Service, British
    (SIS), 20, 128–29, 153, 245,
    269
    Air Ministry conspiracy and,
    227–29
    anti-Hitler conspiracies and,
    173–83
    Hess misison and, 70, 77, 280
    letters to Hamilton intercepted
    by, 263, 272, 285–86, 287
    U.S. entry into war and, 207
Sherman, William Tecumseh,
    53–54, 185, 204
Shirer, William, 156
Signal Corps, 31
Simpson, Wallis, *see* Windsor,
    Duchess of
Sinclair, Sir Archibald, 51
Smuts, Jan Christiaan, 233
socialism, espoused by German
    Workers' Party, 92, 93
Solms, Major, 173, 174, 175
South America, Nazi designs on,
    44, 46
Soviet Union, 20, 25, 49, 113, 124,
    128, 129, 132, 143, 179, 227,
    234, 237, 239, 278–87
    Allied aid to, 282, 283, 284

British alliance with, 160–61
extermination of Jews in, 58
Finland attacked by, 198,
    199–200
Hess mission as viewed in,
    47–48, 279–80, 281–82, 284–87
Nazi invasion of, 13, 21, 22–23,
    26, 35, 41, 47–48, 51–62, 73,
    74, 75, 76, 117, 170, 232–33,
    238, 239, 251, 266–69, 278–82,
    286, 289; *see also* Barbarossa
Nazi nonaggression pact with,
    48, 133–35, 136, 138, 142, 149
Nazi territorial designs on, 103
Poland invaded by, 135, 159–61,
    165
see also Ukraine
Spain, 168, 233
Spandau Prison, 12–17
    Hess's physical examinations at,
    13, 14–16
    impostor at, 16–17, 289
Speer, Albert, 59
SS, *see* Schutzstaffel
Stahmer, Heinrich, 265, 266, 273
Stalin, Josef, 24, 53, 102–3, 214,
    232, 278–87
    Allied aid sought by, 283, 284
    Cold War and, 13, 62, 285, 286
    Hess mission and, 13, 47–48, 62,
    64, 279, 280, 281–82, 284–87
    Hitler's nonaggression pact with,
    48, 133–35, 136, 138, 142, 149
    Nazi invasion and, 22–23, 47–48,
    57, 59, 61, 76, 278–79, 281–82
    Polish invasion and, 159
    suspicious of Allies, 281, 284–87
Stammers, F. G., 272
State Department, U.S., 40, 48, 49,
    71, 72, 77, 288
Stephenson, William, 206–7, 220,
    243, 269
Stevens, R. H.:
    kidnapping of, 181–82, 244
    talks between rebellious German
    generals and, 175–83, 203
Stohrer, Eberhard, 242
Sudetenland, 68, 125, 126, 128, 129,
    193, 194

Sweden:
    in armistice negotiations, 74,
        230, 233, 234, 240, 264
    Nazi iron supplies and, 196,
        198–201
Switzerland, 69, 74
Syria, 22, 278

Templewood, Samuel Hoare, Lord,
    see Hoare, Samuel, Lord
    Templewood
Third Reich, *see* Germany, Nazi
Thomas, Georg, 190
Thomas, Hugh, 11–17, 289
Thomsen, Hans, 237
Thule Society, 83, 91–92
Toland, John, 88
Torch, 283
Troost, Gerdy, 213

Ukraine, 57, 127
    Hitler's designs on, 21, 54, 82,
        114, 124, 231–32, 237, 239, 251
Ultra, 269
United States, 82, 123, 168, 179,
        226, 234, 237
    British propaganda efforts in,
        207, 269–70
    entry into war of, 20–21, 23,
        24–25, 27, 44–46, 47, 54, 56,
        206–8, 219, 243, 269–70
    Hess mission and, 44–47, 48–49,
        60–62, 281
    Hitler's views on, 104
    Nazi leadership investigated by,
        64–76, 77
    Soviet war effort aided by, 282,
        283, 284
University of Munich, 81, 83

Vansittart, Sir Robert, 125–26, 161,
        173, 183, 236
Vatican, 173, 229
    in conspiracy against Hitler,
        191–92, 194–95
Versailles treaty (1919), 68, 80,
        123, 126, 130, 143, 162, 169,
        171, 190
Voitov (K.G.B. agent), 15, 16

völkisch movement, 80, 81, 84, 92
War Office, Nazi, 172
Weddell, Alexander, 241–42
Wednesday Society, 257
Wehrmacht, 131, 156, 202, 216, 232
    in blitzkrieg toward English
        Channel, 172, 183, 202–5,
        208–14, 224, 226
    intelligence services of, 153;
        see also Abwehr
    invasion of England and, 235,
        239
    military strategy of, 184–88
    plots against Hitler in, 173–83
    in Polish campaign, 131, 159, 165
    in Russian campaign, 47, 57–58,
        282
Weimar Republic, *see* Germany,
    Weimar
Weizsäcker, Baron Ernst von,
        52–53, 172, 189, 204, 215, 230,
        237
Welles, Sumner, 46
What Should We Do?, 128–29
Wheeler, Burton, 45
White Russia, 124, 239
Wilhelm II, kaiser of Germany, 80,
        90, 91, 103, 155, 171, 193
Wilhelmina, queen of Netherlands,
        203
Winant, John Gilbert, 39, 41, 281
Windsor, Duchess of (formerly
        Wallis Simpson), 77, 121, 122,
        240–41, 242, 244, 247
Windsor, Duke of (formerly
        Edward VIII), 77, 221, 240–47,
        257, 266
    abdication of, 121, 240–41
    Germany visited by, 121–22
    Hess mission and, 248, 288
    Hitler's admiration for, 240
    kidnap plot and, 243–46
    peace feelers and, 237, 244, 248,
        252, 260–61, 264
    peace sentiments of, 241–42
    posted to Bahamas, 243, 246, 247
    transformation of, 246–47
Winterbotham, Frederick W., 106,
        117–19, 215, 228, 233, 245,

249–50, 254, 272
World War I, 44, 56, 65, 68, 79–80,
    83, 101–2, 103, 136, 155, 164,
    220, 227, 238, 254
  explanations for German loss in,
    80–82, 90
  German reparations payments
    after, 80, 95, 96, 110
  Hess wounded in, 13–14, 16, 83
  Hitler's experiences in, 89–91
  Hitler's views on, 119, 120, 122
  military strategy in, 184–85
  territories stripped from
    Germany after, 130, 142, 169
  World War II as continuation of,
    162
  see also Versailles treaty
World War II:
  air raids on England in, 21, 23–
    24, 26, 27–28, 50, 75, 157–58,
    247–49, 250, 257, 269, 287
  Allied military strategy in,
    282–84
  armistice sought in early days of,
    25–26, 69–75, 77, 164–83, 221–
    222, 226–47, 251, 257–68, 271–
    272, 290; see also Rudolf Hess
    Affair
  British shipping disrupted in, 21,
    27
  British surrender considered in,
    216, 217–19
  British war aims in, 161–62,
    171–83, 217
  as continuation of World War I,
    162
  declarations of war in, 150–53,
    156, 157, 159, 160
  events leading to, 125–148

  Germans' response to start of,
    155–56
  Hitler's radio address at start
    of, 156–57
  Italy's entry into, 137, 163, 197–
    198, 224
  Nazi invasion of Soviet Union in,
    see Barbarossa
  Nazi military strategy in, 184–88,
    202, 204, 222–23, 251, 270
  Nazi mobilization for, 170, 172,
    175, 183
  Nazi strategic weaknesses in,
    196–202
  Nazi strikes against West in,
    see blitzkrieg toward British
    Channel
  North African campaign in,
    21–22, 24, 25, 59, 196–97, 270,
    274, 278, 283
  Norway offensive in, 196,
    198–202
  opening of second front in, 22,
    23, 133, 238, 239, 282–83, 284
  outbreak of, 149
  pause in (summer of 1940),
    226–47
  Phony War phase of, 73,
    159–203, 269
  U.S. entry into, 20–21, 23, 24–25,
    27, 44–46, 47, 54, 56, 206–8,
    219, 243, 269–70

X report, 194–96

Yugoslavia, 76

Zhukov, Georgi, 57, 59